The *New* Daily Study Bible

The Gospel of
Mark

D0756637

Just a reminder of the

28th March, 2004.

Much love from

Grandma & Grandpa

The *New* Daily Study Bible

The Gospel of
Mark

William Barclay

SAINT ANDREW PRESS
Edinburgh

Published by
SAINT ANDREW PRESS
121 George Street, Edinburgh EH2 4YN

© The William Barclay Estate, 1975, 2001

First edition published in 1954 as *The Daily Study Bible: The Gospel of Mark*
Revised edition published in 1975
This third edition fully revised and updated by Saint Andrew Press and
published as *The New Daily Study Bible: The Gospel of Mark* in 2001

The Scripture quotations contained herein are from The New Revised Standard
Version of the Bible, Anglicized Edition, copyright © 1989, 1995 by the Division
of Christian Education of the National Council of the Churches of Christ in the
United States of America, and are used by permission. All rights reserved.

ISBN 0 7152 0782 2

The right of William Barclay to be identified as author of this work has been
asserted according to the Copyright, Designs and Patents Act, 1988.

British Library Cataloguing in Publication Data
A CIP record for this book is available from the British Library

Cover design by McColl Productions Ltd, by courtesy of Saint Andrew Press

All rights reserved. No part of this publication may be reproduced or transmitted
in any form or by any means, electronic or mechanical, including photocopy,
recording, or information storage and retrieval system, without permission in
writing from the publisher. This book is sold subject to the condition that it shall
not, by way of trade or otherwise, be lent, re-sold, hired out or otherwise circulated
without the publisher's prior consent.

Typeset by Waverley Typesetters, Galashiels
Printed in Great Britain by Creative Print & Design, Wales

To

ALL LIBRARIANS

AND KEEPERS OF BOOKS

WITHOUT WHOSE HELP

NO AUTHOR

COULD EVER HOPE TO WRITE A BOOK

AND IN PARTICULAR

TO J.M.

TO WHOM I HAVE CAUSED ENDLESS TROUBLE

AND FROM WHOM I HAVE RECEIVED ENDLESS KINDNESS

CONTENTS

MARK

MARK

MARK

SERIES FOREWORD
(by Ronnie Barclay)

My father always had a great love for the English language and its literature. As a student at the University of Glasgow, he won a prize in the English class – and I have no doubt that he could have become a Professor of English instead of Divinity and Biblical Criticism. In a pre-computer age, he had a mind like a computer that could store vast numbers of quotations, illustrations, anecdotes and allusions; and, more remarkably still, he could retrieve them at will. The editor of this revision has, where necessary, corrected and attributed the vast majority of these quotations with considerable skill and has enhanced our pleasure as we read quotations from Plato to T. S. Eliot.

There is another very welcome improvement in the new text. My mother was one of five sisters, and my grandmother was a commanding figure as the Presbyterian minister's wife in a small village in Ayrshire in Scotland. She ran that small community very efficiently, and I always felt that my father, surrounded by so many women, was more than somewhat overawed by it all! I am sure that this is the reason why his use of English tended to be dominated by the words 'man', 'men' and so on, with the result that it sounded very male-orientated. Once again, the editor has very skilfully improved my father's English and made the text much more readable for all of us by amending the often one-sided language.

It is a well-known fact that William Barclay wrote at break-neck speed and never corrected anything once it was on paper – he took great pride in mentioning this at every possible opportunity! This revision, in removing repetition and correcting the inevitable errors that had slipped through, has produced a text free from all the tell-tale signs of very rapid writing. It is with great pleasure that I commend this revision to readers old and new in the certainty that William Barclay speaks even more clearly to us all with his wonderful appeal in this new version of his much-loved *Daily Study Bible*.

Ronnie Barclay
Bedfordshire
2001

GENERAL INTRODUCTION

(by William Barclay, from the 1975 edition)

The Daily Study Bible series has always had one aim – to convey the results of scholarship to the ordinary reader. A. S. Peake delighted in the saying that he was a 'theological middle-man', and I would be happy if the same could be said of me in regard to these volumes. And yet the primary aim of the series has never been academic. It could be summed up in the famous words of Richard of Chichester's prayer – to enable men and women 'to know Jesus Christ more clearly, to love him more dearly, and to follow him more nearly'.

It is all of twenty years since the first volume of *The Daily Study Bible* was published. The series was the brain-child of the late Rev. Andrew McCosh, MA, STM, the then Secretary and Manager of the Committee on Publications of the Church of Scotland, and of the late Rev. R. G. Macdonald, OBE, MA, DD, its Convener.

It is a great joy to me to know that all through the years *The Daily Study Bible* has been used at home and abroad, by minister, by missionary, by student and by layman, and that it has been translated into many different languages. Now, after so many printings, it has become necessary to renew the printer's type and the opportunity has been taken to restyle the books, to correct some errors in the text and to remove some references which have become outdated. At the same time, the Biblical quotations within the text have been changed to use the Revised Standard Version, but my own original translation of the New Testament passages has been retained at the beginning of each daily section.

There is one debt which I would be sadly lacking in courtesy if I did not acknowledge. The work of revision and correction has been done entirely by the Rev. James Martin, MA, BD, Minister of High Carntyne Church, Glasgow. Had it not been for him this task would never have been undertaken, and it is impossible for me to thank him enough for the selfless toil he has put into the revision of these books.

It is my prayer that God may continue to use *The Daily Study Bible* to enable men better to understand His word.

William Barclay
Glasgow
1975
(Published in the 1975 edition)

GENERAL FOREWORD

(by John Drane)

I only met William Barclay once, not long after his retirement from the chair of Biblical Criticism at the University of Glasgow. Of course I had known about him long before that, not least because his theological passion – the Bible – was also a significant formative influence in my own life and ministry. One of my most vivid memories of his influence goes back to when I was working on my own doctoral research in the New Testament. It was summer 1971, and I was a leader on a mission team working in the north-east of Scotland at the same time as Barclay's Baird Lectures were being broadcast on national television. One night, a young Ph.D. scientist who was interested in Christianity, but still unsure about some things, came to me and announced: 'I've just been watching William Barclay on TV. He's convinced me that I need to be a Christian; when can I be baptized?' That kind of thing did not happen every day. So how could it be that Barclay's message was so accessible to people with no previous knowledge or experience of the Christian faith?

I soon realised that there was no magic ingredient that enabled this apparently ordinary professor to be a brilliant communicator. His secret lay in who he was, his own sense of identity and purpose, and above all his integrity in being true to himself and his faith. Born in the far north of Scotland, he was brought up in Motherwell, a steel-producing town south of Glasgow where his family settled when he was only five, and this was the kind of place where he felt most at home. Though his association with the University of Glasgow provided a focus for his life over almost fifty years, from his first day as a student in 1925 to his retirement from the faculty in 1974, he never became an ivory-tower academic, divorced from the realities of life in the real world. On the contrary, it was his commitment to the working-class culture of industrial Clydeside that enabled him to make such a lasting contribution not only to the world of the university but also to the life of the Church.

He was ordained to the ministry of the Church of Scotland at the age of twenty-six, but was often misunderstood even by other Christians. I doubt that William Barclay would ever have chosen words such as 'missionary' or 'evangelist' to describe his own ministry, but he accomplished what few others have done, as he took the traditional Presbyterian emphasis on spirituality-through-learning and transformed it into a most effective vehicle for evangelism. His own primary interest was in the history and language of the New Testament, but William Barclay was never only a historian or literary critic. His constant concern was to explore how these ancient books, and the faith of which they spoke, could continue to be relevant to people of his own time. If the Scottish churches had known how to capitalize on his enormous popularity in the media during the 1960s and 1970s, they might easily have avoided much of the decline of subsequent years.

Connecting the Bible to life has never been the way to win friends in the world of academic theology, and Barclay could undoubtedly have made things easier for himself had he been prepared to be a more conventional academic. But he was too deeply rooted in his own culture – and too seriously committed to the gospel – for that. He could see little purpose in a belief system that was so wrapped up in arcane and complicated terminology that it was accessible only to experts. Not only did he demystify Christian theology, but he also did it for working people, addressing the kind of things that mattered to ordinary folks in their everyday lives. In doing so, he also challenged the elitism that has often been deeply ingrained in the twin worlds of academic theology and the Church, with their shared assumption that popular culture is an inappropriate vehicle for serious thinking. Professor Barclay can hardly have been surprised when his predilection for writing books for the masses – not to mention talking to them on television – was questioned by his peers and even occasionally dismissed as being 'unscholarly' or insufficiently 'academic'. That was all untrue, of course, for his work was soundly based in reliable scholarship and his own extensive knowledge of the original languages of the Bible. But like One many centuries before him (and unlike most of his peers, in both Church and academy), 'the common people heard him gladly' (Mark 12:37), which no doubt explains why his writings are still inspirational – and why it is a particular pleasure for me personally to commend them to a new readership in a new century.

John Drane
University of Aberdeen
2001

EDITOR'S PREFACE

(by Linda Foster)

When the first volume of the original *Daily Bible Readings*, which later became *The Daily Study Bible* (the commentary on Acts), was published in 1953, no one could have anticipated or envisaged the revolution in the use of language which was to take place in the last quarter of the twentieth century. Indeed, when the first revised edition, to which William Barclay refers in his General Introduction, was completed in 1975, such a revolution was still waiting in the wings. But at the beginning of the twenty-first century, inclusive language and the concept of political correctness are well-established facts of life. It has therefore been with some trepidation that the editing of this unique and much-loved text has been undertaken in producing *The New Daily Study Bible*. Inevitably, the demands of the new language have resulted in the loss of some of Barclay's most sonorous phrases, perhaps best remembered in the often-repeated words 'many a man'. Nonetheless, this revision is made in the conviction that William Barclay, the great communicator, would have welcomed it. In the discussion of Matthew 9:16–17 ('The Problem of the New Idea'), he affirmed the value of language that has stood the test of time and in which people have 'found comfort and put their trust', but he also spoke of 'living in a changing and expanding world' and questioned the wisdom of reading God's word to twentieth-century men and women in Elizabethan English. It is the intention of this new edition to heed that warning and to bring

William Barclay's message of God's word to readers of the twenty-first century in the language of their own time.

In the editorial process, certain decisions have been made in order to keep a balance between that new language and the familiar Barclay style. Quotations from the Bible are now taken from the New Revised Standard Version, but William Barclay's own translation of individual passages has been retained throughout. Where the new version differs from the text on which Barclay originally commented, because of the existence of an alternative reading, the variant text is indicated by square brackets. I have made no attempt to guess what Barclay would have said about the NRSV text; his commentary still refers to the Authorized (King James) and Revised Standard Versions of the Bible, but I believe that the inclusive language of the NRSV considerably assists the flow of the discussion.

For similar reasons, the dating conventions of BC and AD – rather than the more recent and increasingly used BCE (before the common era) and CE (common era) – have been retained. William Barclay took great care to explain the meanings of words and phrases and scholarly points, but it has not seemed appropriate to select new terms and make such explanations on his behalf.

One of the most difficult problems to solve has concerned monetary values. Barclay had his own system for translating the coinage of New Testament times into British currency. Over the years, these equivalent values have become increasingly out of date, and often the force of the point being made has been lost or diminished. There is no easy way to bring these equivalents up to date in a way that will continue to make sense, particularly when readers come from both sides of the Atlantic. I have therefore followed the only known yardstick that gives any feel for the values concerned, namely that a *denarius* was a day's wage for a working man, and I have made alterations to the text accordingly.

One of the striking features of *The Daily Study Bible* is the range of quotations from literature and hymnody that are used by way of illustration. Many of these passages appeared without identification or attribution, and for the new edition I have attempted wherever possible to provide sources and authors. In the same way, details have been included about scholars and other individuals cited, by way of context and explanation, and I am most grateful to Professor John Drane for his assistance in discovering information about some of the more obscure or unfamiliar characters. It is clear that readers use *The Daily Study Bible* in different ways. Some look up particular passages while others work through the daily readings in a more systematic way. The descriptions and explanations are therefore not offered every time an individual is mentioned (in order to avoid repetition that some may find tedious), but I trust that the information can be discovered without too much difficulty.

Finally, the 'Further Reading' lists at the end of each volume have been removed. Many new commentaries and individual studies have been added to those that were the basis of William Barclay's work, and making a selection from that ever-increasing catalogue is an impossible task. It is nonetheless my hope that the exploration that begins with these volumes of *The New Daily Study Bible* will go on in the discovery of new writers and new books.

Throughout the editorial process, many conversations have taken place – conversations with the British and American publishers, and with those who love the books and find in them both information and inspiration. Ronnie Barclay's contribution to this revision of his father's work has been invaluable. But one conversation has dominated the work, and that has been a conversation with William Barclay himself through the text. There has been a real sense of listening to his voice in all the questioning and in the searching for new words to convey the meaning of that text. The aim of *The New Daily Study Bible* is to make clear his message, so that the distinctive voice, which has spoken to so many in past years, may continue to be heard for generations to come.

Linda Foster
London
2001

INTRODUCTION
(by John Drane)

Our understanding of the Gospel of Mark has undergone
several significant developments since William Barclay
wrote about it. At one time, its position as the first gospel
to be written was assumed to give it a historical primacy
over Matthew and Luke, whose gospels were more obviously
crafted in accordance with the interests of their authors. In
5:40-3, Barclay confidently connects Mark with eyewitness
accounts from Peter himself, but today even those who hold
that opinion would acknowledge that the finished text is just
as much a redactional product as the other synoptics, shaped
by the concerns of Mark and his readers in the middle of the
first century.

The overall picture of Jesus would also be slightly different
today. During Jesus' childhood and teenage years, the
Hellenistic city of Sepphoris was under construction not far
from his home town of Nazareth, which suggests that people
in the construction industry (like the household of Joseph)
would be quite prosperous – and also that Galilee was not a
cultural backwater, but central to Hellenistic Palestine, with
Greek regularly spoken on its streets. Barclay's understanding
of the Pharisees as legalists, while still defensible, has also
been challenged in recent discussions, while the role of the
synagogue has undergone some redefinition.

At the same time, Barclay's exposition of Mark still speaks
to today's concerns. He emphasizes the importance of
community for Jesus (on 3:13–19, 'It is significant that

Christianity began with a group . . . a very mixed group'), and his comments on the miracle stories are infused with an insistence that, with Jesus, even life's crises can be transcended. During his lifetime, he was regularly criticized for what some took to be rationalizing 'explanations' of the miracles, though his approach was actually more subtle. The comment on the stilling of the storm (6:45–52) is typical, where he inquires if there might be a 'scientific' explanation, concludes that we don't know – and then asks whether it matters anyway. In some ways, he was ahead of his time by refusing to assume that science could answer such questions.

People today are unlikely to imagine that science ever could say anything worthwhile on matters of faith. For those familiar with the mystical claims of the New Age on the one hand, and charismatic Christianity on the other (neither of which was significant during Barclay's lifetime), his approach of offering background information and then inviting readers to decide such things for themselves is likely to have considerable appeal.

John Drane
University of Aberdeen
2001

INTRODUCTION TO
THE GOSPEL OF MARK

The Synoptic Gospels

The first three gospels, Matthew, Mark and Luke, are always known as the synoptic gospels. The word *synoptic* comes from two Greek words which mean *to see together*; and these three are called the synoptic gospels because they can be set down in parallel columns and their common matter looked at together. It would be possible to argue that of them all Mark is the most important. It would indeed be possible to go further and to argue that it is the most important book in the world, because it is agreed by nearly everyone that it is the earliest of all the gospels and therefore the first life of Jesus that has come down to us. Mark may not have been the first person to write the life of Jesus. Doubtless there were earlier simple attempts to set down the story of Jesus' life; but Mark's gospel is certainly the earliest life of Jesus that has survived.

The Pedigree of the Gospels

When we consider how the gospels came to be written, we must try to think ourselves back to a time when there was no such thing as a printed book. The gospels were written long before printing had been invented, and compiled when every book had to be carefully and laboriously written out by hand. It is clear that, as long as that was the case, only a few copies of any book could exist.

MARK

How do we know, or how can we deduce, that Mark was
the first of all the gospels? When we read the synoptic gospels
even in English we see that there are remarkable similarities
between them. They contain the same incidents often told
in the same words; and they contain accounts of the teaching
of Jesus which are often almost identical. If we compare
the story of the feeding of the 5,000 in the three gospels
(Mark 6:30–44; Matthew 14:12–21; Luke 9:10–17), we
see that it is told in almost exactly the same words and in
exactly the same way. A very clear instance of this is the
story of the healing of the man who was sick with the palsy
(Mark 2:1–12; Matthew 9:1–8; Luke 5:17–26). The accounts
are so similar that even a little parenthesis – 'he said to the
paralytic' – occurs in all three in exactly the same place.
The correspondences are so close that we are forced to one
of two conclusions. Either all three are taking their material
from some common source, or two of the three are based on
the third.

When we study the matter closely we find that Mark can
be divided into 105 sections. Of these, ninety-three occur in
Matthew and eighty-one in Luke. Only four are not included
either in Matthew or in Luke. Even more compelling is this.
Mark has 661 verses; Matthew has 1,068 verses; Luke has
1,149 verses. Of Mark's 661 verses, Matthew reproduces no
fewer than 606. Sometimes he alters the wording slightly but
he even reproduces 51 per cent of Mark's actual words. Of
Mark's 661 verses, Luke reproduces 320, and he actually uses
53 per cent of Mark's actual words. Of the fifty-five verses of
Mark which Matthew does not reproduce, thirty-one are found
in Luke. So the result is that there are only twenty-four verses
in Mark which do not occur somewhere in Matthew and Luke.
This makes it look very much as if Matthew and Luke were
using Mark as the basis of their gospels.

What makes the matter still more certain is this. Both Matthew and Luke very largely follow Mark's order of events. Sometimes Matthew alters Mark's order and sometimes Luke does. But when there is a change in the order Matthew and Luke never agree together against Mark. Always one of them retains Mark's order of events.

A close examination of the three gospels makes it clear that Matthew and Luke had Mark before them as they wrote; and they used his gospel as the basis into which they fitted the extra material which they wished to include.

It is thrilling to remember that when we read Mark's gospel we are reading the first life of Jesus, on which all succeeding lives have necessarily been based.

Mark, the Writer of the Gospel

Who then was this Mark who wrote the gospel? The New Testament tells us a good deal about him. He was the son of a well-to-do lady of Jerusalem whose name was Mary, and whose house was a rallying point and meeting place of the early Church (Acts 12:12). From the very beginning Mark was brought up in the very centre of the Christian fellowship.

Mark was also the nephew of Barnabas, and when Paul and Barnabas set out on their first missionary journey they took Mark with them to be their secretary and attendant (Acts 12:25). This journey was a most unfortunate one for Mark. When they reached Perga, Paul proposed to strike inland up to the central plateau; and for some reason Mark left the expedition and went home (Acts 13:13).

He may have gone home because he was scared to face the dangers of what was notoriously one of the most difficult and dangerous roads in the world, a road hard to travel and haunted by bandits. He may have gone home because it was increasingly clear that the leadership of the expedition was being assumed by Paul, and Mark may have felt with disapproval that his uncle was being pushed into the background. He may have gone home because he did not approve of the work which Paul was doing. Writing in the fourth century, John Chrysostom – perhaps with a flash of imaginative insight – says that Mark went home because he wanted his mother!

Paul and Barnabas completed their first missionary journey and then proposed to set out upon their second. Barnabas was anxious to take Mark with them again. But Paul refused to have anything to do with the man 'who had deserted them in Pamphylia' (Acts 15:37–40). So serious was the difference between them that Paul and Barnabas split company, and, as far as we know, never worked together again.

For some years, Mark vanishes from history. Tradition has it that he went down to Egypt and founded the church of Alexandria there. Whether or not that is true we do not know, but we do know that when Mark re-emerges it is in the most surprising way. We learn to our surprise that when Paul writes the letter to the Colossians from prison in Rome Mark is there with him (Colossians 4:10). In another prison letter, to Philemon, Paul numbers Mark among his fellow workers (verse 24). And, when Paul is waiting for death and very near the end, he writes to Timothy, his right-hand man, and says, 'Get Mark and bring him with you, for he is useful in my ministry' (2 Timothy 4:11). It is a far cry from the time when Paul contemptuously dismissed Mark as a quitter. Whatever had happened, Mark had redeemed himself. He was the one man Paul wanted at the end.

Mark's Sources of Information

The value of any story will depend on the writer's sources of information. Where, then, did Mark get his information about the life and work of Jesus? We have seen that his home was from the beginning a Christian centre in Jerusalem. Often he must have heard people tell of their personal memories of Jesus. But it is most likely that he had a source of information without a superior.

Towards the end of the second century there was a man called Papias who liked to obtain and transmit such information as he could glean about the early days of the Church. He tells us that Mark's gospel is nothing other than a record of the preaching material of Peter, the greatest of the apostles. Certainly Mark stood so close to Peter, and so near to his heart, that Peter could call him 'my son Mark' (1 Peter 5:13). Here is what Papias says:

> Mark, who was Peter's interpreter, wrote down accurately, though not in order, all that he recollected of what Christ had said or done. For he was not a hearer of the Lord or a follower of his. He followed Peter, as I have said, at a later date, and Peter adapted his instruction to practical needs, without any attempt to give the Lord's words systematically. So that Mark was not wrong in writing down some things in this way from memory, for his one concern was neither to omit nor to falsify anything that he had heard.

We may then take it that in his gospel we have what Mark remembered of the preaching material of Peter himself.

So, then, we have two great reasons why Mark is a book of supreme importance. First, it is the earliest of all the gospels; if it was written just shortly after Peter died, its date will be about AD 65. Second, it embodies the record of what Peter preached and taught about Jesus. We may put it this way: Mark is the nearest approach we will ever possess to an eyewitness account of the life of Jesus.

The Lost Ending

There is a very interesting point about Mark's gospel. In its original form it stops at Mark 16:8. We know this for two reasons. First, the verses which follow (Mark 16:9–20) are not in any of the great early manuscripts; only later and inferior manuscripts contain them. Second, the style of the Greek is so different that these verses and the rest of the gospel cannot have been written by the same person.

But the gospel cannot have been *meant* to stop at Mark 16:8. What then happened? It may be that Mark died, perhaps even suffered martyrdom, before he could complete his gospel. More likely, it may be that at one time only one copy of the gospel remained, and that a copy in which the last part of the roll on which it was written had got torn off. There was a time when the Church did not much use Mark, preferring Matthew and Luke. It may well be that Mark's gospel was so neglected that all copies except for a mutilated one were lost. If that is so, we were within an ace of losing the gospel which in many ways is the most important of all.

The Characteristics of Mark's Gospel

Let us look at the characteristics of Mark's gospel so that we may watch for them as we read and study it.

(1) It is the nearest thing we will ever get to a report of Jesus' life. Mark's aim was to give a picture of Jesus as he was. The scholar B. F. Westcott called it 'a transcript from life'. A. B. Bruce of Glasgow's Free Church College said that it was written 'from the viewpoint of loving, vivid recollection', and that its great characteristic was *realism*.

If we are ever to get anything approaching a biography of Jesus, it must be based on Mark, for it is his delight to tell the facts of Jesus' life in the simplest and most dramatic way.

(2) Mark never forgot the divine side of Jesus. He begins
his gospel with the declaration of faith, 'The beginning of
the gospel (good news) of Jesus Christ, the Son of God.' He
leaves us in no doubt what he believed Jesus to be. Again and
again he speaks of the impact Jesus made on the minds and
hearts of those who heard him. The awe and astonishment
which he evoked are always in the forefront of Mark's mind.
'They were astounded at his teaching' (1:22). 'They were all
amazed' (1:27). Such phrases occur again and again. Not
only was this astonishment in the minds of the crowds who
listened to Jesus; it was still more in the minds of the inner
circle of the disciples. 'And they were filled with great awe,
and said to one another, "Who then is this, that even the
wind and the sea obey him?"' (4:41). 'And they were utterly
astounded' (6:51). 'They were greatly astounded' (10:26).

To Mark, Jesus was not simply one of us; he was God
among us, constantly moving people to a wondering amazement with his words and deeds.

(3) At the same time, no gospel gives such a human picture
of Jesus. Sometimes its picture is so human that the later
writers alter it a little because they are almost afraid to say
what Mark said. To Mark, Jesus is simply 'the carpenter' (6:3).
Later Matthew alters that to 'the carpenter's son' (Matthew
13:55), as if to call Jesus a village tradesman is too daring.
When Mark is telling of the temptations of Jesus, he writes,
'The Spirit immediately *drove* him out into the wilderness'
(1:12). Matthew and Luke do not like this word *drove* used of
Jesus, so they soften it down and say, 'Jesus was *led up* by the
Spirit into the wilderness' (Matthew 4:1; cf. Luke 4:1). No
one tells us so much about the emotions of Jesus as Mark
does. Jesus sighed deeply in his spirit (8:12; cf. 7:34). He was
moved with compassion (6:34). He was amazed at their
unbelief (6:6). He was moved with righteous anger (3:5, 8:33,

10:14). Only Mark tells us that when Jesus looked at the rich young ruler he loved him (10:21). Jesus could feel the pangs of hunger (11:12). He could be tired and want to rest (6:31).

It is in Mark's gospel, above all, that we get a picture of a Jesus who shared emotions and passions with us. The sheer humanity of Jesus in Mark's picture brings him very near to us.

(4) One of the great characteristics of Mark is that over and over again he inserts the little vivid details into the narrative which are the hallmark of an eyewitness. Both Matthew and Mark tell of Jesus taking the little child and setting him in the midst. Matthew (18:2) says, 'He called a child, whom he put among them.' Mark adds something which lights up the whole picture (9:36). In the words of the Revised Standard Version, 'And he took a child and put him in the midst of them; and *taking him in his arms*, he said to them . . .' In the lovely picture of Jesus and the children, when Jesus rebuked the disciples for keeping the children from him, only Mark finishes, '*and he took them up in his arms, laid his hands on them, and blessed them*' (10:13–16; cf. Matthew 19:13–15; Luke 18:15–17). All the tenderness of Jesus is in these little vivid additions. When Mark is telling of the feeding of the 5,000, he alone tells how they sat down *in hundreds and in fifties*, looking like vegetable beds in a garden (6:40); and immediately the whole scene rises before us. When Jesus and his disciples were on the last journey to Jerusalem, only Mark tells us, '*and Jesus was walking ahead of them*' (10:32; cf. Matthew 20:17; Luke 18:31); and in that one vivid little phrase all the loneliness of Jesus stands out. When Mark is telling the story of the stilling of the storm, he has one little sentence that none of the other gospel writers have. 'He was in the stern, *asleep on the cushion*' (4:38). And that one touch makes the picture vivid before our eyes.

There can be little doubt that all these details are due to the fact that Peter was an eyewitness and was seeing these things again with the eye of memory.

(5) Mark's realism and his simplicity come out in his Greek style.

(a) His style is not carefully developed and polished. He tells the story as a child might tell it. He adds statement to statement connecting them simply with the word 'and'. In the third chapter of the gospel, in the Greek, there are thirty-four clauses or sentences one after another introduced by 'and' after one principal verb. It is the way in which an eager child would tell the story.

(b) He is very fond of the words 'and straightaway', 'and immediately'. They occur in the gospel almost thirty times. It is sometimes said of a story that 'it marches'. But Mark's story does not so much march; he rushes on in a kind of breathless attempt to make the story as vivid to others as it is to himself.

(c) He is very fond of the historic present. That is to say, in the Greek he talks of events in the present tense instead of in the past. 'And when Jesus heard it, he *says* to them, "Those who are strong do not need a doctor, but those who are ill"' (2:17). 'And when they *come* near to Jerusalem, to Bethphage and to Bethany, to the Mount of Olives, he *sends* two of his disciples, and *says* to them, "Go into the village opposite you . . ."' (11:1-2). 'And immediately, while he was still speaking, Judas, one of The Twelve, *comes*' (14:43).

Generally speaking we do not keep these historic presents in translation, because in English they do not sound well; but they show how vivid and real the thing was to Mark's mind, as if it was happening before his very eyes.

(d) He quite often gives us the very Aramaic words which Jesus used. To Jairus' daughter, Jesus said, '*Talitha cumi*'

(5:41). To the deaf man with the impediment in his speech, he said, *'Ephphatha'* (7:34). The dedicated gift is *'Corban'* (7:11). In the garden, he says, *'Abba*, Father' (14:36). On the cross, he cries, *'Eloi, Eloi, lema sabachthani?'* (15:34).

There were times when Peter could hear again the very sound of Jesus' voice and could not help passing it on to Mark in the very words that Jesus spoke.

The Essential Gospel
It would not be unfair to call Mark *the essential gospel*. We will do well to study with loving care the earliest gospel we possess, the gospel where we hear again the preaching of Peter himself.

MARK

THE BEGINNING OF THE STORY

Mark 1:1–4

> This is the beginning of the story of how Jesus Christ,
> the Son of God, brought the good news to men. There
> is a passage in Isaiah the prophet like this – 'Lo! I send
> my messenger before you and he will prepare your
> road for you. He will be like a voice crying in the wilder-
> ness, "Get ready the road of the Lord. Make straight
> the path by which he will come".' This came true
> when John the Baptizer emerged in the wilderness,
> announcing a baptism which was the sign of a repent-
> ance through which a man might find forgiveness for
> his sins.

MARK starts the story of Jesus a long way back. It did not
begin with Jesus' birth; it did not even begin with John the
Baptizer in the wilderness; it began with the dreams of the
prophets long ago; that is to say, it began long, long ago in
the mind of God.

The Stoics were strong believers in the ordered plan of
God. 'The things of God', said Marcus Aurelius, 'are full of
foresight. All things flow from heaven.' There are things we
may well learn here.

(1) It has been said that 'the thoughts of youth are long,
long thoughts', and so are the thoughts of God. God is

characteristically a God who is working his purposes out. History is not a random kaleidoscope of disconnected events; it is a process directed by the God who sees the end in the beginning.

(2) We are within that process, and because of that we can either help or hinder it. In one sense it is as great an honour to help in some great process as it is a privilege to see the ultimate goal. Life would be very different if, instead of yearning for some distant and at present unattainable goal, we did all that we could to bring that goal nearer.

> In youth, because I could not be a singer,
> I did not even try to write a song;
> I set no little trees along the roadside,
> Because I knew their growth would take so long.

> But now from wisdom that the years have brought me,
> I know that it may be a blessed thing
> To plant a tree for someone else to water,
> Or make a song for someone else to sing.

The goal will never be reached unless there are those who labour to make it possible.

The prophetic quotation which Mark uses is suggestive.

I send my messenger before you and he will prepare your road for you. This is from Malachi 3:1. In its original context it is a threat. In Malachi's day the priests were failing in their duty. The offerings were blemished and shoddy second-bests; the service of the Temple was a weariness to them. The messenger was *to cleanse and purify* the worship of the Temple before the Anointed One of God emerged upon the earth. So then the coming of Christ was a *purification of life*. And the world needed that purification. Seneca called Rome 'a cesspool of iniquity'. Juvenal spoke of her 'as the filthy sewer into which flowed the abominable dregs of every

Syrian and Achaean stream'. Wherever Christianity comes it brings purification.

That happens to be capable of factual demonstration. The journalist Bruce Barton tells how the first important assignment that fell to him was to write a series of articles designed to expose Billy Sunday, the evangelist. Three towns were chosen. 'I talked to the merchants,' Barton writes, 'and they told me that during the meetings and afterward people walked up to the counter and paid bills which were so old that they had long since been written off the books.' He went to visit the president of the chamber of commerce of a town that Billy Sunday had visited three years before. 'I am not a member of any church,' he said. 'I never attend but I'll tell you one thing. If it was proposed now to bring Billy Sunday to this town, and if we knew as much about the results of his work in advance as we do now, and if the churches would not raise the necessary funds to bring him, I could raise the money in half a day from people who never go to church. He took eleven thousand dollars out of here, but a circus comes here and takes out that amount in one day and leaves nothing. He left a different moral atmosphere.' The exposure that Bruce Barton meant to write became a tribute to the cleansing power of the Christian message.

When the evangelist Billy Graham preached in Shreveport, Louisiana, liquor sales dropped by 40 per cent and the sale of Bibles increased 300 per cent. During a mission in Seattle, among the results there is stated quite simply, 'Several impending divorce actions were cancelled.' In Greensboro, North Carolina, the report was that 'the entire social structure of the city was affected'.

One of the great stories of what Christianity can do came out of the mutiny on the *Bounty*. The mutineers were put ashore on Pitcairn Island. There were nine mutineers, six native men, ten native women and a girl, fifteen years old. One of them succeeded in making crude alcohol. A terrible situation ensued. They all died except Alexander Smith. Smith chanced upon a Bible. He read it and he made up his mind to build up a state with the natives of that island based directly on the Bible. It was twenty years before an American sloop called at the island. They found a completely Christian community. There was no jail because there was no crime. There was no hospital because there was no disease. There was no asylum because there was no insanity. There was no illiteracy; and nowhere in the world was human life and property so safe. Christianity had cleansed that society.

Where Christ is allowed to come, the antiseptic of the Christian faith cleanses the moral poison of society and leaves it pure and clean.

John came announcing a *baptism of repentance*. Jews were familiar with ritual washings. Leviticus 11–15 details them. 'The Jew', said Tertullian, 'washes himself every day because every day he is defiled.' Symbolic washing and purifying was woven into the very fabric of Jewish ritual. Gentiles were necessarily unclean for they had never kept any part of the Jewish law. Therefore, when a Gentile became a *proselyte*, that is a convert to the Jewish faith, he had to undergo three things. First, he had to undergo *circumcision*, for that was the mark of the covenant people; second, *sacrifice* had to be made for him, for he stood in need of atonement and only blood could atone for sin; third, he had to undergo *baptism*, which symbolized cleansing from all the pollution of his past life. Naturally, therefore, the baptism was not a mere sprinkling with water, but a bath in which the whole body was bathed.

Jews knew baptism; but the amazing thing about John's baptism was that he, a Jew, was asking Jews to submit to that which only a Gentile was supposed to need. John had made the tremendous discovery that to be a Jew in the racial sense was not to be a member of God's chosen people; a Jew might be in exactly the same position as a Gentile; not the Jewish life, but the cleansed life belonged to God.

The baptism was accompanied by *confession*. In any return to God, confession must be made to three different people.

(1) We must make confession to *ourselves*. It is a part of human nature that we shut our eyes to what we do not wish to see, and above all to our own sins. Someone tells of one man's first step to grace. As he was shaving one morning he looked at his face in the mirror and suddenly said, 'You dirty little rat!' And from that day he began to be a changed man.

No doubt when the prodigal son left home he thought himself a fine and adventurous character. Before he took his first step back home he had to take a good look at himself and say, 'I will get up and go home and say that I am utterly despicable' (cf. Luke 15:17–18).

There is no one in all the world harder to face than ourselves; and the first step to repentance and to a right relationship to God is to admit our sin to ourselves.

(2) We must make confession *to those whom we have wronged*. It will not be much use saying to God that we are sorry until we say we are sorry to those whom we have hurt and grieved. The human barriers have to be removed before the divine barriers can go. In the East African Church, a husband and wife were members of a group. One of them came and made confession that there was a quarrel at home. The minister at once said, 'You should not have come and confessed that quarrel just now; you should have made it up and then come and confessed it.'

It can often be the case that confession to God is easier than confession to others. But there can be no forgiveness without humiliation.

(3) We must make confession to *God*. The end of pride is the beginning of forgiveness. It is when we find it possible to say, 'I have sinned,' that God gets the chance to say, 'I forgive.' It is not those who desire to meet God on equal terms who will discover forgiveness, but those who kneel in humble contrition and whisper through their shame, 'God be merciful to me, a sinner.'

THE HERALD OF THE KING

Mark 1:5–8

> And the whole country of Judaea went out to him, and so did all the people of Jerusalem, and they were baptized by him in the River Jordan, while they confessed their sins. John was clad in a garment of camel's hair, and he had a leather girdle round his waist, and it was his custom to eat locusts and wild honey. The burden of his proclamation was, 'The one who is stronger than I is coming after me. I am not fit to stoop down and to loosen the strap of his sandals. I have baptized you with water, but he will baptize you with the Holy Spirit.'

It is clear that the ministry of John was mightily effective, for they flocked out to listen to him and to submit to his baptism. Why was it that John made an impact such as this upon his nation?

(1) He was a man who lived his message. Not only his words, but also his whole life was a protest. Three things about him marked the reality of his protest against contemporary life.

(a) There was the place in which he stayed – the wilderness. Between the centre of Judaea and the Dead Sea lies one of the most terrible deserts in the world. It is a limestone desert; it looks warped and twisted; it shimmers in the haze of the heat; the rock is hot and blistering and sounds hollow to the feet as if there was some vast furnace underneath; it moves out to the Dead Sea and then descends in dreadful and unscalable precipices down to the shore. In the Old Testament it is sometimes called *Jeshimmon*, which means *The Devastation*. John was no city-dweller. He was a man from the desert and from its solitudes and its desolations. He was a man who had given himself a chance to hear the voice of God.

(b) There were the clothes he wore – a garment woven of camel's hair and a leather belt about his waist. So did Elijah (2 Kings 1:8). To look at the man was to be reminded, not of the fashionable orators of the day, but of the ancient prophets who lived close to the great simplicities and avoided the soft and comfortable luxuries which kill the soul.

(c) There was the food he ate – locusts and wild honey. It so happens that both words are capable of two interpretations. The locusts may be the insects, for the law allowed them to be eaten (Leviticus 11:22–3); but they may also be a kind of bean or nut, the *carob*, which was the food of the poorest of the poor. The honey may be the honey the wild bees make, or it may be a kind of sweet sap that distils from the bark of certain trees. It does not matter what the words precisely mean. In any event John's diet was of the simplest.

So John emerged. People had to listen to a man like that. It was said of Thomas Carlyle that 'he preached the gospel of silence in twenty volumes'. Many come with a message that they themselves deny. Many who possess comfortable bank accounts preach about not laying up treasures upon earth. Many extol the blessings of poverty from comfortable homes.

But in the case of John, the man was the message, and because of that people listened.

(2) His message was effective because he told people what in their heart of hearts they knew and brought them what in the depths of their souls they were waiting for.

(a) The Jews had a saying that 'if Israel would only keep the law of God perfectly for one day the kingdom of God would come'. When John summoned men and women to repentance he was confronting them with a decision that they knew in their heart of hearts they ought to make. Long ago Plato said that education did not consist in telling people new things; it consisted in extracting from their memories what they already knew. No message is so effective as that which speaks to a person's own conscience, and that message becomes well-nigh irresistible when it is spoken by someone who obviously has the right to speak.

(b) The people of Israel were well aware that for 300 years the voice of prophecy had been silent. They were waiting for some authentic word from God. And in John they heard it. In every walk of life the expert is recognizable. A famous violinist tells us that no sooner had Toscanini mounted the rostrum than the orchestra felt his authority flowing over them. We recognize at once a doctor who has real skill. We recognize at once speakers who know their subject. John had come from God, and to hear him was to know it.

(3) His message was effective because he was completely humble. His own verdict on himself was that he was not fit for the duty of a slave. Sandals were composed simply of leather soles fastened to the foot by straps passing through the toes. The roads were unsurfaced. In dry weather they were dust-heaps; in wet weather rivers of mud. To remove the sandals was the work and office of a slave. John asked nothing

for himself but everything for the Christ whom he proclaimed. The man's obvious self-forgottenness, his patent yieldedness, his complete self-effacement, his utter lostness in his message compelled people to listen.

(4) His message was effective because he pointed to something and someone beyond himself. He told men and women that his baptism drenched them in water, but one was coming who would drench them in the Holy Spirit; and while water could cleanse the body, the Holy Spirit could cleanse a person's life and self and heart. The Glasgow minister Dr G. J. Jeffrey had a favourite illustration. When he was making a telephone call through the operator and there was some delay, the operator would often say, 'I'm trying to connect you.' Then, when the connection had been effected, the operator faded out and left him in direct contact with the person to whom he wished to speak.

John's one aim was not to occupy the centre of the stage himself, but to try to connect men and women with the one who was greater and stronger than he; and they listened to him because he pointed, not to himself, but to the one whom we all need.

THE DAY OF DECISION

Mark 1:9–11

> In those days Jesus came from Nazareth in Galilee and was baptized by John in the Jordan; and as soon as he came up out of the water he saw the heavens being riven asunder and the Spirit coming down upon him, as a dove might come down; and there came a voice from heaven, 'You are my beloved Son; I am well pleased with you.'

To any thinking person the baptism of Jesus presents a problem. John's baptism was a baptism of repentance, meant for those who were sorry for their sins and who wished to express their determination to have done with them. What had such a baptism to do with Jesus? Was he not the sinless one, and was not such a baptism unnecessary and quite irrelevant as far as he was concerned? For Jesus the baptism was four things.

(1) It was the moment of *decision*. For thirty years he had stayed in Nazareth. Faithfully he had done his day's work and discharged his duties to his home. For a long time he must have been conscious that the time for him to go out had to come. He must have waited for a sign. The emergence of John was that sign. This, he saw, was the moment when he had to launch out upon his task.

In every life there come moments of decision which may be accepted or rejected. To accept them is to succeed; to reject them, or to shirk them, is to fail. As the American poet, J. R. Lowell, in a poem entitled 'The Present Crisis', had it:

> Once to every man and nation comes the moment to
> decide
> In the strife of Truth with falsehood, for the good or
> evil side;
> Some great cause, God's new Messiah, offering each
> the bloom or blight,
> Parts the goats upon the left hand, and the sheep upon
> the right
> And the choice goes by for ever 'twixt that darkness
> and that light.

To each of us there comes the unreturning decisive moment. As Shakespeare expressed it in the words of Brutus:

There is a tide in the affairs of men,
Which, taken at the flood, leads on to fortune;
Omitted, all the voyage of their lives
Is bound in shallows and in miseries.

The undecided life is the wasted life, the frustrated life, the discontented life and often the tragic life. As John Oxenham saw it when he wrote 'The Ways':

To every man there openeth
A way and ways and a way;
The high soul treads the high way,
And the low soul gropes the low,
And in between on the misty flats,
The rest drift to and fro.

The drifting life can never be the happy life. Jesus knew when John emerged that the moment of decision had come. Nazareth was peaceful and home was sweet, but he answered the summons and the challenge of God.

(2) It was the moment of *identification*. It is true that Jesus did not need to repent from sin; but here was a movement of the people back to God; and with that Godward movement he was determined to identify himself. It is possible to possess ease and comfort and wealth and still to identify with a movement to bring better things to the downtrodden and the poor and the ill-housed and the overworked and the underpaid. The really great identification is when people identify with a movement, not for their own sake, but for the sake of others. In John Bunyan's dream, Christian came in his journeying with Interpreter to the Palace which was heavily guarded and required a battle to seek an entry. At the door there sat the man with the ink horn taking the names of those who would dare the assault. All were hanging back, then Christian saw 'a man of a very stout countenance come up to the man that

sat there to write, saying, "Set down my name, sir" '. When great things are afoot the Christian is bound to say, 'Set down my name, sir,' for that is what Jesus did when he came to be baptized.

(3) It was the moment of *approval*. No one lightly leaves home and sets out on an unknown way. He or she must be very sure that the decision is right. Jesus had decided on his course of action, and now he was looking for the seal of the approval of God. In the time of Jesus, the Jews spoke of what they called the *Bath Qol*, which means *the daughter of a voice*. By this time they believed in a series of heavens, in the highest of which sat God in the light to which no one could approach. There were rare times when the heavens opened and God spoke; but, to them, God was so distant that it was only the faraway echo of his voice that they heard. To Jesus the voice came directly. As Mark tells the story, this was a personal experience which Jesus had and not in any sense a demonstration to the crowd. The voice did not say, 'This is my Son, the Beloved,' as Matthew has it (Matthew 3:17). It said, 'You are my beloved Son,' speaking directly to Jesus. At the baptism Jesus submitted his decision to God and that decision was unmistakably approved.

(4) It was the moment of *equipment*. At that time the Holy Spirit descended upon him. There is a certain symbolism here. The Spirit descended as a dove might descend. The simile is not chosen by accident. The dove is the symbol of *gentleness*. Both Matthew and Luke tell us of the preaching of John (Matthew 3:7–12; Luke 3:7–13). John's was a message of the axe laid to the root of the tree, of the terrible sifting, of the consuming fire. It was a message of doom and not of good news. But from the very beginning the picture of the Spirit likened to a dove is a picture of gentleness. He will conquer, but the conquest will be the conquest of love.

THE TESTING TIME

Mark 1:12–13

> And immediately the Spirit thrust him into the wilder-
> ness. He was in the wilderness forty days, and all the
> time he was being tested by Satan. The wild beasts were
> his companions, and the angels were helping him.

No sooner was the glory of the hour of the baptism over than
there came the battle of the temptations. One thing stands out
here in such a vivid way that we cannot miss it. It was the
Spirit who thrust Jesus out into the wilderness for the testing
time. The very Spirit who came upon him at his baptism now
drove him out for his test.

In this life it is impossible to escape the assault of temptation; but one thing is sure – temptations are not sent to us to
make us fall; they are sent to strengthen the nerve and the
sinew of our minds and hearts and souls. They are not meant
for our ruin, but for our good. They are meant to be tests
from which we emerge better warriors and athletes of God.

Suppose a young boy is a football player; suppose he is
doing well in the second team and showing real signs of
promise, what will the team coach do? He certainly will not
send him out to play for the third team in which he could
walk through the game and never break sweat; he will send
him out to play for the first team where he will be tested as
he never was before and have the chance to prove himself.
That is what temptation is meant to do – to enable us to prove
ourselves and to emerge the stronger for the fight.

Forty days is a phrase which is not to be taken literally. It
is the regular Hebrew phrase for a considerable time. Moses
was said to be on the mountain with God for forty days
(Exodus 24:18); it was for forty days that Elijah went in the

strength of the meal the angel gave him (1 Kings 19:8). Just as we use the phrase *ten days or so*, so here we have the phrase *forty days*, not literally but simply to mean a fair length of time.

It was Satan who tempted Jesus. The development of the conception of Satan is very interesting.

The word *Satan* in Hebrew simply means an *adversary*; and in the Old Testament it is so used of ordinary human adversaries and opponents again and again. The angel of the Lord is the *satan* who stands in Balaam's way (Numbers 22:22); the Philistines fear that David may turn out to be their *satan* (1 Samuel 29:4); David regards Abishai as his *satan* (2 Samuel 19:22); Solomon declares that God has given him such peace and prosperity that he has no *satan* left to oppose him (1 Kings 5:4). The word began by meaning *an adversary* in the widest sense of the term.

But it takes a step on the downward path; it begins to mean *one who pleads a case against a person*. It is in this sense that it is used in the first chapter of Job. In that chapter, Satan is no less than one of the sons of God (Job 1:6); but his particular task was to consider human beings (Job 1:7) and to search for some case that could be pleaded against them in the presence of God. He was the accuser of men and women before God. The word is so used in Job 2:2 and Zechariah 3:2. The task of Satan was to say everything that could be said against anyone.

The other title of Satan is the *devil*; the word *devil* comes from the Greek *diabolos*, which literally means *a slanderer*. It is a small step from the thought of one who searches for everything that can be said against an individual to the thought of one who deliberately and maliciously slanders all human beings in the presence of God. But in the Old Testament, Satan is still an emissary of God and not yet the malignant, supreme enemy of God. He is the *adversary of human beings*.

But now the word takes the last step on its downward course. Through their captivity, the Jews learned something of Persian thought. Persian thought is based on the conception that in this universe there are two powers, a power of the light and a power of the dark, Ormuzd and Ahriman; the whole universe is a battle ground between them, and people must choose one side or the other in that cosmic conflict. In point of fact, that is precisely what life looks like and feels like. To put it in a word, in this world there is God and *God's Adversary*. It was almost inevitable that Satan should come to be regarded as *The Adversary par excellence*. That is what his name means; that is how he was always seen; Satan becomes the essence of everything that is against God.

When we turn to the New Testament we find that it is the devil or Satan who is behind human disease and suffering (Luke 13:16); it is Satan who seduces Judas (Luke 22:3); it is the devil whom we must fight (1 Peter 5:8–9; James 4:7); it is the devil whose power is being broken by the work of Christ (Luke 10:1–19); it is the devil who is destined for final destruction (Matthew 25:41). Satan is the power which is against God.

Here we have the whole essence of the temptation story. Jesus had to decide how he was to do his work. He was conscious of a tremendous task and he was also conscious of tremendous powers. God was saying to him, 'Take my love to men and women; love them till you die for them; conquer them by this unconquerable love even if you finish up upon a cross.' Satan was saying to Jesus, 'Use your power to blast men and women; obliterate your enemies; win the world by might and power and bloodshed.' God said to Jesus, 'Set up a reign of love.' Satan said to Jesus, 'Set up a dictatorship of force.' Jesus had to choose that day between the way of God and the way of the Adversary of God.

Mark's brief story of the Temptations finishes with two vivid touches.

(1) *The animals were his companions*. In the desert there roamed the leopard, the bear, the wild boar and the jackal. This is usually taken to be a vivid detail that adds to the grim terror of the scene. But perhaps it is not so. Perhaps this is a lovely thing, for perhaps it means that the animals were Jesus' friends. Amid the dreams of the golden age when the Messiah would come, the Jews dreamed of a day when the enmity between humanity and the animals would no longer exist. 'I will make for you a covenant on that day with the wild animals, the birds of the air, and the creeping things of the ground' (Hosea 2:18). 'The wolf shall live with the lamb, the leopard shall lie down with the kid . . . The nursing child shall play over the hole of the asp, and the weaned child shall put his hand on the adder's den. They will not hurt or destroy on all my holy mountain' (Isaiah 11:6–9). In later days, St Francis preached to the animals; and it may be that here we have a first foretaste of the loveliness when human beings and all creatures will be at peace. It may be that here we see a picture in which the animals recognized, before the human race did, their friend and their king.

(2) *The angels were helping him*. There are always the divine reinforcements in the hour of trial. When Elisha and his servant were shut up in Dothan with their enemies pressing in upon them and no apparent way of escape, Elisha opened the young man's eyes, and all around he saw the horses and the chariots of fire which belonged to God (2 Kings 6:17). Jesus was not left to fight his battle alone – and neither are we.

THE MESSAGE OF THE GOOD NEWS

Mark 1:14-15

> After John had been committed to prison, Jesus came
> into Galilee, announcing the good news about God, and
> saying, 'The time that was appointed has come; and the
> kingdom of God is here. Repent and believe the good
> news.'

THERE are in this summary of the message of Jesus three
great, dominant words of the Christian faith.

(1) There is *the good news*. It was pre-eminently good
news that Jesus came to bring to all. If we follow the word
evangelion, good news, gospel through the New Testament,
we can see at least something of its content.

(a) It is good news of *truth* (Galatians 2:5; Colossians 1:5).
Until Jesus came, it was possible only to guess and grope
after God. 'O that I knew where I might find him,' cried Job
(Job 23:3). Marcus Aurelius said that the soul can see but
dimly, and the word he uses is the Greek word for seeing
things through water. But with the coming of Jesus we see
clearly what God is like. No longer do we need to guess and
grope; we know.

(b) It is good news of *hope* (Colossians 1:23). The ancient
world was a pessimistic world. Seneca talked of 'our helplessness in necessary things'. In the struggle for goodness,
humanity was defeated. The coming of Jesus brings hope to
the hopeless heart.

(c) It is good news of *peace* (Ephesians 6:15). The penalty
of being human is to have a split personality. In human nature,
the beast and the angel are strangely intermingled. It is told
that once Schopenhauer, the gloomy philosopher, was found
wandering. He was asked, 'Who are you?' 'I wish you could

tell me,' he answered. Robert Burns said of himself, 'My life reminded me of a ruined temple. What strength, what proportion in some parts! What unsightly gaps, what prostrate ruins in others!' The human predicament has always been that we are haunted both by sin and by goodness. The coming of Jesus unifies that disintegrated personality into one. We find victory over our warring selves by being conquered by Jesus Christ.

(d) It is good news of God's *promise* (Ephesians 3:6). It is true that the tendency has been to think of a God of threats rather than a God of promises. Non-Christian religions think of a demanding God; only Christianity tells of a God who is more ready to give than we are to ask.

(e) It is good news of *immortality* (2 Timothy 1:10). To the pagan, life was the road to death; but Jesus came with the good news that we are on the way to life rather than death.

(f) It is good news of *salvation* (Ephesians 1:13). That salvation is not merely a negative thing; it is also positive. It is not simply liberation from penalty and escape from past sin; it is the power to live life victoriously and to conquer sin. The message of Jesus is good news indeed.

(2) There is the word *repent*. Now repentance is not so easy as sometimes we think. The Greek word *metanoia* literally means *a change of mind*. We are very apt to confuse two things – sorrow for the consequences of sin and sorrow for sin. Many people become desperately sorry because of the mess that sin has got them into, but they know very well that, if they could be reasonably sure that they could escape the consequences, they would do the same thing again. It is not the sin that they hate; it is its consequences.

Real repentance means coming not only to be sorry for the consequences of sin but to hate sin itself. Long ago, that wise old writer, Montaigne, wrote in his autobiography,

'Children should be taught to hate vice for its own texture, so that they will not only avoid it in action, but abominate it in their hearts – that the very thought of it may disgust them whatever form it takes.' Repentance means that anyone who was in love with sin comes to hate sin because of its exceeding sinfulness.

(3) There is the word *believe*. 'Believe', says Jesus, 'in the good news.' To believe in the good news simply means to take Jesus at his word, to believe that God is the kind of God that Jesus has told us about, to believe that God so loves the world that he will make any sacrifice to bring us back to himself, to believe that what sounds too good to be true is really true.

JESUS CHOOSES HIS FRIENDS

Mark 1:16–20

> While he was walking beside the Sea of Galilee, he saw Simon and Andrew, Simon's brother, casting their nets into the sea, for they were fishermen. So Jesus said to them, 'Follow me! and I will make you fishers of men.' And immediately they left their nets and followed him. He went a little farther and he saw James, the son of Zebedee, and John, his brother, who were in their boat, mending their nets. Immediately he called them; and they left their father Zebedee in the boat, with the hired servants, and went away after him.

No sooner had Jesus taken his decision and decided his method than he proceeded to build up his staff. Those who seek to lead must begin somewhere. They must gather together kindred souls to whom they can unburden their own hearts and on whose hearts they may write their message. So

29

Mark here shows us Jesus literally laying the foundations of his kingdom and calling his first followers.

There were many fishermen in Galilee. Josephus, who, for a time, was governor of Galilee, and who is the great historian of the Jews, tells us that in his day 330 fishing boats sailed the waters of the lake. Ordinary people in Palestine seldom ate meat, probably not more than once a week. Fish was their staple diet (Luke 11:11; Matthew 7:10; Mark 6:30–44; Luke 24:42). Usually the fish was salt because there was no means of transporting fresh fish. Fresh fish was one of the greatest of all delicacies in the great cities like Rome. The very names of the towns on the lakeside show how important the fishing business was. *Bethsaida* means *House of Fish*; *Tarichaea* means *The Place of Salt-fish*, and it was there that the fish were preserved for export to Jerusalem and even to Rome itself. The salt-fish industry was big business in Galilee.

The fishermen used two kinds of nets, both of which are mentioned or implied in the gospels. They used the net called the *sagēnē*. This was a kind of seine- or trawl-net. It was let out from the end of the boat and was so weighted that it stood, as it were, upright in the water. The boat then moved forward, and, as it moved, the four corners of the net were drawn together, so that the net became like a great bag moving through the water and enclosing the fish. The other kind of net, which Peter and Andrew were using here, was called the *amphiblēstron*. It was a much smaller net. It was skilfully cast into the water by hand and was shaped rather like an umbrella.

It is naturally of the greatest interest to study the men whom Jesus picked out as his first followers.

(1) We must notice *what they were*. They were simple folk. They did not come from the schools and colleges; they were

not drawn from the religious elite or the aristocracy; they were neither learned nor wealthy. They were fishermen. That is to say, they were ordinary people. No one ever believed in ordinary men and women as Jesus did. Once George Bernard Shaw said, 'I have never had any feeling for the working classes, except a desire to abolish them, and replace them by sensible people.' In *The Patrician*, the novelist and playwright John Galsworthy makes Miltoun, one of the characters, say, 'The mob! How I loathe it! I hate its mean stupidity, I hate the sound of its voice, and the look on its face – it's so ugly, so little!' Once, in a fit of temper, Thomas Carlyle declared that there were 27,000,000 people in England – mostly fools! Jesus did not feel like that. Abraham Lincoln said, 'God must love the common people – he made so many of them.' It was as if Jesus said, 'Give me twelve ordinary men and with them, if they will give themselves to me, I will change the world.' We should never think so much of what we are as of what Jesus Christ can make us.

(2) We must notice *what they were doing* when Jesus called them. They were doing their day's work, catching the fish and mending the nets. It was so with many a prophet. 'I am no prophet,' said Amos, 'nor a prophet's son; but I am a herdsman, and a dresser of sycamore trees, and *the Lord took me from following the flock*, and the Lord said to me, "Go, prophesy to my people Israel"' (Amos 7:14–15). The call of God can come to any one of us, not only in the house of God, not only in the secret place, but in the middle of the day's work. As MacAndrew, Rudyard Kipling's Scots engineer, had it:

> From coupler flange to spindle guide
> I see thy hand, O God;
> Predestination in the stride
> Of yon connecting rod.

Those who live in a world that is full of God cannot ever escape him.

(3) We must notice *how he called them*. Jesus' summons was, 'Follow me!' It is not to be thought that on this day he stood before them for the first time. No doubt they had stood in the crowd and listened, no doubt they had stayed to talk long after the rest of the crowd had drifted away. No doubt they already had felt the magic of his presence and the magnetism of his eyes. Jesus did not say to them, 'I have a theological system which I would like you to investigate; I have certain theories that I would like you to think over; I have an ethical system I would like to discuss with you.' He said, 'Follow me!' It all began with a personal reaction to himself; it all began with that tug on the heart which begets the unshakable loyalty. This is not to say that there are none who think themselves into Christianity; but for most of us following Christ is like falling in love. It has been said that 'we admire people for reasons, we love them without reasons'. The thing happens just because they are they and we are we. 'And I,' said Jesus, 'when I am lifted up from the earth, will draw all people to myself' (John 12:32). In by far the greatest number of cases, people follow Jesus Christ not because of anything that Jesus said but because of everything that Jesus is.

(4) Lastly, we must notice *what Jesus offered them. He offered them a task*. He called them not to ease but to service. It has been said that what we all need is something in which to invest our lives. So Jesus called his disciples, not to a comfortable ease and not to a lethargic inactivity; he called them to a task in which they would have to spend themselves and burn themselves up, and, in the end, die for his sake and for the sake of others. He called them to a task wherein they

could win something for themselves only by giving their all to him and to others.

JESUS BEGINS HIS CAMPAIGN

Mark 1:21-2

> So they came into Capernaum; and immediately on the Sabbath day Jesus went into the synagogue and began to teach; and they were completely astonished at the way he taught, for he taught them like one who had personal authority, and not as the experts in the law did.

MARK's story unfolds in a series of logical and natural steps. Jesus recognized in the emergence of John God's call to action. He was baptized and received God's seal of approval and God's equipment for his task. He was tested by the devil and chose the method he would use and the way he would take. He chose his disciples that he might have a little circle of kindred spirits and that he might write his message upon them. And now he had to make a deliberate launching of his campaign. If a man had a message from God to give, the natural place to which he would turn would be the place where God's people met together. That is precisely what Jesus did. He began his campaign in the synagogue.

There are certain basic differences between the synagogue and the church as we know it today.

(a) The synagogue was primarily *a teaching institution*. The synagogue service consisted of only three things – prayer, the reading of God's word and the exposition of it. There was no music, no singing and no sacrifice. It may be said that the *Temple* was the place of *worship and sacrifice*; the synagogue was the place of *teaching and instruction*. The synagogue was by far the more influential, for there was only one Temple. But the law laid it down that wherever there were ten Jewish families there must be a synagogue, and, therefore, wherever there was a colony of Jews, there was a synagogue. If a man had a new message to preach, the synagogue was the obvious place in which to preach it.

(b) The synagogue provided an opportunity to deliver such a message. The synagogue had certain officials. There was the *ruler of the synagogue*. He was responsible for the administration of the affairs of the synagogue and for the arrangements for its services. There were *the distributors of alms*. A collection was taken daily in cash and in kind from those who could afford to give. It was then distributed to the poor; the very poorest were given food for fourteen meals per week. There was *the Chazzan*. He is the man whom the Authorized Version describes as *the minister*. He was responsible for the taking out and storing away of the sacred rolls on which Scripture was written; for the cleaning of the synagogue; for the blowing of the blasts on the silver trumpet which told people that the Sabbath had come; for the elementary education of the children of the community. One thing the synagogue did not have was a permanent preacher or teacher. When the people met at the synagogue service it was open to the ruler to call on any competent person to give the address and the exposition. There was no professional ministry whatsoever. That is why Jesus was able to open his campaign in the synagogues. The opposition had not yet stiffened into hostility. He was known to be a man with a message; and for that very reason the synagogue of every community provided him with a pulpit from which to instruct and to appeal to the people.

When Jesus did teach in the synagogue, the whole method and atmosphere of his teaching was like a new revelation. He did not teach like the scribes, the experts in the law. Who were these scribes?

To the Jews, the most sacred thing in the world was *the Torah*, the law. The core of the law is the Ten Commandments, but the law was taken to mean the first five books of the Old Testament, the Pentateuch, as they are called. To the Jews, this law was completely divine. It had, so they believed, been given directly by God to Moses. It was absolutely holy and absolutely binding. They said, 'He who says that the Torah is not from God has no part in the future world.' 'He who says that Moses wrote even one verse of his own knowledge is a denier and despiser of the word of God.'

If the Torah is so divine, two things emerge. First, it must be the supreme rule of faith and life; and second, it must contain everything necessary to guide and to direct life. If that is so, the Torah demands two things. First, it must obviously be given the most careful and meticulous study. Second, the Torah is expressed in great, wide principles; but, if it contains direction and guidance for *all* life, what is in it implicitly must be brought out. The great laws must become rules and regulations – so their argument ran.

To give this study and to supply this development, a class of scholars arose. These were the *scribes*, the experts in the law. The title of the greatest of them was *Rabbi*. The scribes had three duties.

(1) They set themselves, out of the great moral principles of the Torah, to extract rules and regulations for every possible situation in life. Obviously this was a task that was endless. Jewish religion began with the great moral laws; it ended with an infinity of rules and regulations. It began as religion; it ended as legalism.

(2) It was the task of the scribes to transmit and to teach this law and its developments. These deduced and extracted

rules and regulations were never written down; they are known as *the oral law*. Although never written down, they were considered to be even *more* binding than the written law. From generation to generation of scribes, they were taught and committed to memory. A good student had a memory which was like 'a well lined with lime which loses not one drop'.

(3) The scribes had the duty of giving judgment in individual cases; and, in the nature of things, practically every individual case must have produced a new law.

In what ways did Jesus' teaching differ so much from the teaching of the scribes? He taught with *personal authority*. No scribe ever gave a decision on his own. He would always begin, 'There is a teaching that . . .' and would then quote all his authorities. If he made a statement, he would buttress it with this, that and the next quotation from the great legal masters of the past. The last thing he ever gave was an independent judgment. How different was Jesus! When he spoke, he spoke as if he needed no authority beyond himself. He spoke with utter independence. He cited no authorities and quoted no experts. He spoke with the finality of the voice of God. To the people, it was like a breeze from heaven to hear someone speak like that. The terrific, positive certainty of Jesus was the very antithesis of the careful quotations of the scribes. The note of personal authority rang out – and that is a note which captures everyone's attention.

THE FIRST VICTORY OVER THE POWERS OF EVIL

Mark 1:23–8

There was in the synagogue a man in the grip of an unclean spirit. Immediately he broke into a shout. 'What have we to do with you, Jesus of Nazareth?' he said.

'Have you come to destroy us? I know who you are –
you are the Holy One of God.' Jesus spoke sternly to
him. 'Be silent,' he said, 'and come out of him.' When
the unclean spirit had convulsed the man and had cried
with a great cry it came out of him. They were all so
astonished that they kept asking each other, 'What is
this? This is a new kind of teaching. He gives his orders
with authority even to unclean spirits and they obey
him.' And immediately the report about Jesus went out
everywhere over the whole surrounding district of
Galilee.

IF Jesus' words had amazed the people in the synagogue, his
deeds left them thunderstruck. In the synagogue, there was a
man in the grip of an unclean spirit. He created a disturbance,
and Jesus healed him.

All through the gospels, we keep meeting people who had
unclean spirits and who were possessed by demons or devils.
What lies behind this?

The Jews, and indeed the whole ancient world, believed
strongly in demons and devils. As the German scholar Adolf
von Harnack put it, 'The whole world and the circumambient
atmosphere were filled with devils; not merely idolatry, but
every phase and form of life was ruled by them. They sat on
thrones, they hovered around cradles. The earth was literally
a hell.'

Dr A. Rendle Short, the professor of medicine, cites a fact
which shows the intensity with which the ancient world
believed in demons. In many ancient cemeteries, skulls were
found which had been trepanned. That is to say, a hole had
been bored in the skull. In one cemetery, out of 120 skulls,
six had been trepanned. With the limited surgical technique
available, that was no small operation. Further, it was clear
from the bone growth that the trepanning had been done

during life. It was also clear that the hole in the skull was too small to be of any physical or surgical value; and it is known that the removed disc of bone was often worn as an amulet round the neck. The reason for the trepanning was to allow the demon to escape from the person's body. If primitive surgeons were prepared to undertake that operation, and if people were prepared to undergo it, the belief in demon-possession must have been intensely real.

Where did these demons come from? There were three answers to that question. (1) Some believed that they were as old as creation itself. (2) Some believed that they were the spirits of the wicked who had died and were still carrying on their malignant work. (3) Most people connected the demons with the old story in Genesis 6:1–8 (cf. 2 Peter 2:4–5).

The Jews elaborated the story in this way. There were two angels who forsook God and came to this earth because they were attracted by the beauty of mortal women. Their names were Assael and Shemachsai. One of them returned to God; the other remained on earth and gratified his lust; and the demons are the children that he fathered and their children.

The collective word for demons is *mazzikin*, which means *one who does harm*. So the demons were malignant beings intermediate between God and human beings and who were out to work harm.

The demons, according to Jewish belief, could eat and drink and beget children. They were terrifyingly numerous. There were, according to some, 7,500,000 of them; everyone had 10,000 on the right hand and 10,000 on the left. They lived in unclean places, such as tombs and spots where there was no cleansing water. They lived in the desert where their howling could be heard – hence the phrase *a howling desert*. They were specially dangerous to the lonely traveller, to the woman in childbirth, to the bride and bridegroom, to children who were out after dark, and to those who voyaged at night. They were specially active in the midday heat and between sunset and sunrise. There was a demon of blindness and a demon of leprosy and a demon of heart disease. They could transfer their malign gifts to people. For instance, the evil eye which could turn good fortune into bad and in which all believed was given to an individual by the demons. They worked along with certain animals – the serpent, the bull, the donkey and the mosquito. The male demons were known as *shedim*, and the female as *lilin*, after Lilith. The female demons had long hair and were the enemies of children. That is why children had their guardian angels (Matthew 18:10).

It does not matter whether or not we believe in all this; whether it is true or not is beside the point. The point is that the people in New Testament times did. We still may use the phrase *Poor devil!* That is a relic of the old belief. When a man believed himself to be possessed, he was 'conscious of himself and also of another being who constrains and controls him from within'. That explains why the demon-possessed in Palestine so often cried out when they met Jesus. They knew that Jesus was believed by some at least to be the Messiah; they knew that the reign of the Messiah was the end of the demons; and those who believed themselves to be possessed spoke as demons when they came into the presence of Jesus.

There were many exorcists who claimed to be able to cast out demons. So real was this belief that by AD 340 the Christian Church actually possessed an Order of Exorcists. But there was this difference – the ordinary Jewish and pagan exorcist used elaborate incantations and spells and magical rites. Jesus with one word of clear, simple, brief authority exorcised the demon. No one had ever seen anything like this before. The power was not in the spell, the formula, the incantation, the elaborate rite; the power was in Jesus, and people were astonished.

What are we to say to all this? Paul Tournier in *A Doctor's Casebook* writes, 'Doubtless there are many doctors who in their struggle against disease have had, like me, the feeling that they were confronting, not something passive, but a clever and resourceful enemy.' Dr Rendle Short comes tentatively to the conclusion that 'the happenings in this world, in fact, and its moral disasters, its wars and wickedness, its physical catastrophes, and its sicknesses, may be part of a great warfare due to the interplay of forces such as we see in the book of *Job*, the malice of the devil on one hand and the restraints imposed by God on the other'.

This is a subject on which we cannot dogmatize. We may take three different positions. (1) We may relegate the whole matter of demon-possession to the sphere of primitive thought and say that it was a primitive way of accounting for things in the days before more was known about the human body or the working of the mind. (2) We may accept the fact of demon-possession as being true in New Testament times and as being still true today. (3) If we accept the first position, we have to explain the attitude and actions of Jesus. Either he knew no more on this matter than the people of his day – and that is a thing we can easily accept, for Jesus was not a scientist and did not come to teach science. Or he knew perfectly well that he could never cure the person in trouble unless he assumed the reality of the disease. It was real to the person concerned and had to be treated as such or it could never be cured. In the end we come to the conclusion that there are some answers we do not know.

A PRIVATE MIRACLE

Mark 1:29–31

> And immediately, when they had come out of the
> synagogue, they went, along with Peter and John, into
> the house of Simon and Andrew. Peter's mother-in-law
> was in bed with an attack of fever. Immediately they
> spoke to Jesus about her. He went up to her and took
> her by the hand and raised her up, and the fever left her,
> and she attended to their needs.

IN the synagogue, Jesus had spoken and acted in the most
amazing way. The synagogue service ended and Jesus went
with his friends to Peter's house. According to Jewish custom
the main Sabbath meal came immediately after the synagogue
service, at the sixth hour, that is at 12 noon. (The Jewish day
began at 6 am and the hours are counted from then.) Jesus
might well have claimed the right to rest after the exciting
and exhausting experience of the synagogue service; but once
again his power was appealed to and once again he gave of
himself for others. This miracle tells us something about three
people.

(1) It tells us something about *Jesus*. He did not require
an audience in order to exert his power; he was just as
prepared to heal in the little circle of a cottage as in the great
crowd of a synagogue. He was never too tired to help; the
need of others took precedence over his own desire for rest.
But above all, we see here, as we saw in the synagogue, the
uniqueness of the methods of Jesus. There were many
exorcists in the time of Jesus, but they worked with elaborate
incantations, and formulae, and spells, and magical apparatus.
In the synagogue, Jesus had spoken one authoritative sentence
and the healing was complete.

41

Here we have the same thing again. Peter's mother-in-law
was suffering from what the Talmud called 'a burning fever'.
It was, and still is, very prevalent in that particular part of
Galilee. The Talmud actually lays down the methods of
dealing with it. A knife entirely made of iron was tied by a
braid of hair to a thorn bush. On successive days there was
repeated, first, Exodus 3:2–3; second, Exodus 3:4; and finally
Exodus 3:5. Then a certain magical formula was pronounced,
and thus the cure was supposed to be achieved. Jesus
completely disregarded all the paraphernalia of popular
magic, and with a gesture and a word of unique authority and
power he healed the woman.

The word that the Greek uses for authority in the previous
passage is *exousia*; and *exousia* was defined as unique
knowledge together with unique power; that is precisely what
Jesus possessed, and that is what he was prepared to exercise
in a cottage. Paul Tournier writes, 'My patients very often
say to me, "I admire the patience with which you listen to
everything I tell you." It is not patience at all, but interest.' A
miracle to Jesus was not a means of increasing his prestige;
to help was not a laborious and disagreeable duty; he helped
instinctively, because he was supremely interested in all who
needed his help.

(2) It tells us something about *the disciples*. They had not
known Jesus long, but already they had begun to take all
their troubles to him. Peter's mother-in-law was ill; the home
was upset; and it was for the disciples the most natural thing
in the world to tell Jesus all about it.

Paul Tournier tells how one of life's greatest discoveries
came to him. He used to visit an old Christian pastor who
never let him go without praying with him. He was struck by
the extreme simplicity of the old man's prayers. It seemed
just a continuation of an intimate conversation that the old

saint was always carrying on with Jesus. Tournier goes on, 'When I got back home I talked it over with my wife, and together we asked God to give us also the close fellowship with Jesus the old pastor had. Since then he has been the centre of my devotion and my travelling companion. He takes pleasure in what I do (cf. Ecclesiastes 9:7), and concerns himself with it. He is a friend with whom I can discuss everything that happens in my life. He shares my joy and my pain, my hopes and fears. He is there when a patient speaks to me from his heart, listening to him with me and better than I can. And when the patient is gone I can talk to him about it.'

Therein there lies the very essence of the Christian life. As the hymn has it, 'Take it to the Lord in prayer.' Thus early the disciples had learned what became the habit of a lifetime – to take all their troubles to Jesus and to ask his help for them.

(3) It tells us something about *Peter's wife's mother*. No sooner was she healed than she began to attend to their needs. She used her recovered health for renewed service. A great Scottish family has the motto 'Saved to Serve'. Jesus helps us that we may help others.

THE BEGINNING OF THE CROWDS

Mark 1:32-4

> When evening had come and when the sun had set, they kept bringing to him all those who were ill and demon-possessed. The whole city had crowded together to the door; and he healed many who were ill with various diseases and cast out many demons; and he forbade the demons to speak because they knew him.

THE things that Jesus had done in Capernaum could not be concealed. The emergence of so great a new power and authority was not something which could be kept secret. So the evening found Peter's house besieged with crowds seeking Jesus' healing touch. They waited until evening because the law forbade the carrying of any burden through a town on the Sabbath day (cf. Jeremiah 17:24). That would have been to work, and work was forbidden. They had, of course, no clocks or watches in those days; the Sabbath ran from 6 pm to 6 pm; and the law was that the Sabbath was ended and the day had finished when three stars came out in the sky. So the people of Capernaum waited until the sun had set and the stars were out and then they came, carrying their sick, to Jesus; and he healed them.

Three times we have seen Jesus healing people. First he healed in the synagogue; second, he healed in the house of his friends; and now he healed in the street. Jesus recognized the claim of everyone. It was said of that great eighteenth-century man of letters Dr Johnson that to be in misfortune was to be assured of his friendship and support. Wherever there was trouble Jesus was ready to use his power. He selected neither the place nor the person; he was aware of the universal claim of human need.

The people flocked to Jesus because they recognized in him a man *who could do things*. There were plenty who could talk and expound and lecture and preach; but here was one who dealt not only in words but also in actions. It has been said that 'if a man can make a better mousetrap than his neighbours, the public will beat a path to his house even if he lives in the middle of a wood'. The person people want is the effective person. Jesus could, and can, produce results.

But there is the beginning of tragedy here. The crowds came, but they came *because they wanted something out of*

Jesus. They did not come because they loved him; they did not come because they had caught a glimpse of some new vision; in the last analysis they wanted to use him. That is what nearly everyone wants to do with God and his Son. For one prayer that goes up to God in days of prosperity, 10,000 go up in time of adversity. Many who have never prayed when the sun was shining begin to pray when the cold winds come.

Someone has said that many people regard religion as belonging 'to the ambulance corps and not to the firing line of life'. Religion to them is a crisis affair. It is only when they have got life into a mess, or when life deals them some knock-out blow, that they begin to remember God. We must all go to Jesus, for he alone can give us the things we need for life; but if that going and these gifts do not produce in us an answering love and gratitude there is something tragically wrong. God is not someone to be used in the day of misfortune; he is someone to be loved and remembered every day of our lives.

THE QUIET HOUR AND THE CHALLENGE OF ACTION

Mark 1:35–9

> Very early, when it was still night, Jesus rose and went out. He went away to a deserted place and there he was praying. Simon and his friends tracked him down and said to him, 'They are all searching for you.' Jesus said to them, 'Let us go somewhere else, to the nearby villages, that I may proclaim the good news there too, for that is why I came forth.' So he went to their synagogues, all over Galilee, proclaiming the good news as he went, and casting out demons.

SIMPLY to read the record of the things that happened at Capernaum is to see that Jesus was left with no time alone. Now Jesus knew well that he could not live without God; that if he was going to be forever giving out, he must be at least sometimes taking in, that if he was going to spend himself for others, he must constantly summon spiritual reinforcements to his aid. He knew that he could not live without prayer. In a little book entitled *The Practice of Prayer*, Dr A. D. Belden has some great definitions. 'Prayer may be defined as the appeal of the soul to God.' Not to pray is to be guilty of the incredible folly of ignoring 'the possibility of adding God to our resources'. 'In prayer we give the perfect mind of God an opportunity to feed our mental powers.' Jesus knew this; he knew that if he was to meet people he must first meet God. If prayer was necessary for Jesus, how much more must it be necessary for us?

Even there they sought him out. There was no way in which Jesus could shut the door. Once Rose Macaulay, the novelist, said that all she demanded from this life was 'a room of her own'. That is precisely what Jesus never had. A great doctor has said that the duty of medicine is 'sometimes to heal, often to afford relief, and always to bring consolation'. That duty was always upon Jesus. It has been said that a doctor's duty is 'to help people to live and to die' – and they are always living and dying. It is human nature to try to put up the barriers and to have time and peace to oneself; that is what Jesus never did. Conscious as he was of his own weariness and exhaustion, he was still more conscious of the insistent cry of human need. So when they came for him he rose from his knees to meet the challenge of his task. Prayer will never do our work for us; what it will do is to strengthen us for work which must be done.

Jesus set out on a preaching tour of the synagogues of Galilee. In Mark this tour is dismissed in one verse, but it must have taken weeks and even months to do it. As he went he *preached* and he *healed*. There were three pairs of things which Jesus never separated.

(1) He never separated *words and actions*. He never thought that a work was done when that work was stated; he never believed that his duty was completed when he had exhorted people to God and to goodness. Always the statement and the exhortation were put into action. The American Baptist, Harry Emerson Fosdick, tells of a student who bought the best possible books and the best possible equipment and got a special study chair with a special bookrest to make study easy, and then sat down in the chair – and went to sleep. The person who deals in words with no actions to follow is very like that.

(2) He never separated *soul and body*. There have been types of Christianity which spoke as if the body did not matter. But human beings are *both* soul and body. And the task of Christianity is to redeem the whole person and not just a part. It is indeed blessedly true that it is possible to be starving, living in a hovel and in distress and pain, and yet have sweet times with God; but that is no reason at all to let people live in such a state. Missionaries do not only take the Bible; they take education and medicine; they take the school and the hospital. It is quite wrong to talk about the *social gospel* as if it were an extra, or an option, or even a separate part of the Christian message. The Christian message is one, and it preaches and works for the good of the body as well as the good of the soul.

(3) Jesus never separated *earth and heaven*. There are those who are so concerned with heaven that they forget all about earth and so become impractical visionaries. There are those who are so concerned with earth that they forget about heaven and limit good to material good. The

dream of Jesus was a time when God's will would be done on earth as it is in heaven (Matthew 6:10), and earth and heaven be one.

THE LEPER IS CLEANSED

Mark 1:40–5

A leper came to him, asking him to help him and kneeling before him. 'If you are willing to do so,' he said, 'you are able to cleanse me.' Jesus was moved with pity to the depths of his being.

He stretched out his hand and touched him. 'I am willing,' Jesus said, 'be cleansed.' Immediately the leprosy left him and he was cleansed. Immediately Jesus sent him away with a stern injunction. 'See to it', he said to him, 'that you tell no man anything about this; but go and show yourself to the priest, and bring the offering for cleansing which Moses laid down, so that you may prove to them that you really are healed.' He went away and began to proclaim the story at length and to spread it all over. The result was that it was not possible for Jesus to come openly into any town, but he had to stay outside in the lonely places; and they kept coming to him from all over.

IN the New Testament there is no disease regarded with more terror and pity than leprosy. When Jesus sent out the Twelve he commanded them, 'Heal the sick, cleanse lepers' (Matthew 10:8). The fate of the leper was truly hard. E. W. G. Masterman in his article on leprosy in the *Dictionary of Christ and the Gospels*, from which we have drawn much of the information that follows, says, 'No other disease reduces a human being for so many years to so hideous a wreck.' Let us look first at the facts.

There are three kinds of leprosy.

(1) There is *nodular* or *tubercular leprosy*. It begins with an unaccountable lethargy and pains in the joints. Then there appear on the body, especially on the back, symmetrical discoloured patches. On them little nodules form, at first pink, then turning brown. The skin is thickened. The nodules gather specially in the folds of the cheek, the nose, the lips and the forehead. The whole appearance of the face is changed until the afflicted person loses all human appearance and looks, as the ancients said, like a lion or a satyr. The nodules grow larger and larger; they ulcerate and from them comes a foul discharge. The eyebrows fall out; the eyes become staring; the voice becomes hoarse and the breath wheezes because of the ulceration of the vocal chords. The hands and the feet also ulcerate. Slowly the sufferer becomes a mass of ulcerated growths. The average course of the disease is nine years, and it ends in mental decay, coma and ultimately death. Those suffering from this type of leprosy become utterly repulsive both to themselves and to others.

(2) There is *anaesthetic leprosy*. The initial stages are the same; but the nerve trunks also are affected. The infected area loses all sensation. This may happen without those who suffer from the disease knowing that it has happened; and they may not realize that it has happened until they suffer some burning or scalding and find that there is no feeling whatsoever where pain ought to be. As the disease develops, the injury to the nerves causes discoloured patches and blisters. The muscles waste away; the tendons contract until the hands become like claws. There is always disfigurement of the fingernails. There ensues chronic ulceration of the feet and of the hands and then the progressive loss of fingers and of toes, until in the end a whole hand or a whole foot may drop off. The duration of the disease is anything from

twenty to thirty years. It is a kind of terrible progressive death of the body.

(3) The third kind of leprosy is a type – the commonest of all – where nodular and anaesthetic leprosy are mixed.

That is leprosy proper, and there is no doubt that there were many lepers like that in Palestine in the time of Jesus. From the description in Leviticus 13 it is quite clear that in New Testament times the term *leprosy* was also used to cover other skin diseases. It seems to have been used to include *psoriasis*, a disease which covers the body with white scales, and which would give rise to the phrase 'a leper as white as snow'. It seems also to have included ring-worm, which is still very common in the middle east. The Hebrew word used in Leviticus for leprosy is *tsaraath*. Now Leviticus 13:47 speaks of a *tsaraath* of garments, and a *tsaraath* of houses is dealt with in Leviticus 14:33. Such a blemish on a garment would be some kind of mould or fungus; and on a house it would be some kind of dry rot in the wood or destructive lichen on the stone. The word *tsaraath*, *leprosy* in Jewish thought, seems to have covered any kind of creeping skin disease. Very naturally, with medical knowledge in an extremely primitive state, diagnosis did not distinguish between the different kinds of skin disease and included both the deadly and incurable and the non-fatal and comparatively harmless under the one inclusive title.

Any such skin disease rendered the sufferers unclean. They were banished from the fellowship of others; they must dwell alone outside the camp; they must go with rent clothes, bared heads and a covering upon their upper lips, and as they went they must give warning of their polluted presence with the cry, 'Unclean, unclean!' We see the same thing in the middle ages, which merely applied the Mosaic law. The priest, wearing his stole and carrying a crucifix, led lepers into the church, and read the burial service over them. Lepers were people who were already dead, though still alive. They had to wear black garments that all might recognize and live in a leper- or lazar-house. They must not come into a church service, but while the service went on they might peer through the leper 'squint' cut in the walls. Lepers had not only to bear the physical pain of their disease, they had to bear the mental anguish and the heartbreak of being completely banished from human society and totally shunned.

If ever a leper was cured – and real leprosy was incurable, so it is some of the other skin diseases which must be referred to – he had to undergo a complicated ceremony of restoration which is described in Leviticus 14. He was examined by the priest. Two birds were taken and one was killed over running water. In addition, there were taken cedar, crimson yarn and hyssop. These things and the living bird were dipped in the blood of the dead bird and then the live bird was allowed to go free. The man washed himself and his clothes and shaved himself. Seven days then elapsed and he was re-examined. He had then to shave his hair, his head, his eyebrows. Certain sacrifices were made – two male lambs without blemish and one ewe lamb; a measure of fine flour mixed with oil and one log (a liquid measure) of oil. The amounts were less for the poor. The restored sufferer was touched on the tip of the right ear, the right thumb and the right big toe with blood and oil. He was given a final examination and, if clear of the disease, he was allowed to go with a certificate that he was clean.

Here is one of the most revealing pictures of Jesus.

(1) He did not drive away a man who had broken the law. The leper had no right to have spoken to him at all, but Jesus met the desperation of human need with an understanding compassion.

(2) Jesus stretched out his hand and touched him. He touched the man who was unclean. To Jesus he was not unclean; he was simply a human soul in desperate need.

(3) Having cleansed him, Jesus sent him to fulfil the prescribed ritual. He fulfilled the human law and human righteousness. He did not recklessly defy the conventions, but, when need be, submitted to them.

Here we see compassion, power and wisdom all at work together.

A FAITH THAT WOULD NOT BE DENIED

Mark 2:1-6

> When, some time afterwards, Jesus had come back to Capernaum, the news went round that he was in a house. Such crowds collected that there was no longer any room left, not even round the door. So he was speaking the word to them. A party arrived bringing to him a paralysed man carried by four men. When they could not get near him because of the crowd they unroofed part of the roof of the house in which he was, and when they had dug out part of the roof, they let down the stretcher on which the paralysed man was lying. When Jesus saw their faith, he said to the paralysed man, 'Child, your sins are forgiven.'

AFTER Jesus had completed his tour of the synagogues, he returned to Capernaum. The news of his coming immediately spread abroad. Life in Palestine was very public. In the morning the door of the house was opened and anyone who wished might come out and in. The door was never shut unless someone deliberately wished for privacy; an open door meant an open invitation for all to come in. In the humbler houses, such as this must have been, there was no entrance hall; the door opened directly on to the street. So, in no time, a crowd had filled the house to capacity and jammed the pavement round the door; and they were all eagerly listening to what Jesus had to say.

Into this crowd came four men carrying on a stretcher a friend of theirs who was paralysed. They could not get through the crowd at all, but they were men of resource. The roof of a Palestinian house was flat. It was regularly used as a place of rest and of quiet, and so usually there was an outside stair which ascended to it. The construction of the roof lent itself to what these ingenious four proposed to do. The roof consisted of flat beams laid across from wall to wall, perhaps three feet apart. The space in between the beams was filled with brushwood packed tight with clay. The top was then made watertight. Very largely the roof was of earth and often a flourishing crop of grass grew on the roof of a Palestinian house. It was the easiest thing in the world to dig out the filling between two of the beams; it did not even damage the house very much, and it was easy to repair the breach again. So the four men dug out the filling between two of the beams and let their friend down directly at Jesus' feet. When Jesus saw this faith that laughed at barriers, he must have smiled an understanding smile. He looked at the man, 'Child,' he said, 'your sins are forgiven.'

It may seem an odd way to begin a cure. But in Palestine, in the time of Jesus, it was natural and inevitable. The Jews integrally connected sin and suffering. They argued that if people were suffering they must have sinned. That is in fact the argument that Job's friends produced. 'Who', demanded Eliphaz the Temanite, 'that was innocent ever perished?' (Job 4:7). The Rabbis had a saying, 'There is no sick man healed of his sickness until all his sins have been forgiven him.' To the Jews, a sick person was someone with whom God was angry. It is true that a great many illnesses are due to sin; it is still truer that time and time again they are due not to the sin of the one who is ill, but to the sin of others. We do not make the close connection that the Jews did, but any Jew would have agreed that forgiveness of sins was a prior condition of cure.

It may well be, however, that there is more than this in this story. The Jews made this connection between illness and sin, and it may well be that, in this case, *the man's conscience agreed*. And it may well be that that consciousness of sin had actually produced the paralysis. The power of the mind, especially the subconscious mind, over the body is an amazing thing.

Psychologists quote a case of a girl who played the piano in a cinema in the days of the silent films. Normally she was quite well, but immediately the lights went out and cigarette smoke filled the auditorium she began to be paralysed. She fought against it for a long time, but at last the paralysis became permanent and something had to be done. Examination revealed no physical cause whatever. Under hypnosis it was discovered that when she was very young, only a few weeks old, she had been lying in one of those elaborate old-fashioned cots with an arch of lace over it. Her mother had bent over her smoking a cigarette. The draperies had caught fire. It was immediately extinguished and no physical harm was done to her, but her subconscious mind was remembering this terror. The dark plus the smell of the cigarette smoke in the cinema acted on the unconscious mind and paralysed her body – and she did not know why.

The man in this story may well have been paralysed because consciously or unconsciously his conscience agreed that he was a sinner, and the thought of being a sinner brought the illness which he believed was the inevitable consequence of sin. The first thing that Jesus said to him was, 'Child, God is not angry with you. It's all right.' It was like speaking to a frightened child in the dark. The burden of the terror of God and estrangement from God rolled from his heart, and that very fact made the cure all but complete.

It is a lovely story because the first thing that Jesus does for every one of us is to say, 'Child, God is not angry with you. Come home, and don't be afraid.'

THE UNANSWERABLE ARGUMENT

Mark 2:7–12

Some of the experts in the law were sitting there, and they were debating within themselves, 'How can this fellow speak like this? He is insulting God. Who can forgive sins except one person – God?' Jesus immediately knew in his spirit that this debate was going on in their minds, so he said to them, 'Why do you debate thus in your minds? Which is easier – to say to the paralysed man, "Your sins are forgiven," or to say, "Get up, and lift your bed, and walk around"? Just to let you see that the Son of Man has authority on earth to forgive sins' – he said to the paralysed man – 'I say to you, "Get up! Lift your bed! And go away home!"' And he raised himself, and immediately he lifted his bed, and went out in front of them all. The result was that they were all astonished, and they kept on praising God. 'Never', they kept repeating, 'have we seen anything like this.'

55

JESUS, as we have seen, had already attracted the crowds. Because of that, he had attracted the notice of the official leaders of the Jews. The Sanhedrin was their supreme court. One of its great functions was to be the guardian of orthodoxy. For instance, it was the Sanhedrin's duty to deal with anyone who was a false prophet. It seems that it had sent out a kind of scouting party to check up on Jesus; and they were there in Capernaum. No doubt they had taken up a prominent place in the front of the crowd and were sitting there critically watching everything that was going on.

When they heard Jesus say to the man that his sins were forgiven, it came as a shattering shock. It was an essential of Judaism that only God could forgive sins. For any human being to claim to do so was to insult God; that was blasphemy, and the penalty for blasphemy was death by stoning (Leviticus 24:16). At the moment they were not ready to launch their attack in public, but it was not difficult for Jesus to see how their minds were working. So he determined to fling down a challenge and to meet them on their own ground.

It was their own firm belief that sin and sickness were indissolubly linked together. Those who were sick had sinned. So Jesus asked them: 'Is it easier to say to this man, "Your sins are forgiven," or to say, "Get up and walk"?' Any charlatan could say, 'Your sins are forgiven.' There was no possibility of ever demonstrating whether his words were effective or not; such a statement was completely uncheckable. But to say, 'Get up and walk' was to say something whose effectiveness would either be proved or disproved there and then. So Jesus said in effect: 'You say that I have no right to forgive sins? You hold as a matter of belief that if this man is ill he is a sinner and he cannot be cured till he is forgiven? Very well, then, watch this!' So Jesus spoke the word and the man was cured.

The experts in the law were caught at their own game. On their own stated beliefs the man could not be cured, unless he was forgiven. He *was* cured, therefore he *was* forgiven. Therefore, Jesus' claim to forgive sin *must* be true. Jesus must have left a completely baffled set of legal experts; and, worse, he must have left them in a baffled rage. Here was something that must be dealt with: if this went on, all orthodox religion would be shattered and destroyed. In this incident Jesus signed his own death warrant – and he knew it.

For all that, it is an extremely difficult incident. What does it mean that Jesus can forgive sin? There are three possible ways of looking at this.

(1) We could take it that Jesus was *conveying* God's forgiveness to the man. After David had sinned and Nathan had rebuked him into terror and David had humbly confessed his sin, Nathan said: 'The Lord has put away your sin; you shall not die' (2 Samuel 12:13). Nathan was not forgiving David's sin, but he was conveying God's forgiveness to David and assuring him of it. So we could say that what Jesus was doing was that he was assuring the man of God's forgiveness, conveying to him something which God had already given him. That is certainly true, but it does not read as if it was the whole truth.

(2) We could take it that Jesus was acting as God's representative. John says: 'The Father judges no one but has given all judgement to the Son' (John 5:22). If judgment is committed to Jesus, then so must forgiveness be. Let us take a human analogy. Analogies are always imperfect, but we can think only in human terms. We may give another person *power of attorney*; that means to say that we have given that person the absolute disposal of our goods and property. We agree that the other person should act for us,

and that that person's actions should be regarded precisely as our own. We could take it that that is what God did with Jesus, that he delegated to him his powers and privileges, and that the word Jesus spoke was none other than the word of God.

(3) We could take it in still another way. The whole essence of Jesus' life is that in him we see clearly displayed the attitude of God to men and women. Now that attitude was the very reverse of the way God's attitude had been perceived. It was not an attitude of stern, severe, austere justice, not an attitude of continual demand. It was an attitude of perfect love, of a heart yearning with love and eager to forgive. Again let us use a human analogy. Lewis Hind in one of his essays tells us of the day that he discovered his father. He had always respected and admired his father; but he had always been more than a little afraid of him. He was in church with his father one Sunday. It was a hot drowsy day. He grew sleepier and sleepier. He could not keep his eyes open as the waves of sleep engulfed him. His head nodded. He saw his father's arm go up; and he was sure that his father was going to shake or strike him. Then he saw his father smile gently and put his arm round his shoulder. He cuddled the boy to himself so that he might rest the more comfortably and held him close with the clasp of love. That day, Lewis Hind discovered that his father was not as he had thought him to be and that his father loved him. That is what Jesus did for humanity and for God. He literally brought men and women God's forgiveness upon earth. Without him, they would never have even remotely known about it. 'I tell you,' he said to the man, 'and I tell you here and now, upon earth, you are a forgiven man.' Jesus showed perfectly the attitude of God to all people. He could say, 'I forgive,' because in him God was saying, 'I forgive.'

THE CALL OF THE MAN
WHOM EVERYONE HATED

Mark 2:13–14

> So Jesus went out again to the lakeside, and the whole
> crowd came to him, and he went on teaching them. As
> he walked along, he saw Levi, the son of Alphaeus,
> sitting in the office where he collected the customs
> duties. He said to him, 'Follow me!' He rose and
> followed him.

STEADILY and inexorably the synagogue door was shutting on
Jesus. Between him and the guardians of Jewish orthodoxy,
war had been declared. Now he was teaching, not in the
synagogue, but by the lakeside. The open air was to be his
church, the blue sky his canopy, and a hillside or a fishing
boat his pulpit. Here was the beginning of that dreadful
situation when the Son of God was banned from the place
which was regarded as the house of God.

He was walking by the lakeside and teaching. That was
one of the commonest ways for a Rabbi to teach. As the
Jewish Rabbis walked the roads from one place to another,
or as they strolled in the open air, their disciples grouped
themselves around and walked with them and listened as
they talked. Jesus was doing what any Rabbi might have
done.

Galilee was one of the great road centres of the ancient
world. It has been said that 'Judaea is on the way to nowhere;
Galilee is on the way to everywhere'. Palestine was the land
bridge between Europe and Africa; all land traffic must go
through her. The great Road of the Sea led from Damascus,
by way of Galilee, through Capernaum, down past Carmel,
along the Plain of Sharon, through Gaza and on to Egypt. It

was one of the great roads of the world. Another road led from Acre on the coast away across the Jordan out to Arabia and the frontiers of the empire, a road that was trodden by the regiments and the caravans.

Palestine at this time was divided up. Judaea was a Roman province under a Roman procurator; Galilee was ruled by Herod Antipas, a son of Herod the Great; to the east the territory which included Gaulonitis, Trachonitis and Batanaea was ruled by Philip, another of Herod's sons. On the way from Philip's territory to Herod's domains, Capernaum was the first town to which the traveller came. It was by its very nature a frontier town; because of that it was a customs' centre. In those days there were import and export taxes, and Capernaum must have been the place where they were collected. That is where Matthew worked. True, he was not, like Zacchaeus, in the service of the Romans; he was working for Herod Antipas; but a hated tax-collector he was. (The Authorized Version calls the tax-collectors *publicans*; that is because the Latin word was *publicanus*. The translation *publican*, which is of course nowadays quite misleading, actually goes back to John Wyclif's translation in the fourteenth century.)

This story tells us certain things both about Matthew and about Jesus.

(1) Matthew was a well-hated man. Tax-gatherers can never be a popular section of the community, but in the ancient world they were hated. People never knew just how much they had to pay; the tax-collectors extracted from them as much as they could possibly get and lined their own pockets with the surplus that remained after the demands of the law had been met. Even a Greek writer like Lucian ranks tax-gatherers with 'adulterers, panderers, flatterers and sycophants'. Jesus wanted the man no one else wanted. He offered

his friendship to the man whom all others would have scorned to call friend.

(2) Matthew must have been a man at that moment with an ache in his heart. He must have heard about Jesus; he must have listened often on the outskirts of the crowds to his message; and something must have stirred in his heart. Now he could not possibly have gone to the orthodox good people of his day; to them he was unclean and they would have refused to have anything to do with him.

The story is told of a woman from the dock district in London who came to a women's meeting. She had been living with a Chinese man and had a baby whom she brought with her. She liked the meeting and came back and back again. Then the vicar came to her. 'I must ask you', he said, 'not to come again.' The woman gave him a questioning look. 'The other women', said the vicar, 'say that they will stop coming if you continue to come.' She looked at him with a poignant wistfulness. 'Sir,' she said, 'I know I'm a sinner, but isn't there anywhere a sinner can go?' Fortunately the Salvation Army found that woman and she was reclaimed for Christ.

That is precisely what Matthew was up against until he found the one who came into the world to seek and to save that which was lost.

(3) This story tells us something about Jesus. It was as he walked along the lakeside that he called Matthew. As a great scholar said, 'Even as he was walking along he was looking for opportunities.' Jesus was never off duty. If he could find one man or one woman for God as he walked, he did so. What a harvest we could gather in if we looked for men and women for Christ as we walked!

(4) Of all the disciples, Matthew gave up most. He literally left all to follow Jesus. Peter and Andrew, James and John could go back to the boats. There were always fish to catch

and always the old trade to which to return; but Matthew burned his boats completely. With one action, in one moment of time, by one swift decision he had put himself out of his job forever, for having left his tax-collector's job, he would never get it back. At some time in every life there comes the moment to decide, and we have to be big enough to make the big decisions.

A certain famous man had the habit of going for long country walks on Dartmoor. When he came to a brook that was rather too wide to cross comfortably, the first thing he did was to throw his coat over to the other side. He made sure that there was to be no turning back. He took the decision to cross and made sure he was going to stick to it.

Matthew was the man who staked everything on Christ; and he was not wrong.

(5) From his decision, Matthew got at least three things.

(a) *He got clean hands*. From now on, he could look the world in the face. He might be very much poorer and life must be very much rougher, and the luxuries and the comforts were gone; but from now on his hands were clean and, because his hands were clean, his mind was at rest.

(b) *He lost one job but he got a far bigger one*. It has been said that Matthew left everything but one thing – he did not leave his pen. Scholars do not think that the first gospel, as it stands, is the work of Matthew; but they do think that it embodies one of the most important documents of all history, the first written account of the teaching of Jesus, and that that document was written by Matthew. With his orderly mind, his systematic way of working, his familiarity with the pen, Matthew was the first to give the world a book on the teaching of Jesus.

(c) The odd thing is that Matthew's reckless decision brought him the one thing he can least have been looking for

– it brought him immortal and worldwide fame. Everyone knows the name of Matthew as one forever connected with the transmission of the story of Jesus. Had Matthew refused the call, he would have had a local notoriety as the follower of a disreputable trade which everyone hated; because he answered the call, he gained a worldwide fame as the man who gave us the record of the words of Jesus. God never goes back on those who stake their all on him.

WHERE THE NEED IS GREATEST

Mark 2:15–17

> Jesus was sitting at a meal in Levi's house, and many tax-collectors and sinners were sitting with Jesus and his disciples, for there were many of them, and they sought his company. When the experts in the law, who belonged to the school of the Pharisees, saw that he was eating in the company of sinners and tax-gatherers, they began to say to his disciples, 'It is with tax-collectors and sinners that he is eating and drinking.' Jesus heard them. 'It is not those who are in good health who need a doctor,' he said, 'but those who are ill. I did not come to bring an invitation to people who think that they have no faults but to those who know that they are sinners.'

ONCE again Jesus is flinging down the gauntlet of defiance.

When Matthew had yielded himself to Jesus, he invited him to his house. Naturally, having discovered Jesus for himself, he wished his friends to share his great discovery – and his friends were like himself. It could not be any other way. Matthew had chosen a job which cut him off from the society of all respectable and orthodox people, and he had to find his friends among outcasts like himself. Jesus gladly accepted that invitation; and these outcasts of society sought his company.

Nothing could better show the difference between Jesus and the scribes and Pharisees and orthodox good people of the day. They were not the kind of people whose company sinners would have sought. They would have been looked at with bleak condemnation and arrogant superiority. They would have been frozen out of such company even before they had entered it.

A clear distinction was drawn between those who kept the law and those whom they called *the people of the land*. The people of the land were the common masses who did not observe all the rules and the regulations of conventional Pharisaic piety. By the orthodox it was forbidden to have anything to do with these people. The strict law-keeper must have no fellowship with them at all, must not talk with them nor go on a journey with them. As far as possible, even doing business with them must be avoided; to marry a daughter to one of them was inconceivable; above all, those who adhered to the law must not accept hospitality from or give hospitality to such a person. By going to Matthew's house and sitting at his table and keeping company with his friends, Jesus was defying the orthodox conventions of his day.

We need not for a moment suppose that all these people were sinners in the moral sense of the term. The word *sinner* (*hamartōlos*) had a double significance. It did mean someone who broke the moral law; but it also meant someone who did not observe the scribal law. The person who committed adultery and the person who ate pork were both sinners; those who were guilty of theft and murder and those who did not wash their hands the required number of times and in the required way before they ate were also sinners. These guests of Matthew no doubt included many who had broken the moral law and played fast and loose with life; but no doubt they also included many whose only sin was that they did not observe the scribal rules and regulations.

When Jesus was taxed with this shocking conduct, his answer was quite simple. 'A doctor', he said, 'goes where he is needed. People in good health do not need him; sick people do; I am doing just the same; I am going to those who are sick in soul and who need me most.'

Verse 17 is a highly concentrated verse. It sounds at first hearing as if Jesus had no use for good people. But the point of it is that the very people for whom Jesus can do nothing are those who think themselves so good that they do not need anything done for them; and the very people for whom Jesus can do everything are those who are sinners and know it and who long in their hearts for a cure. To have no sense of need is to have erected a barrier between us and Jesus; to have a sense of need is to possess the passport to his presence.

The attitude of the orthodox Jews to sinners was really compounded of two things.

(1) It was compounded of *contempt*. 'The ignorant man', said the Rabbis, 'can never be pious.' Heraclitus, the Greek philosopher, was an arrogant aristocrat. One called Scythinus undertook to put his discourses into verse so that ordinary uneducated people might read and understand them. The reaction of Heraclitus was put into an epigram. 'Heraclitus am I. Why do ye drag me up and down, ye illiterate? It was not for you I toiled, but for such as understand me. One man in my sight is a match for 30,000, but the countless hosts do not make a single one.' For the masses he had nothing but contempt. The scribes and Pharisees despised the common people; Jesus loved them. The scribes and Pharisees stood on their dignity of formal piety and looked down on sinners;

Jesus came and sat beside them, and by sitting beside them lifted them up.

(2) It was compounded of *fear*. The orthodox were afraid of the contagion of the sinner; they were afraid that they might be infected with sin. They were like doctors who would refuse to attend a case of infectious illness lest they contracted it themselves. Jesus was the one who forgot himself in a great desire to save others. C. T. Studd, the great missionary of Christ, had four lines of doggerel that he loved to quote:

> Some want to live within the sound
>   Of church or chapel bell;
> I want to run a rescue shop
>   Within a yard of hell.

Those who have contempt and fear in their hearts can never be 'fishers of men'.

THE JOYOUS COMPANY

Mark 2:18–20

> The disciples of John were in the habit of fasting, as were the Pharisees. So they came to Jesus and said, 'Why do John's disciples and the disciples of the Pharisees fast, while your disciples do not?' 'Surely', Jesus said to them, 'his closest friends cannot fast while the bridegroom is still with them? So long as they have the bridegroom they do not fast. But the days will come when some day the bridegroom will be taken away from them – and then, in that day, they will fast.'

WITH the stricter Jews, fasting was a regular practice. In Judaism there was only one day in all the year that was a compulsory fast, and that was the Day of Atonement. The day when the nation confessed and was forgiven its sin was The Fast *par excellence*. But the stricter Jews fasted on two days every week, on Mondays and Thursdays. It is to be noted that fasting was not as serious as it sounds, for the fast lasted from 6 am to 6 pm and after that normal food could be eaten.

Jesus is not against fasting as such. There are very good reasons why people might fast. They might deny themselves things they like for the sake of *discipline*, to be certain that they have control over them and not the other way about, to make sure that they never grow to love them so well that they cannot give them up. They might deny themselves comforts and pleasant things so that, after such self-denial, they might appreciate them all the more. One of the best ways to learn to value our homes is to have to stay away from home for a time; and one of the best ways to appreciate God's gifts is to do without them for a period.

These are good reasons for fasting. The trouble about the Pharisees was that in far too many cases their fasting was for self-display. It was to call the attention of *others* to their goodness. They actually whitened their faces and went about with dishevelled garments on their fast days so that no one could miss the fact that they were fasting and so that everyone would see and admire their devotion. It was to call the attention of *God* to their piety. They felt that this special act of extra piety would bring them to the notice of God. Their fasting was a ritual and a self-displaying ritual at that. To be of any value, fasting must not be the result of a ritual; it must be the expression of a feeling in the heart.

Jesus used a vivid picture to tell the Pharisees why his disciples did not fast. After a Jewish wedding, the couple did not go away for a honeymoon; they stayed at home. For a week or so, open house was kept and there was continual feasting and rejoicing. In lives that were hard, a wedding week was the happiest time. To that week of happiness were invited the closest friends of the bride and the bridegroom; and they were called by the name *children of the bridechamber*. Jesus likened his little company to men who were children of the bridechamber, chosen guests at a wedding feast. There was actually a Rabbinic ruling which said, 'All in attendance on the bridegroom are relieved of all religious observances which would lessen their joy.' The wedding guests were actually exempt from all fasting.

This incident tells us that the characteristic Christian attitude to life is joy. The discovery of Christ and the company of Christ are the key to happiness. There was a Japanese criminal called Tokichi Ishii. He was utterly pitiless; he had brutally and callously murdered men, women and children in his career of crime. He was captured and imprisoned. Two Canadian ladies visited the prison. He could not be induced even to speak; he only glowered at them with the face of a wild animal. When they left, they left with him a copy of the Bible in the faint hope that he might read it. He read it, and the story of the crucifixion made him a changed man. Later when the jailer came to lead the doomed man to the gallows, he found not the surly, hardened brute he expected, but a smiling, radiant man, for Ishii the murderer had been born again. The mark of his rebirth was a smiling radiance. The life that is lived in Christ cannot be lived other than in joy.

But the story ends with a foreboding cloud across the sky. No doubt when Jesus spoke of the day when the bridegroom would be taken away his friends did not at the moment see the meaning of it. But here, right at the beginning, Jesus saw the cross ahead. Death did not take him unawares; even now he had counted the cost and chosen the way. Here is courage; here is the picture of a man who would not be deflected from the road at whose end there loomed a cross.

THE NECESSITY OF STAYING YOUNG IN MIND

Mark 2:21-2

> No one sews a patch of new cloth on to an old garment.
> If he does the bit that was meant to fill in the hole tears
> it apart – the new from the old – and the tear is made
> worse. No one puts new wine into old wine skins. If he
> does the wine will burst the wine skins, and the wine
> will be lost as well as the wine skins. New skins for
> new wine!

JESUS knew quite well that he was coming with a message
which was startlingly new; and he also knew that his way of
life was shatteringly different from that of the orthodox
Rabbinic teacher. He also knew how difficult it is for human
minds to accept and to entertain new truth; and here he uses
two illustrations to show how necessary it is to have an
adventurous mind.

No one ever had such a gift as Jesus for the discovery and
the use of homely illustrations. Over and over again he finds
in the simple things pathways and pointers to God. No one
was ever such an expert in getting from the 'here and now' to
the 'there and then'. For Jesus, 'earth was crammed with
heaven'. He lived so close to God that everything spoke to
him of God. Someone tells how, on Saturday afternoons, he
used to go for country walks with one of the most famous of
Scottish preachers. They used to have long talks together.
Telling of it afterwards he said, 'Wherever the conversation
started, he had a way of cutting straight across country to
God.' Wherever Jesus' gaze fell, it had a way of flashing
straight on to God.

(1) He speaks of the danger of sewing a new patch on an
old garment. The word used means that the new cloth was

still undressed; it had never been shrunk; so when the garment got wet in the rain the new patch shrank, and being much stronger than the old, it tore the old apart. There comes a time when the day of patching is over, and re-creating must begin. In the time of Martin Luther, it was not possible to patch up the abuses of the Roman Catholic Church; the time for *reformation* had come. In the time of John Wesley, for Wesley at least, the time for patching the Church of England was done. He did not want to leave it, but in the end he had to, for only a new fellowship would suffice. It may well be that there are times when we try to patch, when what is wanted is the complete abandonment of the old and the acceptance of something new.

(2) Wine was kept in wine skins. There was no such thing as a bottle in our sense of the term. When these skins were new they had a certain elasticity; as they grew old they became hard and unyielding. New wine is still fermenting; it gives off gases; these gases cause pressure; if the skin is new it will yield to the pressure, but if it is old and hard and dry it will explode, and wine and skin alike will be lost. Jesus is pleading for a certain elasticity in our minds. It is fatally easy to become set in our ways. J. A. Findlay, the Principal of Didsbury Methodist College in Manchester, quotes a saying of one of his friends – 'When you reach a conclusion you're dead.' What he meant was that when our minds become fixed and settled in their ways, when they are quite unable to accept new truth and to contemplate new ways, we may be physically alive but we are mentally dead.

As they grow older almost everyone develops a constitutional dislike of that which is new and unfamiliar. We grow very unwilling to make any adjustments in our habits and ways of life. Lesslie Newbigin, who was involved in the discussions about the formation of the United Church of South

India, tells how one of the things that most often held things up was that people kept asking, 'Now, if we do that, just where are we going?' In the end someone had to say bluntly, 'Christians have no right to ask where they are going.' Abraham went out not knowing whither he went (Hebrews 11:8). There is a great verse in that same chapter of Hebrews: 'By faith Jacob, when dying, blessed each of the sons of Joseph "bowing in worship over the top of his staff"' (Hebrews 11:21). With the very breath of death upon him, the old traveller still had his pilgrim staff in his hand. To the end of the day, with the evening now upon him, he was still ready for the road. If we are really to rise to the height of the Christian challenge, we must retain the adventurous mind. I received a letter once which ended, 'Yours aged 83 and still growing' – and with the inexhaustible riches of Christ before us, why not?

PIETY, REAL AND FALSE

Mark 2:23-8

> One Sabbath day Jesus was going through the corn fields. His disciples began to pluck the ears of corn as they made their way along. The Pharisees began to say to him, 'Look! Why are they doing what is not allowed on the Sabbath?' 'Have you never read', he said, 'what David did when he and his friends were in need and hungry? Have you never read how he went into the house of God, when Abiathar was high priest, and ate the shewbread – which none is allowed to eat except the priests – and gave it to his friends as well?' 'The Sabbath', he said to them, 'was made for the sake of man and not man for the sake of the Sabbath. Therefore the Son of Man is lord also of the Sabbath.'

ONCE again Jesus cut right across the scribal rules and
regulations. When he and his disciples were going through
the corn fields one Sabbath day, his disciples began to pluck
the ears of corn and to eat them. On any ordinary day, the
disciples were doing what was freely permitted (Deuteronomy
23:25). So long as the traveller did not put a sickle into the
field, he was free to pluck the corn. But this was done on the
Sabbath, and the Sabbath was hedged around with literally
thousands of petty rules and regulations. All work was forbidden. Work had been classified under thirty-nine different
heads, and four of these heads were reaping, winnowing,
threshing and preparing a meal. By their action, the disciples
had technically broken all these four rules and were to be
classified as law-breakers. It seems fantastic to us; but to the
Jewish Rabbis it was a matter of deadly sin and of life and
death.

The Pharisees immediately launched their accusation and
pointed out that Jesus' disciples were breaking the law. They
obviously expected him to stop them on the spot. Jesus
answered them in their own language. He cited the story
which is told in 1 Samuel 21:1–6. David was fleeing for his
life; he came to the tabernacle in Nob; he demanded food
and there was none except the shewbread. Exodus 25:23–30
tells of the shewbread. It consisted of twelve loaves placed
on a golden table three feet long, one and a half feet wide,
and one and a half feet high. The table stood in the tabernacle
in front of the Holy of Holies, and the bread was a kind of
offering to God. It was changed once a week; when it was
changed it became the property of the priests and of the priests
alone, and no one else might eat it (Leviticus 24:9). Yet in his
time of need David took and ate that bread. Jesus showed
that Scripture itself supplies a precedent in which human need
took precedence over human and even divine law.

'The Sabbath', he said, 'was made for the sake of man and not man for the sake of the Sabbath.' That was self-evident. Human life was created before ever the elaborate Sabbath law came into existence. Human beings were not created to be the victims and the slaves of Sabbath rules and regulations, which were in the beginning created to make life fuller and better for them. Men and women are not to be enslaved by the Sabbath; the Sabbath exists to make their lives better.

This passage confronts us with certain essential truths which we forget at our peril.

(1) Religion does not consist in rules and regulations. To take the matter in question – Sunday observance is important, but there is a great deal more to religion than Sunday observance. If it were possible to become a Christian simply by abstaining from work and pleasure on the Sunday, and by attending church on that day, and saying prayers and reading the Bible, being a Christian would be a very easy thing. Whenever we forget the love and the forgiveness and the service and the mercy that are at the heart of religion and replace them by the performance of rules and regulations, religion is in a decline. Christianity has at all times consisted far more in doing things than in refraining from doing things.

(2) The first claim on anyone is the claim of human need. Even the catechisms and the confessions admit that works of necessity and *mercy* are quite legal on the Sabbath. If ever the performance of our religion stops us helping someone who is in need, our religion is not religion at all. People matter far more than systems. Persons are far more important than rituals. The best way to worship God is to help people.

(3) The best way to use sacred things is to use them to help one another. That, in fact, is the only way to give them to God. One of the loveliest of all stories is that of *The Fourth Wise Man*. His name was Artaban. He set out to follow the

star and he took with him a sapphire, a ruby and a pearl beyond price as gifts for the King. He was riding hard to meet his three friends, Caspar, Melchior and Balthasar, at the agreed place. The time was short; they would leave if he was late. Suddenly he saw a dim figure on the ground before him. It was a traveller stricken with fever. If he stayed to help, he would miss his friends. He did stay, he helped and healed the man. But now he was alone. He needed camels and bearers to help him across the desert because he had missed his friends and their caravan. He had to sell his sapphire to get them; and he was sad because the King would never have his gem.

He journeyed on and in due time came to Bethlehem, but again he was too late. Joseph and Mary and the baby had gone. Then there came the soldiers to carry out Herod's command that the children should be slain. Artaban was in a house where there was a little child. The tramp of the soldiers came to the door; the weeping of stricken mothers could be heard. Artaban stood in the doorway, tall and dark, with the ruby in his hand and bribed the captain not to enter. The child was saved; the mother was overjoyed; but the ruby was gone; and Artaban was sad because the King would never have his ruby.

For years, he wandered looking in vain for the King. More than thirty years afterwards, he came to Jerusalem. There was a crucifixion that day. When Artaban heard of the Jesus being crucified, he sounded wondrously like the King, and Artaban hurried towards Calvary. Maybe his pearl, the loveliest in all the world, could buy the life of the King. Down the street came a girl fleeing from a band of soldiers. 'My father is in debt,' she cried, 'and they are taking me to sell as a slave to pay the debt. Save me!' Artaban hesitated; then sadly he took out his pearl, gave it to the soldiers and bought the girl's freedom.

All at once the skies were dark; there was an earthquake and a flying tile hit Artaban on the head. He sank half-conscious to the ground. The girl pillowed his head on her lap. Suddenly his lips began to move. 'Not so, my Lord. For when saw I thee anhungered and fed thee? Or thirsty, and gave thee drink? When saw I thee a stranger, and took thee in? Or naked and clothed thee? When saw I thee sick in prison, and came unto thee? Thirty and three years have I looked for thee; but I have never seen thy face, nor ministered to thee, my King.' And then like a whisper from very far away, there came a voice. 'Verily I say unto you, inasmuch as thou hast done it unto one the least of these my brethren, thou hast done it unto me.' And Artaban smiled in death because he knew that the King had received his gifts.

The best way to use sacred things is to use them for others. It has been known for children to be barred from a church because that church was considered too ancient and sacred for such as they. It can be that a church is more concerned with the elaboration of its services than with the help of its community and the relief of its poor. But the sacred things are only truly sacred when they are used for human benefit. The shewbread was never so sacred as when it was used to feed a starving man. The Sabbath was never so sacred as when it was used to help those who needed help. The decisive factor in the use of all things is love and not law.

THE CLASH OF IDEAS

Mark 3:1–6

> Jesus went into the synagogue again; and there was a
> man there who had a hand which had withered; and
> they were watching him closely to see if he would heal

him on the Sabbath day, so that, if he did, they might be able to formulate a charge against him. He said to the man who had the withered hand, 'Stand up and come out in to the middle of the congregation.' He said to them, 'Is it lawful to do good on the Sabbath day? Or to do evil? To save a life? Or to kill it?' But they remained silent. He looked round on them with anger, for he was grieved at the obtuseness of their hearts. He said to the man, 'Stretch out your hand!' He stretched it out; and his hand was restored. The Pharisees immediately went out and began to concoct a plot with Herod's entourage against Jesus, with a view to killing him.

THIS is a crucial incident in the life of Jesus. It was already clear that he and the orthodox leaders of the Jews were quite at variance. For him to go back into the synagogue at all was a brave thing to do. It was the act of a man who refused to seek safety and who was determined to look a dangerous situation in the face. In the synagogue there was a deputation from the Sanhedrin. No one could miss them, for, in the synagogue, the front seats were the seats of honour and they were sitting there. It was the duty of the Sanhedrin to deal with anyone who was likely to mislead the people and seduce them from the right way; and that is precisely what this deputation conceived of themselves as doing. The last thing they were there to do was to worship and to learn; they were there to scrutinize Jesus' every action.

In the synagogue there was a man with a paralysed hand. The Greek word means that he had not been born that way but that some illness had taken the strength from him. The Gospel according to the Hebrews, a gospel which is lost except for a few fragments, tells us that the man was a stone mason and that he entreated Jesus to help him, for his livelihood was in his hands and he was ashamed to beg. If

Jesus had been a cautious, prudent person he would have conveniently arranged not to see the man, for he knew that to heal him was asking for trouble.

It was the Sabbath day; all work was forbidden, and to heal was to work. The Jewish law was definite and detailed about this. Medical attention could be given only if a life was in danger. To take some examples – a woman in child-birth might be helped on the Sabbath; an infection of the throat might be treated; if a wall fell on anyone, enough might be cleared away to see whether the person was dead or alive; anyone found alive might be helped, but a dead body must be left until the next day. A fracture could not be attended to. Cold water might not be poured on a sprained hand or foot. A cut finger might be bandaged with a plain bandage but not with ointment. That is to say, at the most an injury could be kept from getting worse; it must not be made better.

It is extraordinarily difficult for us to grasp this. The best way in which we can see the strict orthodox view of the Sabbath is to remember that a strict Jew would not even defend his life on the Sabbath. In the wars of the Maccabees, when resistance broke out, some of the Jewish rebels took refuge in caves. The Syrian soldiers pursued them. Josephus, the Jewish historian, tells us that they gave them the chance to surrender and they would not, so 'they fought against them on the Sabbath day, and they burned them as they were in caves, without resistance and without so much as stopping up the entrances of the caves. They refused to defend themselves on that day because they were not willing to break in upon the honour they owed to the Sabbath, even in such distress; for our law requires that we rest on that day.' When Pompey, the Roman general, was besieging Jerusalem, the defenders took refuge in the Temple precincts. Pompey proceeded to

build a mound which would overlook them and from which
he might bombard them. He knew the beliefs of the Jews and
he built on the Sabbath day, and the Jews lifted not one hand
to defend themselves or to hinder the building, although they
knew that by their Sabbath inactivity they were signing their
own death warrant. The Romans, who had compulsory
military service, had in the end to exempt the Jews from army
service because no strict Jew would fight on the Sabbath. The
orthodox Jewish attitude to the Sabbath was completely rigid
and unbending.

Jesus knew that. This man's life was not in the least danger.
Physically he would be no worse off if he were left until the
next day. For Jesus this was a test case, and he met it fairly
and squarely. He told the man to rise and to come out of his
place and stand where everyone could see him. There were
probably two reasons for that. Very likely Jesus wished to
make one last effort to waken sympathy for the stricken man
by showing everyone his wretchedness. Quite certainly Jesus
wished to take the step he was going to take in such a way
that no one could possibly fail to see it.

He asked the experts in the law two questions. *Is it lawful
to do good or to do evil on the Sabbath day?* He put them in a
dilemma. They were bound to admit that it was lawful to do
good; and it was a good thing he proposed to do. They were
bound to deny that it was lawful to do evil; and, yet, surely it
was an evil thing to leave a man in wretchedness when it was
possible to help him. Then he asked, *Is it lawful to save a
life or to kill it?* Here he was driving the point home. *He*
was taking steps to save this wretched man's life; *they* were
thinking out methods of killing himself. On any reckoning it
was surely a better thing to be thinking about helping a man
than it was to be thinking of killing a man. No wonder they
had nothing to say!

Then Jesus with a word of power healed the man; and the Pharisees went out and tried to hatch a plot with the Herodians to kill him. This shows the lengths to which the Pharisees would go. No Pharisee would normally have anything to do with a Gentile or someone who did not keep the law; such people were unclean. The Herodians were the court entourage of Herod; they were continually coming into contact with Romans. For all normal purposes the Pharisees would have considered them unclean; but now they were prepared to enter into what was for them an unholy alliance. In their hearts, there was a hate which would stop at nothing.

This passage is fundamental because it shows the clash of two ideas of religion.

(1) To the Pharisee, religion was *ritual*: it meant obeying certain rules and regulations. Jesus broke these regulations and they were genuinely convinced that he was a bad man. It is like those who believe that religion consists in going to church, reading the Bible, saying grace at meals, having family worship, and carrying out all the external acts which are looked on as religious, and who yet never put themselves out to do anything for anyone, who have no sense of sympathy, no desire to sacrifice, who are serene in their rigid orthodoxy, and deaf to the call of need and blind to the tears of the world.

(2) To Jesus, religion was *service*. It was love of God *and* love of others. Ritual was irrelevant compared with love in action. A verse from J. G. Whittier's hymn, 'O Lord and Master of us All', sums it up:

> Our Friend, our Brother, and our Lord,
> What may Thy service be?
> Nor name, nor form, nor ritual word,
> But simply following Thee.

To Jesus, the most important thing in the world was not the correct performance of a ritual but the spontaneous answer to the cry of human need.

IN THE MIDST OF THE CROWDS

Mark 3:7–12

> So Jesus withdrew to the lakeside with his disciples, and a great multitude from Galilee followed him; and from Judaea and from Jerusalem, and from Idumaea and from the Transjordan country, and from the territory round Tyre and Sidon, there came to him a great crowd of people, for they were hearing about what great things he was doing. He told his disciples to have a boat ready waiting for him because of the crowd, so that they would not crush him; for he healed many, and the result was that all who were suffering from the scourges of disease rushed upon him to touch him. And as often as unclean spirits saw him, they kept flinging themselves down before him and shouting, 'You are the Son of God.' Many times he sternly forbade them to make him known.

UNLESS Jesus wished to be involved in a head-on collision with the authorities, he had to leave the synagogues. It was not that he withdrew through fear; it was not the retreat of a man who feared to face the consequences. But his hour had not yet come. There was much that he had still to do and say before the time of final conflict.

So he left the synagogues and went out to the lakeside and the open sky. Even there the crowds flocked to him from far afield. From all over Galilee they came; many made the 100-mile journey from Jerusalem in Judaea to see him and to

listen to him. Idumaea was the ancient realm of Edom, away
in the deep south, between the southern borders of Palestine
and Arabia. From the east side of Jordan they came; and even
from foreign territory, for people came from the Phoenician
cities of Tyre and Sidon, which lie on the Mediterranean coast,
north-west of Galilee.

So large were the crowds that it became dangerous and a
boat had to be kept ready, just off the shore, in case he might
be overwhelmed with the crushing of the throng. His cures
brought him into even greater danger, for the sick people did
not even wait for him to touch them; they rushed to touch
him.

At this time he was faced with one special problem, the
problem of those who were possessed by demons. Let us
remember that, whatever our belief about demons may be,
these people were convinced they were possessed by an alien
and evil power external to themselves. They called Jesus *the
Son of God*. What did they mean by that? They certainly did
not use the term in what we might call a philosophical or a
theological sense. In the ancient world, *son of God* was by no
means an uncommon title. The kings of Egypt were said to
be the sons of Ra, their god. From Augustus onwards, many
of the Roman emperors were described on inscriptions as
sons of God.

The Old Testament has four ways in which it uses this
term. (1) *The angels* are *the sons of God*. The story in Genesis
6:2 says that *the sons of God* saw the daughters of mortals
and were fatally attracted to them. Job 1:6 tells of the day
when *the sons of God* came to present themselves before
the Lord. It was a regular title for the angels. (2) *The nation
of Israel* is *the son of God*. God called *his son* out of Egypt
(Hosea 11:1). In Exodus 4:22, God says of the nation, '*Israel
is my firstborn son*'. (3) *The king of the nation* is *the son of*

God. In 2 Samuel 7:14, the promise to the king is, 'I will be a father to him, and he shall be *a son to me*. (4) In the later books, which were written between the Testaments, *the good man* is *the son of God*. In Ecclesiasticus (Sirach) 4:10, the promise to the man who is kind to the fatherless is:

> You will then be like *a son of the Most High*,
> and he will love you more than does your mother.

In all these cases, the term *son* describes someone who is specially near and close to God. We get a parallel to this which shows something of its meaning in the New Testament. Paul calls Timothy *his son* (1 Timothy 1:2, 18). Timothy was no blood relation to Paul at all, but there was no one, as Paul says (Philippians 2:19–22), who knew his mind so well. Peter calls Mark *his son* (1 Peter 5:13), because there was no one who could interpret his mind so well. When we meet this title in the simplicity of the gospel story, we are not to think in terms of philosophy or theology or of the doctrine of the Trinity; we are to think of it as expressing the fact that Jesus' relationship to God was so close that no other word could describe it. Now those who were demon-possessed felt that in them there was an independent evil spirit; they somehow felt that Jesus was closely related to God; they felt that in the presence of this nearness to God the demons could not live and therefore they were afraid.

We must ask, 'Why did Jesus so sternly bid them to remain silent?' The reason was very simple and very compelling. Jesus was the Messiah, God's anointed king; but his idea of Messiahship was quite different from the popular idea. He saw in Messiahship a way of service, of sacrifice and of love with a cross at the end of it. The popular idea of the Messiah was of a conquering king who, with his mighty armies, would blast the Romans and lead the Jews to world power. Therefore, if a rumour were to go out that the Messiah had arrived, the inevitable consequence would be rebellions and uprisings, especially in Galilee, where the people were always ready to follow a nationalist leader.

Jesus thought of Messiahship in terms of love; the people thought of Messiahship in terms of Jewish nationalism. Therefore, before there could be any proclamation of his Messiahship, Jesus had to educate the people into the true idea of what it meant. At this stage, nothing but harm and trouble and disaster could come from the proclamation that the Messiah had arrived. It would have issued in nothing but useless war and bloodshed. First of all, the true conception of what the Messiah was had to be learned; a premature announcement such as this could have wrecked Jesus' whole mission.

THE CHOSEN COMPANY

Mark 3:13-19

> Jesus went up into the mountain and invited to his service the men of his choice; and he appointed twelve that they might be with him, and that he might send them out to act as his heralds, and to have power to cast out demons. He chose Simon, and to him he gave the name of Peter; he chose James, Zebedee's son, and John, James' brother, and to them he gave the name Boanerges, which means Sons of Thunder; he chose Andrew and Philip and Bartholomew and Matthew and Thomas, and James, Alphaeus' son, and Thaddaeus and Simon, the Cananaean, and Judas Iscariot, who also betrayed him.

JESUS had come to a very important moment in his life and work. He had emerged with his message; he had chosen his method; he had gone throughout Galilee preaching and healing. By this time he had made a very considerable impact on the public mind. Now he had to face two very practical problems. First, he had to find some way of making his message permanent if anything happened to him – and that something would happen he did not doubt. Second, he had to find some way of disseminating his message, and in an age when there was no such thing as a printed book or newspaper, and no way of reaching large numbers of people at the one time, that was no easy task. There was only one way to solve these two problems: he had to choose those on whose hearts and lives he could write his message and who would go out from his presence to carry that message abroad. Here we see him doing exactly that.

It is significant that *Christianity began with a group*. The Christian faith is something which from the beginning had to be discovered and lived out in a fellowship. The whole essence of the way of the Pharisees was that it separated them from their fellows; the very name *Pharisee* means *the separated one*; the whole essence of Christianity was that it bound men and women to their fellows, and presented them with the task of living with each other and for each other.

Further, Christianity began with a very mixed group. In it the two extremes met. Matthew was a tax-collector and, therefore, an outcast; he was a renegade and a traitor to his fellow countrymen. Simon the Cananaean is correctly called by Luke 'Simon the Zealot'; and the Zealots were a band of fiery, violent nationalists who were pledged even to murder and assassination to clear their country of the foreign yoke. The man who was lost to patriotism and the fanatical patriot came together in that group, and no doubt between them there were all kinds of backgrounds and opinions. Christianity began by insisting that the most diverse people should live together

and by enabling them to do so, because they were all living
with Jesus.

Judging them by worldly standards, the men whom Jesus
chose had no special qualifications at all. They were not
wealthy; they had no special social position; they had no
special education; they were not trained theologians; they
were not high-ranking religious leaders; they were twelve
ordinary men. But they *had* two special qualifications. First,
they had felt the magnetic attraction of Jesus. There was
something about him that made them wish to take him as
their Master. And second, they had the courage to show that
they were on his side. Make no mistake, that did require
courage. Here was Jesus calmly crashing through the rules
and regulations; here was Jesus heading for an inevitable
collision with the orthodox leaders; here was Jesus already
branded as a sinner and labelled as a heretic; and yet
they had the courage to attach themselves to him. No band of
men ever staked everything on such a forlorn hope as these
Galilaeans, and no band of men ever did it with more open
eyes. These twelve had all kinds of faults, but whatever else
could be said about them, they loved Jesus and they were not
afraid to tell the world that they loved him – and that is being
a Christian.

Jesus called them to him for two purposes. First, he called
them *to be with him*. He called them to be his steady and consistent companions. Others might come and go; the crowd
might be there one day and gone the next; others might be
fluctuating and spasmodic in their attachment to him, but these
twelve were to identify their lives with his life and live with
him all the time. Second, he called them *to send them out*. He
wanted them to be his representatives. He wanted them to
tell others about him. They themselves had been won in order
to win others.

For their task, Jesus equipped them with two things. First, he gave them *a message*. They were to be his heralds. A wise man said that no one has any right to be a teacher unless he has a teaching of his own to offer, or the teaching of another that with all the passion of his heart he wishes to propagate. People will always listen to the man or woman with a message. Jesus gave these friends of his something to say. Second, he gave them *a power*. They were also to cast out demons. Because they kept company with him, something of his power was on their lives.

If we would learn what discipleship is, we will do well to think again of these first disciples.

THE VERDICT OF HIS FAMILY

Mark 3:20–1

> Jesus went into a house, and once again so dense a crowd collected that they could not even eat bread. When his own people heard what was going on, they went out to restrain him, for they said, 'He has taken leave of his senses.'

SOMETIMES someone drops a remark which cannot be interpreted otherwise than as the product of bitter experience. Once when Jesus was enumerating the things which might have to be faced for following him, he said, 'One's foes will be members of one's own household' (Matthew 10:36). His own family had come to the conclusion that he had taken leave of his senses and that it was time he was taken home. Let us see if we can understand what made them feel like that.

(1) Jesus had left home and the carpenter's business at Nazareth. No doubt it was a flourishing business from which he could at least have made a living; and quite suddenly he

had flung the whole thing up and gone out to be a wandering preacher. No one with any sense, they must have been thinking, would throw up a business where the money came in every week to become a vagrant who had nowhere even to sleep.

(2) Jesus was obviously on the way to a head-on collision with the orthodox leaders of his day. There are certain people who can do a great deal of harm, people on whose right side it is better to keep, people whose opposition can be very dangerous. No one, they must have been thinking, would ever get up against the powers that be, because it was obvious that in any collision with them people always came off second best. No one could take on the scribes and the Pharisees and the orthodox leaders and hope to get away with it.

(3) Jesus had newly started a little society of his own – and a very strange society it was. There were some fishermen; there was a reformed tax-collector; there was a fanatical nationalist. They were not the kind of people whom anyone with ambitions would particularly want to know. They certainly were not the kind of people who would be any good to anyone who was set on a career. They must have been thinking, 'How could anyone pick a crowd of friends like that?' They were definitely not the kind of people a prudent person would want to get mixed up with.

By his actions Jesus had made it clear that the three laws by which most people tend to organize their lives meant nothing to him.

(1) He had thrown away *security*. The one thing that most people in this world want more than anything else is just that. They want above all things a job and a position which are secure, and where there are as few material and financial risks as possible.

(2) He had thrown away *safety*. Most people tend at all times to play safe. They are more concerned with the safety of any course of action than with its moral quality, its rightness or its wrongness. A course of action which involves risk is something from which they instinctively shrink.

(3) He had shown himself utterly indifferent to *the verdict of society*. He had shown that he did not much care what people said about him. In point of fact, as the writer H. G. Wells said, for most people 'the voice of their neighbours is louder than the voice of God'. 'What will people say?' is one of the first questions that most of us are in the habit of asking.

What appalled Jesus' friends was the risks that he was taking, risks which, as they thought, no one with any sense would take.

When John Bunyan was in prison, he was quite frankly afraid. 'My imprisonment', he thought, 'might end on the gallows for aught that I could tell.' He did not like the thought of being hanged. Then came the day when he was ashamed of being afraid. 'Methought I was ashamed to die with a pale face and tottering knees for such a cause as this.' So finally he came to a conclusion as he thought of himself climbing up the ladder to the gallows: 'Wherefore, thought I, I am for going on and venturing my eternal state with Christ whether I have comfort here or no; if God doth not come in, thought I, I will leap off the ladder even blindfold into eternity, sink or swim, come heaven, come hell; Lord Jesus, if thou wilt catch me, do: if not, *I will venture for thy name*.' That is precisely what Jesus was willing to do. *I will venture for thy name*. That was the essence of the life of Jesus, and that – not safety and security – should be the motto of every Christian and the mainspring of the Christian life.

ALLIANCE OR CONQUEST?

Mark 3:22–7

> The experts in the law from Jerusalem came down. They
> said, 'He has Beelzebul on his side.' They said, 'It is by
> the ruler of the demons that he casts out the demons.'
> Jesus called them and spoke to them by way of analogy.
> 'How can Satan cast out Satan? If a kingdom is divided
> against itself, that kingdom cannot stand. And if a house
> is divided against itself that house will not be able to
> stand. And if Satan had risen up against himself, and is
> divided, he cannot stand – he is finished. No one can go
> into the house of a strong man and plunder his gear
> unless he first binds the strong man – then he will
> plunder his house.'

THE orthodox officials never questioned Jesus' power to
exorcise demons. They did not need to, for exorcism was
a common phenomenon at that time. What they did say
was that Jesus' power was due to the fact that he was in
league with the king of the demons, that, as one commentator puts it, 'it was by the great demon he cast out the
little demons'. People have always believed in 'black magic',
and that is what they claimed Jesus was practising.

Jesus had no difficulty in exploding that argument. The
essence of exorcism has always been that the exorcist calls
on some stronger power to drive out the weaker demon. So
Jesus says: 'Just think! If there is internal dissension in a
kingdom, that kingdom cannot last. If there are quarrels in a
house, that house will not endure long. If Satan is actually
making war with his own demons then he is finished as an
effective power, because civil war has begun in the kingdom
of Satan.' 'Put it another way,' Jesus said. 'Suppose you want

to rob a strong man. You have no hope of doing so until you have got the strong man under subjection. Once you have got him tied up you can plunder his goods – but not until then.' The defeat of the demons did not show that Jesus was in alliance with Satan; it showed that Satan's defences had been breached. A stronger name had arrived; the conquest of Satan had begun. Two things emerge here.

(1) Jesus accepts life as a struggle between the power of evil and the power of God. He did not waste his time in speculation about problems to which there is no answer. He did not stop to argue about where evil came from; but he did deal with it most effectively. One of the odd things is that we spend a good deal of time discussing the origin of evil; but we spend less time working out practical methods of tackling the problem. Someone put it this way – suppose we wake up to find the house on fire, we do not sit down and embark upon the reading of a treatise entitled 'The Origin of Fires in Private Houses'. We grab such defences as we can muster and deal with the fire. Jesus saw the essential struggle between good and evil which is at the heart of life and raging in the world. He did not speculate about it; he dealt with it and gave to others the power to overcome evil and do the right.

(2) Jesus regarded the defeat of disease as part of the conquest of Satan. This is an essential part of Jesus' thought. He desired, and was able, to save bodies as well as souls. The doctor and the scientist who meet the challenge of disease are sharing in the defeat of Satan as much as the preacher of the word. The doctor and the minister are not doing different work but the same work. They are not rivals but allies in God's warfare against the power of evil.

THE SIN FOR WHICH THERE IS
NO FORGIVENESS

Mark 3:28–30

> 'This is the truth I tell you – all sins will be forgiven to
> the sons of men – I mean all the insulting things that
> they say; but whoever insults the Holy Spirit will not
> be forgiven forever but he has made himself guilty of
> the sin that not even eternity can wipe out.' This he
> said because they were saying, 'He has an unclean
> spirit.'

IF we are to understand what this terrible saying means, we
must first understand the circumstances in which it was said.
It was said by Jesus when the scribes and Pharisees had
declared that the cures he performed were performed not by
the power of God, but by the power of the devil. These men
had been able to look at the incarnate love of God and to
think it the incarnate power of Satan.

We must begin by remembering that Jesus could not have
used the phrase 'the Holy Spirit' in the full Christian sense of
the term. The Spirit in all his fullness did not come until
Jesus had returned to his glory. It was not until Pentecost
that there came to men and women the supreme experience
of the Holy Spirit. Jesus must have used the term in the *Jewish*
sense of the term. Now in Jewish thought the Holy Spirit had
two great functions. First, he revealed God's truth; second,
he enabled that truth to be recognized. That will give us the
key to this passage.

(1) The Holy Spirit enabled men and women to recognize
God's truth when it entered their lives. But if people refuse
to exercise any God-given faculty they will in the end lose it.
If they live in the dark long enough they will lose the ability

to see. If they stay in bed long enough they will lose the power to walk. If they refuse to do any serious study they will lose the power to study. And if people refuse the guidance of God's Spirit often enough they will become in the end incapable of recognizing that truth when they see it. In their eyes, evil becomes good and good evil. They can look on the goodness of God and call it the evil of Satan.

(2) Why should such a sin have no forgiveness? The biblical scholar H. B. Swete says, 'To identify the source of good with the embodiment of all evil implies a moral wreck for which the Incarnation itself provides no remedy.' The 1920s Bishop of Derby, A. J. Rawlinson, calls it 'essential wickedness', as if here we see the quintessence of all evil. The Lutheran scholar Johannes Bengel said that all other sins are *human* but this sin is *Satanic*. Why should all this be so?

Consider the effect of Jesus on people. The very first effect is to make them see their own utter unworthiness in comparison with the beauty and the loveliness of the life of Jesus. 'Go away from me, Lord,' said Peter, 'for I am a sinful man!' (Luke 5:8). When Tokichi Ishii first read the story of the gospel he said, 'I stopped. I was stabbed to the heart as if pierced by a five-inch nail. Shall I call it the love of Christ? Shall I call it his compassion? I do not know what to call it. I only know that I believed and my hardness of heart was changed.' The first reaction was that he was stabbed to the heart. The result of that sense of unworthiness and the result of that stabbed heart is a heartfelt penitence, and penitence is the only condition of forgiveness. But, if people have got themselves into such a state, by repeated refusals to listen to the promptings of the Holy Spirit, that they cannot see anything lovely in Jesus at all, then the sight of Jesus will not give them any sense of sin; because they have no sense of sin they cannot be penitent, and because they are not penitent they cannot be forgiven.

One of the Lucifer legends tells how one day a priest noticed in his congregation a magnificently handsome young man. After the service, the young man stayed for confession. He confessed so many and such terrible sins that the priest's hair stood on end. 'You must have lived long to have done all that,' the priest said. 'My name is Lucifer and I fell from heaven at the beginning of time,' said the young man. 'Even so,' said the priest, 'say that you are sorry, say that you repent and even you can be forgiven.' The young man looked at the priest for a moment and then turned and strode away. He would not and could not say it; and therefore he had to go on still desolate and still damned.

There is only one condition of forgiveness and that is penitence. As long as people see loveliness in Christ, as long as they hate sin even if they cannot leave it, even if they are in the mud and the mire, they can still be forgiven. But if people, by repeated refusals of God's guidance, have lost the ability to recognize goodness when they see it, if they have got their moral values inverted until evil to them is good and good to them is evil, then, even when they are confronted by Jesus, they are conscious of no sin; they cannot repent and therefore they can never be forgiven. That is the sin against the Holy Spirit.

THE CONDITIONS OF KINSHIP

Mark 3:31–5

> His mother and his brothers came. They stood outside and sent someone in with a message to him. The crowd were sitting round him. 'Look!' they said, 'your mother

and your brothers are outside inquiring for you.' 'Who',
he answered, 'is my mother and my brothers?' He
looked round those who were sitting in a circle round
about him. 'Look!' he said, 'my mother and my
brothers! Whoever does God's will, he is my brother,
my sister and my mother.'

HERE Jesus lays down the conditions of true kinship. It is not
solely a matter of flesh and blood. It is possible to be much
nearer to someone who is no blood relation at all than to
those who are bound to us by the closest ties of kin and blood.
Wherein lies this true kinship?

(1) True kinship lies in a *common experience*, especially
when it is an experience where two people have really come
through things together. It has been said that two people really
become friends when they are able to say to each other, 'Do
you remember?' and then to go on and talk about the things
they have come through together. Someone once met an old
woman. An acquaintance of hers had died. 'You will be sorry',
he said, 'that Mrs So-and-so is dead.' 'Yes,' she said, but
without showing any great grief. 'I saw you just last week,'
he said, 'laughing and talking with each other. You must have
been great friends.' 'Yes,' she said, 'I was friendly with her. I
used to laugh with her; but to be real friends folks have got
to weep together.' That is profoundly true. The basis of true
kinship lies in a common experience, and Christians have the
common experience of being forgiven sinners.

(2) True kinship lies in *a common interest*. The ecumenical
activist A. M. Chirgwin tells us a very interesting thing in
The Bible in World Evangelism. One of the greatest difficulties
that booksellers and distributors of the Scriptures have is not
so much to sell their books as to keep people reading them.
He goes on, 'A colporteur [bookseller] in pre-Communist
China had for years been in the habit of going from shop to

shop and house to house. But he was often disappointed because many of his new Bible readers lost their zeal, until he hit upon the plan of putting them in touch with one another and forming them into a worshipping group which in time became a duly organized Church.' Only when these isolated units became part of a group which was bound together by a common interest did real kinship come into being. Christians have that common interest because they are all people who desire to know more about Jesus Christ.

(3) True kinship lies in *a common obedience*. The disciples were a very mixed group. All kinds of beliefs and opinions were mixed up among them. A tax-collector like Matthew and a fanatical nationalist like Simon the Zealot ought to have hated each other like poison and no doubt at one time did. But they were bound together because both had accepted Jesus Christ as Master and Lord. Any platoon of soldiers will be made up of men from different backgrounds and from different walks of life and holding very different opinions: yet, if they are long enough together, they will be welded into a band of comrades because of the common obedience which they all share. Those who share a common leader can become friends. We can love each other only when we all love Jesus Christ.

(4) True kinship lies in *a common goal*. There is nothing for binding people together like a common aim. Here there is a great lesson for the Church. A. M. Chirgwin, talking of renewed interest in the Bible, asks, does this 'point to the possibility of a new approach to the ecumenical problem based on biblical rather than on ecclesiastical considerations'? The churches will never draw together so long as they argue about the ordination of their ministers, the form of church government, the administration of the sacraments and all the rest of it. The one thing on which they can all come

together is the fact that all of them are seeking to win men and women for Jesus Christ. If kinship comes from a common goal then Christians above all others possess its secret, for all are seeking to know Christ better and to bring people within his kingdom. Wherever else we differ, on that we can agree.

TEACHING IN PARABLES

Mark 4:1–2

> Jesus began again to teach by the lakeside. A very great crowd collected to hear him, so great that he had to go on board a boat and sit in it on the lake. The whole crowd was on the land facing the lake. He began to teach them many things in parables, and in his teaching he began to say to them, 'Listen! Look! The sower went out to sow.'

IN this section we see Jesus making a new departure. He was no longer teaching in the synagogue; he was teaching by the lakeside. He had made the orthodox approach to the people; now he had to take unusual methods.

We do well to note that Jesus was prepared to use new methods. He was willing to take religious preaching and teaching out of its conventional setting in the synagogue into the open air and among the crowds of ordinary men and women. John Wesley was for many years a faithful and orthodox servant of the Church of England. Down in Bristol his friend George Whitefield was preaching to the miners, to as many as 20,000 of them at a time, in the open air; and his hearers were being converted by the hundred. He sent for John Wesley. Wesley said, 'I love a commodious room, a soft cushion, a handsome pulpit.' This whole business of open-air preaching rather offended him. He said himself, 'I could scarcely reconcile myself at first to this strange way – having been all my life (till very lately) so tenacious of every point relating to decency and order, that I should have thought the saving of souls almost a sin if it had not been done in a church.' But Wesley saw that field preaching won souls and said, 'I cannot argue against a matter of fact.'

There must have been many among the orthodox Jews who regarded this new departure as sensationalism; but Jesus was wise enough to know when new methods were necessary and adventurous enough to use them. It would be well if his Church was equally wise and equally adventurous.

This new departure needed a new method; and the new method Jesus chose was to speak to the people *in parables. A parable* is literally *something thrown beside something else*; that is to say, it is basically *a comparison*. It is an *earthly story with a heavenly meaning*. Something on earth is compared with something in heaven, that the heavenly truth may be better grasped in light of the earthly illustration. Why did Jesus choose this method? And why did it become so characteristic of him that he is known forever as the master of the parable?

(1) First and foremost, Jesus chose the parabolic method simply to make people listen. He was not now dealing with an assembly of people in a synagogue who were more or less bound to remain there until the end of the service. He was dealing with a crowd in the open air who were quite free to walk away at any time. Therefore, the first essential was *to interest them*. Unless their interest was aroused, they would simply drift away. The eighteenth-century poet Sir Philip Sidney speaks of the poet's secret: 'With a tale forsooth he cometh unto you, with a tale that holdeth children from play and old men from the chimney-corner.' The surest way to

awaken people's interest is to tell them stories, and Jesus knew that.

(2) Further, when Jesus used the parabolic method he was using something with which Jewish teachers and audiences were entirely familiar. There are parables in the Old Testament of which the most famous is the story of the one ewe-lamb that Nathan told to David when he had treacherously eliminated Uriah and taken possession of Bathsheba (2 Samuel 12:1–7). The Rabbis habitually used parables in their teaching. It was said of Rabbi Meir that he spoke one-third in legal decisions, one-third in exposition, and one-third in parables.

Here are two examples of Rabbinic parables. The first is the work of Rabbi Judah the Prince (c. AD 190). Antoninus, the Roman emperor, asked him how there could be punishment in the world beyond, for since body and soul after their separation could not have committed sin they could blame each other for the sins committed upon earth. The Rabbi answered in a parable:

> A certain king had a beautiful garden in which was excellent fruit; and over it he appointed two watchmen, one blind and one lame. The lame man said to the blind man, 'I see exquisite fruit in the garden. Carry me thither that I may get it and we will eat it together.' The blind man consented and both ate of the fruit. After some days the Lord of the garden came and asked the watchmen concerning the fruit. Then the lame man said, 'As I have no legs I could not go to it, so it is not my fault.' And the blind man said, 'I could not even see it so it is not my fault.' What did the Lord of the garden do? He made the blind man carry the lame and thus passed judgment on them both. So God will replace the souls in their bodies and will punish both together for their sins.

When Rabbi Chiyya's son Abin died at the early age of twenty-eight, Rabbi Zera delivered the funeral oration, which he put in the form of a parable:

> A king had a vineyard for which he engaged many labourers, one of whom was specially apt and skilful. What did the king do? He took this labourer from his work, and walked through the garden conversing with him. When the labourers came for their hire in the evening the skilful labourer appeared among them and received a full day's wages from the king. The other labourers were very angry at this, and said, 'We have toiled the whole day, while this man has worked but two hours. Why does the king give him the full hire even as unto us?' The king said to them, 'Why are you angry? Through his skill he has done more in the two hours than you have done all day.' So it is with Rabbi Abin ben Chiyya. In the twenty-eight years of his life he has learned more than others learn in 100 years. Hence he has fulfilled his life work, and is entitled to be called to Paradise earlier than others from his work on earth; nor will he miss aught of his reward.

When Jesus used the parabolic method of teaching, he was using a method with which the Jews were familiar and which they could understand.

(3) Still further, when Jesus used the parabolic method of teaching he was making the abstract idea concrete. Few people can grasp abstract ideas. Most people think in pictures. We could talk about *beauty* for long enough and no one would be any the wiser; but, if we can point to a person and say, 'That is a beautiful person,' beauty becomes clear. We could talk about goodness for long enough and fail to arrive at a definition of it; but we all recognize a good deed when

we see one. There is a sense in which *every* word must become flesh; every idea must be actualized in a person. When the New Testament talks about faith it takes the example of Abraham so that the idea of faith becomes flesh in the person of Abraham. Jesus was a wise teacher. He knew that it was useless to expect simple minds to cope with abstract ideas, and so he put the abstract ideas into concrete stories; he showed them in action; he made them into persons, so that those who heard him might grasp and understand them.

(4) Lastly, the great virtue of the parable is that it compels people to think for themselves. It does not do their thinking for them. It compels them to make their own deductions and to discover the truth for themselves. The worst way to help children is to do their work for them. It does not help them at all to do their maths, write their essays or work out their problems. It does help greatly to give them the necessary help to do it *for themselves*. That is what Jesus was aiming at. Truth always has a double impact when it is a personal discovery. Jesus did not wish to save people the mental sweat of thinking; he wished to make them think. He did not wish to make their minds lazy; he wished to make them active. He did not wish to take the responsibility from them; he wished to lay the responsibility on them. So he used the parabolic method, not to do his audience's thinking for them, but to encourage them to do their own thinking. He presented them with truth which, if they would make the right effort in the right frame of mind, they could discover for themselves, and therefore possess it in a way that made it really and truly theirs.

FROM EARTH TO HEAVEN

Mark 4:3-9

'Listen! Look! The sower went out to sow. As he was
sowing, some seed fell along the roadside; and the birds
came and devoured it. Some fell upon rocky ground
where it did not have much earth; and it sprang up
immediately, because it had no depth of earth, but,
when the sun rose, it was scorched, and it was withered
away, because it had no root. Some fell among thorns;
and the thorns crowded in on it until they choked the
life out of it, and it did not yield any fruit. And some
fell on good ground; and, as it grew up and grew greater,
it yielded fruit and bore as much as thirtyfold and
sixtyfold and a hundredfold.' And he said, 'Who has
ears to hear, let him hear.'

WE leave the interpretation of this parable until we come to
the interpretation Mark gives us, and for the moment we
consider it only as a specimen of Jesus' parabolic teaching
in action. The scene is the lakeside; Jesus is sitting in the
boat just off the shore. The shore shelves gently down to the
water's edge, and makes a natural amphitheatre for the crowd.
Even as he talks, Jesus sees a sower busy sowing seed in the
fields beside the lake. 'Look!' he said, 'The sower went out
to sow.' Herein is the whole essence of the parabolic method.

(1) Jesus started from the *here and now* to get to the *there
and then*. He started from a thing that was happening at that
moment on earth in order to lead people's thoughts to heaven;
he started from something which everyone could see to get
to the things that are invisible; he started from something
which everyone knew to get to something which no one had
ever realized. That was the very essence of Jesus' teaching.
He did not bewilder people by starting with things which

were strange and abstruse and involved; he started with the simplest things that even a child could understand.

(2) By so doing, Jesus showed that he believed that there was a real kinship between earth and heaven. Jesus would not have agreed that 'earth was a desert drear'. He believed that in the ordinary, common, everyday things of life it was possible to see God. As Archbishop William Temple put it: 'Jesus taught men to see the operation of God in the regular and the normal – in the rising of the sun and the falling of the rain and the growth of the plant.' Long ago, Paul had the same idea when he said that the visible world is designed to make known the invisible things of God (Romans 1:20). For Jesus, this world was not a lost and evil place; it was the garment of the living God. Sir Christopher Wren lies buried in St Paul's Cathedral, the great church that his own genius planned and built. On his tombstone there is a simple Latin inscription which means, 'If you wish to see his monument, look around you.' Jesus would have said, 'If you wish to see God, look around you.' Jesus finds in the common things of life a countless source of signs which lead men and women to God if they will only read them aright.

(3) The very essence of the parables is that they were spontaneous, of the moment and unrehearsed. Jesus looks round, seeking a point of contact with the crowd. He sees the sower and on the spur of the moment that sower becomes his text. The parables were not stories worked out in the quiet of a study: they were not carefully thought out and polished and rehearsed. Their supreme greatness is that Jesus composed these immortal short stories on the spur of the moment. They were produced by the demand of the occasion and in the cut and thrust of debate.

In his book, *The Parables of Jesus*, C. J. Cadoux said of the parables: 'A parable is art harnessed for service and conflict . . . Here we find the reason why the parable is so rare. It requires a considerable degree of art, but art exercised under hard conditions. In the three typical parables of the Bible the speaker takes his life in his hands. Jotham (Judges 9:8–15) spoke his parable of the trees to the men of Shechem and then fled for his life. Nathan (2 Samuel 12:1–7), with the parable of the ewe-lamb, told an oriental despot of his sin. Jesus in the Parable of the Wicked Husbandmen used his own death sentence as a weapon for his cause . . . In its most characteristic use the parable is a weapon of controversy, not shaped like a sonnet in undisturbed concentration but improvised in conflict to meet the unpremeditated situation. In its highest use it shows the sensitiveness of the poet, the penetration, rapidity and resourcefulness of the protagonist, and the courage that allows such a mind to work unimpeded by the turmoil and danger of mortal conflict.'

When we bear in mind that the parables of Jesus were flashed out spontaneously, their wonder is increased a hundredfold.

(4) That brings us to a point we must always remember in our attempts to interpret the parables. They were, in the first instance, not meant to be read but to be *heard*. That is to say, in the first instance, no one could sit down and study them phrase by phrase and word by word. They were spoken not to be studied at length and at leisure, but to produce an immediate impression and reaction. That is to say, *the parables must never be treated as allegories*. In an allegory, every part and action and detail of the story has an inner significance. *The Pilgrim's Progress* and the *Faerie Queene* are allegories; in them every event and person and detail has a symbolic meaning. Clearly an allegory is something to be read and studied and examined; but a parable is something which was heard once and once only. Therefore

what we must look for in a parable is not a situation in which every detail stands for something but a situation in which one great idea leaps out and shines like a flash of lightning. It is always wrong to attempt to make every detail of a parable mean something. It is always right to say: 'What one idea would flash into someone's mind on hearing this story for the first time?'

THE MYSTERY OF THE KINGDOM

Mark 4:10–12

> When Jesus was alone, his own circle of people, together with the Twelve, asked him about the parables. He said to them, 'To you there is given the knowledge of the kingdom of God which only the initiated can know. To those who are outside, everything is expounded by means of parables, so that they may indeed see and yet not perceive the meaning of things, and may indeed hear and not understand, lest at any time they should turn and be forgiven.'

THIS has always been one of the most difficult passages in all the gospels. The Authorized Version speaks of the *mystery* of the kingdom of God. This word *mystery* has in Greek a technical meaning; it does not mean something which is complicated and mysterious in our sense of the term. It means something which is quite unintelligible to the person who has not been initiated into its meaning, but is perfectly plain to the person who has been so initiated.

In New Testament times in the pagan world, one of the great features of popular religion was what were called the *mystery religions*. These religions promised communion with and even identity with some god, whereby all the terrors of life and of death would be taken away. Nearly all these mystery religions were based on the story of some god who had suffered and died and risen again; they nearly all found their expression in the form of passion plays.

One of the most famous was called the Mystery of Isis. Osiris was a wise and good king. Seth, his wicked brother, hated him and along with seventy-two conspirators persuaded him to come to a banquet. There he induced him to enter a cunningly made coffin which exactly fitted him. When he was inside, the lid was snapped down and the coffin was cast into the Nile. Isis, his faithful wife, after a long and weary search, found the coffin and brought it home in mourning. When she was absent the wicked Seth came again, stole away the body, cut it into fourteen pieces and scattered them throughout all Egypt. Once again Isis set out on her sad and weary search. In the end she discovered all the pieces and by her magical powers put them together and restored Osiris to life again; and from that time he became the immortal king of the living and the dead.

What happened was this. The candidate underwent a long preparation of purification and of fasting and of asceticism and of instruction as to the inner meaning of the story. Then the dramatic story with its grief and its sorrow and its resurrection and its triumphal ending was played out as a passion play. Music and incense and lighting and a splendid liturgy were all used to enhance the emotional atmosphere. As the play was played out, the worshipper felt at one with the god both in suffering and in triumph, and passed through death to immortality by union with the god. The point is that to the uninitiated the whole thing would have been meaningless; but to the initiated the thing was full of meaning which they had been taught to see.

That is the technical meaning of this Greek word *mustērion*. When the New Testament talks of the *mystery* of the kingdom, it does not mean that the kingdom is remote and abstruse and hard to understand; but it does mean that it is quite unintelligible to those who have not given their hearts to Jesus, and that only those who have taken Jesus as Master and Lord can understand what the kingdom of God means.

The real difficulty of the passage lies in the section that follows. If we take it at its face value, it sounds as if Jesus taught in parables deliberately to cloak his meaning, purposely to hide it from ordinary men and women. Whatever else the passage originally meant, it cannot have meant that; for, if one thing is crystal clear, it is that Jesus used parables not to cloak his meaning and to hide his truth but to enable men and women to see it and to compel them to recognize it.

How then did this passage come to be in the form it is? It is a quotation from Isaiah 6:9–10. From the beginning, it worried people. It was worrying them more than 200 years before Jesus made use of it. The Hebrew literally runs (the following two translations are by W. O. E. Oesterley):

> And he said, Go, and say to this people, 'Go on hearkening, but understand not; go on looking, but perceive not.' Make fat the heart of this people, and its ears make heavy, and its eyes besmear; lest it see with its eyes, and with its ears hear, and its heart understand, so that it should be healed again.

It seems on the face of it that God is telling Isaiah that he is to pursue a course deliberately designed to make the people fail to understand.

In the third century BC the Hebrew Scriptures were translated into Greek, and the Greek version, the Septuagint, as it is called, became one of the most influential books in the world, for it carried the Old Testament everywhere Greek was spoken. The Septuagint translators were worried at this strange passage and they translated it differently:

> And he said, Go and say to this people, 'Ye shall hear indeed, but ye shall not understand; and seeing, ye shall see, and not perceive.' For the heart of this people has become gross, and with their ears they hear heavily, and their eyes they have closed; lest at any time they should see with their eyes and hear with their ears, and understand with their heart, and should be converted, and I should heal them.

The Greek version does not say that God intended that the people should be so dull that they would not understand; it says that they had made themselves so dull that they could not understand – which is a very different thing. The explanation is that no one can translate or set down in print a tone of voice. When Isaiah spoke, he spoke half in irony and half in despair and altogether in love. He was thinking, 'God sent me to bring his truth to this people; and for all the good I am doing I might as well have been sent to shut their minds to it. I might as well be speaking to a brick wall. You would think that God had shut their minds to it.'

So Jesus spoke his parables; he meant them to flash into people's minds and to illuminate the truth of God. But in so many eyes he saw a dull incomprehension. He saw so many people blinded by prejudice, deafened by wishful thinking, too lazy to think. He turned to his disciples and he said to them: 'Do you remember what Isaiah once said? He said that when he came with God's message to God's people Israel in his day they were so dully un-understanding that you would have thought that God had shut instead of opening their minds; I feel like that today.' When Jesus said this, he did not say it in anger, or irritation, or bitterness, or exasperation. He said it with the wistful longing of frustrated love, the poignant sorrow of a man who had a tremendous gift to give which people were too blind to take.

If we read this, hearing not a tone of bitter exasperation, but a tone of regretful love, it will sound quite different. It will tell us not of a God who deliberately caused blindness and hid his truth, but of people who were so dully uncomprehending that it seemed no use even for God to try to penetrate the iron curtain of their lazy incomprehension. God save us from hearing his truth like that!

THE HARVEST IS SURE

Mark 4:13–20

'Don't you understand this parable?' he said to them. 'How then will you understand all the parables? What the sower is sowing is the word. The kind of people represented by the case in which the seed fell by the side of the road are those in whose case the word is sown, and whenever they hear it, immediately Satan comes, and snatches away the word that was sown into them. Just so, the kind of people represented by the case in which the seed was sown on the rocky ground are those, who, whenever they hear the word, immediately gladly welcome it. They have no root in themselves, but they are quite impermanent; and then, when trouble or persecution happens because of the word, they immediately stumble and collapse. Then there are the others who are represented by the case in which the seed was sown among thorns. These are the people who hear the word, but the anxieties of this world and the deceptive attraction of wealth and the desires for other things enter into them and choke the life out of the word, and it never gets a chance to bear fruit. The kind of people who are represented by the case in which the seed fell on good ground are such as hear the word and receive it and bring forth fruit, thirty and sixty and a hundredfold.'

EVERY detail of this parable would be real to its hearers because every detail came from everyday life. Four kinds of ground are mentioned.

(1) There was the hard ground at the side of the road. The seed might fall on this kind of ground in two ways. The fields in Palestine were in the form of long, narrow strips; these strips were divided by little grass paths, which were rights of way; the result was that they became beaten as hard as stone by the feet of those who used them. As the sower scattered his seed, some might well fall there; and there it had no chance to grow.

But there was another way of sowing. Sometimes a sack of seed was put on the back of a donkey; a hole was cut in the corner of the sack; and then the animal was led up and down as the seed flowed out. Inevitably as the donkey was brought along the road to the field some of the seed fell on the road; and just as inevitably the birds swooped and gobbled it up.

There are some people into whose hearts Christian truth can find no entry. This is due to the hearer's lack of interest; and that lack of interest comes from a failure to realize how important the Christian decision is. Christianity fails to make an impact on so many people, not because they are hostile to it, but because they are indifferent. They think that it is irrelevant to life and that they can get on well enough without it. That might be true if life was always an easy way where there were neither tensions nor tears; but in fact there comes to each one of us a time when we need a power that is not our own. It is the tragedy of life that so many discover that too late.

(2) There was the rocky ground. This was not ground full of stones; it was a narrow skin of earth over a shelf of limestone rock. Much of Galilee was like that. In many fields, the outcrop of the rock through the shallow soil could be seen. Seed which fell there germinated all right; but because the soil was so shallow and held so little nourishment and moisture, the heat of the sun soon withered the sprouting seed and it died.

It is always easier to begin a thing than to finish it. A certain famous evangelist said: 'We have learned that it takes about five per cent effort to win a man to Christ, and ninety-five per cent to keep him in Christ and growing into maturity in the church.' Many begin the Christian way only to fall by the wayside.

There are two troubles which cause this collapse. One is the failure to think the thing out and to think it through, the failure to realize what it means and what it costs before the start is made. The other is the fact that there are thousands of people who are attracted by Christianity but who never let it get beyond the surface of their lives. The fact is that with Christianity it is a case of all or nothing. We are safe only when we have given ourselves in total commitment to Christ, as John Wesley's translation of a German hymn has it:

> Is there a thing beneath the sun,
>> That strives with thee my heart to share?
> Ah! tear it thence, and reign alone,
>> The Lord of every motion there.

(3) There was the ground that was full of thorns. The Palestinian farmer was lazy. He cut off the top of the fibrous rooted weeds: he even burned off the top; and the field might look clean; but below the surface the roots were still there;

and in due time the weeds revived in all their strength. They grew with such rapidity and such virulence that they choked the life out of the seed.

It is easy to pack life with such a multiplicity of interests that there is no time left for Christ. As Matthew Arnold's poem 'Absence' put it, the cares of life can be like the clogging dust until 'we forget because we must and not because we will'. The more complicated life becomes, the more necessity there is to see that our priorities are right, for there are so many things which seek to push Christ on to the sidelines.

(4) There was the good, clean, deep soil in which the seed flourished.

If we are really to benefit by the Christian message, the parable tells us that we must do three things.

(a) We must *hear* it; and we cannot hear unless we listen. It is characteristic of so many of us that we are so busy talking that we have no time to hear, so engaged in arguing that we have no time to listen, so occupied in advancing our own opinions that we have no time to attend to the opinions of Christ, so much on the move that we have no time for the essential stillness.

(b) We must *receive* it. When we hear the Christian message, we must really take it into our minds. The human mind is an odd and dangerous machine. We are so constructed, in the wise providence of creation, that, whenever a foreign body threatens to enter the eye, the eye automatically closes. That is an instinctive, reflex action. Whenever the mind hears something that it does not want to hear, it automatically closes its door. There are times when truth can hurt; but sometimes a distasteful drug or an unpleasant treatment must be accepted if health is to be preserved. To shut the mind to truth we do not want to hear is the straight road to disaster and to tragedy.

(c) We must *put it into action*. The yield in the parable was thirty-, sixty- and a hundredfold. That is a large yield, but the volcanic soil of Galilee was famous for its crops. Christian truth must always emerge in action. In the last analysis the Christian is challenged, not to speculate, but to act.

All that is the meaning of this parable *when we sit down and study it at leisure*. But it is quite impossible that all that would flash into the minds of those who heard it for the first time. What, then, would be the one thing which struck the crowd who heard it for the first time beside the Sea of Galilee? Surely this – that, *although part of the seed never grew, the fact remained that at the end of the day there was a splendid harvest*. This is the parable to end despair. It may seem that much of our effort achieves no result; it may seem that much of our labour is wasted. That is how the disciples were feeling, when they saw Jesus banished from the synagogue and regarded with suspicion. In many places his message seemed to have failed, and they were discouraged and downhearted. But this parable said to them, and says to us, 'Patience! Do your work. Sow the seed. Leave the rest to God. The harvest is sure.'

THE LIGHT WHICH MUST BE SEEN

Mark 4:21

> This was one of Jesus' sayings: 'Surely a lamp is not brought in to be put under a peck measure or under the bed? Is it not brought in to be set upon a lamp stand?'

VERSES 21–5 are interesting because they show the problems that confronted the writers of the gospels. These verses give

us four different sayings of Jesus. In verse 21 there is the
saying about the lamp. In verse 22 there is the saying about
the revealing of secret things. In verse 24 there is the saying
which lays it down that we shall receive back with the same
measure as we have given. In verse 25 there is the saying that
to the one who has, still more will be given. In Mark these
verses come one after another in immediate succession. But
verse 21 is repeated in Matthew 5:15; verse 22 is repeated in
Matthew 10:26; verse 24 is repeated in Matthew 7:2; and verse
25 is repeated in Matthew 13:12 and also in Matthew 25:29.
The four consecutive verses in Mark are scattered all over
Matthew. One practical thing emerges for our study. We must
not try to find any connection between them. Clearly they are
quite disconnected and we must take them one by one.

How did it come about that these sayings of Jesus are given
by Mark one after another and scattered by Matthew all over
his gospel? The reason is just this. Jesus had a unique
command of language. He could say the most vivid and pithy
things. He could say things that stuck in the memory and
refused to be forgotten. Further, he must have said many of
these things far more than once. He was moving from place
to place and from audience to audience; and he must have
repeated much of his teaching wherever he went. The consequence was that the things that Jesus said were remembered
– they were said with such vividness that they could not be
forgotten – but the occasion on which they were said was
forgotten. The result was a great many of what one might
call 'orphan' sayings of Jesus. A saying was embedded in
people's minds and remembered forever, but the context and
the occasion were forgotten. So then we have to take these
vivid sayings individually and examine them.

The first was that no one lights a lamp and puts it under
a peck measure, which would be like putting a bowl on top

of it, nor is it ever put under a bed. A lamp is meant to be seen and to help people to see; and it is put in a place where it will be visible to all. From this saying, we may learn two things.

(1) *Truth is meant to be seen*; it is not meant to be concealed. There may be times when it is dangerous to tell the truth; there may be times when to tell the truth is the quickest way to persecution and to trouble. But the true man or woman and the true Christian will stand by the truth in face of all.

When Martin Luther decided to take up his stand against the Roman Catholic Church, he decided first of all to attack *indulgences*. *Indulgences* were to all intents and purposes remissions of sins which could be bought from a priest at a price. He drew up ninety-five theses against these indulgences. And what did he do with his ninety-five theses? There was a church in Wittenberg called the Church of All Saints. It was closely connected with the university; on its door university notices were posted, and the subject of academic debates displayed. There was no more public noticeboard in the town. To that door Luther affixed his theses. When did he do it? The day when the largest congregation came to the church was All Saints' Day, 1st November. It happened to be the anniversary of the founding of that church, and many services were held and crowds came. It was on All Saints' Day that Luther nailed his ninety-five theses to the church door. If he had been a prudent man, he would not have drawn up his ninety-five theses at all. If he had been a man with an eye on safety, he would never have nailed them to the church door. And, if he must nail them to the door, with any thought of personal safety he would never have chosen All Saints' Day to make his declaration. But Luther felt that he had discovered the truth; and his one thought was to display the truth and to align his life with it.

In every walk of life, there are times when we know quite
well what the truth demands, what is the right thing to do,
what a Christian ought to do. In every walk of life, there are
times when we fail to do it, because it would be to court
unpopularity and perhaps worse. We ought to remember that
the lamp of truth is something to be held aloft and not
concealed in the interests of a cowardly safety.

(2) *Our Christianity is meant to be seen.* In the early
Church, sometimes to show one's Christianity meant death.
The Roman Empire was as vast as the world. In order to get
some sort of binding unity into that vast empire, emperor-
worship was started. The emperor was the embodiment of
the state and he was worshipped as a god. On certain stated
days it was demanded that everyone should come and sacrifice
to the godhead of the emperor. It was really a test of political
loyalty. After doing so, people received a certificate to say
they had done so; and, having got that certificate, they could
go away and worship any god they liked.

We still have many of these certificates. They run like this:

> To those who have been put in charge of the sacrifices
> from Inareus Akeus from the village of Theoxenis,
> together with his children Aias and Hera, who stay in
> the village of Theadelpheia. We sacrifice regularly to
> the gods and now in your presence, as the regulations
> demand, we have sacrificed and poured our libation and
> have tasted the offerings, and we ask you to give us the
> required certificate. May you fare well.

Then there follows the attestation.

> We, Serenas and Hermas, have witnessed your sacri-
> ficing.

All that Christians had to do was to go through that formal
act, receive the certificate, and they were safe. And the fact

of history is that thousands of Christians died rather than do so. They could have concealed the fact that they were Christians with the greatest of ease; they could have gone on being Christians, as it were, privately, with no trouble at all. But to them their Christianity was something which had to be attested and witnessed to in presence of all. They were proud that everyone should know where they stood. To such men and women we owe our Christian faith today.

It is often easier to keep quiet the fact that we belong to Christ and his Church; but our Christianity should always be like the lamp that can be seen by everyone.

THE TRUTH THAT CANNOT BE SUPPRESSED

Mark 4:22-3

> For there is nothing secret that will not be brought into
> the open; nothing is done that it should be hidden away,
> but that it should lie open for all to see. If a man has
> ears to hear, let him hear.

IT was Jesus' certain conviction that the truth cannot ultimately be hidden. This saying applies in two directions.

(1) *It applies to truth itself.* There is something about the truth which is indestructible. Some people may refuse to face it; they may try to suppress it; they may even try to obliterate it; they may refuse to accept it, but 'great is the truth and in the end it will prevail'.

In the early sixteenth century, an astronomer called Copernicus made the discovery that the earth is not the centre of the universe, that in fact the earth goes round the sun and not the sun round the earth. He was a cautious man and for thirty years he kept this discovery to himself. Then in 1543, when death's breath was on him, he persuaded a terrified printer to print his great work, *Revolutions of Heavenly Bodies*. Soon Copernicus died but others inherited the storm.

In the early seventeenth century, Galileo accepted the theory of Copernicus and stated publicly his belief in it. In 1616, he was summoned to the Inquisition in Rome and his beliefs were condemned. Judgment was passed. 'The first proposition, that the sun is the centre and does not revolve about the earth, is foolish, absurd, false in theology, and heretical because contrary to Holy Scripture . . . The second proposition, that the earth is not the centre, but revolves about the sun, is absurd, false in philosophy, and from a theological point of view at least, opposed to the true faith.' Galileo gave in. It was easier to conform than to die, and for years he remained silent.

A new pope came to the papal throne, and Galileo thought that Urban VIII was a man of wider sympathy and greater culture than his predecessor, so once again he came out into the open with his theory. He was mistaken in his hopes. This time he had to sign a recantation or undergo torture. He signed. 'I, Galileo, being in my seventieth year, being a prisoner and on my knees, and before your Eminences, having before my eyes the Holy Gospel, which I touch with my hands, abjure, curse and detest the error and the heresy of the movement of the earth.' His recantation saved him from death but not from prison. And in the end he was even denied burial in the family tomb.

It was not only the Roman Catholic Church which tried to avoid the truth. Martin Luther wrote: 'People gave ear to an upstart astrologer [he meant Copernicus] who strove to show that the earth revolves, not the heavens or the firmament, the sun and the moon . . . This fool wishes to reverse the entire science of astronomy: but sacred Scripture tells us that Joshua commanded the sun to stand still, and not the earth.'

But time goes on. You can threaten to torture a man for discovering the truth; you can call him a fool and try to laugh him out of court; but that does not alter the truth. 'It lies not in your power', said the religious reformer Andrew Melville, 'to hang or exile the truth.' Truth may be attacked, delayed, suppressed, mocked at; but time brings in its revenges, and in the end truth prevails. Each of us must take care that we are not fighting against the truth.

(2) *It applies to ourselves and to our own life and conduct.* When we do a wrong thing, our first instinct is to hide. That is what Adam and Eve did when they broke the commandment of God (Genesis 3:8). But truth has a way of emerging. In the last analysis we cannot hide the truth from ourselves, and those who harbour secrets are never happy. The web of deception is never a permanent concealment. And, when it comes to ultimate things, we cannot have any secrets from God. In the end, it is literally true that there is nothing which will not be revealed in the presence of God. When we remember that, we are bound to be filled with the desire to make life such that everyone may look on it and God survey it without shame to ourselves.

THE BALANCE OF LIFE

Mark 4:24

> This was another of Jesus' sayings: 'Pay attention to what you hear! What you get depends on what you give. What you give you will get back, only more so.'

IN life there is always a balance. Our getting will be determined by our giving.

(1) This is true of *study*. The more study we are prepared to give to any subject, the more we will get from it. The

ancient nation of the Parthians would never give their young men a meal until they had broken sweat. They had to work before they ate. All subjects of study are like that. They give pleasure and satisfaction in proportion to the effort that we are prepared to spend upon them. It is specially so in regard to the study of the Bible. We may sometimes feel that there are certain parts of the Bible with which we are out of sympathy; if we study these parts they will often be the very parts which end by giving us the richest harvest. A superficial study of a subject will often leave us quite uninterested whereas a really intensive study will leave us thrilled and fascinated.

(2) It is true of *worship*. The more we bring to the worship of God's house, the more we will get from it. When we come to worship in the house of God, there are three wrong ways in which we may come.

(a) We may come entirely to get. If we come in such a way, the likelihood is that we will criticize the organist and the choir and find fault with the minister's preaching. We will regard the whole service as a performance laid on for our special entertainment. We must come prepared to give; we must remember that worship is a corporate act, and that each of us can contribute something to it. If we ask, not, 'What can I get out of this service?' but, 'What can I contribute to this service?' we will in the end get far more out of it than if we simply came to take.

(b) We may come without expectation. Our coming may be the result of habit and routine. It may be simply part of the timetable into which we have divided the week. But, after all, we should be coming to meet God, and when we meet him anything may happen.

(c) We may come without preparation. It is so easy to leave for the worship of God's house with no preparation of mind or heart at all because often it is a rush to get there at all. But it would make all the difference in the world, if, before we came, we were for a moment or two still and quiet and engaged with God in prayer. As the Jewish Rabbis told their disciples: 'They pray best together who first pray alone.'

(3) It is true of *personal relationships*. One of the great facts of life is that we see our reflection in other people. If we are cross and irritable and bad-tempered, we will probably find other people equally unpleasant. If we are critical and fault-finding, the chances are that we will find other people the same. If we are suspicious and distrustful, the likelihood is that others will be so to us. If we wish others to love us, we must first love them. Those who would have friends must show themselves to be friendly. It was because Jesus believed in men and women that they believed in him.

THE LAW OF INCREASE

Mark 4:25

> To him who already has still more will be given: and from him who has not, even what he has will be taken away.

THIS may seem a hard saying; but the whole lesson of life is that it is inevitably and profoundly true.

(1) It is true of *knowledge*. The more we know the more we are capable of knowing. We cannot enter into the riches of Greek literature before we have ploughed through Greek grammar. When we have the basic grammar, still more will be given to us. We cannot really get the best out of music without learning something of the structure of a symphony. But possession of that knowledge yields still more and more loveliness. It is equally true that unless we are consistently

bent on the task of increasing our knowledge, such knowledge as we have will in the end be taken away from us. Many of us in our youth had a working knowledge of French at school and have now forgotten even the little that we knew because we made no attempt to develop it.

The more knowledge we have, the more we can acquire. And, if we are not always out to increase it, such knowledge as we have will soon slip from our grasp. The Jewish teachers had an oddly expressive saying. They said that the scholar should be treated like a young heifer – because every day a little heavier burden should be laid upon him. In knowledge we cannot stand still; we are gaining or losing it all the time.

(2) It is true of *effort*. The more physical strength we have, the more, within the limits of our bodily frame, we can acquire. The more we train our bodies, the more our bodies will be able to do. On the other hand, if we allow our physical frame to grow slack and flabby and soft we will end by losing even the fitness that we had. We would sometimes do well to remember that our bodies belong to God as much as our souls. Many of us have been hindered from doing the work we might do because we have made ourselves physically unfit to do it.

(3) It is so with *any skill or craft*. The more we develop the skill of hand, or eye, or mind, the more we are able to develop it. If we are content to drift along, never trying anything new, never adopting any new technique, we remain stuck in the one job with no progress. If we neglect our particular skill, we will find in the end that we have lost it altogether.

(4) It is so with *the ability to bear responsibility*. The more responsibility we take on, the more we are able to bear; the more decisions we compel ourselves to take, the better we are able to take them. But if we shirk our responsibilities, if we evade decisions and waver all the time, in the end we

will become flabby, spineless creatures totally unfit for responsibility and totally unable to come to any decision at all. Again and again in his parables, Jesus goes on the assumption that the reward of good work is still more work to do. It is one of the essential laws of life, a law which we forget at our peril, that the more we have won the more we can win, and that, if we will not make the effort, we will lose even that which once we had won.

THE UNSEEN GROWTH AND THE CERTAIN END

Mark 4:26–9

> He said to them: 'This is what the kingdom of God is like. It is like what happens when a man casts seed upon the earth. He sleeps and he wakes night and day, and the seed sprouts and grows – and he does not know how it does it. The earth produces fruit with help from no one, first the shoot, then the ear, then the full corn in the ear. When the time allows it, immediately he despatches the sickle, for the time to harvest has come.'

THIS is the only parable which Mark alone relates to us. The kingdom of God really means *the reign of God*; it means the day when God's will will be done as perfectly on earth as it is in heaven. That is the goal of God for the whole universe. This parable is short but it is filled with unmistakable truths.

(1) It tells us of *human helplessness*. The farmer does not make the seed grow. In the last analysis he does not even understand how it grows. It has the secret of life and of growth within itself. No one has ever possessed the secret of life; no one has ever created anything in the full sense of the

term. We can discover things; we can rearrange them; we can develop them; but create them we cannot. We do not create the kingdom of God; the kingdom is God's. It is true that we can frustrate it and hinder it, or we can make a situation in the world where it is given the opportunity to come more fully and more speedily. But behind all things is God and the power and will of God.

(2) It tells us something about the *kingdom*. It is a notable fact that Jesus so often uses illustrations from the growth of nature to describe the coming of the kingdom of God.

(a) Nature's growth is often *imperceptible*. If we see a plant every day, we cannot see its growth taking place. It is only when we see it, and then see it again after an interval of time, that we notice the difference. It is so with the kingdom. There is not the slightest doubt that the kingdom is on the way if we compare, not today with yesterday, but this century with the century which went before.

When Elizabeth Fry, the Quaker prison reformer, went to Newgate Prison in 1817, she found in the women's quarters 300 women and numberless children crammed into two small wards. They lived and cooked and ate and slept on the floor. The only attendants were one old man and his son. They crowded, half-naked, almost like animals, begging for money, which they spent on drink at a bar in the prison itself. She found there a boy of nine who was waiting to be hanged for poking a stick through a window and stealing paints valued at twopence. In 1853 the weavers of Bolton and the miners of Stafford were striking over pay because they could not earn a living wage.

Nowadays things like that are unthinkable. Why? Because the kingdom is on the way. The growth of the kingdom may, like that of the plant, be imperceptible from day to day; but over the years it is plain.

(b) Nature's growth is *constant*. Night and day, while we sleep, growth goes on. There is nothing spasmodic about God. The great trouble about human effort and human goodness is that they are spasmodic. One day we take one step forward; the next day we take two steps back. But the work of God goes on quietly; unceasingly God unfolds his plan. In the words of the well-known hymn,

> God is working his purpose out, as year succeeds to
>   year:
> God is working his purpose out, and the time is
>   drawing near –
> Nearer and nearer draws the time – the time that shall
>   surely be,
> When the earth shall be filled with the glory of God as
>   the waters cover the sea.

(c) Nature's growth is *inevitable*. There is nothing so powerful as growth. A tree can split a concrete pavement with the power of its growth. A weed can push its green head through an asphalt path. Nothing can stop growth. It is so with the kingdom. In spite of human rebellion and disobedience, God's work goes on; and nothing in the end can stop the purposes of God.

(3) It tells us that there is *a consummation*. There is a day when the harvest comes. Inevitably when the harvest comes, two things happen – which are opposite sides of the same thing. The good fruit is gathered in, and the weeds and the tares are destroyed. Harvest and judgment go hand in hand. When we think of this coming day, three things are laid upon us.

(a) It is a summons to *patience*. We are creatures of the moment and inevitably we think in terms of the moment. God has all eternity in which to work. 'A thousand years in your sight are like yesterday when it is past, or like a watch in the night' (Psalm 90:4). Instead of our petulant, fretful, irritable human hastiness we should cultivate in our souls the patience which has learned to wait on God.

(b) It is a summons to *hope*. We are living today in an atmosphere of despair. People despair of the Church; they despair of the world; they look with shuddering dread on the future. 'Man', said H. G. Wells, 'who began in a cave behind a windbreak will end in the disease-soaked ruins of a slum.' Between the two World Wars, Sir Philip Gibbs wrote a book in which he looked forward, thinking of the possibility of a war of poison gas. He said something like this. 'If I smell poison gas in High Street, Kensington, I am not going to put on a gas-mask. I am going to go out and breathe deeply of it, because I will know that *the game is up*.' So many people feel that for humanity the game is up. Now no one can think like that *and* believe in God. If God is the God we believe him to be, there is no room for pessimism. There may be remorse, regret; there may be penitence, contrition; there may be heart-searching, the awareness of failure and of sin; but there can never be despair. The hymn-writer F. W. Faber wrote:

> Workman of God! O lose not heart,
>   But learn what God is like,
> And, in the darkest battle-field,
>   Thou shalt know where to strike.

> For right is right, since God is God,
>   And right the day must win:
> To doubt would be disloyalty,
>   To falter would be sin.

(c) It is a summons to *preparedness*. If there comes the consummation, we must be ready for it. It is too late to prepare for it when it is upon us. We have literally to prepare to meet our God.

If we live in patience which cannot be defeated, in hope which cannot despair, and in preparation which always sees life in the light of eternity, we shall, by the grace of God, be ready for his consummation when it comes.

FROM SMALL TO GREAT

Mark 4:30–2

> He said: 'How shall we find something with which to compare the kingdom of God, or what picture will we use to represent it? It is like a grain of mustard seed, which, when it is sown upon the ground, is the least of all the seeds upon the earth. But, when it is sown, it springs up and it becomes greater than all the herbs; and it sends out great branches so that the birds of the heaven can find a lodging under its shade.'

THERE are in this parable two pictures which every Jew would readily recognize.

First, in Palestine a grain of mustard seed stood proverbially for the smallest possible thing. For instance, 'faith as a grain of mustard seed' means 'the smallest conceivable amount of faith'. This mustard seed did in fact grow into something very like a tree. A traveller in Palestine speaks of seeing a mustard plant which, in its height, was higher than a horse and its rider. The birds were very fond of the little black seeds of the tree, and a cloud of birds over a mustard plant was a common sight.

Second, in the Old Testament one of the commonest ways to describe a great empire was to describe it as a tree, and the tributary nations within it were said to be like birds finding shelter within the shadow of its branches (Ezekiel 17:22ff., 31:1ff.; Daniel 4:10, 21). The figure of a tree with birds in the branches therefore stands for a great empire and the nations which form part of it.

(1) This parable says, *Never be daunted by small beginnings*. It may seem that at the moment we can produce only a very small effect; but if that small effect is repeated and repeated it will become very great. There is a scientific experiment to show the effect of dyes. A large vessel of clear water is taken and a little phial of dye. Drop by drop the dye is dropped into the clear water. At first it seems to have no effect at all and the water does not seem to be coloured in the least. Then quite suddenly the water begins to tinge with the colour; bit by bit the colour deepens, until the whole vessel is coloured. It is the repeated drops that produce the effect.

We often feel that for all that we can do, it is hardly worth while starting a thing at all. But we must remember this – *everything* must have a beginning. Nothing emerges full-grown. It is our duty to do what we can; and the cumulative effect of all the small efforts can in the end produce an amazing result.

(2) This parable speaks of *the empire of the Church*. The tree and the birds, we have seen, stand for the great empire and for all the nations which find shelter within it. The Church began with an individual and it is meant to end with the world. There are two directions in which this is true.

(a) The Church is an empire in which all kinds of opinions and all kinds of theologies can find a place. We have a tendency to brand as a heretic anyone who does not think as we do. John Wesley was the greatest example of tolerance in the world. 'We think', he said, 'and we let think.' 'I have no more right', he said, 'to object to a man for holding a different opinion from mine than I have to differ with a man because he wears a wig and I wear my own hair.' Wesley had one greeting, 'Is thy heart as my heart? Then give me thy hand!' It is good to have the assurance of being right, but that is no reason to hold the conviction that everyone else is wrong.

(b) The Church is an empire in which all nations meet. Once a new church was being built. One of its great features was to be a stained-glass window. The committee in charge searched for a subject for the window and finally decided on the lines from Ann Shepherd's hymn:

> Around the throne of God in heaven
> Thousands of children stand.

They employed a great artist to paint the picture from which the window would be made. He began the work and fell in love with the task. Finally he finished it. He went to bed and fell asleep but in the night he seemed to hear a noise in his studio: he went into the studio to investigate; and there he saw a stranger with a brush and a palette in his hands working at his picture. 'Stop!' he cried. 'You'll ruin my picture.' 'I think', said the stranger, 'that you have ruined it already.' 'How is that?' said the artist. 'Well,' said the stranger, 'you have many colours on your palette but you have used only one for the faces of the children. Who told you that in heaven there were only children whose faces were white?' 'No one,' said the artist. 'I just thought of it that way.' 'Look!' said the stranger. 'I will paint their faces in every colour and shade of every race. They are all there, for they have all answered my call.' '*Your* call?' said the artist. 'Who are you?' The stranger smiled. 'Once long ago I said, "Let the children come to me and don't stop them, for of such is the kingdom of heaven" – and I'm still saying it.' Then the artist realized that it was the Master himself, and as he did so, he vanished from his sight.

The picture looked so much more wonderful now with its children with faces of every shade and colour as well as white.

In the morning, the artist awoke and rushed through to his studio. His picture was just as he had left it; and he knew that it had all been a dream. Although that very day the committee was coming to examine the picture, he seized his brushes and his paints, and began to paint the children of every colour and of every race throughout all the world. When the committee arrived, they thought the picture very beautiful, and one whispered gently, 'Why! It's God's family at home.'

The Church is the family of God; and that Church which began in Palestine, small as the mustard seed, has room in it for every nation in the world. There are no barriers in the Church of God. The barriers are of our own making, and God in Christ has torn them down.

THE WISE TEACHER AND THE WISE SCHOLAR

Mark 4:33-4

It was with many such parables that he kept speaking the word to them, suiting his instruction to their ability to hear it. It was his custom not to speak to them without a parable; and when they were by themselves, he unfolded the meaning of everything to his own disciples.

HERE we have a short but perfect definition of both the wise teacher and the wise learner. Jesus suited his instruction to the ability of those who were listening to him. That is the first essential in wise teaching.

There are two dangers that wise teachers must at all costs avoid.

(a) They must avoid all *self-display*. Their duty as teachers is not to draw attention to themselves but to draw attention to their subject. A love of self-display can result in attempts to scintillate at the expense of truth. Finding clever ways of saying a thing becomes more important than the thing itself. Or, it can result in a desire to display erudition so that the teaching becomes so obscure and elaborate and involved that few people can understand it at all. There is no virtue in talking over the head of an audience. As someone said, 'The fact that a man shoots above the target only proves that he is a bad shot.' Good teachers must be in love with their subject and not in love with themselves.

(b) Teachers must avoid *a sense of superiority*. True teaching does not consist in telling people things. It consists in learning things together. It was Plato's idea that teaching simply meant extracting from people's minds and memories what they already knew. Teachers who stand on a pedestal and talk down will never be successful. True teaching consists in sharing and discovering truth together. It is a joint exploration of the countries of the mind.

There are certain qualities which those who would teach must constantly seek to acquire.

(a) Teachers must possess *understanding*. One of the great difficulties of the expert is to understand why the non-expert finds a thing so difficult to understand or to do. It is necessary for teachers to think with the learners' minds and to see with the learners' eyes, before they can really explain and impart any kind of knowledge.

(b) Teachers must possess *patience*. The Jewish Rabbi Hillel laid it down, 'An irritable man cannot teach', and insisted that the first essential of a teacher is to be even-tempered. The Jews laid it down that if a teacher found that his scholars did not understand a thing he must begin again without rancour and without irritation and explain it all over again. That is precisely what Jesus did all his life.

(c) Teachers must possess *kindness*. Jewish teaching regulations forbade all excessive punishment. Especially they forbade all punishment which would humiliate the scholar. Teachers have a duty always to encourage, and never to discourage. Anna Buchan tells how her old grandmother had a favourite phrase, 'Never daunton [discourage] youth.' It is all too easy to speak sharply to a less able pupil; it is often a temptation to score a cheap triumph by making such pupils the target of such sarcasms and witticisms as will make them a laughing-stock. The teacher who is kind will never do that.

This passage also shows us the wise learner. It gives us a picture of an inner circle to whom Jesus could really and fully explain things.

(a) Wise learners *do not go away to forget*. They go away to think over what they have heard. They chew it over until they have finally digested it. Epictetus, the wise Stoic teacher, used to be grieved by some of his pupils. He said that people ought to use the philosophy they learned, not to talk about, but to live by. In a crude metaphor, he said that sheep do not vomit up the grass in order to show the shepherd how much they have eaten; they digest it and use it to produce wool and milk. Wise scholars go away, not to forget what they have learned, and not to display what they have learned, but quietly to think it over until they have discovered what it means for life and for living for themselves.

(b) Above all, wise learners *seek the teacher's company*. After Jesus had spoken the crowds dispersed; but there was a little company who lingered with him and did not want to leave him. It was to them that he unfolded the meaning of everything. In the last analysis, if someone is a really great teacher, it is not so much the teaching but the person that we wish to know. The message will always lie not so much in what is said as in what that teacher is. Those who wish to learn from Christ must keep company with Christ. If we do that we will win not only learning but life itself.

THE PEACE OF THE PRESENCE

Mark 4:35–41

> When on that day evening had come, he said to them, 'Let us cross over to the other side.' So they left the crowds and took him, just as he was, in their boat. And there were other boats with him. A great storm of wind got up and the waves dashed upon the boat, so that the boat was on the point of being swamped. And he was in the stern sleeping upon a pillow. They woke him. 'Teacher,' they said, 'don't you care that we are perishing?' So, when he had been wakened, he spoke sternly to the wind and said to the sea, 'Be silent! Be muzzled!' and the wind sank to rest and there was a great calm. He said to them, 'Why are you afraid? Have you still no faith?' And they were stricken with a great awe, and kept saying to each other, 'Who then can this be, because the wind and the sea obey him?'

THE Lake of Galilee was notorious for its storms. They came literally out of the blue with shattering and terrifying suddenness. A writer describes them like this: 'It is not unusual to see terrible squalls hurl themselves, even when the sky is perfectly clear, upon these waters which are ordinarily so calm. The numerous ravines which to the north-east and east debouch [open out] upon the upper part of the lake operate as so many dangerous defiles in which the winds from the heights of Hauran, the plateaux of Trachonitis, and the summit of Mount Hermon are caught and compressed in such a way that, rushing with tremendous force through a narrow space and then being suddenly released, they agitate the little Lake of Gennesaret in the most frightful fashion.' The voyager across the lake was always liable to encounter just such sudden storms as this.

Jesus was in the boat in the position in which any distinguished guest would be conveyed. We are told that, 'In these boats . . . the place for any distinguished stranger is on the little seat placed at the stern, where a carpet and cushion are arranged. The helmsman stands a little farther forward on the deck, though near the stern, in order to have a better look-out ahead.'

It is interesting to note that the words Jesus addressed to the wind and the waves are exactly the same as he addressed to the demon-possessed man in Mark 1:25. Just as an evil demon possessed that man, so the destructive power of the storm was, so people in Palestine believed in those days, the evil power of the demons at work in the realm of nature.

We do this story far less than justice if we merely take it in a literalistic sense. If it describes no more than a physical miracle in which an actual storm was stilled, it is very wonderful and it is something at which we must marvel, but it is something which happened once and cannot happen again. In that case it is quite external to us. But if we read it in a symbolic sense, it is far more valuable. When the disciples realized the presence of Jesus with them, the storm became a calm. Once they knew he was there, fearless peace entered their hearts. To voyage with Jesus was to voyage in peace even in a storm. Now that is universally true. It is not something which happened once; it is something which still happens and which can happen for us. In the presence of Jesus, we can have peace even in the wildest storms of life.

(1) He gives us peace in the storm of *sorrow*. When sorrow comes as come it must, he tells us of the glory of the life to come. He changes the darkness of death into the sunshine of

the thought of life eternal. He tells us of the love of God. There is an old story of a gardener who in his garden had a favourite flower which he loved much. One day he came to the garden to find that flower gone. He was vexed and angry and full of complaints. In the midst of his resentment he met the master of the garden and hurled his complaints at him. 'Hush!' said the master, 'I plucked it for myself.' In the storm of sorrow Jesus tells us that those we love have gone to be with God, and gives us the certainty that we shall meet again those whom we have loved and lost awhile.

(2) He gives us peace when life's *problems* involve us in a tempest of doubt and tension and uncertainty. There come times when we do not know what to do; when we stand at some crossroads in life and do not know which way to take. If then we turn to Jesus and say to him, 'Lord, what will you have me to do?' the way will be clear. The real tragedy is not that we do not know what to do; but that often we do not humbly submit to Jesus' guidance. To ask his will and to submit to it is the way to peace at such a time.

(3) He gives us peace in the storms of *anxiety*. The chief enemy of peace is worry, worry for ourselves, worry about the unknown future, worry about those we love. But Jesus speaks to us of a Father whose hand will never cause his child a needless tear and of a love beyond which neither we nor those we love can ever drift. In the storm of anxiety, he brings us the peace of the love of God.

THE BANISHING OF THE DEMONS

Mark 5:1–13

> They came to the other side of the lake, to the territory of the Gerasenes. Immediately Jesus had disembarked from the boat, there met him from the tombs a man in

the grip of an unclean spirit. This man lived among the tombs. No one had ever been able to bind him with a chain, because he had often been bound with fetters and chains, and the chains had been wrenched apart by him and the fetters shattered; and no one was strong enough to tame him. Continually, night and day, in the tombs and in the hills, he kept shrieking and gashing himself with stones. He saw Jesus when he was still a long way away, and he ran and knelt before him. 'What', he said, 'have you and I to do with each other, Jesus, you son of the most high God? In God's name, I adjure you, do not torture me!' For Jesus had been saying to him, 'Unclean spirit, come out of the man!' 'What is your name?' he asked him. 'Legion is my name,' he said, 'for we are many.' And he kept begging Jesus with many an entreaty not to send them out of the country. Now a great herd of swine was feeding on the mountainside. 'Send us into the swine,' they urged him, 'that we may go into them.' And Jesus permitted them to go into them. And the unclean spirits came out and entered into the swine and the herd – there were about 2,000 of them – rushed down the precipice into the lake, and were drowned in the lake.

HERE is a vivid and rather eerie story. It is the kind of story in which we have to do our best to read between the lines, because it is thinking and speaking in terms quite familiar to people in Palestine in the days of Jesus but quite alien to us.

If this is to be taken in close connection with what goes before – and that is Mark's intention – it must have happened late in the evening or even when the night had fallen. The story becomes all the more weird and frightening when it is seen as happening in the shadows of the night.

Verse 35 tells us that it was late in the evening when Jesus and his friends set sail. The Lake of Galilee is thirteen miles long at its longest, and eight miles wide at its widest. At this particular part it was about five miles across. They had made the journey and, on the way, they had encountered the storm, and now had reached land. It was a part of the lakeside where there were many caves in the limestone rock, and many of these caves were used as tombs in which bodies were laid. At the best of times it was an eerie place; as night fell it must have been grim indeed.

Out of the tombs there came a demon-possessed man. It was a fitting place for him to be, for demons, so they believed in those days, dwelt in woods and gardens and vineyards and dirty places, in lonely and desolate spots and among the tombs. It was in the night-time and before cock-crow that the demons were specially active. To sleep alone in an empty house at night was dangerous; to greet any person in the dark was perilous, for he might be a demon. To go out at night without a lantern or a torch was to court trouble. It was a perilous place and a perilous hour, and the man was a dangerous man.

How completely this man felt himself to be possessed is seen in his way of speaking. Sometimes he uses the singular, as if he himself was speaking; sometimes he uses the plural, as if all the demons in him were speaking. He was so convinced that the demons were in him that he felt they were speaking through him. When asked his name, he said his name was Legion. There were probably two reasons for that.

A legion was a Roman regiment of 6,000 troops. Very likely the man had seen one of these Roman regiments clanking along the road, and he felt that there was a whole battalion of demons inside him. In any event, the Jews believed that it was not possible to survive if you realized the number of demons with which you were surrounded. They were 'like the earth that is thrown up around a bed that is sown'. There were 10,000 at a person's right hand and 10,000 at the left hand. The queen of the female spirits had no fewer than 180,000 followers. There was a Jewish saying, 'A legion of hurtful spirits is on the watch for men, saying, "When shall he fall into the hands of one of these things and be taken?"' No doubt this wretched man knew all about this, and his poor, wandering mind was certain that a mass of those demons had taken up their residence in him.

Further, Palestine was an occupied country. The legions, at their wildest and most irresponsible, could sometimes be guilty of atrocities that would make the blood run cold. It may well be that this man had seen, perhaps even witnessed his loved ones suffer from, the murder and plundering that could sometimes follow the legions. It may well be that it was some such terrible experience which had driven him insane. The word *Legion* conjured up for him a vision of terror and death and destruction. He was convinced that demons like that were inside him.

We shall not even begin to understand this story unless we see how serious a case of demon-possession this man was. It is clear that Jesus made more than one attempt to heal him. Verse 8 tells us that Jesus had begun by using his usual method – an authoritative order to the demon to come out. On this occasion that was not successful. Next, he demanded what the demon's name was. It was always supposed in those days that, if a demon's name could be discovered, it gave a certain power over it. An ancient magical formula says, 'I adjure thee, every demonic spirit, say whatsoever thou art.' The belief was that if the name was known the demon's power was broken. In this case even that did not prove enough.

Jesus saw that there was only one way to cure this man – and that was to give him unanswerable demonstration that the demons had gone out of him, at least, unanswerable as far as his own mind was concerned. It does not matter whether we believe in demon-possession or not; the man believed in it. Even if it all lay in his disordered mind, the demons were terribly real to him. Dr Rendle Short, speaking about the supposed evil influence of the moon (Psalm 121:6) which emerges in the words *lunatic* and *moonstruck*, says, 'Modern science does not recognize any particular harm as coming from the moon. Yet it is a very widespread belief that the moon does affect people mentally . . . It is good to know that the Lord can deliver us from imaginary dangers as well as from real ones. Often the imaginary are harder to face.'

This man needed deliverance; whether that deliverance was from literal demon-possession or from an all-powerful delusion does not matter. This is where the herd of swine comes in. They were grazing on the hillside. The man felt that the demons were asking to be not totally destroyed but sent into the swine. All the time he was uttering the shrieks and going through the convulsions which were the sign of his malady. Suddenly, as his yells reached a new pitch of intensity, the whole herd took flight and plunged down a steep slope into the sea. *There* was the very proof that the man needed. This was almost the only thing on earth that could have convinced him that he was cured. Jesus, like a wise healer who understood so kindly and sympathetically the psychology of a diseased mind, used the event to help the man climb back to sanity, and his disordered mind was restored to peace.

There are some people who will blame Jesus because the healing of the man involved the death of the pigs. Surely it is a singularly blind way to look at things? How could the fate of the pigs possibly be compared with the fate of a man's immortal soul? We do not, presumably, have any objections to eating meat for dinner or refuse pork because it involved

the killing of some pig. Surely if we kill animals to avoid
going hungry, we can raise no objection if the saving of a
man's mind and soul involved the death of a herd of these
same animals? There is a cheap sentimentalism which will
languish in grief over the pain of an animal and never turn a
hair at the wretched state of millions of God's men and
women. This is not to say that we need not care what happens
to God's animal creation, for God loves every creature whom
his hands have made, but it is to say that we must preserve a
sense of proportion; and in God's scale of proportions, there
is nothing so important as a human soul.

BIDDING CHRIST BE GONE

Mark 5:14-17

> The men who were feeding the pigs fled, and brought
> news of what had happened to the town and to the farms.
> They came to see what it was that had happened. They
> came to Jesus, and they saw the demon-possessed man
> – the man who had had the legion of demons – sitting
> fully clothed and in his senses, and they were afraid;
> and those who had seen what had taken place told them
> what had happened to the demon-possessed man, and
> told them about the pigs; and they began to urge Jesus
> to get out of their territory.

VERY naturally the men who had been in charge of the pigs
went to the town and to the farms with news of this astounding
happening. When the curious people arrived on the spot they
found the man who had once been so mad sitting fully clothed
and in full possession of his faculties. The wild and naked
madman had become a sane and sensible citizen. And then
comes the surprise, the paradox, the thing that no one would

really expect. One would have thought that they would have regarded the whole matter with joy; but they regarded it with terror. And one would have thought that they would have urged Jesus to stay with them and exercise still further his amazing power; but they urged him to get out of their district as quickly as possible. Why? A man had been healed but their pigs had been destroyed, and therefore they wanted no more of this. The routine of life had been unsettled, and they wanted the disturbing element removed as quickly as possible.

A frequent cry of the human mind is, 'Please don't disturb me.' On the whole, the one thing people want is to be left alone.

(1) Instinctively people say, *Don't disturb my comfort.* If someone came to us and said, 'I can give you a world that will be better for the mass of people in general, but it will mean that your comfort will, at least for a time, be disturbed and upset, and you will have to do with less for the sake of others,' most of us would say, 'I would much rather that you would leave things as they are.' In point of fact that is almost precisely the situation which has developed over past decades. We are living through a time of redistribution, not only in this country but in the developing nations as well. We are living through a time when life is a great deal better than it ever was for a great many. But it has meant that life is not so comfortable as it was for some people; and for that very reason there is resentment because some of the comforts of life have gone.

There is a great deal of talk about what life *owes* us. Life owes us precisely nothing; the debt is all the other way round. It is we who owe life all that we have to give. We are followers of one who gave up the glory of heaven for the narrowness of earth, who gave up the joy of God for the pain of the cross. It is human not to want to have our comfort disturbed; it is divine to be willing to be disturbed that others may have more.

(2) Instinctively people say, '*Don't disturb my posses-sions.*' Here is another aspect of the same thing. None of us really willingly gives up anything we may possess. The older we get the more we want to clutch it to us. The author, George Borrow, who knew the gipsies, tells us that it is the fortune-telling gipsy's policy to promise to the young various pleasures, and to foretell to the old riches and only riches 'for they have sufficient knowledge of the human heart to be aware that avarice is the last passion that becomes extinct within'. We can soon see whether people really accept their faith and whether they really believe in their principles, by seeing if they are willing to become poorer for them.

(3) Instinctively people say, '*Don't disturb my religion.*'

(a) People say, 'Don't let unpleasant subjects disturb the pleasant decorum of my religion.' The poet and critic Edmund Gosse points out a curious omission in the sermons of the famous seventeenth-century cleric Jeremy Taylor. 'These sermons are amongst the most able and profound in the English language, but they hardly ever mention the poor, hardly ever refer to their sorrows, and show practically no interest in their state. The sermons were preached in South Wales where poverty abounded. The cry of the poor and the hungry, the ill-clothed and the needy ceaselessly ascended up to heaven, and called out for pity and redress, but this eloquent divine never seemed to hear it, he lived and wrote and preached surrounded by the suffering and the needy, and yet remained scarcely conscious of their existence.'

It is much less disturbing to preach about the niceties of theological beliefs and doctrines than it is to preach about human need and the abuses of life. We have actually known of congregations who informed ministers that it was a con-dition of their call that they would not preach on certain subjects. It was a notable thing that it was not what Jesus said about God that got him into trouble; it was what he said about *people* and about human need that disturbed the orthodox of his day.

(b) People have been known to say, 'Don't let personal relationships disturb my religion.' An amazing thing in this connection has been discovered from the life of Angela di Foligras, the famous Italian mystic. She had the gift of completely withdrawing herself from this world, and of returning from her trances with tales of ineffably sweet communion with God. It was she herself who said: 'In that time, and by God's will, there died my mother, who was a great hindrance unto me in following the way of God; my husband died likewise, and in a short time there died all my children. And because I had commenced to follow the aforesaid way, and had prayed God that he would rid me of them, I had great consolation of their deaths, albeit I did also feel some grief.' Her family was a trouble to her religion.

There is a type of religion which is fonder of committees than it is of housework, which is more set on quiet times than it is on human service. It prides itself on serving the Church and spending itself in devotion – but in God's eyes it has got things the wrong way round.

(c) People say, 'Don't disturb my beliefs.' There is a type of religion which says, 'If it has been good enough up to now, it is good enough for me.' There are people who do not want to know anything new, for they know that if they did they might have to go through the mental sweat of rethinking things and coming to new conclusions. There is a cowardice of thought and a lethargy of mind and a sleep of the soul which are terrible things.

The Gerasenes banished the disturbing Christ – and still there are people who seek to do the same.

A WITNESS FOR CHRIST

Mark 5:18–20

> As Jesus was getting into the boat, the man who had
> been demon-possessed kept begging him that he might
> be allowed to stay with him. He did not allow him, but
> said to him, 'Go back to your home and your own people,
> and tell them all that the Lord has done for you.' And he
> went away and began to proclaim the story throughout
> the Decapolis of all that Jesus had done for him.

THE interesting thing about this passage is that it tells us that
this incident happened in the Decapolis. Decapolis literally
means the Ten Cities. Near to the Jordan and on its east side,
there were ten cities mainly of rather a special character. They
were essentially Greek. Their names were Scythopolis, which
was the only one on the west side of the Jordan, Pella, Dion,
Gerasa, Philadelphia, Gadara, Raphana, Kanatha, Hippos and
Damascus. With the conquests of Alexander the Great, there
had been a Greek penetration into Palestine and Syria.

The Greek cities which had been then founded were in
rather a curious position. They were within Syria; but they
were very largely independent. They had their own councils
and their own coinage; they had the right of local administration, not only of themselves but of an area around them;
they had the right of association for mutual defence and for
commercial purposes. They remained in a kind of semi-
independence down until the time of the Maccabees, about
the middle of the second century BC. The Maccabees were
the Jewish conquerors and they subjected most of these cities
to Jewish rule.

They were liberated from Jewish rule by the Roman
emperor Pompey about 63 BC. They were still in a curious

position. They were to some extent independent, but were
liable to Roman taxation and Roman military service. They
were not garrisoned, but frequently were the headquarters
of Roman legions in the eastern campaigns. Now Rome
governed most of this part of the world by a system of
tributary kings. The result was that Rome could give these
cities very little actual protection; and so they banded
themselves together into a kind of corporation to defend
themselves against Jewish and Arab encroachment. They
were stubbornly Greek. They were beautiful cities; they
had their Greek gods and their Greek temples and their
Greek amphitheatres; they were devoted to the Greek way of
life.

Here, then, is a most interesting thing. If Jesus was in the
Decapolis, it is one of the first hints of things to come. There
would be Jews there, but it was fundamentally a Greek area.
Here is a foretaste of a world for Christ. Here is the first sign
of Christianity bursting the bonds of Judaism and going out
to all the world. Just how Greek these cities were and just
how important they were can be seen from the fact that from
Gadara alone there came Philodemus, the great Epicurean
philosopher, who was a contemporary of Cicero, Meleager,
the master of the Greek epigram, Menippus, the famous
satirist, and Theodorus, the rhetorician, who was no less a
person than the tutor of Tiberius, the reigning Roman emperor.
Something happened on that day that Jesus set foot in the
Decapolis.

There is now good reason to see why Jesus sent the man
back.

(1) He was to be a witness for Christianity. He was to be
a living, walking, vivid, unanswerable demonstration of
what Christ can do for us. Our glory must always be not in
what we can do for Christ but in what Christ can do for us.

The unanswerable proof of Christianity is a re-created human being.

(2) He was to be the first seed of what in time was to become a mighty harvest. The first contact with Greek civilization was made in the Decapolis. Everything must start somewhere; and the glory of all the Christianity which one day flowered in the Greek mind and genius began with a man who had been possessed by demons and whom Christ healed. Christ must always begin with someone. In our own circle and society, why should he not begin with us?

IN THE HOUR OF NEED

Mark 5:21-4

> When Jesus had crossed over in the boat back again to the other side, a great crowd gathered together to him; and he was by the lakeside. One of the rulers of the synagogue, Jairus by name, came to him; and, when he saw Jesus, he threw himself at his feet. He pled with him, 'My little daughter is lying at death's door. Come and lay your hands on her, that she may be cured and live.' Jesus went away with him; and the crowd were following him, and crushing in upon him on all sides.

THERE are all the elements of tragedy here. It is always tragic when a child is ill. The story tells us that the ruler's daughter was twelve years of age. According to the Jewish custom, a girl became a woman at twelve years and one day. This girl was just on the threshold of womanhood, and when death comes at such a time it is doubly tragic.

The story tells us something about this man who was the ruler of the synagogue. He must have been a person of some considerable importance. The ruler was the administrative head of the synagogue. He was the president of the board of elders responsible for the good management of the synagogue. He was responsible for the conduct of the services. He did not usually take part in them himself, but he was responsible for the allocation of duties and for seeing that they were carried out with all seemliness and good order. The ruler of the synagogue was one of the most important and most respected men in the community. But something happened to him when his daughter fell ill and he thought of Jesus.

(1) His *prejudices* were forgotten. There can be no doubt that he must have regarded Jesus as an outsider, as a dangerous heretic, as one to whom the synagogue doors were rightly closed, and one whom anyone who valued his orthodoxy would do well to avoid. But he was a big enough man to abandon his prejudices in his hour of need. Prejudice really means *a judging beforehand*. It is a judging before the evidence has been examined, or a verdict given because of refusal to examine it. Few things have done more to hold things up than this. Nearly every forward step has had to fight against initial prejudice. When Sir James Simpson discovered its use as an anaesthetic, especially in the case of childbirth, chloroform was held to be 'a decoy of Satan, apparently opening itself to bless women, but in the end hardening them, and robbing God of the deep, earnest cries, that should arise to him in time of trouble'. A prejudiced mind shuts out many a blessing.

(2) His *dignity* was forgotten. He, the ruler of the synagogue, came and threw himself at the feet of Jesus, the wandering teacher. He was not the first man who had to forget his dignity to save his life and to save his soul.

In the old story, that is precisely what Naaman had to do (2 Kings 5). He had come to Elisha to be cured of his leprosy.

Elisha's prescription was that he should go and wash in the Jordan seven times. That was no way to treat the Syrian prime minister! Elisha had not even delivered the message personally; he had sent it by a messenger! And, had they not far better rivers in Syria than the muddy little Jordan? These were Naaman's first thoughts; but he swallowed his pride and lost his leprosy.

There is a famous story of Diogenes, the Cynic philosopher. He was captured by pirates and was being sold as a slave. As he gazed at the bystanders who were bidding for him, he looked at a man. 'Sell me to that man,' he said. 'He needs a master.' The man bought him and handed over the management of his household and the education of his children to him. 'It was a good day for me', he used to say, 'when Diogenes entered my household.' True, but that required a certain loss of dignity.

It frequently happens that those who stand on their dignity fall from grace.

(3) His *pride* was forgotten. It must have taken a conscious effort of humiliation for this ruler of the synagogue to come and ask for help from Jesus of Nazareth. No one wishes to be indebted to anyone else; we would like to run our lives on our own. The very first step of the Christian life is to become aware that we cannot be anything other than indebted to God.

(4) Here we enter the realm of speculation, but it seems to me that we can say of this man that his *friends* were forgotten. It may well be that, to the end, they objected to him calling in Jesus. It is rather strange that he came himself and did not send a messenger. It seems unlikely that he would consent to leave his daughter when she was on the point of death. Maybe he came because no one else would go. His household were suspiciously quick to tell him not to trouble Jesus any more. It sounds almost as if they were glad not to call upon his

help. It may well be that this ruler defied public opinion and home advice in order to call in Jesus. It is often the case that we are wisest when our worldly-wise friends think we are acting like fools.

Here was a man who forgot everything except that he wanted the help of Jesus; and because of that forgetfulness he would remember forever that Jesus is a Saviour.

A SUFFERER'S LAST HOPE

Mark 5:25-9

> Now there was a woman who was suffering from a haemorrhage which had lasted for twelve years. She had gone through many things at the hands of many doctors; she had spent everything she had; and it had not helped her at all. Indeed she rather got worse and worse. When she heard the stories about Jesus, she came up behind him in the crowd, and she touched his robe, for she said, 'If I touch even his clothes I will be cured.' And immediately the fountain of her blood was staunched, and she knew in her body that she was healed from her scourge.

THE woman in this story suffered from a trouble which was very common and very hard to deal with. The Talmud itself gives no fewer than eleven cures for such a trouble. Some of them are tonics and astringents, but some of them are sheer superstitions like carrying the ashes of an ostrich egg in a linen rag in summer and a cotton rag in winter; or carrying a barley corn which had been found in the dung of a white she-ass. No doubt this poor woman had tried even these desperate remedies. The trouble was that not only did this affect a woman's health, it also rendered her continuously unclean and shut her off from the worship of God and the fellowship of her friends (Leviticus 15:25–7).

Mark here has a gentle gibe at the doctors. She had tried them all and had suffered much and had spent everything she had, and the result was that she was worse instead of better. Jewish literature is interesting on the subject of doctors. 'I went to physicians', says one person, 'to be healed, but the more they treated me with ointments, the more my vision was obscured by the white films, until I became completely blind' (Tobit 2:10). There is a passage in the *Mishnah*, which is the written summary of the traditional law, which is talking about the trades that a man may teach his son. 'Rabbi Judah says: "Ass-drivers are most of them wicked, camel-drivers are most of them proper folk, sailors are most of them saintly, the best among physicians is destined for Gehenna, and the most seemly among butchers is a partner of Amalek."' But, fortunately and justly, there are voices on the other side. One of the greatest of all tributes to doctors is in the Book of Ecclesiasticus (Sirach) (one of the apocryphal books written in the time between the Old and the New Testaments) in chapter 38:1–4, 7–8, 12–14:

> Honour physicians for their services,
>   for the Lord created them;
> for their gift of healing comes from the Most High,
>   and they are rewarded by the king.
> The skill of physicians makes them distinguished,
>   and in the presence of the great they are admired.
> The Lord created medicines out of the earth,
>   and the sensible will not despise them.
>
> By them the physician heals and takes away pain;
>   the pharmacist makes a mixture from them.
> God's works will never be finished;
>   and from him health spreads over all the earth.

Then give the physician his place, for the Lord created him;
  do not let him leave you, for you need him;
There may come a time when recovery lies in the hands of
    physicians,
    for they too pray to the Lord
  that he grant them success in diagnosis
    and in healing, for the sake of preserving life.

The physicians had had no success with the treatment of
this woman's case, and she had heard of Jesus. But she had
this problem – her trouble was an embarrassing thing; to go
in the crowd and to state it openly was something she could
not face, and so she decided to try to touch Jesus in secret.
Every devout Jew wore an outer robe with four tassels on it,
one at each corner. These tassels were worn in obedience to
the command in Numbers 15:38–40, and they were to signify
to others, and to remind the man himself, that the wearer was
a member of the chosen people of God. They were the badge
of a devout Jew. It was one of these tassels that the woman
slipped through the crowd and touched; and, having touched
it, she was thrilled to find herself cured.

Here was a woman who came to Jesus as a last resort;
having tried every other cure that the world had to offer, she
finally tried him. So many people have come to seek the help
of Jesus because they have reached their wits' end. They may
have battled with temptation until they could fight no longer
and stretched out a hand, crying, 'Lord, save me! I perish!'
They may have struggled on with some exhausting task until
reaching breaking point and then cried out for a strength
which was not their own. They may have laboured to attain
the goodness which haunted them, only to see it recede ever
further away, until they became utterly frustrated. No one
should need to be driven to Christ by the force of circumstances, and yet many come that way; and, even if it is thus

we come, he will never send us empty away. As that best-
loved of all hymns puts it:

> When other helpers fail and comforts flee,
> Help of the helpless, O abide with me.

THE COST OF HEALING

Mark 5:30-4

Jesus was well aware in himself that the power which
issued from him had gone out of him; and immediately,
in the middle of the crowd, he turned and said: 'Who
touched my clothes?' The disciples said to him: 'Look
at the crowd that are crushing you on every side – what's
the point of saying, "Who touched me?"' He kept
looking all round to see who had done this. The woman
was terrified and trembling. She knew well what had
happened to her. She came and threw herself down
before him, and told him the whole truth. 'Daughter!'
he said to her, 'Your faith has cured you! Go, and be in
good health, free from the trouble that was your
scourge.'

THIS passage tells us something about three people.

(1) It tells us something about Jesus. It tells us *the cost of
healing*. Every time Jesus healed anyone, it took something
out of him. Here is a universal rule of life. We will never
produce anything great unless we are prepared to put
something of ourselves, of our very life, of our very soul into
it. No pianist will ever give a really great performance if
she glides through a piece of music with faultless technique
and nothing more. The performance will not be great
unless at the end of it there is the exhaustion which comes
of the outpouring of self. No actor will ever give a great

performance who repeats his words with every inflection right and every gesture correct like a perfectly designed automaton. His tears must be real tears; his feelings must be real feelings; something of himself must go into the acting. No preacher who ever preached a real sermon descended from the pulpit without a feeling of being drained of something.

If we are ever to help one another, we must be ready to give of ourselves. It all comes from our attitude to others. Once Matthew Arnold, the great literary critic, said of the middle classes: 'Look at these people; the clothes they wear; the books they read; the texture of mind that composes their thoughts; would any amount of money compensate for being like one of these?' Now the *sense* of that saying may or may not be true; but the point is that it was *contempt* that gave it birth. He looked on those around him with a kind of shuddering loathing; and no one who looks on people like that can ever help them.

Think on the other hand of Moses, after the people had made the golden calf when he was on the mountain top. Remember how he begged God to blot him out of the book of remembrance if only the people might be forgiven (Exodus 32:30–2). Think of how the nineteenth-century poet, F. W. H. Myers, makes Paul speak when he looks upon the lost and pagan world:

> Then, with a thrill, the intolerable craving,
> > Shivers throughout me like a trumpet call –
> O to save these, to perish for their saving –
> > Die for their life, be offered for them all.

The greatness of Jesus was that he was prepared to pay the price of helping others, and that price was the outgoing of his very life. We follow in his steps only when we are prepared to spend, not our substance, but our souls and strength for others.

(2) It tells us something about the disciples. It shows us very vividly the limitations of what is called common sense. The disciples took the common-sense point of view. How could Jesus avoid being touched and jostled in a crowd like that? That was the sensible way to look at things. There emerges the strange and poignant fact that they had never realized that it cost Jesus anything at all to heal others.

One of the tragedies of life is the strange insensitiveness of the human mind. We so often utterly fail to realize what others are going through. Because we may have no experience of something, we never think what that something is costing someone else. Because something may be easy for us, we never realize what a costly effort it may be for someone else. That is why we so often hurt worst of all those we love. We may pray for common sense, but sometimes we would do well to pray for that sensitive, imaginative insight which can see into the hearts of others.

(3) It tells us something about the woman. It tells us of the relief of confession. It was all so difficult; it was all so humiliating. But once she had told the whole truth to Jesus, the terror and the trembling were gone and a wave of relief flooded her heart. And when she had made her pitiful confession she found him very kind.

> Let not conscience make you linger,
>   Nor of fitness fondly dream;
> All the fitness he requireth
>   Is to feel your need of him.

It is never hard to confess to one who understands like Jesus.

DESPAIR AND HOPE

Mark 5:35–9

> While he was still speaking, messages came from the
> household of the ruler of the synagogue. 'Your
> daughter', they said, 'has died. Why trouble the teacher
> any more?' Jesus overheard this message being given.
> He said to the ruler of the synagogue, 'Don't be afraid!
> Only keep on believing!' He allowed no one to accom-
> pany him except Peter and James and John, James'
> brother. They came to the house of the ruler of the
> synagogue. He saw the uproar. He saw the people
> weeping and wailing. He came in. 'Why', he said to
> them, 'are you so distressed? And what are you weeping
> for? The little girl has not died – she is sleeping.' They
> laughed him to scorn.

JEWISH mourning customs were vivid and detailed, and
practically all of them were designed to stress the desolation
and the final separation of death. The triumphant victorious
hope of the Christian faith was totally absent.

Immediately death had taken place, a loud wailing was set
up so that all might know that death had struck. The wailing
was repeated at the graveside. The mourners hung over the
dead body, begging for a response from the silent lips. They
beat their breasts; they tore their hair; and they rent their
garments.

The rending of garments was done according to certain
rules and regulations. It was done just before the body was
finally hidden from sight. Garments were to be rent to the
heart, that is, until the skin was exposed, but were not to be
rent beyond the navel. For fathers and mothers the rent was
on the left side, over the heart; for others it was on the right
side. A woman was to rend her garments in private; she was

then to reverse the inner garment, so that it was worn back to front; she then rent her outer garment, so that her body was not exposed. The rent garment was worn for thirty days. After seven days the rent might be roughly sewn up, in such a way that it was still clearly visible. After the thirty days the garment was properly repaired.

Flute-players were essential. Throughout most of the ancient world, in Rome, in Greece, in Phoenicia, in Assyria and in Palestine, the wailing of the flute was inseparably connected with death and tragedy. It was laid down that, however poor a man was, he must have at least two flute-players at his wife's funeral. W. Taylor Smith in Hastings' *Dictionary of Christ and the Gospels* quotes two interesting instances of the use of flute-players, which show how widespread the custom was. There were flute-players at the funeral of Claudius, the Roman emperor. When in AD 67 news reached Jerusalem of the fall of Jotapata to the Roman armies, Josephus tells us that 'most people engaged flute-players to lead their lamentations'.

The wail of the flutes, the screams of the mourners, the passionate appeals to the dead, the rent garments and the torn hair must have made a Jewish house a poignant and emotional place on the day of mourning.

When death came, a mourner was forbidden to work, to anoint himself or to wear shoes. Even the poorest man must cease from work for three days. He must not travel with goods; and the prohibition of work extended even to his servants. He must sit with head bound up. He must not shave or 'do anything for his comfort'. He must not read the law or the prophets, for to read these books is joy. He was allowed to read Job, Jeremiah and Lamentations. He must eat only in his own house, and he must abstain altogether from meat and wine. He must not leave the town or village for thirty days. It was the custom not to eat at a table, but to eat sitting on the floor, using a chair as a table. It was the custom, which still survives, to eat eggs dipped in ashes and salt.

There was one curious custom. All water from the house, and from the three houses on each side, was emptied out, because it was said that the Angel of Death procured death with a sword dipped in water taken from close at hand. There was one peculiarly moving custom. In the case of a young life cut off too soon, if the young person had never been married, a form of marriage service was part of the burial rites. For the time of mourning, the mourner was exempt from the keeping of the law, because he was supposed to be beside himself, mad with grief.

The mourner must go the synagogue; and when he entered the people faced him and said, 'Blessed is he that comforteth the mourner.' The Jewish prayer book has a special prayer to be used before a meal in the house of the mourner:

> Blessed art thou, O God, our Lord, King of the Universe, God of our fathers, our Creator, our Redeemer, our Sanctifier, the Holy One of Jacob, the King of Life, who art good and doest good; the God of truth, the righteous Judge who judgest in righteousness, who takest the soul in judgment, and rulest alone in the universe, who doest in it according to his will and all his ways are in judgment, and we are his people, and his servants, and in everything we are bound to praise him and to bless him, who shields all the calamities of Israel, and will shield us in this calamity, and from this mourning will bring us to life and peace. Comfort, O God, our Lord, all the mourners of Jerusalem that mourn in our sorrow. Comfort them in their mourning, and make them rejoice in their agony as a man is comforted by his mother. Blessed art thou, O God, the Comforter of Zion, thou that buildest again Jerusalem.

That prayer is later than New Testament times, but it is against the background of the earlier, unrestrained expressions of grief that we must read this story of the girl who had died.

THE DIFFERENCE FAITH MAKES

Mark 5:40-3

> But he put them all out, and he took with him the father of the little girl, and the mother and his own friends, and went into the room where the little girl was. He took the little girl by the hand, and he said to her, 'Maid! I say to you, arise!' Immediately the maid arose and walked around, for she was about twelve years of age. And immediately they were amazed with a great astonishment. He gave them strong injunctions that no one should know about this. And he ordered that something to eat should be given to her.

THERE is a very lovely thing here. In the gospel itself, 'Maid! Arise' is '*Talitha cumi*', which is Aramaic. How did this little bit of Aramaic get itself embedded in the Greek of the gospels? There can be only one reason. Mark got his information from Peter. For the most part, outside of Palestine at least, Peter, too, would have to speak in Greek. But Peter had been there; he was one of the chosen three, the inner circle, who had seen this happen. And he could never forget Jesus' voice. In his mind and memory he could hear that '*Talitha cumi*' all his life. The love, the gentleness, the caress of it lingered with him forever, so much so that he was unable to think of it in Greek at all, because his memory could hear it only in the voice of Jesus and in the very words that Jesus spoke.

This passage is a story of contrasts.

(1) There is the contrast between *the despair* of the mourners and *the hope* of Jesus. 'Don't bother the Teacher,' they said. 'There's nothing anyone can do now.' 'Don't be afraid,' said Jesus, 'only believe.' In the one place it is the voice of despair that speaks, in the other the voice of hope.

(2) There is the contrast between *the unrestrained distress* of the mourners and *the calm serenity* of Jesus. They were wailing and weeping and tearing their hair and rending their garments in a paroxysm of distress; he was calm and quiet and serene and in control.

Why this difference? It was due to Jesus' perfect confidence and trust in God. The worst human disaster can be met with courage and gallantry when we meet it with God. They laughed him to scorn because they thought his hope was groundless and his calm mistaken. But the great fact of the Christian life is that what looks completely impossible to us is possible with God. What on merely human grounds is far too good to be true becomes blessedly true when God is there. They laughed him to scorn, but their laughter must have turned to amazed wonder when they realized what God can do. There is nothing beyond facing, and there is nothing beyond conquest – not even death – when it is faced and conquered in the love of God which is in Christ Jesus our Lord.

WITHOUT HONOUR IN HIS OWN COUNTRY

Mark 6:1–6

> Jesus left there and came into his own native place, and his disciples went with him. When the Sabbath came he began to teach in the synagogue. Many, as they listened, were amazed. 'Where', they said, 'did this man get this knowledge? What wisdom is this that has been

given to him? And how can such wonderful things keep
happening through his hands? Is not this the carpenter,
Mary's son, the brother of James and Joses and Judah
and Simon? Are his sisters not here with us?' And they
took offence at him. So Jesus said to them, 'A prophet
is not without honour except in his own native place,
and among his own kinsmen and in his own family.'
And he was not able to do any wonderful deeds there,
except that he laid his hands on a few sick people and
healed them. And he was amazed by their unwillingness
to believe. He made a tour of the villages teaching.

WHEN Jesus came to Nazareth, he put himself to a very severe
test. He was coming to his home town; and there are no
severer critics than those who have known us since childhood.
It was never meant to be a private visit simply to see his old
home and his own people. He came attended by his disciples.
That is to say he came as a Rabbi. The Rabbis moved about
the country accompanied by their little circle of disciples,
and it was as a teacher, with his disciples, that Jesus came.

He went into the synagogue and he taught. His teaching
was greeted not with wonder but with a kind of contempt.
'They took offence at him.' They were scandalized that a
man who came from a background like Jesus should say and
do things such as he did. Familiarity had bred a mistaken
contempt.

They refused to listen to what he had to say for two reasons.

(1) They said, 'Is not this the carpenter?' The word used
for *carpenter* is *tektōn*. Now *tektōn* does mean a worker in
wood, but it means more than merely a joiner. It means a
craftsman. In Homer, the *tektōn* is said to build ships and
houses and temples. In the past, there could be found in little
towns and villages a craftsman who would build you anything
from a chicken-coop to a house; the kind of man who could

build a wall, mend a roof, repair a gate; the craftsman, the handyman, who with few or no instruments and with the simplest tools could turn his hand to any job. That is what Jesus was like. But the point is that the people of Nazareth despised Jesus *because he was a working man*. He was a man of the people, a layman, an ordinary man – and therefore they despised him.

One of the leaders of the British Labour movement was that great soul Will Crooks. He was born into a home where one of his earliest recollections was seeing his mother crying because she had no idea where the next meal was to come from. He started work in a blacksmith's shop at five shillings a week. He became a fine craftsman and one of the bravest and straightest men who ever lived. He entered municipal politics and became the first Labour Mayor of any London borough. There were people who were offended when Will Crooks became Mayor of Poplar. In a crowd one day a lady said with great disgust, 'They've made that common fellow, Crooks, Mayor, and he's no better than a working man.' A man in the crowd – Will Crooks himself – turned round and raised his hat. 'Quite right, madam,' he said. 'I am not better than a working man.'

The people of Nazareth despised Jesus because he was a working man. To us that is his glory, because it means that God, when he came to earth, claimed no exemptions. He took upon himself the common life with all its common tasks.

The accidents of birth and fortune and pedigree have nothing to do with our true worth. As Alexander Pope had it:

> Worth makes the man, and want of it the fellow;
> The rest is all but leather or prunello.

As Robert Burns had it:

A prince can mak' a belted knight,
   A marquis, duke, an' a' that!
But an honest man's aboon his might –
   Guid faith, he mauna fa' that!
For a' that, an' a' that,
Their dignities an' a' that,
The pith o' sense an' pride o' worth
Are higher rank than a' that.

We must always beware of the temptation to evaluate one another by externals and incidentals, and not by native worth.

(2) They said, 'Is not this Mary's son? Do we not know his brothers and his sisters?' The fact that they called Jesus *Mary's son* tells us that Joseph must have been dead. Therein we have the key to one of the enigmas of Jesus' life. Jesus was only thirty-three when he died; and yet he did not leave Nazareth until he was thirty (Luke 3:23). Why this long delay? Why this lingering in Nazareth while a world waited to be saved? The most likely reason was that Joseph died young and Jesus took upon himself the support of his mother and of his brothers and sisters; and only when they were old enough to fend for themselves did he go forth. He was faithful in this small matter, and therefore in the end God gave him much to do.

But the people of Nazareth despised him because they knew his family. Thomas Campbell was a very considerable poet. His father had no sense of poetry at all. When Thomas' first book emerged with his name on it, he sent a copy to his father. The old man took it up and looked at it. It was really the binding and not the contents at all that he was looking at. 'Who would have thought', he said in wonder, 'that our Tom could have made a book like that?' Sometimes when familiarity should breed a growing respect it breeds an increasing and easy-going familiarity. Sometimes we are too near people to see their greatness.

The result of all this was that Jesus could do no mighty works in Nazareth. The atmosphere was wrong, and there are some things that cannot be done unless the atmosphere is right.

(1) It is still true that people cannot be healed if they refuse to be healed. Margot Asquith tells of the death of Neville Chamberlain. It is well known that his policy turned out in such a way that it broke his heart. Margot Asquith met his doctor, Lord Horder. 'You can't be much of a doctor,' she said, 'as Neville Chamberlain was only a few years older than Winston Churchill, and I should have said he was a strong man. Were you fond of him?' Lord Horder replied, 'I was very fond of him. I like all unlovable men. I have seen too many of the other kind. Chamberlain suffered from shyness. He did not want to live; and when a man says that, *no doctor can save him.*' We may call it faith; we may call it the will to live; but without it none of us can survive.

(2) There can be no preaching in the wrong atmosphere. Our churches would be different places if congregations would only remember that they preach far more than half the sermon. In an atmosphere of expectancy, the poorest effort can catch fire. In an atmosphere of critical coldness or bland indifference, the most Spirit-packed utterance can fall lifeless to the earth.

(3) There can be no peace-making in the wrong atmosphere. If those gathered together have come together to hate, they will hate. If they have come together to refuse to understand, they will misunderstand. If they have come together to see no other point of view but their own, they will see no other. But if they have come together, loving Christ

and seeking to love each other, even those who are most widely separated can come together in him.

There is laid on us the tremendous responsibility that we can either help or hinder the work of Jesus Christ. We can open the door wide to him – or we can slam it in his face.

HERALDS OF THE KING

Mark 6:7-11

Jesus called the Twelve to him and he began to send them out in twos. He gave them power over unclean spirits. He ordered them to take nothing for the road except a staff. He ordered them not to take bread, or a wallet, or a copper coin in their belts. He ordered them to wear sandals and, he said, 'You must not put on two tunics.' He said to them, 'Wherever you enter into a house, stay there, until you leave that place, and, if any place refuses to give you hospitality, and, if in any place they will not listen to you, when you leave there, shake off the dust from the soles of your feet, to bear witness to the fact that they were guilty of such conduct.'

WE will understand all the references in this passage better if we have in our minds a picture of what a Jew in Palestine in the time of Jesus ordinarily wore. There were five articles of dress.

(1) The innermost garment was the *chitōn*, or *sindōn*, or *tunic*. It was very simple. It was simply a long piece of cloth folded over and sewn down one side. It was long enough to reach almost to the feet. Holes were cut in the top corners for the arms. Such garments were commonly sold without any hole for the head to go through. That was to prove that the garment was in fact new, and it was to allow the buyer to

arrange the neckline as he or she wished. For instance, the
neckline was different for men and women. It had to be lower
in the case of women so that a mother could suckle her baby.
At its simplest, this inner garment was little more than a sack
with holes cut in the corners. In a more developed form it
had long close-fitting sleeves; and sometimes it was opened
up so that it was made to button down the front like a cassock.

(2) The outer garment was called the *himation*. It was used
as a cloak by day and as a blanket by night. It was composed
of a piece of cloth seven feet from left to right and four and a
half feet from top to bottom. One and a half feet at each side
was folded in, and in the top corner of the folded part holes
were cut for the arms to go through. It was therefore almost
square. Usually it was made of two strips of cloth, each seven
feet by a little more than two feet, sewn together. The seam
came down the back. But a specially carefully made *himation*
might be woven of one piece, as Jesus' robe was (John 19:23).
This was the main article of dress.

(3) There was the *girdle*. It was worn over the two garments
we have already described. The skirts of the tunic could be
hitched up under the girdle for work or for running. Sometimes
the tunic was hitched above the girdle, and in the hollow place
so made above the girdle a parcel or a package could be
carried. The girdle was often double for the eighteen inches
from each end. The double part formed a pocket in which
money was carried.

(4) There was the *head-dress*. It was a piece of cotton or
linen about a yard square. It could be white, or blue, or black.
Sometimes it was made of coloured silk. It was folded diagon-
ally and then placed on the head so that it protected the back
of the neck, the cheekbones and the eyes from the heat and
glare of the sun. It was held in place by a circlet of easily
stretched, semi-elastic wool round the head.

(5) There were the *sandals*. They were merely flat soles of leather, wood or matted grass. The soles had thongs at the edges through which a strap passed to hold the sandal on to the foot.

The wallet may be one of two things.

(a) It may be the ordinary traveller's bag. This was made of a goat's skin. Often the animal was skinned whole and the skin retained the original shape of the animal, legs, tail, head and all! It had a strap at each side and was slung over the shoulder. In it the shepherd, or pilgrim, or traveller carried bread and raisins, and olives, and cheese enough to last him for a day or two.

(b) There is a very interesting suggestion. The Greek word is *pēra*; and it can mean a *collecting bag*. Very often the priests and devotees went out with these bags to collect contributions for their temple and their god. They have been described as 'pious robbers with their booty growing from village to village'. There is an inscription in which a man who calls himself a slave of the Syrian goddess says that he brought in seventy bags full each journey for his lady.

If the first meaning is taken, Jesus meant that his disciples must take no supplies for the road, but must trust God for everything. If the second meaning is taken, it means that they must not be like the grasping priests. They must go about giving and not getting.

There are two other interesting things here.

(1) It was the Rabbinic law that when a man entered the Temple courts he must put off his staff and shoes and money girdle. All ordinary things were to be set aside on entering the sacred place. It may well be that Jesus was thinking of this, and that he meant his disciples to see that the humble homes they were to enter were every bit as sacred as the Temple courts.

(2) Hospitality was a sacred duty in the middle east. When a stranger entered a village, it was not his duty to search for hospitality; it was the duty of the village to offer it. Jesus told his disciples that if hospitality was refused, and if doors and ears were shut, they must shake off the dust of that place from their feet when they left. The Rabbinic law said that the dust of a Gentile country was defiled, and that when a man entered Palestine from another country he must shake off every particle of dust of the unclean land. It was a pictorial formal denial that a Jew could have any fellowship even with the dust of a heathen land. It is as if Jesus said, 'If they refuse to listen to you, the only thing you can do is to treat them as a strict Jew would treat a Gentile house. There can be no fellowship between them and you.'

So we can see that the mark of the Christian disciple was to be utter simplicity, complete trust and the generosity which is out always to give and never to demand.

THE MESSAGE AND THE MERCY OF THE KING

Mark 6:12–13

> So they went out and heralded forth the summons to repentance; and they cast out many demons, and anointed many sick people with oil and healed them.

HERE in brief summary is an account of the work that the Twelve did when Jesus sent them out.

(1) To the people they brought Jesus' message. The word used is literally that used for *a herald's proclamation*. When the apostles went out to preach, they did not *create* a message; they *brought* a message. They did not tell people what they believed and what they considered probable; they told people what Jesus had told them. It was not their opinions they

brought to people; it was God's truth. The message of the prophets always began, 'Thus says the Lord.' Those who would bring an effective message to others must first receive it from God.

(2) To the people they brought *the King's message*; and the King's message was, 'Repent!' Clearly that was a disturbing message. To repent means to change one's mind and then to fit one's actions to this change. Repentance means a change of heart and a change of action. It is bound to *hurt*, for it involves the bitter realization that the way we were following is wrong. It is bound to *disturb*, because it means a complete reversal of life.

That is precisely why so few people do repent – for the last thing most people desire is to be disturbed. Lady Asquith, wife of the Liberal statesman, in a vivid phrase, speaks of people who 'dawdle towards death'. So many people do that. They resent all strenuous activity. Life for them is 'a land where it is always afternoon'. In some ways the positive, vivid, daring sinners who are crashing their way to some self-chosen goal are more attractive than negative, vague loiterers who drift spinelessly and without direction through life.

There is a passage in the novel *Quo Vadis?* Vinicius, the young Roman, has fallen in love with a girl who is a Christian. Because he is not a Christian she will have nothing to do with him. He follows her to the secret night gathering of the little group of Christians, and there, unknown to anyone, he listens to the service. He hears Peter preach, and, as he listens, something happens to him. 'He felt that if he wished to follow that teaching, he would have to place on a burning pile all his thoughts, habits and character, his whole nature up to that moment, burn them into ashes and then fill himself with a life altogether different, and an entirely new soul.'

That *is* repentance. But what if someone simply wants to be left alone? The change is not necessarily from robbery, theft, murder, adultery and glaring sins. The change may be from a life that is completely selfish, instinctively demanding, totally inconsiderate, the change from a self-centred to a God-centred life – and a change like that hurts. Professor W. M. Macgregor of Trinity College, Glasgow, quotes a saying of the Bishop in *Les Misérables*. 'I always bothered some of them; for through me the outside air came at them; my presence in their company made them feel as if a door had been left open and they were in a draught.' Repentance is no sentimental feeling sorry; repentance is a revolutionary thing – that is why so few repent.

(3) To the people they brought *the King's mercy*. Not only did they bring this shattering demand upon people's lives; they brought also help and healing. They brought liberation to poor, demon-possessed men and women. From the beginning, Christianity has aimed to bring health to body and to soul; it has always aimed not only at soul salvation, but at whole salvation. It brought not only a hand to lift from moral wreckage, but a hand to lift from physical pain and suffering. It is most suggestive that they anointed with oil. In the ancient world, oil was regarded as a panacea. Galen, the great Greek doctor, said, 'Oil is the best of all instruments for healing diseased bodies.' In the hands of the servants of Christ, the old cures acquired a new quality. The strange thing is that they used the things which their limited knowledge knew at that time; but the spirit of Christ gave the healer a new power and the old cure a new quality. The power of God became available in common things to the faith of men and women.

So the Twelve brought to people the message and the mercy of the King, and that remains the Church's task today and every day.

THREE VERDICTS ON JESUS

Mark 6:14-15

> King Herod heard about Jesus, for his name was known
> everywhere. He said, 'John the Baptizer has risen from
> the dead. That is why these wonderful powers work
> through him.' Others said, 'It is Elijah.' Others said,
> 'He is a prophet, like one of the famous prophets.'

BY this time, news of Jesus had penetrated all over the
country. The tale had reached the ears of Herod. The reason
why he had not up to this time heard of Jesus may well be
due to the fact that his official residence in Galilee was in
Tiberias. Tiberias was largely a Gentile city, and, as far as we
know, Jesus never set foot in it. But the mission of the Twelve
had taken Jesus' fame all over Galilee, so that his name was
upon everyone's lips. In this passage, we have three verdicts
upon Jesus.

(1) There is the verdict of a guilty conscience. Herod had
been guilty of allowing the execution of John the Baptizer,
and now he was haunted by what he had done. Whenever
people commit evil acts, the whole world becomes their
enemy. Inwardly, they cannot command their thoughts; and,
whenever they allow themselves to think, their thoughts return
to the wicked things that they have done. We cannot avoid
living with ourselves; and when we are filled with self-
accusations, life becomes intolerable. Outwardly, we live in
the fear that we will be found out and that some day the
consequences of our evil deeds will catch up with us.

Some time ago, a convict escaped from a Glasgow prison.
After forty-eight hours of liberty he was recaptured, cold and
hungry and exhausted. He said that it was not worth it. 'I
didn't have a minute,' he said. 'Hunted, hunted all the time.

You don't have a chance. You can't stop to eat. You can't stop to sleep.'

Hunted – that is the word which so well describes the lives of those who have done some evil thing. When Herod heard of Jesus, the first thing that flashed into his mind was that this was John the Baptizer whom he had killed, come back to reckon with him. Because the sinning life is the haunted life, sin is never worth the cost.

(2) There is the verdict of the nationalist. Some thought that this Jesus was Elijah come again. The Jews waited for the Messiah. There were many ideas about the Messiah, but the commonest of all was that he would be a conquering king who would first give the Jews back their liberty and who would then lead them on a triumphant campaign throughout the world. It was an essential part of that belief that, before the coming of the Messiah, Elijah, the greatest of the prophets, would come again to be his herald and his forerunner. Even to this day, when Jews celebrate the Passover Feast, they leave at the table an empty chair called Elijah's chair. They place it there with a glass of wine before it, and at one part of their celebration they go to the door and fling it wide open, that Elijah may come in and bring at last the long-awaited news that the Messiah has come.

This is the verdict of those who desire to find in Jesus the realization of *their own ambitions*. They think of Jesus not as someone to whom they must submit and whom they must obey; they think of Jesus as someone they can use. Such people think more of their own ambitions than of the will of God.

(3) There is the verdict of those who are waiting for the voice of God. There were those who saw in Jesus a prophet. In those days, the Jews were only too well aware that for 300 years the voice of prophecy had been silent. They had listened

to the arguments and the legal disputations of the Rabbis; they had listened to the moral lectures of the synagogue; but it was three long centuries since they had listened to a voice which proclaimed, 'Thus says the Lord.' People in those days were listening for the authentic voice of God – and in Jesus they heard it. It is true that Jesus was more than a prophet. He did not bring only the voice of God. He brought the very power and the very life and the very being of God. But those who saw in Jesus a prophet were at least more right than the conscience-stricken Herod and the expectant nationalists. If they had got that far in their thoughts of Jesus, it was not impossible that they might take the further step and see in him the Son of God.

AN EVIL WOMAN'S REVENGE

Mark 6:16–29

But when Herod heard about it, he said, 'This is John, whom I beheaded, risen from the dead.' For Herod had sent and seized John and had bound him in prison because of the affair of Herodias, his brother Philip's wife – because he had married her. For John had said to Herod, 'It is not right for you to have your brother's wife.' Herodias set herself against him, and wished to kill him, and she could not succeed in doing so, for Herod was afraid of John, because he well knew that he was a just and holy man, and he kept him safe. When Herod listened to John he did not know what to do, and yet he found a certain pleasure in listening to him. But a day of opportunity came, when, on his birthday, Herod was giving a banquet to his courtiers and to his captains and to the leading men of Galilee. Herodias' daughter herself came in and danced before them, and she pleased

Herod and those who were reclining at table with him. The king said to the maiden, 'Ask me for anything you like and I will give it to you.' He swore to her, 'Whatever you ask me for, I will give you, even up to half of my kingdom.' She went out and said to her mother, 'What am I to ask for myself?' She said, 'John the Baptizer's head.' At once she hurried into the king and made her request. 'I wish', she said, 'that here and now you will give me the head of John the Baptizer on a plate.' The king was grief-stricken, but, because of the oath he had taken, and because he had taken it in front of his guests, he did not wish to break his word to her. So immediately the king despatched an executioner with orders to bring his head. The executioner went away and beheaded him in prison, and brought his head on a plate, and gave it to the maiden, and the maiden gave it to her mother. When his disciples heard about it, they came and took away his body and laid it in a tomb.

THIS story has all the simplicity of tremendous drama.

First, let us look at *the scene*. The scene was the fortress of Machaerus. Machaerus stood on a lonely ridge, surrounded by terrible ravines, overlooking the east side of the Dead Sea. It was one of the loneliest and grimmest and most unassailable fortresses in the world. To this day the dungeons are there, and the traveller can still see the staples and the iron hooks in the wall to which John must have been bound. It was in that bleak and desolate fortress that the last act of John's life was played out.

Second, let us look at *the characters*. The marriage tangles of the Herod family are quite incredible, and their interrelations are so complicated that they become almost impossible to work out. When Jesus was born, Herod the Great was king. He was the king who was responsible for the massacre of the children in Bethlehem (Matthew 2:16–18). Herod the

Great was married many times. Towards the end of his life he became almost insanely suspicious, and murdered member after member of his own family, until it became a Jewish saying, 'It is safer to be Herod's pig than Herod's son.'

First, he married Doris, by whom he had a son, Antipater, whom he murdered. Then he married Mariamne, the Hasmonean, by whom he had two sons, Alexander and Aristobulus, whom he also murdered. Herodias, the villainess of the present passage, was the daughter of this Aristobulus. Herod the Great then married another Mariamne, called the Boethusian. By her he had a son called Herod Philip. Herod Philip married Herodias, who was the daughter of his half-brother, Aristobulus, and who was therefore his own niece. By Herodias, Herod Philip had a daughter called Salome, who is the girl who danced before Herod of Galilee in our passage. Herod the Great then married Malthake, by whom he had two sons – Archelaus and Herod Antipas, who is the Herod of our passage and the ruler of Galilee. The Herod Philip who married Herodias originally, and who was the father of Salome, inherited none of Herod the Great's dominions. He lived as a wealthy private citizen in Rome. Herod Antipas visited him in Rome. There he seduced Herodias and persuaded her to leave her husband and marry him.

Note who Herodias was: (a) she was the daughter of his half-brother, Aristobulus, and therefore his niece; and (b) she was the wife of his half-brother Herod Philip, and therefore his sister-in-law. Previously Herod Antipas had been married to a daughter of the king of the Nabataeans, an Arabian country. She escaped to her father, who invaded Herod's territory to avenge his daughter's honour and heavily defeated Herod. To complete this astounding picture – Herod the Great finally married Cleopatra of Jerusalem, by whom he had a son called Philip the Tetrarch. This Philip married Salome who was at one and the same time (a) the daughter of Herod Philip, his half-brother, and (b) the daughter of Herodias, who herself was the daughter of Aristobulus, another of his half-brothers. Salome was therefore at one and the same time his niece and his great-niece. If we put this in the form of a table it will be easier to follow – see opposite page.

Seldom in history can there have been such a series of matrimonial entanglements as existed in the Herod family. By marrying Herodias, his brother's wife, Herod had broken the Jewish law (Leviticus 18:16, 20:21) and had outraged the laws of decency and of morality.

Because of this adulterous marriage and because of Herod's deliberate seduction of his brother's wife, John had publicly rebuked him. It took courage to rebuke in public a despot who had the power of life and death, and John's courage in rebuking evil wherever he saw it is commemorated in the Prayer Book collect for St John the Baptist's Day.

> Almighty God, by whose providence thy servant, John
> the Baptist, was wonderfully born, and sent to prepare
> the way of thy Son our Saviour, by preaching of repent-
> ance; make us so to follow his doctrine and holy life,
> that we may truly repent according to his preaching;
> and after his example constantly speak the truth, boldly
> rebuke vice, and patiently suffer for the truth's sake.

In spite of John's rebuke Herod still feared and respected him, for John was so obviously a man of sincerity and of goodness; but with Herodias it was different. She was implacably hostile to John and determined to eliminate him. She got her chance at Herod's birthday feast, which he was celebrating with his courtiers and his captains. Into that feast

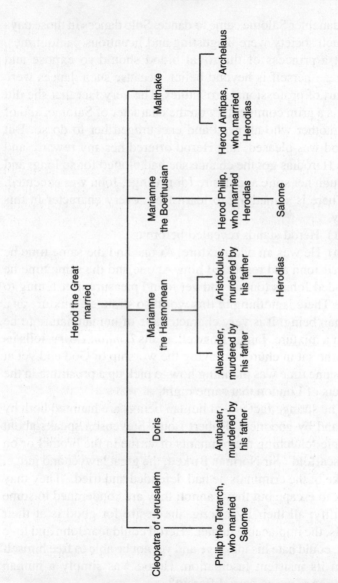

her daughter Salome came to dance. Solo dances in those days in such society were disgusting and licentious pantomimes. That a princess of the royal blood should so expose and demean herself is beyond belief, because such dances were the art of professional prostitutes. The very fact that she did this is a grim commentary on the character of Salome, and of the mother who allowed and encouraged her to do so. But Herod was pleased; and Herod offered her any reward; and thus Herodias got the chance she had plotted for so long; and through her spite and desire for revenge, John was executed.

There is something to learn from every character in this story.

(1) Herod stands revealed before us.

(a) He was an odd mixture. At one and the same time he feared John and respected him. At one and the same time he dreaded John's tongue and yet found pleasure in listening to him. There is nothing in this world so strange a mixture as a human being. It is very characteristic of human nature to be such a mixture. James Boswell, in his *London Diary*, tells us how he sat in church enjoying the worship of God and yet at the same time was planning how to pick up a prostitute in the streets of London that same night.

The strange fact is that human beings are haunted both by sin and by goodness. Robert Louis Stevenson speaks about people 'clutching the remnants of virtue in the brothel or on the scaffold'. Sir Norman Birkett, the great lawyer and judge, spoke of the criminals he had defended and tried. 'They may seek to escape but they cannot; they are condemned to some nobility; all their lives long, the desire for good is at their heels, the implacable hunter.' Herod could fear John and love him, could hate his message and yet not be able to free himself from its insistent fascination. Herod was simply a human being. Are we so very different?

(b) Herod was a man who acted on impulse. He made his reckless promise to Salome without thinking. It may well be that he made it when he was more than a little drunk and bloated with wine. Let us take care. Let us think before we speak. Let us never by self-indulgence get into a state when we lose our powers of judgment and are liable to do things for which afterwards we will be very sorry.

(c) Herod feared what others might say. He kept his promise to Salome because he had made it in front of his cronies and was unwilling to break it. He feared their jeers, their laughter; he feared that they would think him weak. Many have done things they afterwards bitterly regretted because they had not the moral courage to do the right. Many have made themselves far worse than they might otherwise have been because they feared the laughter of their so-called friends.

(2) Salome and Herodias stand revealed before us. There is a certain greatness about Herodias. Years after this, her Herod sought the title of King. He went to Rome to plead for it; instead of giving him the title, the emperor banished him to Gaul for having the insolence and the insubordination to ask for such a title. Herodias was told that she need not share this exile, that she might go free, and she proudly answered that where her husband went she went too.

Herodias shows us what an embittered person can do. The Jewish Rabbis had a saying. They said that a *good woman* might marry a *bad man*, for by so doing she would end by making him as good as herself. But they said that a *good man* might never marry a *bad woman*, for she would inevitably drag him down to her own level. The trouble with Herodias was that she wished to eliminate the one man who had the courage to confront her with her sin. She wished to do as she liked with no one to remind her of the moral law.

She murdered John that she might sin in peace. She forgot that while she need no longer meet John, she still had to meet God.

(3) John the Baptizer stands revealed before us. He stands as the man of courage. He was a child of the desert and of the wide-open spaces, and to imprison him in the dark dungeons of Machaerus must have been the last refinement of torture. But John preferred death to falsehood. He lived for the truth and he died for it. Those who bring to others the voice of God act like a conscience. Many would silence their consciences if they could, and therefore those who speak for God must always take their lives and their fortune in their hands.

THE PATHOS OF THE CROWD

Mark 6:30–4

> The apostles came together again to Jesus, and they told him all that they had done and taught. He said to them, 'Come you by yourselves into a lonely place, and rest for a while.' For there were many coming and going and they could not find time even to eat. So they went away in the boat to a lonely place all by themselves. Now many saw them going away and recognized them; and they ran together there on foot from all the towns and went on ahead of them. When Jesus disembarked he saw a great crowd, and he was moved to the depths of his being with pity for them, because they were like sheep who had no shepherd; and he began to teach them many things.

WHEN the disciples came back from their mission, they reported to Jesus all that they had done. The demanding crowds were so insistent that they had no time even to eat; so

Jesus told them to come with him to a lonely place on the other side of the lake that they might have peace and rest for a little time.

Here we see what might be called *the rhythm of the Christian life*. The Christian life is a continuous going into the presence of God from the presence of men and women and coming out into the presence of men and women from the presence of God. It is like the rhythm of sleep and work. We cannot work unless we have our time of rest; and sleep will not come unless we have worked until we are tired.

There are two dangers in life. First, there is the danger of a too constant activity. We cannot work without rest; and we cannot live the Christian life unless we give ourselves time with God. It may well be that the whole trouble in our lives is that we give God no opportunity to speak to us, because we do not know how to be still and to listen; we give God no time to recharge us with spiritual energy and strength, because there is no time when we wait upon him. How can we bear life's burdens if we have no contact with him who is the Lord of all good life? How can we do God's work unless in God's strength? And how can we receive that strength unless we seek in quietness and in loneliness the presence of God?

Second, there is the danger of too much withdrawal. Devotion that does not issue in action is not real devotion. Prayer that does not issue in work is not real prayer. We must never seek God's fellowship in order to avoid human fellowship but in order to fit ourselves better for it. The rhythm of the Christian life is the alternate meeting with God in the secret place and serving one another in the market place.

But the rest which Jesus sought for himself and for his disciples was not to be. The crowds saw Jesus and the Twelve going away. At this particular place, it was four miles across the lake by boat and ten miles round the top of the lake on foot. On a windless day, or with a contrary wind, a boat might take some time to make the passage, and an energetic person could walk round the top of the lake and be there before the boat arrived. That is exactly what happened; and when Jesus and his disciples stepped out of the boat, the very crowd from which they had sought some little peace was there waiting for them.

Any ordinary man would have been intensely annoyed. The rest Jesus so much desired and which he had so well earned was denied to him. His privacy was invaded. Any ordinary man would have resented it all, but Jesus was moved with pity at the pathos of the crowd. He looked at them; they were so desperately in earnest; they wanted so much what he alone could give them; to him they were like sheep who had no shepherd. What did he mean?

(1) A sheep without the shepherd cannot find the way. Left to ourselves, we get lost in life. John Cairns, Principal of the United Presbyterian Trinity Hall, Edinburgh, spoke of people who feel like 'lost children out in the rain'. In the *Inferno*, Dante has a line where he says, 'I woke up in the middle of the wood, and it was dark, and there was no clear way before me.' Life can be so bewildering. We can stand at some crossroads and not know which way to take. It is only when Jesus leads and we follow that we can find the way.

(2) A sheep without the shepherd cannot find its pasture and its food. In this life, we are bound to seek for sustenance. We need the strength which can keep us going; we need the inspiration which can lift us out of ourselves and above ourselves. When we seek it elsewhere, our minds are still unsatisfied, our hearts still restless, our souls still unfed. We can gain strength for life only from him who is the living bread.

(3) A sheep without the shepherd has no defence against the dangers which threaten it. It can defend itself neither from

robbers nor from wild animals. If life has taught us one thing, it must be that we cannot live it alone. No one has a sure defence against the temptations which assail us and from the evil of the world which attacks us. Only in the company of Jesus can we walk in the world and remain untainted by it. Without him we are defenceless; with him we are safe.

LITTLE IS MUCH IN THE HANDS OF JESUS

Mark 6:35-44

> When it was now late the disciples came to Jesus. 'The place', they said, 'is lonely, and it is now late. Send them away that they may go into the surrounding countryside and villages and buy themselves something to eat.' He answered, 'You give them something to eat.' 'Are we', they said to him, 'to go away and buy 200 denarii worth of loaves and so give them something to eat?' 'How many loaves have you?' he said to them. 'Go and see!' When they had found out, they said, 'Five and two fishes.' He ordered them to make them all sit down in groups on the green grass. So they sat down in sections of hundreds and of fifties. He took the five loaves and the two fishes, and he looked up into the heaven and blessed them and broke the loaves. He gave them to the disciples to serve the people with them. And he divided up the two fishes among them all. And they all ate until they were completely satisfied; and they gathered up the broken pieces of bread and what was left of the fishes – twelve basketsful. And those who ate the loaves amounted to 5,000 men.

IT is a notable fact that no miracle seems to have made such an impression on the disciples as this, because this is the only miracle of Jesus which is related in all four gospels. We have already seen how Mark's gospel really embodies the preaching material of Peter. To read this story, so simply and yet so dramatically told, is to read something that reads exactly like an eyewitness account. Let us note some of the vivid and realistic details.

They sat down on *the green grass*. It is as if Peter was seeing the whole thing in his mind's eye again. It so happens that this little descriptive phrase provides us with quite a lot of information. The only time when the grass would be green would be in the late springtime, in mid-April. So it is then that this miracle must have taken place. At that time the sun set at 6 pm, so this must have happened at some time in the late afternoon.

Mark tells us that they sat down in *sections* of 100 and of 50. The word used for *sections* (*prasiai*) is a very pictorial word. It is the normal Greek word for the rows of vegetables in a vegetable garden. When you looked at the little groups, as they sat there in their orderly rows, they looked for all the world like the rows of vegetables in a series of garden plots.

At the end they took up *twelve basketsful* of fragments. No orthodox Jew travelled without his basket (*kophinos*). The Romans made a jest of the Jew and his basket. There were two reasons for the basket, which was a wickerwork affair shaped like a narrow-necked pitcher, broadening out as it went down. First, the very orthodox Jew carried his own food supplies in his basket, so that he would be certain of eating food that was ceremonially clean and pure. Second, many a Jew was an accomplished beggar, and into his basket went the proceeds of his begging. The reason that there were *twelve* baskets is simply that there were *twelve* disciples. It was into their own baskets that they frugally gathered up the fragments so that nothing would be lost.

The wonderful thing about this story is that all through it runs an implicit contrast between the attitude of Jesus and the attitude of the disciples.

(1) It shows us *two reactions to human need*. When the disciples saw how late it was, and how tired and hungry the crowd were, they said, 'Send them away so that they can find something to eat.' In effect they said, 'These people are tired and hungry. Get rid of them and let someone else worry about them.' Jesus said, '*You* give them something to eat.' In effect Jesus said, 'These people are tired and hungry. We must do something about it.' There are always the people who are quite aware that others are in difficulty and trouble, but who wish to push the responsibility for doing something about it on to someone else; and there are always the people who when they see someone up against it feel compelled to do something about it themselves. There are those who say, 'Let others worry.' And there are those who say, '*I* must worry about my brother's or my sister's need.'

(2) It shows us *two reactions to human resources*. When the disciples were asked to give the people something to eat, they insisted that 200 denarii, or what the Authorized Version calls 200 'pence', was not enough to buy bread for them. The word the Authorized Version translates as *penny* is *denarius*. This was a Roman silver coin and was the standard day's wage of a working man. In effect the disciples were saying, 'We could not earn enough in more than six months' work to give this crowd a meal.' They really meant, 'Anything we have got is no use at all.'

Jesus said, 'What have you got?' They had five loaves. These were not like the loaves with which we are familiar: they were more like rolls. John (6:9) tells us they were barley loaves; and barley loaves were the food of the poorest of the poor. Barley bread was the cheapest and the coarsest of all bread. They had two fishes, which would be about the size of sardines. Tarichaea – which means the salt-fish town – was a well-known place on the lake from which salt-fish went out to all over the world. The little salt-fishes were eaten as relish with the dry rolls.

It did not seem much. But Jesus took it and worked wonders with it. In the hands of Jesus, little is always much. We may think that we have little of talent or substance to give to Jesus. That is no reason for a hopeless pessimism such as the disciples had. The one fatal thing to say is, 'For all I could do, it is not worth my while trying to do anything.' If we put ourselves into the hands of Jesus Christ, there is no telling what he can do with us and through us.

THE CONQUEST OF THE STORM

Mark 6:45–52

Immediately he made the disciples embark on the boat and go across ahead to Bethsaida while he sent the crowd away. When he had taken leave of them, he went away into a mountain to pray. When it was late the boat was half-way across the lake and Jesus was alone upon the land. He saw that they were sore beset as they rowed, for the wind was against them. About the fourth watch of the night he came to them walking on the sea, and it looked as if he meant to pass them by. When they saw him walking on the sea they thought it was a ghost, and they cried out in terror, for they all saw him and they were distracted with fear. At once he spoke with them. 'Courage!' he said. 'It is I. Don't be afraid.' And he

came into the boat with them, and the wind sank to rest.
And they were exceedingly astonished within themselves, because they did not understand about the loaves
because their minds were obtuse.

AFTER the hunger of the crowd had been satisfied, Jesus
immediately sent his disciples away before he dismissed the
crowd. Why should he do that? Mark does not tell us, but
most probably we have the explanation in John's account.
John tells us that after the crowd had been fed there was a
move to take Jesus and to make him king. That was the last
thing Jesus desired. It was that very way of power that once,
finally and for all, he had rejected at the time of his
temptations. He could see it coming. He did not want his
disciples to be infected and caught up in this nationalistic
outburst. Galilee was the hotbed of revolution. If this
movement was not checked, there might well emerge among
the excitable people a rebellion which would wreck
everything and lead to disaster for all concerned. So Jesus
sent away his disciples lest they too should become inflamed
by this movement, and then he calmed the crowd and bade
them farewell.

When he was alone, he went up into a mountain to pray.
Thick and fast the problems were descending upon him.
There was the hostility of the orthodox people; there was
the frightened suspicion of Herod Antipas; there were the
political hotheads who would make him a nationalistic
Messiah against his will. At this particular time there was
many a problem on Jesus' mind and many a burden on his
heart.

For some hours he was alone amid the hills with God. As
we have seen, this must have happened about mid-April, and
mid-April was the Passover time. Now the Passover was

deliberately fixed for the full moon, as Easter still is. The Jewish night ran from 6 pm to 6 am, and it was divided into four watches – 6 pm to 9 pm, 9 pm to 12 midnight, 12 midnight to 3 am, and 3 am to 6 am. About 3 am, Jesus looked from the mountainside out across the lake. The lake was only four miles across at that point, and in the light of the moon it lay stretched out before him. The wind was up and he saw the boat, with his disciples in it, having a hard struggle to reach the other side.

See what happened. Immediately Jesus saw his friends in trouble, his own problems were set aside; the moment for prayer was past; the time for action had come; he forgot himself and went to the help of his friends. That is of the very essence of Jesus. The cry of human need to him surpassed all other claims. His friends needed him; he must go.

What happened we do not know, and will never know. The story is shrouded in mystery which defies explanation. What we do know is that he came to them and their storm became a calm. With him beside them nothing mattered any more.

When St Augustine was writing about this incident he said, 'He came treading the waves; and so he puts all the swelling tumults of life under his feet. Christians – why afraid?' It is the simple fact of life, a fact which has been proved by countless thousands of men and women in every generation, that when Christ is there the storm becomes a calm, the tumult becomes a peace, what cannot be done is done, the unbearable becomes bearable, and we pass the breaking point and do not break. To walk with Christ will be for us also the conquest of the storm.

THE DEMANDING CROWDS

Mark 6:53-6

> When they had crossed over and reached land they came
> to Gennesareth, and moored the boat there. When they
> had disembarked from the boat the people immediately
> recognized him; and they ran all over that countryside,
> and, wherever they knew he was, they began to carry to
> him on pallets those who were ill. And whenever he
> came into villages or towns or country places, they laid
> the sick in the open spaces, and they kept begging him
> to be allowed to touch even the tassel of his robe; and
> all who touched it were restored to health.

No sooner had Jesus landed on the other side of the lake than
once again he was surrounded by crowds. Just sometimes he
must have looked on the crowds with a certain wistfulness,
because there was hardly a person in them who had not come
to get something out of him. They came to get. They came
with their insistent demands. They came – to put it bluntly –
to use him. What a difference it would have made if, among
these crowds, there had been some few who came to give
and not to get. In a way it is natural that we should come to
Jesus to get things from him, for there are so many things
that he alone can give: but it is always shameful to take
everything and to give nothing, and yet it is very characteristic
of human nature.

(1) There are those who simply make use of their *homes*.
It is specially so with young people. They regard their homes
as being there to cater for their comfort and their convenience.
It is there they eat and sleep and get things done for them; but
surely home is a place to which we ought to contribute, from
which we ought not only to be taking all the time?

(2) There are those who simply make use of their *friends*. There are some people from whom we never hear unless they want something from us. There are those who regard other people as existing to help them when they need their help, and to be forgotten when they cannot be of use.

(3) There are those who simply make use of the *church*. They desire the church to baptize their children, marry their young people and bury their dead. They are seldom to be seen there unless they wish some service. It is their unconscious attitude that the church exists to serve them, but that they have no duty whatever towards it.

(4) There are those who seek simply to make use of *God*. They never remember him unless they need him. Their only prayers are requests, or even demands, made of God. Someone has put it this way. In some hotels, there is a boy called the 'bell-hop'. The hotel guest rings the bell, and the bell-hop appears; he will fetch anything the guest wishes on demand. Some people regard God as a kind of universal bell-hop, only to be summoned when something is needed.

If we examine ourselves, we are all, to some extent, guilty of these things. It would rejoice the heart of Jesus if more often we came to him to offer our love, our service, our devotion, and less often to demand from him the help we need.

CLEAN AND UNCLEAN

Mark 7:1-4

> There gathered together to Jesus the Pharisees, and some
> of the experts in the law who had come down from
> Jerusalem. They saw that some of his disciples ate their
> bread with hands which were ceremonially unclean, that

is to say hands which had not undergone the prescribed washings; for the Pharisees, and all the Jews, who hold to the traditions of the elders, do not eat unless they wash their hands, using the fist as the law prescribes; and when they come in from the market place they do not eat unless they immerse their whole bodies; and there are many other traditions which they observe which relate to the prescribed washings of cups and pitchers and vessels of bronze.

THE difference and the argument between Jesus and the Pharisees and the experts in the law, which this chapter relates, are of tremendous importance, for they show us the very essence and core of the divergence between Jesus and the orthodox Jews of his time.

The question asked was, 'Why do Jesus and his disciples not observe the tradition of the elders?' What was this tradition, and what was its moving spirit?

Originally, for a Jew, the law meant two things: it meant, first and foremost, the Ten Commandments, and, second, the first five books of the Old Testament, or, as they are called, the Pentateuch. Now it is true that the Pentateuch contains a certain number of detailed regulations and instructions; but, in the matter of moral questions, what is laid down is a series of great moral principles which individuals must interpret and apply for themselves. For a long time, the Jews were content with that. But in the fourth and fifth centuries before Christ, there came into being a class of legal experts whom we know as the *scribes*. They were not content with great moral principles; they had what can only be called a passion for definition. They wanted these great principles amplified, expanded and broken down until they issued in thousands and thousands of little rules and regulations governing every possible action and every possible situation in life. These rules and regulations were not written down until long after the time of Jesus. They are what is called the *oral law*; these rules make up *the tradition of the elders*.

The word *elders* does not mean, in this phrase, the officials of the synagogue; rather it means *the ancients*, the great legal experts of the old days, like Hillel and Shammai. Much later, in the third century after Christ, a summary of all these rules and regulations was made and written down, and that summary is known as the *Mishnah*.

There are two aspects of these scribal rules and regulations which emerge in the argument in this passage. One is about *the washing of hands*. The scribes and Pharisees accused the disciples of Jesus of eating with unclean hands. The Greek word is *koinos*. Ordinarily, *koinos* means common; then it comes to describe something which is ordinary in the sense that it is not sacred, something that is *profane* as opposed to sacred things; and finally it describes something, as it does here, which is ceremonially unclean and unfit for the service and worship of God.

There were definite and rigid rules for the washing of hands. Note that this handwashing was *not* in the interests of hygienic purity; it was *ceremonial cleanness* which was at stake. Before every meal, and between each of the courses, the hands had to be washed, and they had to be washed in a certain way. The hands, to begin with, had to be free of any coating of sand or mortar or gravel or any such substance. The water for washing had to be kept in special large stone jars, so that it itself was clean in the ceremonial sense and so that it might be certain that it had been used for no other purpose, and that nothing had fallen into it or had been mixed with it. First, the hands were held with fingertips *pointing upwards*; water was poured over them and had to run at least down to the wrist; the minimum amount of water was one quarter of a log, which is equal to one and a half eggshells full of water. While the hands were still wet, each hand had to be cleansed with the fist of the other. That is what the phrase about using the fist means; the fist of one hand was rubbed into the palm and against the surface of the other. This meant that at this stage the hands were wet with water; but that water was now unclean because it had touched unclean hands. So, next, the hands had to be held with fingertips pointing downwards and water had to be poured over them in such a way that it began at the wrists and ran off at the fingertips. After all that had been done, the hands were clean.

To fail to do this was in Jewish eyes not to be guilty of bad manners, not to be dirty in the health sense, but to be unclean in the sight of God. Anyone who ate with unclean hands was subject to the attacks of a demon called Shibta. To omit so to wash the hands was to become liable to poverty and destruction. Bread eaten with unclean hands was not better than excrement. A Rabbi who once omitted the ceremony was buried in excommunication. Another Rabbi, imprisoned by the Romans, used the water given to him for handwashing rather than for drinking and in the end nearly perished of thirst, because he was determined to observe the rules of cleanliness rather than satisfy his thirst.

That, to the Pharisaic and scribal Jew, was religion. It was ritual, ceremonial, and regulations like that which they considered to be the essence of the service of God. Ethical religion was buried under a mass of tabus and rules.

The last verses of the passage deal further with this conception of uncleanness. A thing might in the ordinary sense be completely clean and yet in the legal sense be unclean. There is something about this conception of uncleanness in Leviticus 11-15 and in Numbers 19. Nowadays we would talk rather of things being *tabu* than of being *unclean*. Certain

animals were unclean (Leviticus 11). A woman after child-
birth was unclean; a leper was unclean; anyone who touched
a dead body was unclean. And those who had become unclean
in this way made unclean anything they in turn touched. A
Gentile was unclean; food touched by a Gentile was unclean;
any vessel touched by a Gentile was unclean. So, then, when
a strict Jew returned from the market place he immersed his
whole body in clean water to take away the taint he might
have acquired.

Obviously vessels could easily become unclean; they might
be touched by an unclean person or by unclean food. This is
what our passage means by the washings of cups and pitchers
and vessels of bronze. In the *Mishnah* there are no fewer
than twelve treatises on this kind of uncleanness. If we take
some actual examples, we will see how far this went. A *hollow*
vessel made of pottery could contract uncleanness *inside* but
not outside; that is to say, it did not matter who or what
touched it outside, but it did matter what touched it inside. If
it became unclean it must be broken; and no unbroken piece
must remain which was big enough to hold enough oil to
anoint the little toe. A flat plate without a rim could not
become unclean at all; but a plate with a rim could. If vessels
made with leather, bone or glass were *flat* they could not
contract uncleanness at all; if they were *hollow* they could
become unclean *outside and inside*. If they were unclean they
must be broken; and the break must be a hole at least big
enough for a medium-sized pomegranate to pass through. To
cure uncleanness, earthen vessels must be broken; other
vessels must be immersed, boiled, purged with fire – in the
case of metal vessels – and polished. A three-legged table
could contract uncleanness; if it lost one or two legs it could
not; if it lost three legs it could, for then it could be used as a
board, and a board could become unclean. Things made of

metal could become unclean, except a door, a bolt, a lock, a hinge, a knocker and a gutter. Wood used in metal utensils could become unclean; but metal used in wood utensils could not. Thus a wooden key with metal teeth could become unclean; but a metal key with wooden teeth could not.

We have taken some time over these scribal laws, this tradition of the elders, because *that is what Jesus was up against*. To the scribes and Pharisees, these rules and regulations were the essence of religion. To observe them was to please God; to break them was to sin. This was their idea of goodness and of the service of God. In the religious sense, Jesus and these people spoke different languages. It was precisely because he had no use for all these regulations that they considered him a bad man. There is a fundamental split here – that between those who see religion as ritual, ceremonial, rules and regulations, and those who see in religion loving God and loving their fellow men and women.

The next passage will develop this; but it is clear that Jesus' idea of religion and that of the scribes and Pharisees had nothing in common at all.

GOD'S LAWS AND HUMAN RULES

Mark 7:5–8

> So the Pharisees and the experts in the law asked him, 'Why do your disciples not conduct themselves as the tradition of the elders prescribes, but eat bread with hands that are unclean?' He said to them, 'Isaiah did well when he prophesied about you hypocrites, as it stands written, "This people honour me with their lips, but their heart is far away from me. This so-called reverence of men is an empty thing, for they teach as

> doctrine human rules and regulations." While you hold
> fast the tradition of men you abandon the command of
> God.'

THE scribes and Pharisees saw that the disciples of Jesus did
not observe the niceties of the tradition and the code of the
oral law in regard to the washing of hands before and during
meals, and they asked why. Jesus began by quoting to them a
passage from Isaiah 29:13. There, Isaiah accused the people
of his day of honouring God with their lips while their hearts
were really far away. In principle, Jesus accused the scribes
and Pharisees of two things.

(1) He accused them of *hypocrisy*. The word *hupokritēs*
has an interesting and revealing history. It begins by meaning
simply *one who answers*; it goes on to mean one who answers
in a set dialogue or a set conversation, that is to say *an actor*;
and finally it means, not simply an actor on the stage, but *one
whose whole life is a piece of acting without any sincerity
behind it at all*. Anyone to whom religion is a legal thing,
anyone to whom religion means carrying out certain external
rules and regulations, anyone to whom religion is entirely
connected with the observation of a certain ritual and the
keeping of a certain number of tabus is in the end bound to
be, in this sense, a hypocrite. The reason is this – such people
believe that they are good if they carry out the correct acts
and practices, *no matter what their hearts and their thoughts
are like*.

To take the case of the legalistic Jew in the time of Jesus,
he might hate those around him with all his heart, he might
be full of envy and jealousy and concealed bitterness and
pride; that did not matter so long as he carried out the correct
handwashings and observed the correct laws about cleanness
and uncleanness. Legalism takes account of outward actions;
but it takes no account at all of people's inward feelings.

They may well be meticulously serving God in outward things, and bluntly disobeying God in inward things – and that is hypocrisy.

There is no greater religious peril than that of identifying religion with outward observance. There is no commoner religious mistake than to identify goodness with certain so-called religious acts. Church-going, Bible-reading, careful financial giving, even timetabled prayer do not make us good. The fundamental question is, how are our hearts towards God and towards others? And if in our hearts there are enmity, bitterness, grudges and pride, not all the outward religious observances in the world will make us anything other than hypocrites.

(2) The second accusation that Jesus implicitly levelled against these legalists was that *they substituted the efforts of human ingenuity for the laws of God*. For their guidance for life they did not depend on listening to God; they depended on listening to the clever arguments and debates, the fine-spun niceties, the ingenious interpretations of the legal experts. Cleverness can never be the basis of true religion. True religion can never only be the basis of human thought. It must always come, not from their ingenious discoveries, but from the simple listening to and accepting the voice of God.

AN INIQUITOUS REGULATION

Mark 7:9–13

> He said to them, 'You make an excellent job of completely nullifying the command of God in order to observe your own tradition. For Moses said, "Honour your father and your mother." And, "He who speaks evil of his father or mother shall certainly die." But you

say, that, if a man says to his father or mother, "That by which you might have been helped by me is *Corban*," – that is to say, *God-dedicated* – you no longer allow him to do anything for his father and mother, and you thereby render invalid the word of God by your tradition which you hand on. You do many things like that.'

THE exact meaning of this passage is very difficult to discover. It hinges on the word *Corban*, which seems to have undergone two stages of meaning in Jewish usage.

(1) The word meant a *gift*. It was used to describe something which was specially dedicated to God. A thing which was *Corban* was as if it had already been laid upon the altar. That is to say, it was completely set apart from all ordinary purposes and usages and became the property of God. If a man wished to dedicate some of his money or his property to God, he declared it *Corban*, and thereafter it might never again be used for any ordinary or secular purpose.

It does seem that, even at this stage, the word was capable of very shrewd usage. For instance, a creditor might have a debtor who refused or was unwilling to pay. The creditor might then say, 'The debt you owe me is *Corban*,' that is to say, 'The debt you owe me is dedicated to God.' From then on, the debtor ceased to be in debt to another person and began rather to be in debt to God, which was far more serious. It may well be that the creditor could discharge his part of the matter by making a quite small symbolic payment to the Temple, and then keeping the rest for himself. In any event, to introduce the idea of *Corban* into this kind of debt was a kind of religious blackmail transforming a debt owed to another person into a debt owed to God.

It does seem that the idea of *Corban* was already capable of misuse. If that is the idea behind this, the passage speaks of a man declaring his property *Corban*, sacred to God, and then when his father or mother in dire need comes to him for help, saying, 'I am sorry that I cannot give you any help because nothing that I have is available for you because it is dedicated to God.' The vow was made an excuse to avoid helping a parent in need. The vow which the scribal legalist insisted upon involved breaking one of the Ten Commandments which are the very law of God.

(2) There came a time when *Corban* became a much more generalized oath. When a person declared anything *Corban* he entirely alienated it from the person to whom he was talking. A man might say, '*Corban* that by which I might be profited by you,' and, in so doing, he bound himself never to touch, taste, have or handle anything possessed by the person so addressed. Or, he might say, '*Corban* that by which you might be profited by me,' and, in so saying, he bound himself never to help or to benefit the person so addressed by anything that belonged to himself. If that is the use here, the passage means that, at some time, perhaps in a fit of anger or rebellion, a man had said to his parents, '*Corban* anything by which you may ever be helped by me,' and that afterwards, even if he repented from his rash vow, the scribal legalists declared that it was unbreakable and that he might never again render his parents any assistance.

Whichever is the case – and it is not possible to be certain – this much is sure, that there were cases in which the strict performance of the scribal law made it impossible to carry out the law of the Ten Commandments.

Jesus was attacking a system which put rules and regulations before the claim of human need. The commandment of God was that the claim of human love should come first; the commandment of the scribes was that the claim of legal rules and regulations should come first. Jesus was quite sure that any regulation which prevented anyone from giving help where help was needed was nothing less than a contradiction of the law of God.

We must take care that we never allow rules to paralyse the claims of love. Nothing that prevents us helping another person can ever be a rule approved by God.

THE REAL DEFILEMENT

Mark 7:14-23

> He called the crowd to him again and said, 'Listen to me, all of you and understand. There is nothing which goes into a man from outside which can render him unclean; but it is the things which come out of a man which render the man unclean.' When he came into the house, away from the crowd, his disciples asked him about this hard saying. He said to them, 'So, then, are you too unable to grasp things? Do you not understand that everything that goes into a man from outside cannot render him unclean, because it does not go into his heart, but into his stomach, and it is then evacuated from him by natural bodily processes?' (The effect of this saying is to render all foods clean.) But he went on to say, 'What comes out of a man, *that is* what renders the man unclean. It is from within, from the heart, that there come evil designs, fornications, thefts, murders, adulteries, covetous deeds, evil deeds, guile, wanton wickedness, envy, slander, pride, folly. All these evil things come from within, and they render a man unclean.'

ALTHOUGH it may not seem so now, this passage, when it was first spoken, was well-nigh the most revolutionary passage in the New Testament. Jesus has been arguing with the legal experts about different aspects of the traditional law. He has shown the irrelevance of the elaborate handwashings. He has shown how rigid adherence to the traditional law can actually mean disobedience to the law of God. But here he says something more startling yet. He declares that nothing that goes into a person can possibly cause defilement, for it is received only into the body, which rids itself of it in the normal, physical way.

No Jew ever believed that, and orthodox Jews do not believe it even now. Leviticus 11 has a long list of animals that are unclean and may not be used for food. How very seriously this was taken can be seen from many an incident in Maccabaean times. At that time the Syrian king, Antiochus Epiphanes, was determined to root out the Jewish faith. One of the things he demanded was that the Jews should eat pork, pig's flesh; but they died in their hundreds rather than do so. 'But many in Israel were resolved in their hearts not to eat unclean food. They chose to die rather than to be defiled by food or to profane the holy covenant; and they did die' (1 Maccabees 1:62–3). Fourth Maccabees (chapter 7) tells the story of a widow and her seven sons. It was demanded that they should eat pig's flesh. They refused. The first had his tongue cut out and the ends of his limbs cut off; he was then roasted alive in a pan. The second had his hair and the skin of his skull torn off. One by one they were tortured to death while their aged mother looked on and cheered them on; they died rather than eat meat which to them was unclean.

Against this, Jesus made his revolutionary statement that nothing that goes into a person can make that person unclean. He was wiping out at one stroke the laws for which Jews had suffered and died. No wonder the disciples were amazed.

In effect, Jesus was saying that *things* cannot be either unclean or clean in any real religious sense of the term. Only *persons* can be really defiled; and what defiles people are

their own actions, which are the product of their own hearts.
This was new doctrine and shatteringly new doctrine. Jews
had, and still have, a whole system of *things* which are clean
and unclean. With one sweeping pronouncement, Jesus
declared the whole thing irrelevant and that uncleanness has
nothing to do with what people take into their bodies but
everything to do with what comes out of their hearts.

Let us look at the things Jesus lists as coming from the
heart and making people unclean.

He begins with *evil designs* (*dialogismoi*). Every outward
act of sin is preceded by an inward act of choice; therefore
Jesus begins with the evil thought from which the evil action
comes. Next come *fornications* (*porneiai*); later he is to list
acts of *adultery* (*moicheiai*); but this first word is a wide
word – it means every kind of traffic in sexual vice. There
follow *thefts* (*klopai*). In Greek, there are two words for a
robber – *kleptēs* and *lēstēs*. *Lēstēs* is a *brigand*; Barabbas was
a *lēstēs* (John 18:40), and a brigand may be a very brave man
although an outlaw. *Kleptēs* is a thief; Judas was a *kleptēs*
when he pilfered from the box (John 12:6). A *kleptēs* is a
mean, deceitful, dishonourable pilferer, without even the redeeming quality of a certain audacious gallantry that a brigand
must have. *Murders* (*phonoi*) and *adulteries* come next in
the list and their meaning is clear.

Then come *covetous deeds* (*pleonexiai*). *Pleonexia* comes
from two Greek words meaning *to have more*. It has been
defined as *the accursed love of having*. It has been defined
as 'the spirit which snatches at that which it is not right to
take', 'the baneful appetite for that which belongs to
others'. It is the spirit which snatches at things, not to hoard
them like a miser, but to spend them in lust and luxury. It has
been defined as 'Rapacious appetite for gain, not for its own
sake, but for the pleasure of refunding it immediately through

all the channels of pride and luxury.' It is not the desire for money and things; it includes the desire for power, the insatiable lust of the flesh. Plato said, 'The desire of man is like a sieve or pierced vessel which he ever tries to, and can never fill.' *Pleonexia* is that lust for having which is in the heart of the person who sees happiness in things instead of in God.

There follow *evil deeds*. In Greek, there are two words for evil – *kakos*, which describes a thing which in itself is evil, and *ponēros*, which describes a person or a thing which is *actively* evil. *Ponēriai* is the word used here. The person who is *ponēros* is the one in whose heart there is the desire to harm. That person is, as the eighteenth-century German theologian Johann Bengel said, 'trained in every crime and completely equipped to inflict evil on any man'. In the seventeenth century, Jeremy Taylor defined this *ponēria* as 'aptness to do shrewd turns, to delight in mischiefs and tragedies; loving to trouble our neighbour, and to do him ill offices; crossness, perverseness and peevishness of action in our intercourse'. *Ponēria* not only corrupts the person who has it; it corrupts others too. *Ponēros* – the evil one – is the title of Satan. The worst people of all, those who are doing Satan's work, are those who, being bad themselves, make others as bad as they are.

Next comes *dolos*, translated *guile*. It comes from a word which means *bait*; it is used for trickery and deceit. It is used for instance of a mousetrap. When the Greeks were besieging Troy and could not gain entry, they sent the Trojans the present of a great wooden horse, as if it was a token of goodwill. The Trojans opened their gates and took it in. But the horse was filled with Greeks who in the night broke out and dealt death and devastation to Troy. That exactly is *dolos*. It is crafty, cunning, deceitful, clever treachery.

Next on the list is *wanton wickedness (aselgeia).* The Greeks defined *aselgeia* as 'a disposition of soul that resents all discipline', as 'a spirit that acknowledges no restraints, dares whatsoever its caprice and wanton insolence may suggest'. The great characteristic of people who are guilty of *aselgeia* is that they are lost to decency and to shame. Evil men and women may hide their sin, but those who have *aselgeia* sin without a qualm and never hesitate to shock other people. Jezebel was the classic instance of *aselgeia* when she built a pagan shrine in Jerusalem the holy city.

Envy is literally *the evil eye,* the eye that looks on the success and happiness of another in such a way that it would cast an evil spell upon it if it could. The next word is *blasphēmia.* When this is used of words against others, it means *slander*; when it is used of words against God, it means *blasphemy.* It means insulting other people or God.

There follows *pride (huperēphania).* The Greek word literally means 'showing oneself above'. It describes the attitude of people 'who have a certain contempt for everyone except themselves'. The interesting thing about this word, as the Greeks used it, is that it describes an attitude that may never become *public.* It may be that in their heart of hearts these people are always secretly comparing themselves with others. They might even ape humility and yet in their hearts be proud. Sometimes, of course, the pride is evident. The Greeks had a legend of this pride. They said that the Giants, the sons of Tartarus and Gē, in their pride sought to storm heaven and were cast down by Hercules. That is *huperēphania.* It is setting oneself up against God; it is 'invading God's prerogatives'. That is why it has been called 'the peak of all the vices', and why 'God opposes the proud' (James 4:6).

Last comes *folly* (*aphrosunē*). This does not mean the
foolishness that is due to weakness of intellect and lack of
brains; it means moral folly. It describes not those who are
brainless fools, but those who choose to play the fool.

It is a truly terrible list which Jesus cites of the things that
come from the human heart. When we examine it, a shudder
surely passes over us. Nonetheless it is a summons, not to a
fastidious shrinking from such things, but to an honest self-
examination of our own hearts.

THE FORECAST OF A WORLD FOR CHRIST

Mark 7:24–30

> He left there and went away into the regions of Tyre
> and Sidon. He went into a house and he did not wish
> anyone to know about it, but he could not be there
> without people knowing about it. When a woman whose
> daughter had an unclean spirit heard about him, she
> immediately came and threw herself at his feet. The
> woman was a Greek, a Syrophoenician by birth. She
> asked him to cast the demon out of her daughter. He
> said to her, 'First of all you must let the children eat
> their fill; it is not right to take the bread that belongs to
> the children and to throw it to the dogs.' 'True, sir,' she
> answered, 'but even the dogs below the table eat some
> of the bits of bread that the children throw away.' He
> said to her, 'Because of this word, go your way! The
> demon has come out of your daughter!' She went away
> and found the child thrown upon her bed and the demon
> gone.

WHEN this incident is seen against its background, it becomes
one of the most moving and extraordinary in the life of
Jesus.

First, let us look at the geography of the incident. Tyre and Sidon were cities of Phoenicia, which was a part of Syria. Phoenicia stretched north from Carmel, right along the coastal plain. It lay between Galilee and the sea coast. Phoenicia indeed, as Josephus puts it, 'encompassed Galilee'.

Tyre lay forty miles north-west of Capernaum. Its name means *the Rock*. It was so called because off the shore lay two great rocks joined by a 3,000-foot-long ridge. This formed a natural breakwater, and Tyre was one of the great natural harbours of the world from the earliest times. Not only did the rocks form a breakwater, they also formed a defence; and Tyre was not only a famous harbour, it was also a famous fortress. It was from Tyre and Sidon that there came the first sailors who steered by the stars. Until sailors learned to find their way by the stars, ships had to hug the coast and to lay up by night; but the Phoenician sailors circumnavigated the Mediterranean and found their way through the Pillars of Hercules until they came to Britain and the tin mines of Cornwall. It may well be that in their adventuring they had even circumnavigated Africa.

Sidon was twenty-six miles north-east of Tyre and sixty miles north of Capernaum. Like Tyre it had a natural breakwater, and its origin as a harbour and a city was so ancient that no one knew who had founded it.

Although the Phoenician cities were part of Syria, they were all independent, and they were all rivals. They had their own kings, their own gods and their own coinage. Within a radius of fifteen or twenty miles, they were supreme. Outwardly they looked to the sea; inland they looked to Damascus, and the ships of the sea and the caravans of many lands flowed into them. In the end, Sidon lost trade and greatness to Tyre and sank into a demoralized degeneracy. But the Phoenician sailors will always be famous as the men who first found their way by following the stars.

(1) So, then, the first tremendous thing which meets us is that *Jesus is in Gentile territory*. Is it any accident that this incident comes here? The previous incident shows Jesus wiping out the distinction between clean and unclean foods. Can it be that here, in symbol, we have him wiping out the difference between clean and unclean people? Just as Jews would never soil their lips with forbidden foods, so they would never soil their lives by contact with the unclean Gentile. It may well be that here Jesus is saying by implication that the Gentiles are not unclean but that they, too, have their place within the kingdom.

Jesus must have come north to this region for temporary escape. In his own country, he was under attack from every side. Long ago, the scribes and Pharisees had branded him as a sinner because he broke through their rules and regulations. Herod regarded him as a menace. The people of Nazareth treated him with scandalized dislike. The hour would come when he would face his enemies with blazing defiance, but that was not yet. Before it came, he would seek the peace and quiet of seclusion, and in that withdrawal from the enmity of the Jews the foundation of the kingdom of the Gentiles was laid. It is the forecast of the whole history of Christianity. The Jews' rejection had become the opportunity of the Gentiles.

(2) But there is more to it than that. Ideally, these Phoenician cities were part of the realm of Israel. When, under Joshua, the land was being partitioned out, the tribe of Asher was allocated the land "as far as Great Sidon . . . to the fortified city of Tyre' (Joshua 19:28–9). They had never been able to subdue their territory and they had never entered into it. Again is it not symbolic? Where the might of arms was helpless, the conquering love of Jesus Christ was victorious.

The earthly Israel had failed to gather in the people of Phoenicia; now the true Israel had come upon them. It was not a strange land into which Jesus came; it was a land which long ago God had given him for his own. He was not so much coming among strangers as entering into his inheritance.

(3) The story itself must be read with insight. The woman came asking Jesus' help for her daughter. His answer was that it was not right to take the children's bread and give it to dogs. At first it is an almost shocking saying.

The dog was not the well-loved companion that it is today; more commonly it was a symbol of dishonour. To a Greek, the word *dog* meant a shameless and audacious woman. To a Jew, it was equally a term of contempt. 'Do not give to dogs what is holy' (Matthew 7:6; cf. Philippians 3:2; Revelation 22:15).

The word *dog* was in fact sometimes a Jewish term of contempt for the Gentiles. Rabbi Joshua ben Levi had a parable. He saw the blessings of God which the Gentiles enjoy; he asked, 'If the Gentiles without the law enjoy blessings like that, how many more blessings will Israel, the people of God, enjoy?' 'It is like a king who made a feast and brought in the guests and placed them at the door of his palace. They saw the dogs come out, with pheasants, and heads of fatted birds, and calves in their mouths. Then the guests began to say, "If it be thus with the dogs, how much more luxurious will the meal itself be?" And the nations of the world are compared to dogs, as it is said (Isaiah 56:11), "The dogs have a mighty appetite".'

No matter how you look at it, the term *dog* is an insult. How, then, are we to explain Jesus' use of it here?

(a) He did not use the usual word; he used a diminutive word which described not the wild dogs of the streets, but the little pet lap-dogs of the house. In Greek, diminutives are characteristically affectionate. Jesus took the sting out of the word.

(b) Without a doubt, his tone of voice made all the difference. The same word can be a deadly insult and an affectionate address, according to the tone of voice. We can call someone 'an old rascal' in a voice of contempt or a voice of affection. Jesus' tone took all the poison out of the word.

(c) In any event, Jesus did *not* shut the door. *First*, he said, the children must be fed, but only first; there is meat left for the household pets. True, Israel had the *first* offer of the gospel, but only the first; there were others still to come. The woman was a Greek, and the Greeks had a gift of repartee; and she saw at once that Jesus was speaking with a smile. She knew that the door was swinging on its hinges. In those days, people did not have knives or forks or table-napkins. They ate with their hands; they wiped the soiled hands on chunks of bread and then flung the bread away and the house-dogs ate it. So the woman said, 'I know the children are fed first, but can't I even get the scraps the children throw away?' And Jesus loved it. Here was a sunny faith that would not take no for an answer, here was a woman with the tragedy of an ill daughter at home, and there was still light enough in her heart to reply with a smile. Her faith was tested and her faith was real, and her prayer was answered. Symbolically, she stands for the Gentile world which so eagerly seized on the bread of heaven which the Jews rejected and threw away.

DOING ALL THINGS WELL

Mark 7:31-7

> He went away again from the regions of Tyre and came
> through Sidon to the Sea of Galilee, through the regions
> of the Decapolis. They brought to him a man who was
> deaf and who had an impediment in his speech, and

they asked him to lay his hands on him. He took him aside from the crowd all by himself. He thrust his fingers into his ears, and spat, and touched his tongue. Then he looked up into heaven, and sighed, and said to him, 'Ephphatha!' which means, 'Be opened!' And his ears were opened, and the bond which held his tongue was loosed, and he spoke correctly. He enjoined them to tell no one; but the more he enjoined them the more exceedingly they proclaimed the story of what he had done. They were all amazed beyond measure. 'He has done all things well,' they said. And he made the deaf to hear and the dumb to speak.

THIS story begins by describing what is on the face of it an amazing journey. Jesus was going from Tyre to the territory around the Sea of Galilee. He was going from Tyre in the north to Galilee in the south; and he started by going to Sidon. That is to say, he started going due south by going due north! As one scholar has put it, it would be like going from London to Cornwall via Manchester; or from Glasgow to Edinburgh via Perth; or from Philadelphia to Atlanta by way of New York.

Because of that difficulty, some have thought that the text is wrong and that Sidon should not enter into it at all. But almost certainly the text is correct as it stands. Another thinks that this journey took no less than eight months; and that, indeed, is far more likely.

It may well be that this long journey is the peace before the storm, a long communion with the disciples before the final tempest breaks. In the very next chapter, Peter makes the great discovery that Jesus is the Christ (Mark 8:27–9), and it may well be that it was in this long, lonely time together that this impression became a certainty in Peter's heart. Jesus needed this long time with his disciples before the strain and tension of the approaching end.

When Jesus did arrive back in the regions of Galilee, he came into the district of the Decapolis, and there they brought to him a man who was deaf and who had an impediment in his speech. As William Tyndale vividly translates it, the man was 'deffe and stambed in his speech'. No doubt the two things went together; it was the man's inability to hear which made his speech so imperfect. There is no miracle which so beautifully shows Jesus' way of treating people.

(1) He took the man aside from the crowd, all by himself. Here is the most tender considerateness. Deaf people are always a little embarrassed. In some ways, it is more embarrassing to be deaf than it is to be blind. Deaf people know they cannot hear; and when someone in a crowd shouts at them and tries to make them hear, in their excitement they can become all the more helpless. Jesus showed the most tender consideration for the feelings of a man for whom life was very difficult.

(2) Throughout the whole miracle, Jesus acted what he was going to do in dumb show. He put his hands in the man's ears and touched his tongue with spittle. In those days, people believed that spittle had a curative quality. Suetonius, the Roman historian, tells of an incident in the life of Vespasian, the emperor. 'It fortuned that a certain mean commoner stark-blind, another likewise with a feeble and lame leg, came together unto him as he sat upon his tribunal, craving that help and remedy for their infirmities which had been shown unto them by Serapis in their dreams; that he should restore the one to his sight, if he did but spit into his eyes, and strengthen the other's leg, if he vouchsafed only to touch it with his heel. Now when as he could hardly believe that the thing any way would find success and speed accordingly, and therefore durst not so much as put it to the venture, at the last, through the persuasion of his friends, openly before the

assembly he assayed both means, neither missed he of the effect' (Suetonius, *Life of Vespasian* 7, Holland's translation). Jesus looked up to heaven to show that it was from God that help was to come. Then he spoke the word and the man was healed.

The whole story shows us most vividly that Jesus did not consider the man merely *a case*; he considered him as *an individual*. The man had a special need and a special problem, and with the most tender considerateness Jesus dealt with him in a way that spared his feelings and in a way that he could understand.

When it was completed, the people declared that he had done all things well. That is none other than the verdict of God upon his own creation in the very beginning (Genesis 1:31). When Jesus came, bringing healing to broken bodies and salvation to human souls, he had begun the work of creation all over again. In the beginning, everything had been good; human sin had spoiled it all; and now Jesus was bringing back the beauty of God to the world which human sin had rendered ugly.

COMPASSION AND CHALLENGE

Mark 8:1–10

> In those days, when there was again a great crowd, and when they had nothing to eat, Jesus called his disciples to him and said, 'My heart is moved with pity for the crowd, because they have stayed with me now for three days, and they have nothing to eat. If I send them away to their homes still fasting, they will faint on the road; and some of them have come from a long distance.' His disciples answered him, 'Where could anyone get

bread to satisfy them in a desert place like this?' He
asked them, 'How many loaves have you?' They said,
'Seven.' He ordered the crowd to sit down on the
ground. He took the seven loaves and gave thanks for
them and broke them, and gave them to his disciples to
set before the people. So they set them before the crowd,
and they had a few small fishes. So he blessed them and
told them to set them before them too. So they ate until
they were completely satisfied. They gathered up what
remained over of the broken pieces – seven baskets.
There were about 4,000 people there. So he sent them
away, and immediately he embarked on the boat with
his disciples and came to the district of Dalmanutha.

THERE are two things closely intertwined in this incident.

(1) There is the compassion of Jesus. Over and over again
we see Jesus moved with compassion. The most amazing
thing about him is his sheer considerateness. Now considerateness is a virtue which never forgets the details of life. Jesus
looked at the crowd; they had been with him for three days;
and he remembered that they had a long walk home. He whose
task it was to bring the splendour and the majesty of the truth
and love of God to men and women might have had a mind
above thinking of what was going to happen to his congregation on their walk home. But Jesus was not like that.
Confront Jesus with a lost soul or a tired body, and his first
instinct was to help.

It is all too true that the first instinct of too many people is
not to help. I met a man once at a conference and was
discussing with him the dangers of a certain stretch of road
on the way to the town where we were. 'Yes,' he said. 'It's a
right bad bit of road. I saw a crash on it as I drove here today.'
'Did you stop and help?' I asked. 'Not me,' he said, 'I wasn't
going to be held up by getting mixed up in a thing like that.'

It is human to want to avoid the trouble of giving help; it is divine to be moved with such compassion and pity that we are compelled to help.

(2) There is the challenge of Jesus. When Jesus had pity on the crowd and wished to give them something to eat, the disciples immediately pointed out the practical difficulty that they were in a desert place and that there was nowhere within miles where any food could be got. At once Jesus flashed the question back at them, 'What have *you* got with which you may help?' Compassion became a challenge. In effect Jesus was saying, 'Don't try to push the responsibility for helping onto someone else. Don't say that you would help if you had only something to give. Don't say that in these circumstances to help is impossible. Take what you have and give it and see what happens.'

One of the most joyous of all Jewish feasts is the Feast of Purim. It falls on 14th March and commemorates the deliverance of which the Book of Esther tells. Above all it is a time of giving gifts; and one of its regulations is that, no matter how poor people are, they must seek out someone poorer than themselves and give them a gift. Jesus has no time for the spirit which waits until all the circumstances are perfect before it thinks of helping. Jesus says, 'If you see someone in trouble, help him with what you have. You never know what you may do.'

There are two interesting things in the background of this story.

The first is this. This incident happened on the far side of the Sea of Galilee in the district called the Decapolis. Why did this tremendous crowd of 4,000 assemble? There is no doubt that the healing of the deaf man with the impediment in his speech would help to arouse interest and to collect the crowd.

But one commentator has made a most interesting
suggestion. In Mark 5:1–20, we have already read how Jesus
cured the Gerasene demoniac. That incident also happened
in the Decapolis. Its result was that they urged Jesus to go
away. But the cured demoniac wished to follow Jesus, and
Jesus sent him back to his own people to tell them what great
things the Lord had done for him. Is it just possible that part
of this great crowd was due to the missionary activity of the
healed demoniac? Have we got here a glimpse of what the
witness of one man can do for Christ? Were there people in
the crowd that day who came to Christ and found their souls
because a man had told them what Christ had done for him?
John Bunyan tells how he owed his conversion to the fact
that he heard three or four old women talking, as they sat in
the sun, 'about a new birth, the work of God in their hearts'.
They were talking of what God had done for them. It may
well be that there were many that day in that crowd in the
Decapolis who were there because they had heard a man
telling what Jesus Christ had done for him.

The second thing is this. It is odd that the word for *basket*
is different in this story from the word used in the similar
story in Mark 6. In Mark 6:44, the word for basket is *kophinos*,
which describes the basket in which Jews carried their food,
a basket narrow at the top and wider at the foot, and rather
like a water pot. The word used here is *sphuris*, which
describes a basket like a hamper; a *frail* is the technical term.
It was in that kind of basket that Paul was let down over the
wall of Damascus (Acts 9:25); and the word describes the
basket which the Gentiles used. This incident happened in
the Decapolis, which was on the far side of the lake and had
a large Gentile population. Is it possible that we are to see in
the feeding of the multitude in Mark 6 the coming of the
bread of God to the Jews, and in this incident the coming of

the bread of God to the Gentiles? When we put these two stories together, is there somewhere at the back of them the suggestion and the forecast and the symbol that Jesus came to satisfy the hunger of Jew and Gentile alike, that in him, in truth, was the God who opens his hand and satisfies the desire of every living thing?

THE BLINDNESS WHICH DESIRES A SIGN

Mark 8:11–13

> The Pharisees came out and began to ask him questions. They were looking for a sign from heaven, and they were trying to test him. He sighed in his spirit and said to them, 'Why does this generation look for a sign? This is the truth I tell you – no sign will be given to this generation.' He sent them away and he again embarked on the boat, and went away to the other side.

THE whole tendency of the age in which Jesus lived was to look for God in the abnormal. It was believed that when the Messiah came the most startling things would happen. Before we reach the end of this chapter, we shall examine more closely, and in detail, the kind of signs which were expected. We may note just now that when false Messiahs arose, as they frequently did, they lured the people to follow them by promising astonishing signs. They would promise, for instance, to cleave the waters of the Jordan in two and leave a pathway through it, or they would promise, with a word, to make the city walls fall down.

It was a sign like that that the Pharisees were demanding. They wished to see some shattering event blazing across the horizon, defying the laws of nature and astonishing everyone. To Jesus, such a demand was not due to the desire to see the hand of God; it was due to the fact that they were blind to his hand. To Jesus, the whole world was full of signs; the corn in the field, the leaven in the loaf, the scarlet anemones on the hillside all spoke to him of God. He did not think that God had to break in from outside the world; he knew that God was already in the world for anyone who had eyes to see. The sign of truly religious people is not that they come to church to find God but that they find God everywhere, not that they make a great deal of sacred places but that they sanctify common places.

That is what the poets knew and felt, and that is why they were poets. In 'Aurora Leigh', Elizabeth Barrett Browning wrote:

> Earth's crammed with heaven,
> And every common bush afire with God;
> But only he who sees, takes off his shoes,
> The rest sit round it and pluck blackberries.

Thomas Edward Brown wrote the poem 'My Garden':

> A garden is a lovesome thing, God wot!
>   Rose plot,
>   Fringed pool,
> Fern's grot –
>   The veriest school
>   Of peace: and yet the fool
> Contends that God is not –
> Not God! In gardens! when the eve is cool?
>   Nay, but I have a sign;
>   'Tis very sure God walks in mine.

And still another poet wrote:

> One asked a sign from God; and day by day
>   The sun arose in pearl; in scarlet set;

Each night the stars appeared in bright array;
  Each morn the thirsty grass with dew was wet;
  The corn failed not its harvest, nor the vine –
  And yet he saw no sign!

For anyone who has eyes to see and a heart to understand, the daily miracle of night and day and the daily splendour of all common things are sign enough from God.

THE FAILURE TO LEARN FROM EXPERIENCE

Mark 8:14–21

They had forgotten to bring loaves, and they had only one loaf with them in the boat. Jesus enjoined them, 'Look to it! Beware of the evil influence of the Pharisees and of the evil influence of Herod!' They kept discussing the situation among themselves, and saying, 'We have no loaves.' Jesus knew what they were saying. 'Why', he said, 'do you keep talking about the fact that you have no loaves? Do you not yet see and understand? Is your mind completely obtuse? Do you not see although you have eyes? Do you not hear although you have ears? Do you not remember? When I broke the five loaves and gave them to the 5,000 how many basketsful of broken pieces did you take up?' 'Twelve,' they said to him. 'When I broke the seven loaves among the 4,000 how many basketsful of broken pieces did you take up?' 'Seven,' they said to him. So he said to them, 'Do you still not understand?'

This passage sheds a very vivid light on the minds of the disciples. They were crossing over to the other side of the Sea of Galilee, and they had forgotten to bring bread with them. We will best get the meaning of this passage if we connect it closely with what goes before. Jesus was thinking of the demand of the Pharisees for a sign and also thinking of Herod's terrified reaction to himself. 'Beware', he said, to translate it literally, 'of the leaven of the Pharisees and the leaven of Herod.' To a Jew, leaven was the symbol of evil. Leaven was a piece of dough kept over from a previous baking and fermented. To a Jew, fermentation was identified with putrefaction, and therefore leaven stood for evil.

Sometimes Jews used the word *leaven* much as we would use the term *original sin*, or the natural evil of human nature. Rabbi Alexander said, 'It is revealed before thee that our will is to do thy will. And what hinders? The leaven that is in the dough and slavery to the kingdoms of the world. May it be thy will to deliver us from their hand.' It was, so to speak, the taint of human nature, original sin, the corrupting leaven which kept human beings from doing the will of God. So when Jesus said this, he was saying, 'Be on your guard against the evil influence of the Pharisees and of Herod. Don't you go the same way that the Pharisees and Herod have already gone.'

What is the point? What possible connection is there between the Pharisees and Herod? The Pharisees had just asked for a sign. For a Jew – we shall see this more fully shortly – nothing was easier than to think of the Messiah in terms of wonders and conquests and miraculous happenings and nationalistic triumphs and political supremacy. Herod had tried to build up happiness through the gaining of power and wealth and influence and prestige. In one sense, for both the Pharisees and Herod the kingdom of God was an earthly kingdom; it was based on earthly power and greatness, and on the victories that force could win. It was as if Jesus by this detached hint was already preparing the disciples for something very soon to come. It was as if he was saying, 'Maybe soon it will dawn on you that I am God's Anointed One, the Messiah. When that thought does come, don't think in terms of earthly power and glory as the Pharisees and Herod do.' Of the true meaning, at the moment he said nothing. That grim revelation was still to come.

In point of fact, this hint of Jesus passed clean over the disciples' heads. They could think of nothing but the fact that they had forgotten to bring loaves, and that, unless something happened, they would go hungry. Jesus saw their preoccupation with bread. It may well be that he asked his questions not with anger, but with a smile, like one who tries to lead a slow child to see a self-evident truth. He reminded them that twice he had satisfied the hunger of huge crowds with food enough and to spare. It is as if he said, 'Why all the worry? Don't you remember what happened before? Hasn't experience taught you that you don't need to worry about things like that if you are with me?'

The odd fact is that we learn only half the lessons of experience. Too often experience fills us with pessimism, teaches us what we cannot do, teaches us to view life with a kind of resigned hopelessness. But there are other experiences. Sorrow came – and we came through it still erect. Temptation came – and somehow we did not fall. Illness took us – and somehow we recovered. A problem seemed insoluble – and somehow it was solved. We were at our wits' end – and somehow we went on. We reached the breaking point – and somehow we did not break. We, too, are blind. If we would only read the lessons of experience aright, it would teach us not the pessimism of the things that cannot be, but the hope which stands amazed that God has brought us thus far in safety and in certainty, and the confidence that God can bring us through anything that may happen.

A BLIND MAN LEARNS TO SEE

Mark 8:22–6

> They came to Bethsaida; and they brought a blind man
> to him and asked him to touch him. He took the blind
> man's hand and took him outside the village. He spat
> into his eyes and laid his hands on him, and asked him,
> 'Do you see anything?' He looked up and said, 'I see
> men, but I see them walking looking like trees.' Again
> he laid his hands on his eyes. He gazed intently, and his
> sight was restored and he saw everything clearly. He
> sent him away to his home. 'Do not', he said, 'even
> enter into the village.'

BLINDNESS was, and still is, one of the great curses of the
middle east. It was caused partly by ophthalmia and partly
by the pitiless glare of the sun. It was greatly aggravated by
the fact that people knew nothing of hygiene and of cleanliness. It was common to see a person with matter-encrusted
eyes on which the flies persistently settled. Naturally this
carried the infection far and wide, and blindness was a
scourge.

Only Mark tells us this story, and yet there are certain
extremely interesting things in it.

(1) Again we see the unique considerateness of Jesus. He
took the blind man out of the crowd and out of the village
that he might be alone with him. Why? Think about it.
This man was blind and apparently had been born blind. If
he had been suddenly given back his sight in the middle of a
crowd, there would have flashed upon his newly seeing eyes
hundreds of people and things, and dazzling colours, so that
he would have been completely bewildered. Jesus knew it
would be far better if he could be taken to a place where the
thrill of seeing would break less suddenly upon him.

All great doctors and great teachers have one outstanding characteristic. Great doctors are able to enter into the very minds and hearts of their patients; they understand their fears and their hopes; they literally sympathize – suffer – with them. Great teachers enter into the very minds of their pupils. They see their problems, their difficulties, their stumbling-blocks. That is why Jesus was so supremely great. He could enter into the minds and hearts of the people whom he sought to help. He had the gift of considerateness, because he could think with their thoughts and feel with their feelings. God grant to us this Christlike gift.

(2) Jesus used methods that the man could understand. The ancient world believed in the healing power of spittle. The belief is not so strange when we remember that it is a first instinct to put a cut or burned finger into our mouth to ease the pain. Of course the blind man knew of this, and Jesus used a method of curing him which he could understand. Jesus was wise. He did not begin with words and methods which were far above the heads of ordinary people. He spoke to them and acted on them in a way that their minds could grasp and understand. There have been times when unintelligibility has been accounted a virtue and a sign of greatness. Jesus had the still greater greatness – the greatness which could be easily grasped.

(3) In one thing, this miracle is unique – it is the only miracle which can be said to have happened gradually. Usually Jesus' miracles happened suddenly and completely. In this miracle, the blind man's sight came back in stages.

There is symbolic truth here. No one ever sees all God's truth all at once. One of the dangers of a certain type of evangelism is that it encourages the idea that taking a personal decision for Christ makes someone a full-grown Christian. One of the dangers of Church membership is that it can be presented in such a way as to imply that when a person becomes a pledged member of the Church he or she has come to the end of the road. So far from that being the case, the decision and the pledge of membership are the beginning of the road. They are the discovery of the riches of Christ which are inexhaustible, and if any of us lived 100, or 1,000, or 1,000,000 years, we would still have to go on growing in grace, and learning more and more about the infinite wonder and beauty of Jesus Christ. F. W. H. Myers, in his poem 'Saint Paul', makes Paul say:

> Let no man think that sudden in a minute
>   All is accomplished and the work is done –
> Though with thine earliest dawn thou shouldst begin it
>   Scarce were it ended in thy setting sun.

It is gloriously true that sudden conversion is a gracious possibility, but it is equally true that every day we should be reconverted. With all God's grace and glory before us, we can go on learning for a lifetime and still need eternity to know as we are known.

THE GREAT DISCOVERY

Mark 8:27-30

> Jesus and his disciples went away to the villages of Caesarea Philippi. On the road he asked his disciples a question. 'Who', he said to them, 'do men say that I am?' They said to him, 'Some say, John the Baptizer; others say, Elijah; others, one of the prophets.' He asked them, 'You – who do you say that I am?' Peter answered him, 'You are God's Anointed One.' And he insisted that they should tell no man about him.

CAESAREA PHILIPPI was outside Galilee altogether. It was not
in the territory of Herod, but in the territory of Philip. It was
a town with an amazing history. In the oldest days it was
called *Balinas*, for it had once been a great centre of the
worship of Baal. To this day it is called *Banias*, which is a
form of *Panias*. It is so called because up on the hillside
there was a cavern which was said to be the birthplace of the
Greek god Pan, the god of nature. From a cave in the hillside
gushed forth a stream which was held to be the source of the
River Jordan. Further up on the hillside rose a gleaming
temple of white marble which Philip had built to the godhead
of Caesar, the Roman emperor, the ruler of the world, who
was regarded as a god.

It is an amazing thing that it was here of all places that
Peter saw in a homeless Galilaean carpenter the Son of God.
The ancient religion of Palestine was in the air, and the
memories of Baal clustered around. The gods of classical
Greece brooded over the place, and no doubt people heard
the pipes of Pan and caught a glimpse of the woodland
nymphs. The Jordan would bring back to memory episode
after episode in the history of Israel and the conquest of the
land. And clear in the eastern sun gleamed and glinted the
marble of the holy place which reminded everyone that Caesar
was a god. There, of all places, as it were against the
background of all religions and all history, Peter discovered
that a wandering teacher from Nazareth, who was heading
for a cross, was the Son of God. There is hardly anything in
all the gospel story which shows the sheer force of the
personality of Jesus as does this incident. It comes in the
very middle of Mark's gospel and it does so by design, for it
comes at the gospel's peak moment. In one way at least, this
moment was the crisis of Jesus' life. Whatever his disciples
might be thinking, he knew for certain that ahead lay an

inescapable cross. Things could not go on much longer. The opposition was gathering itself to strike. The problem confronting Jesus was this – had he had any effect at all? Had he achieved anything? Or, to put it another way, had anyone discovered who he really was? If he had lived and taught and moved among the people and no one had glimpsed God in him, then all his work had gone for nothing. There was only one way he could leave a message behind, and that was to write it on someone's heart.

So, in this moment, Jesus put all things to the test. He asked his disciples what people were saying about him, and he heard from them the popular rumours and reports. Then came a breathless silence, and he put the question which meant so much, 'Who do *you* say that I am?' And suddenly Peter realized what he had always known deep down in his heart. This was the Messiah, the Christ, the Anointed One, the Son of God. And with that answer, Jesus knew that he had not failed.

Now we come to a question which has been half-put and half-answered more than once before, but which now must be answered in detail or the whole gospel story is not fully intelligible. No sooner had Peter made this discovery than Jesus told him he must tell no one of it. Why? Because, first and foremost, Jesus had to teach Peter and the others what Messiahship really meant. To understand the task that Jesus had in hand and to understand the real meaning of this necessity, we have to inquire at some length what the messianic ideas of the time of Jesus really were.

The Jewish Ideas of the Messiah

Throughout all their existence, the Jews never forgot that they were in a very special sense God's chosen people. Because of that, they naturally looked to a very special place in the world. In the early days, they looked forward to achieving that position by what we might call natural means. They always regarded the greatest days in their history as the days of David; and they dreamed of a day when there would arise another king of David's line, a king who would make them great in righteousness and in power (Isaiah 9:7, 11:1; Jeremiah 22:4, 23:5, 30:9).

But as time went on, it came to be pitilessly clear that this dreamed-of greatness would never be achieved by natural means. The ten tribes were carried off to Assyria and lost forever. The Babylonians conquered Jerusalem and carried the Jews away captive. Then came the Persians as their masters; then the Greeks; then the Romans. So far from knowing anything like dominion, for centuries the Jews never even knew what it was to be completely free and independent.

So another line of thought grew up. It is true that the idea of a great king of David's line never entirely vanished and was always intertwined in some way with their thought; but more and more they began to dream of a day when God would intervene in history and achieve by supernatural means that which natural means could never achieve. They looked for divine power to do what human power was helpless to do.

In between the Testaments were written a whole flood of books which were dreams and forecasts of this new age and the intervention of God. As a class, they are called *Apocalypses*. The word literally means *unveilings*. These books were meant to be unveilings of the future. It is to them that we must turn to find out what the Jews believed in the time of Jesus about the Messiah and the work of the Messiah and the new age. It is against their dreams that we must set the dream of Jesus.

In these books, certain basic ideas occur. We follow here the classification of these ideas given by Emil Schürer, who wrote *A History of the Jewish People in the Time of Jesus Christ.*

(1) Before the Messiah came, there would be a time of terrible tribulation. There would be a messianic travail. It would be the birth-pangs of a new age. Every conceivable terror would burst upon the world; every standard of honour and decency would be torn down; the world would become a physical and moral chaos.

> And honour shall be turned into shame,
> And strength humiliated into contempt,
> And probity destroyed,
> And beauty shall become ugliness . . .
> And envy shall rise in those who had not thought
>   aught of themselves,
> And passion shall seize him that is peaceful,
> And many shall be stirred up in anger to injure many,
> And they shall rouse up armies in order to shed blood,
> And in the end they shall perish together with them.

> (2 Baruch 50:35f.)

There would be 'earthquakes, tumult of peoples, intrigues of nations, waverings of leaders, confusion of princes' (4 Ezra [2 Esdras] 9:3).

> From heaven shall fall fiery swords down to the earth.
> Lights shall come, bright and great, flashing into the
> midst of men; and earth, the universal mother, shall
> shake in these days at the hand of the Eternal. And the
> fishes of the sea and the beasts of the earth and the
> countless tribes of flying things and all the souls of men
> and every sea shall shudder at the presence of the Eternal
> and there shall be panic. And the towering mountain
> peaks and the hills of the giants he shall rend, and the
> murky abyss shall be visible to all. And the high ravines
> in the lofty mountains shall be full of dead bodies and

> rocks shall flow with blood and each torrent shall flood
> the plain . . . And God shall judge all with war and
> sword, and there shall be brimstone from heaven, yea
> stones and rain and hail incessant and grievous. And
> death shall be upon the four-footed beasts . . . Yea the
> land itself shall drink of the blood of the perishing and
> beasts shall eat their fill of flesh. (Sibylline Oracles
> 3:669ff.)

The Mishnah enumerates as signs that the coming of the
Messiah is near:

> That arrogance increases, ambition shoots up, that the
> vine yields fruit yet wine is dear. The government turns
> to heresy. There is no instruction. The synagogue is
> devoted to lewdness. Galilee is destroyed, Gablan laid
> waste. The inhabitants of a district go from city to city
> without finding compassion. The wisdom of the learned
> is hated, the godly despised, truth is absent. Boys insult
> old men, old men stand in the presence of children. The
> son depreciates the father, the daughter rebels against
> the mother, the daughter-in-law against the mother-in-
> law. A man's enemies are his house-fellows.

The time which preceded the coming of the Messiah was
to be a time when the world was torn in pieces and every
bond relaxed. The physical and the moral order would
collapse.

(2) Into this chaos there would come Elijah as the forerunner and herald of the Messiah. He was to heal the breaches
and bring order into the chaos to prepare the way for the
Messiah. In particular he was to mend disputes. In fact the
Jewish oral law laid it down that money and property whose
ownership was disputed, or anything found whose owner was
unknown, must wait 'till Elijah comes'. When Elijah came,
the Messiah would not be far behind.

226

(3) Then there would enter the Messiah. The word *Messiah* and the word *Christ* mean the same thing. *Messiah* is the Hebrew and *Christ* is the Greek for the Anointed One. A king was made king by anointing, and the Messiah was God's anointed king. It is important to remember that *Christ* is not a *name*; it is a *title*. Sometimes the Messiah was thought of as a king of David's line, but more often he was thought of as a great, superhuman figure crashing into history to remake the world and in the end to vindicate God's people.

(4) The nations would ally themselves and gather themselves together against the champion of God.

> The kings of the nations shall throw themselves against this land bringing retribution on themselves. They shall seek to ravage the shrine of the mighty God and of the noblest men whensoever they come to the land. In a ring round the city the accursed kings shall place each one his throne with his infidel people by him. And then with a mighty voice God shall speak unto all the undisciplined, empty-minded people and judgment shall come upon them from the mighty God, and all shall perish at the hand of the Eternal. (Sibylline Oracles 3:663-72)

> Then when all the nations hear his voice, all the nations shall leave their own lands and the warfare that they have against one another; and an innumerable multitude shall be gathered together, as you saw, wishing to come and conquer him. (4 Ezra [2 Esdras] 13:33-5)

(5) The result would be the total destruction of these hostile powers. The Jewish philosopher Philo said that the Messiah would 'take the field and make war and destroy great and populous nations'.

He will denounce them for their ungodliness, and for their wickedness, and will display before them their contemptuous dealings ... and when he has reproved them, then he will destroy them.

(4 Ezra [2 Esdras] 12:32–3)

And it shall come to pass in those days that none shall
    be saved,
Either by gold or by silver,
And none shall be able to escape.
And there shall be no iron for war,
Nor shall one clothe oneself with a breastplate.
Bronze shall be of no service,
And tin shall not be esteemed,
And lead shall not be desired.
And all things shall be destroyed from the surface of
    the earth.

(1 Enoch 52:7–9)

The Messiah will be the most destructive conqueror in history, smashing his enemies into utter extinction.

(6) There would follow the renovation of Jerusalem. Sometimes this was thought of as the purification of the existing city. More often it was thought of as the coming down of the new Jerusalem from heaven. The old house was to be folded up and carried away, and in the new one, 'All the pillars were new and the ornaments larger than those of the first' (1 Enoch 90:28).

(7) The Jews who were dispersed all over the world would be gathered into the city of the new Jerusalem. To this day, the Jewish daily prayer includes the petition, 'Lift up a banner to gather our dispersed and assemble us from the four ends of the earth.' The eleventh of the Psalms of Solomon has a noble picture of that return.

Blow ye in Zion on the trumpet to summon the saints,
　Cause ye to be heard in Jerusalem the voice of him
　　that bringeth good tidings;
　For God hath had pity on Israel in visiting them.
Stand on the height, O Jerusalem, and behold thy
　　children,
　From the East and the West, gathered together by
　　the Lord;
From the North they come in the gladness of their
　　God,
　From the isles afar off God hath gathered them.
High mountains hath he abased into a plain for them;
　The hills fled at their entrance.
The woods gave them shelter as they passed by;
　Every sweet-smelling tree God caused to spring up
　　for them,
　That Israel might pass by in the visitation of the
　　glory of their God.
Put on, O Jerusalem, thy glorious garments;
　Make ready thy holy robe;
　For God hath spoken good for Israel forever and
　　ever,
Let the Lord do what he hath spoken concerning Israel
　　and Jerusalem;
　Let the Lord raise up Israel by his glorious name.
The mercy of the Lord be upon Israel forever and ever.

It can easily be seen how Jewish this new world was to be.
The nationalistic element is dominant all the time.

(8) Palestine would be the centre of the world and the rest
of the world subject to it. All the nations would be subdued.
Sometimes it was thought of as a peaceful subjugation.

And all the isles and the cities shall say, How doth the
Eternal love those men! For all things work in sympathy
with them and help them . . . Come let us all fall upon

> the earth and supplicate the eternal King, the mighty,
> everlasting God. Let us make procession to his Temple,
> for he is the sole Potentate. (Sibylline Oracles 3:710ff.)

More often, the fate of the Gentiles was utter destruction at which Israel would exult and rejoice.

> And he will appear to punish the Gentiles,
> And he will destroy all their idols.
> Then, thou, O Israel, shalt be happy.
> And thou shalt mount upon the necks and the wings of
>   the eagle [that is, Rome, the eagle, is to be destroyed]
> And they shall be ended and God will exalt thee.
>
>   . . .
>
> And thou shalt look from on high
> And see thine enemies in Gehenna,
> And thou shalt recognize them and rejoice.
>
>   (Assumption of Moses 10:7–10)

It was a grim picture. Israel would rejoice to see her enemies broken and in hell. Even the dead Israelites were to be raised up to share in the new world.

(9) Finally, there would come the new age of peace and goodness which would last forever.

These are the messianic ideas which were in people's minds when Jesus came. They were violent, nationalistic, destructive, vengeful. True, they ended in the perfect reign of God, but they came to it through a bath of blood and a career of conquest. Think of Jesus set against a background like that. No wonder he had to re-educate his disciples in the meaning of Messiahship; and no wonder he was crucified in the end as a heretic. There was no room for a cross and there was little room for suffering love in a picture like that.

THE TEMPTER SPEAKS IN THE VOICE
OF A FRIEND

Mark 8:31-3

> He began to teach them that it was necessary that the
> Son of Man should suffer many things, and should be
> rejected by the elders and chief priests and scribes, and
> be killed and rise again after three days. He kept telling
> them this plainly. And Peter caught him and began to
> rebuke him. He turned round; he looked at his disciples;
> and he rebuked Peter. 'Get behind me, Satan,' he said.
> 'These are not God's thoughts but men's.'

IT is against the background of what we have just seen of the
common conception of the Messiah that we must read this.
When Jesus connected Messiahship with suffering and death,
he was making statements that were to the disciples both
incredible and incomprehensible. All their lives they had
thought of the Messiah in terms of irresistible conquest, and
they were now being presented with an idea which staggered
them. That is why Peter protested so violently. To him the
whole thing was impossible.

Why did Jesus rebuke Peter so sternly? Because he was
putting into words the very temptations which were assailing
Jesus. Jesus did not want to die. He knew that he had powers
which he could use for conquest. At this moment, he was
refighting the battle of temptations in the wilderness. This
was the devil tempting him again to fall down and worship
him, to take his way instead of God's way.

It is a strange thing, and sometimes a terrible thing, that
the tempter sometimes speaks to us in the voice of a
well-meaning friend. We may have decided on a course which
is the right course but which will inevitably bring trouble,

loss, unpopularity, sacrifice. And some well-meaning friend tries with the best intentions in the world to stop us. I knew a man who decided to take a course which would almost inevitably land him in trouble. A friend came to him and tried to dissuade him. 'Remember', said the friend, 'that you have a wife and a family. You can't do this.' It is quite possible for our friends to love us so much that they want us to avoid trouble and to play safe.

In 'Gareth and Lynette', Tennyson tells the story of the youngest son of Lot and Bellicent. He has seen the vision and he wishes to become one of Arthur's knights. Bellicent, his mother, does not wish to let him go.

'Hast thou no pity on my loneliness?' she asks. His father, Lot, is old and 'lies like a log and all but smouldered out'. Both his brothers are already at Arthur's court. 'Stay, my best son,' she says, 'ye are yet more boy than man.' If he stays she will arrange the hunt to keep him happy in the chase and find some princess to be his bride. The boy has had the vision, and one by one the mother, who loves him dearly, produces reasons, excellent reasons, why he should stay at home. Someone who loves him speaks with the tempter's voice, all unaware that she is doing it. But Gareth answers,

> O Mother,
> How can ye keep me tethered to you – Shame.
> Man am I grown, a man's work must I do.
> Follow the deer? Follow the Christ, the King,
> Live pure, speak true, right wrong, follow the King –
> Else, wherefore born?

So Gareth went when the vision called.

The tempter can make no more terrible attack than in the voice of those who love us and who think they seek only our good. That is what happened to Jesus that day; that is why he

answered so sternly. Not even the pleading voice of love must
silence for us the imperious voice of God.

THE WAY OF THE DISCIPLE

Mark 8:34–5

> He called the crowd to him, together with his disciples,
> and said to them, 'If anyone wishes to come after me,
> let him deny himself, and let him take up his cross, and
> let him follow me.'

THIS part of Mark's gospel is so near the heart and centre of
the Christian faith that we must take it almost sentence by
sentence. If each day we could go out with only one of these
sentences locked in our hearts and dominating our lives, it
would be far more than enough to be going on with.

Two things stand out here even at first sight.

(1) There is the almost startling honesty of Jesus. No one
could ever say that they were induced to follow Jesus by
false pretences. Jesus never tried to bribe anyone by the offer
of an easy way. He did not offer peace; he offered glory. To
tell the disciples they must be ready to take up a cross was to
tell them they must be ready to be regarded as criminals and
to die.

The honesty of great leaders has always been one of their
characteristics. In the days of the Second World War, when
Sir Winston Churchill took over the leadership of the country,
all that he offered was 'blood, toil, tears and sweat'. Garibaldi,
the great Italian patriot, appealed for recruits in these terms:
'I offer neither pay, nor quarters, nor provisions; I offer
hunger, thirst, forced marches, battles and death. Let him who
loves his country in his heart, and not with his lips only, follow
me.' 'Soldiers, all our efforts against superior forces have

been unavailing. I have nothing to offer you but hunger and
thirst, hardship and death; but I call on all who love their
country to join with me.'

Jesus never sought to lure anyone to him by the offer of
an easy way; he sought to challenge men and women, to
waken the boldness and moral courage in their souls, by the
offer of a way than which none could be higher and harder.
He came not to make life easy but to challenge people to
greatness.

(2) There is the fact that Jesus never called on anyone to
do or face anything which he was not prepared to do and face
himself. That indeed is the characteristic of the leader whom
people will follow.

When Alexander the Great set out in pursuit of Darius,
he made one of the wonder marches of history. In eleven
days he marched his men more than 400 miles. They were
very nearly giving up, mainly because of thirst, for there
was no water. Plutarch relates the story. 'While they were in
this distress, it happened that some Macedonians who had
fetched water in skins upon their mules from a river they had
found out came about noon to the place where Alexander
was, and seeing him almost choked with thirst, presently
filled a helmet and offered it to him. He asked them to whom
they were carrying the water; they told him to their children,
adding, that if his life were but saved, it was no matter for
them, they should be well enough able to repair that loss,
though they all perished. Then he took the helmet into his
hands, and looking round about, when he saw all those
who were near him stretching their heads out and looking
earnestly after the drink, he returned it again with thanks
without tasting a drop of it. "For," he said, "if I alone should
drink, the rest would be out of heart." The soldiers no
sooner took notice of his temperance and magnanimity upon

this occasion, but they, one and all, cried out to him to lead them forward boldly, and began whipping on their horses. For while they had such a king they said they defied both weariness and thirst, and looked upon themselves to be little less than immortal.' It was easy to follow a leader who never demanded from his men what he would not endure himself.

There was a famous Roman general, Quintus Fabius Cunctator. He was discussing with his staff how to take a difficult position. Someone suggested a certain course of action. 'It will only cost the lives of a few men,' this counsellor said. Fabius looked at him. 'Are you', he said, 'willing to be one of the few?'

Jesus was not the kind of leader who sat remote and played with people's lives like expendable pawns. What he demanded that they should face, he, too, was ready to face. Jesus had a right to call on us to take up a cross, for he himself first bore one.

(3) Jesus said of those who would be his disciples, 'Let them deny themselves.' We will understand the meaning of this demand best if we take it very simply and literally. 'Let them say no to self.' If we would follow Jesus Christ we must say no to ourselves and yes to Christ. We must say no to our own natural love of ease and comfort. We must say no to every course of action based on self-seeking and self-will. We must say no to the instincts and the desires which prompt us to touch and taste and handle the forbidden things. We must unhesitatingly say yes to the voice and the command of Jesus Christ. We must be able to say with Paul, 'It is no longer I who live, but it is Christ who lives in me' (Galatians 2:20). We live no longer to follow our own will, but to follow the will of Christ, and in that service we find perfect freedom.

FINDING LIFE BY LOSING LIFE

Mark 8:36

> Whoever seeks to save his life shall lose it; and whoever
> loses his life for my sake and for the sake of the gospel
> shall save it.

THERE are certain things which are lost by being kept and
saved by being used. Any individual talent is like that. If it is
used, it will develop into something still greater. If someone
refuses to use it, in the end that talent will be lost. Supremely
so, life is like that.

History is full of examples of men and women who, by
throwing away their lives, gained life eternal. Late in the fourth
century, there was in the east a monk called Telemachus. He
had determined to leave the world and to live all alone in
prayer and meditation and fasting, and so to save his soul. In
his lonely life he sought nothing but contact with God. But
somehow he felt there was something wrong. One day as he
rose from his knees, it suddenly dawned upon him that his
life was based not on a self-less but on a selfish love of God.
It came to him that if he was to serve God he must serve others,
that the desert was no place for a Christian to live, that the
cities were full of sin and therefore full of need.

He determined to bid farewell to the desert and set out to
the greatest city in the world, Rome, at the other side of the
world. He begged his way across lands and seas. By this time,
Rome was officially Christian. He arrived at a time when
Stilicho, the Roman general, had gained a mighty victory
over the Goths. To Stilicho was granted a Roman triumph.
There was this difference from the old days – now it was to
the Christian churches the crowds poured and not to the pagan
temples. There were the processions and the celebrations, and

Stilicho rode in triumph through the streets, with the young Emperor Honorius by his side.

But one thing had lingered on into Christian Rome. There was still the arena; there were still the gladiatorial games. Christians were no longer thrown to the lions; but still those captured in war had to fight and kill each other to make a Roman holiday for the masses. Still the spectators roared with blood lust as the gladiators fought.

Telemachus found his way to the arena. There were 80,000 people there. The chariot races were ending; and there was a tenseness in the crowd as the gladiators prepared to fight. Into the arena they came with their greeting, 'Hail, Caesar! We who are about to die salute you!' The fight was on and Telemachus was appalled. Men for whom Christ had died were killing each other to amuse an allegedly Christian populace. He leapt the barrier. He was in between the gladiators, and for a moment they stopped. 'Let the games go on,' roared the crowd. They pushed the old man aside; he was still in his hermit's robes. Again he came between them. The crowd began to hurl stones at him; they urged the gladiators to kill him and get him out of the way. The commander of the games gave an order; a gladiator's sword rose and flashed; and Telemachus lay dead.

Immediately the crowd were silent. They were suddenly shocked that a holy man should have been killed in such a way. Suddenly there was a mass realization of what this killing really was. The games ended abruptly that day – and they never began again. Telemachus, by dying, had ended them. As the author of *The Decline and Fall of the Roman Empire*, Edward Gibbon, said of him, 'His death was more useful to mankind than his life.' By losing his life, he had done more than he could ever have done by living it out in lonely devotion in the desert.

God gave us life to spend and not to keep. If we live carefully, always thinking first of our own profit, ease, comfort and security, if our sole aim is to make life as long and as trouble-free as possible, if we will make no effort except for ourselves, we are losing life all the time. But if we spend life for others, if we forget health and time and wealth and comfort in our desire to do something for Jesus and for those for whom Jesus died, we are winning life all the time.

What would have happened to the world if doctors and scientists and inventors had not been prepared to risk experiments often on their own bodies? What would have happened to life if everyone had wished for nothing but to remain comfortably at home, and there had been no such person as an explorer or a pioneer? What would happen if every mother refused to take the risk of bearing a child? What would happen if everyone spent all they had upon themselves?

The very essence of life is in risking life and spending life, not in saving it and hoarding it. True, it is the way of weariness, of exhaustion, of giving to the uttermost – but it is better any day to burn out than to rust out, for that is the way to happiness and the way to God.

THE SUPREME VALUE IN LIFE

Mark 8:37

> What profit is it for a man to gain the whole world and
> to forfeit his life? For what is a man to give in exchange
> for his life?

IT is quite possible for a person in one sense to make a huge success of life and in another sense to be living a life that is not worth living. The real question Jesus asks is, 'Where do you put your values in life?' It is possible to put our values on the wrong things and to discover it too late.

(1) It is possible to sacrifice honour for profit. We may desire material things and not be over-particular how we get them. The world is full of temptations towards profitable dishonesty. The novelist George Macdonald tells in one of his books about a draper who always used his thumb to make the measure just a little short. 'He took from his soul', he said, 'and put it in his siller-bag.' The real question, the question which sooner or later will have to be answered, is, 'How does life's balance sheet look in the sight of God?' God is the auditor whom, in the end, we all must face.

(2) It is possible to sacrifice principle for popularity. It may happen that those who are easy-going, agreeable and pliable will save themselves a lot of trouble. It may happen that those who are inflexibly devoted to principle will find themselves disliked. Shakespeare paints the picture of Wolsey, the great Cardinal, who served Henry VIII with all the ingenuity and wit he possessed.

> Had I but serv'd my God with half the zeal
> I serv'd my king, he would not in mine age
> Have left me naked to mine enemies.

The real question, the question that we all in the end will have to face, is not, 'What did others think of this?' but, 'What does God think of it?' It is not the verdict of public opinion but the verdict of God that settles destiny.

(3) It is possible to sacrifice the lasting things for the cheap things. It is always easier to have a cheap success. An author may sacrifice that which would be really great for the cheap success of a moment. A musician may produce ephemeral trifles when something real and lasting might have been produced. We might choose a job which will bring us more

money and more comfort, and turn our backs on one where we could render more service to others. It is all too easy to spend life in little things and let the big things go. Some people might prefer a life of pleasure and of so-called freedom to the service of a home and the upbringing of a family.

But life has a way of revealing the true values and condemning the false as the years pass on. A cheap thing never lasts.

(4) We may sum it all up by saying that it is possible to sacrifice eternity for the moment. We would be saved from all kinds of mistakes if we always looked at things in the light of eternity. Many things are pleasant for the moment but ruinous in the long run. The test of eternity, the test of seeking to see things as God sees them, is of all tests the most real.

Those who see things as God sees them will never spend their lives on the things that are literally soul-destroying.

WHEN THE KING COMES INTO HIS OWN

Mark 8:38–9:1

> 'Whoever is ashamed of me and of my words in this adulterous and sinful generation, of him also shall the Son of Man be ashamed when he comes in the glory of his Father with the holy angels.' And he used to say to them, 'This is the truth I tell you – there are some of those who are standing here who will not taste of death until they shall see the kingdom of God coming with power.'

ONE thing leaps out from this passage – the confidence of Jesus. He has just been speaking of his death; he has no doubt that the cross stands ahead of him; but nonetheless he is absolutely sure that in the end there will be triumph.

The first part of the passage states a simple truth. When the king comes into his kingdom, he will be loyal to those who have been loyal to him. No one can expect to dodge all the trouble of some great undertaking and then reap all the benefit of it. No one can expect to refuse service in some campaign and then share in the decorations when it is brought to a successful conclusion. Jesus is saying, 'In a difficult and hostile world, Christianity is up against it these days. If you are ashamed under such conditions to show that you are a Christian, if you are afraid to show what side you are on, you cannot expect to gain a place of honour when the kingdom comes.'

The last part of this passage has caused much serious thought. Jesus says that many who are standing there will not die until they see the kingdom coming with power. What worries some people is that they take this as a reference to the second coming; but if it is, Jesus was mistaken, because he did *not* return in power and glory in the lifetime of those who were there.

But this is not a reference to the second coming at all. Consider the situation. At that moment, Jesus had only once been outside Palestine, and on that occasion he was just over the border in Tyre and Sidon. Only a very few people in a very small country had ever heard of him. Palestine was only about 120 miles from north to south and about 40 miles from east to west; its total population was 4,000,000 or thereby. To speak in terms of world conquest when he had scarcely ever been outside such a small country was strange. To make matters worse, even in that small country, he had so provoked the enmity of the orthodox leaders and of those in whose hands lay power that it was quite certain that he could hope for nothing other than death as a heretic and an outlaw. In face of a situation like that, there must have been many who felt despairingly that Christianity had no possible future, that in a short time it would be wiped out completely and eliminated from the world. Humanly speaking, these pessimists were right.

Now consider what did happen. Scarcely more than thirty years later, Christianity had swept through Asia Minor; Antioch had become a great Christian church. It had penetrated to Egypt; the Christians were strong in Alexandria. It had crossed the sea and come to Rome and swept through Greece. Christianity had spread like an unstoppable tide throughout the world. It was astonishingly true that in the lifetime of many there, against all expectations, Christianity had come with power. So far from being mistaken, Jesus was absolutely right.

The amazing thing is that Jesus never knew despair. In face of the dullness of human minds, in face of the opposition, in face of crucifixion and of death, he never doubted his final triumph – because he never doubted God. He was always certain that what human beings find impossible is completely possible with him.

THE GLORY OF THE MOUNTAIN TOP

Mark 9:2–8

Six days after, Jesus took Peter and James and John along with him and brought them up into a high mountain, all by themselves, alone. And he was transfigured in their presence. His clothes became radiant, exceedingly white, such that no fuller on earth could have made them so white. And Elijah and Moses appeared to them, and they were talking with Jesus. Peter said to Jesus. 'Teacher, it is good for us to be

here. So let us make three booths, one for you, and one
for Moses and one for Elijah.' He said this because he
did not know what he was saying, for they were awe-
struck. And there came a cloud overshadowing them.
And there came a voice from the cloud, 'This is my
beloved Son. Hear Him!' And immediately, when they
had looked round, they saw no one any more except
Jesus alone with them.

WE are face to face with an incident in the life of Jesus that is
cloaked in mystery. We can only try to understand. Mark says
that this happened six days after the incidents near Caesarea
Philippi. Luke says that it happened eight days afterwards.
There is no discrepancy here. They both mean what we might
express by saying, 'about a week afterwards'. Both the eastern
and the western Churches hold their remembrance of the
transfiguration on 6th August. It does not matter whether or
not that is the actual date, but it is a time we do well to
remember.

Tradition says that the transfiguration took place on the
top of Mount Tabor. The eastern Church actually calls the
Festival of the Transfiguration the *Taborion*. It may be that
the choice is based on the mention of Mount Tabor in Psalm
89:12, but it is unfortunate. Tabor is in the *south* of Galilee
and Caesarea Philippi is away to the north. Tabor is no more
than 1,000 feet high, and, in the time of Jesus, there was a
fortress on the top. It is much more likely that this event took
place amid the eternal snows of Mount Hermon, which is
9,200 feet high and much nearer Caesarea Philippi and where
the solitude would be much more complete.

What happened we cannot tell. We can only bow in
reverence as we try to understand. Mark tells us that the
garments of Jesus became radiant. The word he uses (*stilbein*)
is the word used for the glistening gleam of burnished brass

or gold or of polished steel or of the golden glare of the sunlight. When the incident came to an end, a cloud overshadowed them.

In Jewish thought, the presence of God is regularly connected with the cloud. It was in the cloud that Moses met God. It was in the cloud that God came to the Tabernacle. It was the cloud which filled the Temple when it was dedicated after Solomon had built it. And it was the dream of the Jews that when the Messiah came the cloud of God's presence would return to the Temple (Exodus 16:10, 19:9, 33:9; 1 Kings 8:10; 2 Maccabees 2:8). The descent of the cloud is a way of saying that the Messiah had come, and any Jew would understand it like that.

The transfiguration has a double significance.

(1) It did something very precious for Jesus. Jesus had to take his own decisions. He had taken the decision to go to Jerusalem, and that was the decision to face and accept the cross. Obviously he had to be absolutely sure that was right before he could go on. On the mountain top, he received a double approval of his decision.

(a) Moses and Elijah met with him. Now Moses was the *supreme law-giver* of Israel. To him the nation owed the laws of God. Elijah was *the first and the greatest of the prophets*. People always looked back to him as the prophet who brought to them the very voice of God. When these two great figures met with Jesus, it meant that the greatest of the law-givers and the greatest of the prophets said to him, 'Go on!' It meant that they saw in Jesus the consummation of all that they had dreamed of in the past. It meant that they saw in him all that history had longed for and hoped for and looked forward to. It is as if at that moment Jesus was assured that he was on the right way because all history had been leading up to the cross.

(b) God spoke with Jesus. As always, Jesus did not consult his own wishes. He went to God and said, 'What will you have me do?' He put all his plans and intentions before God. And God said to him, 'You are acting as my own beloved Son should act and must act. Go on!' On the mountain of the transfiguration, Jesus was assured that he had not chosen the wrong way. He saw not only the inevitability but the essential rightness of the cross.

(2) It did something very precious for the disciples.

(a) They had been shattered by Jesus' statement that he was going to Jerusalem to die. That seemed to them the complete negation of all that they understood of the Messiah. They were still bewildered and uncomprehending. Things were happening which not only baffled their minds but were also breaking their hearts. What they saw on the mountain of the transfiguration would give them something to hold on to, even when they could not understand. Cross or no cross, they had heard God's voice acknowledge Jesus as his Son.

(b) It made them in a special sense witnesses of the glory of Christ. A witness has been defined as someone who first *sees* and then *shows*. This time on the mountain had shown them the glory of Christ, and now they had the story of this glory to hide in their hearts and to tell to others, not at the moment, but when the time came.

THE FATE OF THE FORERUNNER

Mark 9:9–13

> As they were coming down from the mountain, Jesus enjoined them that they must not relate to anyone what they had seen, except when the Son of Man should have risen from the dead. They clung to this word, asking

among themselves, what this phrase about rising from
the dead could mean. They asked Jesus, 'Do the experts
in the law not say that Elijah must come first?' 'It is
true,' he said to them, 'Elijah comes first and sets all
things in order. And yet how does it stand written about
the Son of Man that he must suffer many things and be
treated with contempt? But, I say to you, Elijah, too,
has come, and they treated him as they wished, even as
it stands written about him.'

NATURALLY the three disciples were thinking hard as they came
down the mountainside.

First, Jesus began with an injunction. They must tell no
one of what they had seen. Jesus knew quite well that their
minds were still haunted by the conception of a Messiah of
might and power. If they were to tell of what had happened
on the mountain top, of how the glory of God had appeared,
of how Moses and Elijah had appeared, how that could be
made to chime in with popular expectations! How it could
be made to seem a prelude to the burst of God's avenging
power on the nations of the world! The disciples still had to
learn what Messiahship meant. There was only one thing that
could teach them that – the cross and the resurrection to
follow. When the cross had taught them what Messiahship
meant and when the resurrection had convinced them that
Jesus was the Messiah, *then*, and then only, they might tell of
the glory of the mountain top, for then, and then only, would
they see it as it ought to be seen – as the prelude, not to the
unleashing of God's force, but to the crucifying of God's
love.

Still their minds worked on. They could not understand
what Jesus' words about resurrection meant. Their whole
attitude shows that in fact they never understood them. Their
whole outlook when the cross came was that of men to whom

the end had come. We must not blame the disciples. It was
simply that they had been so schooled in a completely
different idea of Messiahship that they could not take in what
Jesus had said.

Then they asked something that was puzzling them. Jews
believed that before the Messiah came Elijah would come to
be his herald and forerunner (Malachi 4:5–6). They had a
Rabbinic tradition that Elijah would come three days before
the Messiah. On the first day he would stand on the mountains
of Israel, lamenting the desolation of the land. And then in a
voice that would be heard from one end of the world to the
other, he would cry, '*Peace* cometh to the world. *Peace*
cometh to the world.' On the second day he would cry, '*Good*
cometh to the world. *Good* cometh to the world.' And on the
third day he would cry, '*Jeshuah* [*salvation*] cometh to the
world. *Jeshuah* cometh to the world.' He would restore all
things. He would mend the family breaches of the grim last
days. He would settle all doubtful points of ritual and
ceremonial. He would cleanse the nation by bringing back
those wrongfully excluded and driving out those wrongfully
included. Elijah had an amazing place in the thought of Israel.
He was conceived of as being continuously active in heaven
and on earth in their interest, and being the herald of the final
consummation.

Inevitably the disciples were wondering, 'If Jesus is the
Messiah, what has happened to Elijah?' Jesus' answer was in
terms that any Jew would understand. 'Elijah', he said, 'has
come and people treated him as they willed. They took him
and they arbitrarily applied their will to him and forgot God's
will.' He was referring to the imprisonment and death of John
the Baptist at the hands of Herod. Then, by implication, he
drove them back to that thought they would not face and
that he was determined they must face. By implication he

demanded, 'If they have done that to the forerunner, what will they do to the Messiah?'

Jesus was overturning all the preconceived notions and ideas of his disciples. They looked for the emergence of Elijah, the coming of the Messiah, the irruption of God into time and the shattering victory of heaven, which they identified with the triumph of Israel. He was trying to compel them to see that in fact the herald had been cruelly killed and the Messiah must end on a cross. They still did not understand, and their failure to understand was due to the cause which always makes people fail to understand – they clung to their way and refused to see God's way. They wished things as they desired them and not as God had ordered them. The error of their thoughts had blinded them to the revelation of God's truth.

COMING DOWN FROM THE MOUNT

Mark 9:14-18

> When they came to the disciples, they saw a great crowd gathered around them, and the experts in the law engaged in discussion with them. And as soon as they saw him the whole crowd were amazed and ran to him and greeted him. He asked them, 'What are you discussing among yourselves?' And one of the crowd answered him, 'Teacher, I brought my son to you because he has a spirit which makes him dumb. And whenever the spirit seizes him, it convulses him, and he foams at the mouth and grinds his teeth, and he is wasting away. And I asked your disciples to cast it out and they could not.'

THIS is the kind of thing that Peter had wanted to avoid. On the mountain top, in the presence of the glory, Peter had said,

'This is a good place for us to be.' Then he had wanted to build three booths for Jesus and Moses and Elijah, and to stay there. Life was so much better, so much nearer God, there on the mountain top. Why ever come down again? But it is of the very essence of life that we *must* come down from the mountain top. It has been said that in religion there must be *solitude*, but not *solitariness*. The solitude is necessary, for each of us must keep contact with God; but if, in our search for the essential solitude, we shut ourselves off from others, shut our ears to their appeal for help, shut our hearts to the cry of their tears, that is not religion. The solitude is not meant to make us solitary. It is meant to make us better able to meet and cope with the demands of everyday life.

Jesus came down to a delicate situation. A father had brought his boy to the disciples, and the boy was an epileptic. All the symptoms were there. The disciples had been quite unable to deal with his case, and that had given the scribes their chance. The helplessness of the disciples was a first-rate opportunity to belittle not only them but their Master. That is what made the situation so delicate, and that is what makes every human situation so delicate for the Christian. Our conduct, our words, our ability or inability to cope with the demands of life, are used as a yardstick, not only to judge us, but to judge Jesus Christ.

A. Victor Murray, in his book *Christian Education*, writes, 'There are those into whose eyes comes a far-away look when they talk about the church. It is a supernatural society, the body of Christ, his spotless bride, the custodian of the oracles of God, the blessed company of the redeemed, and a few more romantic titles, none of which seem to tally with what the outsider can see for himself in "St Agatha's Parish Church", or "High Street Methodists".' It does not matter how high-sounding our professions may be, it is by our actions that people judge us, and, in judging us, judge our Master. That was the situation here.

Then Jesus arrived. When the people saw him, they were astonished. We are not for one moment to think that the radiance of the transfiguration still lingered on him. That would have been to undo his own instructions that it be kept as yet a secret. The crowd had thought him away up in the lonely slopes of Hermon. They had been so engrossed in their argument that they had not seen him come, and now, just when the moment was right, here he was in the middle of them. It was at his sudden, unexpected but opportune arrival that they were surprised.

Here we learn two things about Jesus.

(1) He was ready to face the cross and he was ready to face the common problem just as either came. It is characteristic of human nature that we can face the great crisis moments of life with honour and dignity, but allow the routine demands of everyday life to irritate and annoy us. We can face the shattering blows of life with a certain heroism, but allow the petty pinpricks to upset us. Many of us can face a great disaster or a great loss with calm serenity and yet lose our tempers if a meal is badly cooked or a train late. The amazing thing about Jesus was that he could serenely face the cross and just as calmly deal with the day-to-day emergencies of life. The reason was that he did not keep God only for the crisis as so many of us do. He walked the daily paths of life with him.

(2) He had come into the world to save the world, and yet he could give himself in his entirety to the helping of one single person. It is much easier to preach the gospel of love for all the world than it is to love individual, not-very-lovable sinners. It is easy to be filled with a sentimental affection for the human race, and just as easy to find it too much bother to

go out of our way to help an individual member of it. Jesus
had the gift, which is the gift of a regal nature, of giving
himself entirely to every person with whom he happened to
be.

THE CRY OF FAITH

Mark 9:19-24

'O faithless generation!' Jesus answered. 'How long
am I to be with you? How long am I to bear you? Bring
him to me!' They brought him to Jesus. When he saw
Jesus, the spirit immediately sent the boy into a con-
vulsion, and he fell upon the ground, and rolled about,
foaming at the mouth. Jesus asked his father, 'How long
is it since this happened to him?' He said, 'He has been
like this since he was a child. Often it throws him into
the fire and into waters for it is out to destroy him. But,
if you can, let your heart be moved with pity, and help
us.' Jesus said to him, 'You say, "If you can." All things
are possible to him who believes.' Immediately the
father of the boy cried out, 'I *do* believe. Help my
unbelief.'

THIS passage begins with a cry wrung from the heart of Jesus.
He had been on the mountain top and had faced the tremendous task that lay ahead of him. He had decided to stake his
life on the redemption of the world. And now he had come
back down to find his nearest followers, his own chosen
disciples, beaten and baffled and helpless and ineffective. The
thing, for the moment, must have daunted even Jesus.
Looking at the Twelve, he must have had a sudden realization
of what anyone else would have called the hopelessness of
his task. He must at that moment have almost despaired of

the attempt to change human nature and to make men of the world into men of God.

How did he meet the moment of despair? 'Bring the boy to me,' he said. When we cannot deal with the ultimate situation, the thing to do is to deal with the situation which at the moment confronts us. It was as if Jesus said, 'I do not know how I am ever to change these disciples of mine, but I *can* at this moment help this boy. Let me get on with the present task, and not despair of the future.'

Again and again that is the way to avoid despair. If we sit and think about the state of the world, we may well become very depressed; then let us get to action in our small corner of the world. We may sometimes despair of the Church; then let us get to action in our own small part of the Church. Jesus did not sit appalled and paralysed at the slowness of people's minds; he dealt with the immediate situation. As Charles Kingsley had it:

> Do the work that's nearest.
> Though it's dull at whiles,
> Helping when we meet them
> Lame dogs over stiles.

The surest way to avoid pessimism and despair is to take what immediate action we can – and there is always something to be done.

To the father of the boy, Jesus stated the conditions of a miracle. 'To the one who believes,' said Jesus, 'all things are possible.' It was as if Jesus said, 'The cure of your boy depends not on me but on you.' This is not a specially theological truth; it is universal. To approach anything in the spirit of hopelessness is to make it hopeless; to approach anything in the spirit of faith is to make it a possibility. The Italian statesman Cavour once said that what a statesman needed above all was 'a sense of the possible'. Most of us are cursed with a sense of the impossible, and that is precisely why miracles do not happen.

The whole attitude of the father of the boy is most illuminating. Originally he had come seeking for Jesus himself. Since Jesus was on the mountain top, he had had to deal with the disciples, and his experience of them was discouraging. His faith was badly shaken, so badly shaken that when he came to Jesus all he could say at first was, 'Help me, *if you can.*' Then, face to face with Jesus, suddenly his faith blazed up again. 'I believe,' he cried. 'If there is still some discouragement in me, still some doubts, take them away and fill me with an unquestioning faith.'

It sometimes happens that people get less than they hoped for from some church or from some servant of the Church. When that happens, they ought to press beyond the Church to the Master of the Church, beyond the servant of Christ to Christ himself. The Church may at times disappoint us, and God's servants on earth may disappoint us. But when we battle our way face to face with Jesus Christ, he never disappoints us.

THE CAUSE OF FAILURE

Mark 9:25-9

> When Jesus saw that the crowd was running together, he rebuked the unclean spirit. 'Spirit of dumbness and deafness,' he said, 'I order you, come out of him, and don't go into him again.' When it had cried and violently convulsed him it came out, and he became like a dead man, so that many said, 'He is dead.' But Jesus took him by the hand, and raised him up, and he stood up.

253

> When he had gone into the house, and when they were
> by themselves, his disciples asked him, 'Why were we
> not able to cast it out?' 'This kind', he said to them,
> 'cannot come out except by prayer.'

JESUS must have taken father and son aside. But the crowd, hearing their cries, came running up, and Jesus acted. There was one last struggle, a struggle to complete exhaustion, and the boy was cured.

When they were by themselves, the disciples asked the cause of their failure. They were no doubt remembering that Jesus had sent them out to preach and heal and cast out devils (Mark 3:14–15). Why, then, had they this time so signally failed? Jesus answered quite simply that this kind of cure demanded prayer.

In effect he said to them, 'You don't live close enough to God.' They had been equipped with power, but it needed prayer to maintain it.

There is a deep lesson here. God may have given us a gift, but unless we maintain close contact with him it may wither and die. That is true of any gift. God may give a man great natural gifts as a preacher, but unless he maintains contact with God, he may in the end become only a man of words and not a man of power. God may give a woman a gift of music or of song, but unless she maintains contact with God, she may become a mere professional, who uses the gift only for gain, which is a dreary thing. That is not to say that gifts should not be used for gain. It is right to capitalize on any talent. But it does mean that, even when those blessed with such talent are using it, they should be finding joy in it because they are also using it for God. It is told of Jenny Lind, the famous Swedish soprano, that before every performance she would stand alone in her dressing-room and pray, 'God, help me to sing true tonight.'

Unless we maintain this contact with God, we lose two things, however great our gift may be.

(1) We lose *vitality*. We lose that living power, that something extra which makes for greatness. The thing becomes a performance instead of an offering to God. What should be a vital, living body becomes a beautiful corpse.

(2) We lose *humility*. What should be used for God's glory we begin to use for our own, and the virtue goes out of it. What should have been used to set God before others is used to set ourselves before them, and the breath of loveliness is gone.

Here is a warning thought. The disciples had been equipped with power direct from Jesus, but they had not nurtured power with prayer, and power had vanished. Whatever gifts God has given us, we lose them when we use them for ourselves. We keep them when we enrich them by continual contact with the God who gave them.

FACING THE END

Mark 9:30–1

> When they left there, they made their way through Galilee, and Jesus did not wish anyone to know where he was, for he kept teaching the disciples and saying to them, 'The Son of Man is being delivered into the hands of men, and they will kill him, and, when he has been killed, after three days he will rise again.' But they did not understand what he said, and they were afraid to ask him what it meant.

THIS passage marks a milestone. Jesus had now left the north country where he was safe and was taking the first step towards Jerusalem and to the cross which awaited him there.

For once he did not want the crowds around him. He knew quite clearly that unless he could write his message on the hearts of his chosen disciples, he had failed. Any teacher can leave behind a series of propositions, but Jesus knew that that was not enough. He had to leave behind him a band of persons on whom these propositions were written. He had to make sure, before he left this world in the body, that there were some who understood, however dimly, what he had come to say.

This time the tragedy of his warning is even more poignant. If we compare it with the previous passage in which he foretold his death (Mark 8:31), we see that one phrase is added, 'The Son of Man is being delivered into the hands of men.' There was a traitor in the little band, and Jesus knew it. He could see the way in which the mind of Judas was working. Maybe he could see it better than Judas could himself. And when he said, 'The Son of Man is being delivered into the hands of men,' he was not only announcing a fact and giving a warning, he was also making a last appeal to the man in whose heart was forming the purpose of betrayal.

Still the disciples did not understand. The thing they did not understand was the bit about rising again. By this time they were aware of the atmosphere of tragedy, but to the end of the day they never grasped the certainty of the resurrection. That was a wonder that was too great for them, a wonder that they grasped only when it became an accomplished fact.

When they did not understand, they were afraid to ask any further questions. It was as if they knew so much that they were afraid to know more. Any one of us might receive a verdict from our doctor. We might think the general gist of the verdict bad, but not understand all the details, and we might be afraid to ask questions, for the simple reason that we are afraid to know any more. The disciples were like that.

Sometimes we are amazed that they did not grasp what was so plainly spoken. The human mind has an amazing faculty for rejecting what it does not wish to see. Are we so very different? Over and over again we have heard the Christian message. We know the glory of accepting it and the tragedy of rejecting it, but many of us are just as far off as we ever were from giving it our full allegiance and moulding our lives to fit it. People still accept the parts of the Christian message which they like and which suit them, and refuse to understand the rest.

THE TRUE AMBITION

Mark 9:32-5

> So they came to Capernaum. When Jesus was in the house he asked them, 'What were you arguing about on the road?' They remained silent, for on the road they had been arguing with each other who was to be greatest. So Jesus sat down, and called the Twelve, and said to them, 'If anyone wishes to be first, he must be the last of all, and the servant of all.'

NOTHING so well shows how far the disciples were from realizing the real meaning of Jesus' Messiahship as this does. Repeatedly he had told them what awaited him in Jerusalem, and yet they were still thinking of his kingdom in earthly terms and of themselves as his chief ministers of state. There is something heartbreaking in the thought of Jesus going towards a cross and his disciples arguing about who would be greatest.

Yet in their heart of hearts they knew they were wrong. When he asked them what they had been arguing about, they had nothing to say. It was the silence of shame. They had no defence. It is strange how a thing takes its proper place and acquires its true character when it is set in the eyes of Jesus. So long as they thought that Jesus was not listening and that Jesus had not seen, the argument about who should be greatest seemed fair enough, but when that argument had to be stated in the presence of Jesus it was seen in all its unworthiness.

If we took everything and set it in the sight of Jesus, it would make all the difference in the world. If of everything we did, we asked, 'Could I go on doing this if Jesus was watching me?'; if of everything we said, we asked, 'Could I go on talking like this if Jesus was listening to me?', there would be many things which we would be saved from doing and saying. And the fact of Christian belief is that there is no 'if' about it. All deeds are done, all words are spoken in his presence. God keep us from the words and deeds which we would be ashamed that he should hear and see.

Jesus dealt with this very seriously. It says that he sat down and called the Twelve to him. When a Rabbi was teaching as a Rabbi, as a master teaches his scholars and disciples, when he was really making a pronouncement, he sat to teach. Jesus deliberately took up the position of a Rabbi teaching his pupils before he spoke. And then he told them that if they sought for greatness in his kingdom they must find it, not by being first but by being last, not by being masters but by being servants of all. It was not that Jesus abolished ambition. Rather, he re-created and sublimated ambition. For the ambition to rule, he substituted the ambition to serve. For the ambition to have things done for us, he substituted the ambition to do things for others.

So far from being an impossibly idealistic view, this is a view of the soundest common sense. The really great people, those who are remembered as having made a real contribution to life, are the ones who said to themselves, not, 'How can I use the state and society to further my own prestige and my own personal ambitions?' but, 'How can I use my personal gifts and talents to serve the state?'

Stanley Baldwin paid a noble tribute to the former Viceroy of India, Lord Curzon, when he died. In it he said, 'I want, before I sit down, to say one or two things that no one but I can say. A Prime Minister sees human nature bared to the bone, and it was my chance to see him twice when he suffered great disappointment – the time when I was preferred to him as Prime Minister, and the time when I had to tell him that he could render greater service to the country as chairman of the Committee of Imperial Defence than in the Foreign Office. Each of these occasions was a profound and bitter disappointment to him, but never for one moment did he show by word, look or innuendo, or by any reference to the subject afterwards, that he was dissatisfied. He bore no grudge, and he pursued no other course than the one I expected of him, of doing his duty where it was decided he could best render service.' Here was a man whose greatness lay not in the fact that he reached the highest offices of state, but in the fact that he was ready to serve his country anywhere.

True selflessness is rare, and when it is found it is remembered. The Greeks had a story of a Spartan called Paedaretos. Three hundred men were to be chosen to govern Sparta, and Paedaretos was a candidate. When the list of the successful was announced his name was not on it. 'I am sorry', said one of his friends, 'that you were not elected. The people ought to have known what a wise officer of state you would have made.' 'I am glad', said Paedaretos, 'that in Sparta there are 300 men better than I am.' Here was a man who became a legend because he was prepared to give to others the first place and to bear no ill-will.

Every economic problem would be solved if people lived for what they could do for others and not for what they could get for themselves. Every political problem would be solved if human ambition was only to serve the state and not to enhance individual prestige. The divisions and disputes which tear the Church asunder would for the most part never occur if the only desire of its office-bearers and its members was to serve it without caring what position they occupied. When Jesus spoke of the supreme greatness and value of the one whose ambition was to be a servant, he laid down one of the greatest practical truths in the world.

HELPING THE HELPLESS IS HELPING CHRIST

Mark 9:36–7

> Jesus took a little child and set him in the midst of them. And he took him up in the crook of his arm and said to them, 'Whoever receives one little child like this in my name receives me, and whoever receives me, receives not me, but him who sent me.'

JESUS is here still dealing with the worthy and the unworthy ambition.

He took a child and set him in front of them. Now children have no influence at all; they cannot advance a career nor enhance a person's prestige; children cannot give us things. It is the other way round. Children need things; they must have things done for them. So Jesus says, 'Whoever welcomes the poor, ordinary people, the people who have no influence and no wealth and no power, the people who need things done for them, is welcoming me. More than that, that person is welcoming God.' The child is typical of the person who needs things, and it is the society of the person who needs things that we must seek.

There is a warning here. It is easy to cultivate the friendship of the person who can do things for us, and whose influence can be useful to us. And it is equally easy to avoid the society of the person who inconveniently needs our help. It is easy to curry favour with the influential and the great, and to neglect the simple, humble, ordinary people. It is easy at some function to seek the society and the notice of some distinguished person, and to avoid the poor relation. In effect, Jesus here says that we ought to seek out not those who can do things for us, but those for whom we can do things, for in this way we are seeking the society of himself. This is another way of saying, 'Just as you did it to one of the least of these who are members of my family, you did it to me' (Matthew 25:40).

A LESSON IN TOLERANCE

Mark 9:38-40

> John said to Jesus, 'Teacher, we saw a man casting out demons by the use of your name, and we tried to stop him because he is not one of our company.' 'Don't stop him,' said Jesus. 'There is no one who can do a work of power in the strength of my name and lightly speak evil of me. He who is not against us is for us.'

As we have seen over and over again, in the time of Jesus everyone believed in demons. Everyone believed that both mental and physical illness was caused by the malign influence of these evil spirits. Now there was one very common way to exorcise them. If one could get to know the name of a still more powerful spirit and command the evil demon in that name to come out of a person, the demon was supposed to be powerless to resist. It could not stand against the might of the more powerful name. This is the kind of picture we have here. John had seen a man using the all-powerful name of Jesus to defeat the demons and he had tried to stop him, because he was not one of the intimate band of the disciples. But Jesus declared that no one could do a mighty work in his name and be altogether his enemy. Then Jesus laid down the great principle that 'Whosoever is not against us is for us.'

Here is a lesson in tolerance, and it is a lesson that nearly everyone needs to learn.

(1) We all have a right to our own thoughts. We all have a right to think things out and to think them through until we come to our own conclusions and our own beliefs. And that is a right we should respect. We are often too apt to condemn what we do not understand. The Quaker William Penn once said, 'Neither despise nor oppose what thou dost not understand.' Kingsley Williams, in *The New Testament in Plain English*, translates a phrase in Jude 10 like this – 'Those who speak abusively of everything they do not understand.'

There are two things we must remember.

(a) There is far more than one way to God. 'God', as Tennyson has it, 'fulfils himself in many ways.' The Spanish novelist Cervantes once said, 'Many are the roads by which God carries his own to heaven.' The world is round, and two people can get to precisely the same destination by starting out in precisely opposite directions. All roads, if we pursue them long enough and far enough, lead to God. It is a fearful thing for any individual or any church to claim a monopoly on salvation.

(b) It is necessary to remember that truth is always bigger than any individual's grasp of it. No one can possibly grasp all truth. The basis of tolerance is not a lazy acceptance of anything. It is not the feeling that there cannot be assurance anywhere. The basis of tolerance is simply the realization of the magnitude of truth itself. The politician and journalist John Morley wrote, 'Toleration means reverence for all the possibilities of truth, it means acknowledgment that she dwells in divers mansions, and wears vesture of many colours, and speaks in strange tongues. It means frank respect for freedom of indwelling conscience against mechanical forms, official conventions, social force. It means the charity that is greater than faith or hope.' Intolerance is a sign both of arrogance and ignorance, for it is a sign that people believe that there is no truth beyond the truth they see.

(2) Not only must we concede the right of each one of us to do our own thinking, we must also concede the right to do our own speaking. Of all democratic rights, the dearest is that of liberty of speech. There are, of course, limits. If people are spreading doctrines calculated to destroy morality and to remove the foundations from all civilized and Christian society, they must be combated. But the way to combat them is certainly not to eliminate them by force but to prove them wrong. Once Voltaire laid down the conception of freedom of speech in a vivid sentence. 'I hate what you say,' he said, 'but I would die for your right to say it.'

(3) We must remember that any doctrine or belief must finally be judged by the kind of people it produces. Thomas Chalmers once put the matter in a nutshell. 'Who cares', he demanded, 'about any Church but as an instrument of Christian good?' The question must always ultimately be, not, 'How is a Church governed?' but, 'What kind of people does a Church produce?'

There is an old eastern fable. A man possessed a ring set with a wonderful opal. Whoever wore the ring became so sweet and true in character that everyone loved him. The ring was a charm. Always it was passed down from father to son, and always it did its work. As time went on, it came to a father who had three sons whom he loved with an equal love. What was he to do when the time came to pass on the ring? The father got other two rings made precisely the same so that none could tell the difference. On his deathbed he called each of his sons in, spoke some words of love and to each, without telling the others, gave a ring. When the three sons discovered that each had a ring, a great dispute arose as to which was the true ring that could do so much for its owner. The case was taken to a wise judge. He examined the rings and then he spoke. 'I cannot tell which is the magic ring,' he said, 'but you yourselves can prove it.' 'We?' asked the sons in astonishment. 'Yes,' said the judge, 'for if the true ring gives sweetness to the character of the man who wears it, then I and all the other people in the city will know the man who possesses the true ring by the goodness of his life. So, go your ways, and be kind, be truthful, be brave, be just in your dealings, and he who does these things will be the owner of the true ring.'

The matter was to be proved by life. No one can entirely condemn beliefs which make people good. If we remember that, we may be less intolerant.

(4) We may hate a person's beliefs, but we must never hate the person. We may wish to eliminate the teaching, but we must never wish to eliminate the teacher.

> He drew a circle that shut me out –
> Rebel, heretic, thing to flout.
> But love and I had the wit to win –
> We drew a circle that took him in.

REWARDS AND PUNISHMENTS

Mark 9:41–2

> Whoever gives you a cup of water to drink on the ground
> that you belong to Christ, I tell you truly he will not
> lose his reward. And whoever puts a stumbling-block
> in the path of one of these little ones who believe in me,
> it is better for him that a great millstone hang about his
> neck and he be cast into the sea.

THE teaching of this passage is simple, unmistakable and
salutary.

(1) It declares that any kindness shown, any help given,
to the people of Christ will not lose its reward. The
reason for helping is that the person in need belongs to
Jesus. Everyone in need has a claim upon us because he
or she is dear to Christ. Had Jesus still been here in the
flesh, he would have helped that person in the most practical
way, and the duty of help has devolved on us. It is to be
noted how simple the help is. The gift is a cup of cold water.
We are not asked to do great things for others, things beyond
our power. We are asked to give the simple things that anyone
can give.

A missionary tells a lovely story. She had been telling a
class of African schoolchildren about giving a cup of cold
water in the name of Jesus. She was sitting on the verandah
of her house. Into the village square came a company of native
bearers. They had heavy packs. They were tired and thirsty,
and they sat down to rest. Now they were men of another
tribe, and had they asked the ordinary non-Christian native
for water they would have been told to go and find it for
themselves, because of the barrier between the tribes. But as
the men sat wearily there, and as the missionary watched,

from the school emerged a little line of tiny African girls. On their heads they had pitchers of water. Shyly and fearfully they approached the tired bearers, knelt and offered their pitchers of water. In surprise the bearers took them and drank and handed them back, and the girls took to their heels and ran to the missionary. 'We have given a thirsty man a drink', they said, 'in the name of Jesus.' The little children took the story and the duty literally.

Would that more would do so! It is the simple kindnesses that are needed. As Muhammad said long ago, 'Putting a lost man on the right road, giving a thirsty man a drink of water, smiling in your brother's face – that, too, is charity.'

(2) But the converse is also true. To help is to win the eternal reward. To cause a weaker brother or sister to stumble is to win the eternal punishment. The passage is deliberately stern. The millstone that is mentioned is a great millstone. There were two kinds of mills in Palestine. There was the hand-mill that the women used in the house. And there was the mill whose stone was so great that it took a donkey to turn it.

The millstone here is literally a millstone turned by a donkey. To be cast into the sea with that attached was certainly to have no hope of return. This was in fact a punishment and a means of execution both in Rome and in Palestine. Josephus tells us that when certain Galilaeans had made a successful revolt 'they took those of Herod's party and drowned them in the lake'. Suetonius, the Roman historian, tells us of Augustus that, 'Because the tutor and attendants of his son Gaius took advantage of their master's illness to commit acts of arrogance and greed to his province, he had them thrown into a river with heavy weights about their necks.'

To sin is terrible but to teach another to sin is infinitely worse. The American writer O. Henry has a story in which he tells of a little girl whose mother was dead. Her father used to come home from work and sit down and take off his jacket and open his paper and light his pipe and put his feet on the mantelpiece. The little girl would come in and ask him to play with her for a little, for she was lonely. He told her he was tired, to let him be at peace. He told her to go out to the street and play. She played on the streets. The inevitable happened – she took to the streets. The years passed on and she died. Her soul arrived in heaven. Peter saw her and said to Jesus, 'Master, here's a girl who was a bad lot. I suppose we send her straight to hell?' 'No,' said Jesus gently, 'let her in. Let her in.' And then his eyes grew stern, 'But look for a man who refused to play with his little girl and sent her out to the streets – *and send him to hell*.' God is not hard on the sinner, but he will be stern to the person who makes it easier for another to sin, and whose conduct, either thoughtless or deliberate, puts a stumbling-block in the path of a weaker brother or sister.

THE GOAL WHICH IS WORTH ANY SACRIFICE

Mark 9:43–8

> If your hand proves a stumbling-block to you, cut it off. It is better for you to enter life maimed than to go away to Gehenna with two hands, to the fire that can never be quenched. And if your foot is a stumbling-block to you, cut it off. For it is better for you to enter life lame than to be cast into Gehenna with two feet. And if your eye proves a stumbling-block to you, cast it away. For it is

better for you to enter into the kingdom of God with
one eye than to be cast into Gehenna with two eyes,
where their worm does not die and the fire is never
quenched.

THIS passage lays down in vivid language the basic truth that
there is one goal in life worth any sacrifice. In physical
matters, it may be that someone may have to part with a limb
or with some part of the body to preserve the life of the whole
body. The amputation of a limb or the excision of a part of
the body by surgical means is sometimes the only way to
preserve the life of the whole body. In the spiritual life, the
same kind of thing can happen.

The Jewish Rabbis had sayings based on the way in which
some parts of the body can lend themselves to sin. 'The eye
and the heart are the two brokers of sin.' 'The eye and the
heart are the two handmaids of sin.' 'Passions lodge only in
him who sees.' 'Woe to him who goes after his eyes, for the
eyes are adulterous.' There are certain human instincts, and
certain parts of our physical constitution, which minister to
sin. This saying of Jesus is not to be taken literally, but is a
vivid way of saying that there is a goal in life worth any
sacrifice to attain it.

There are in this passage repeated references to *Gehenna*.
Gehenna is spoken of in the New Testament in Matthew 5:22,
29–30; 10:28; 18:9; 23:15, 33; Luke 12:5; James 3:6. The
word is regularly translated as *hell* (as in the New Revised
Standard Version). It is a word with a history. It is a form of
the word *Hinnom*. The valley of Hinnom was a ravine outside
Jerusalem. It had an evil past.

It was the valley in which Ahaz, in the old days, had instituted fire-worship and the sacrifice of little children in the
fire. 'He made offerings in the valley of the son of Hinnom,
and made his sons pass through fire' (2 Chronicles 28:3).

That terrible pagan worship was also followed by Manasseh (2 Chronicles 33:6). The valley of Hinnom, Gehenna, therefore, was the scene of one of Israel's most terrible lapses into pagan customs. In his reforms Josiah declared it an unclean place. 'He defiled Topheth, which is in the valley of Ben-hinnom, so that no one would make a son or a daughter pass through fire as an offering to Molech' (2 Kings 23:10).

When the valley had been so declared unclean and had been so desecrated, it was set apart as the place where the refuse of Jerusalem was burned. The consequence was that it was a foul, unclean place, where loathsome worms bred on the refuse, and which smoked and smouldered at all times like some vast incinerator. The actual phrase about the worm which does not die, and the fire which is not quenched, comes from a description of the fate of Israel's evil enemies in Isaiah 66:24.

Because of all this, Gehenna had become a kind of type or symbol of hell, the place where the souls of the wicked would be tortured and destroyed. It is so used in the Talmud. 'The sinner who desists from the words of the Law will in the end inherit Gehenna.' So Gehenna stands as the place of punishment, and the word roused in the mind of every Israelite the grimmest and most terrible pictures.

But what was the goal for which everything must be sacrificed? It is described in two ways. Twice it is called *life*, and once it is called *the kingdom of God*. How may we define *the kingdom of God*? We may take our definition from the Lord's Prayer. In that prayer, two petitions are set beside each other. 'Your kingdom come. Your will be done on earth as it is in heaven.' There is no literary device so characteristic of Jewish style as *parallelism*. In parallelism, two phrases are set side by side, the one of which either restates the other or amplifies, explains and develops it. Any verse of the Psalms will show this device in action. So, then, we may take it that in the Lord's Prayer the one petition is an explanation and amplification of the other. When we set the two together, we get the definition that: 'The kingdom of heaven is a society upon earth in which God's will is as perfectly done in earth as it is in heaven.'

We may then go on to say quite simply that perfectly to do God's will is to be a citizen of the kingdom of heaven. And if we take that and apply it to the passage we are now studying, it will mean that *it is worth any sacrifice and any discipline and any self-denial to do the will of God*, and only in doing that will is there real life and ultimate and completely satisfying peace.

The third-century biblical scholar Origen takes this symbolically. He says that it may be necessary to excise some heretic or some evil person from the fellowship of the Church in order to keep the body of the Church pure. But this saying is meant to be taken very personally. It means that it may be necessary to excise some habit, to abandon some pleasure, to give up some friendship, to cut out some thing which has become very dear to us, in order to be fully obedient to the will of God. This is not a matter with which anyone can deal for anyone else. It is solely a matter of a person's individual conscience, and it means that, if there is anything in our lives which is coming between us and a perfect obedience to the will of God, however much habit and custom may have made it part of our lives, it must be rooted out. The rooting out may be as painful as a surgical operation; it may seem like cutting out part of our own body; but if we are to know real *life*, real happiness and real peace it must go. This may sound bleak and stern, but in reality it is only facing the facts of life.

THE SALT OF THE CHRISTIAN LIFE

Mark 9:49-50

> Everyone must be salted with fire,
> Salt is good, but, if the salt has become saltless, with
>   what will you season it?
> Have salt in yourselves, and so live at peace with each
>   other.

THESE three verses are among the most difficult in the New Testament. The commentators produce scores of different interpretations. The interpretation will become easier if we remember something we have already had cause to note. Often Jesus dropped pithy sayings which stuck in people's minds because they could not possibly forget them. But often, although the saying was remembered, the occasion on which it was said was forgotten. The result is that we often get a series of quite disconnected sayings of Jesus set together because they stuck in the writer's mind in that order.

Here is an instance of this. We will not make sense of these two verses at all unless we recognize that here we have *three quite separate sayings of Jesus* which have nothing to do with each other. They came together in the compiler's mind and stuck there together in this order because they all contain the word *salt*. They are a little collection of sayings of Jesus in which he used *salt* in various ways as metaphor or illustration. All this is to say that we must not try to find some remote connection between these sayings. We must take them individually and interpret each as it comes.

(1) Everyone must be salted by fire. According to the Jewish law every sacrifice must be salted with salt before it was offered to God on the altar (Leviticus 2:13). That

sacrificial salt was called *the salt of the covenant* (Numbers 18:19; 2 Chronicles 13:5). It was the addition of that salt which made the sacrifice acceptable to God, and which his covenant law laid down as necessary. This saying of Jesus will then mean, 'Before a Christian life becomes acceptable to God it must be treated with fire just as every sacrifice is treated with salt.' The fire is the salt which makes the life acceptable to God.

What does that mean? In ordinary New Testament language, fire has two connections.

(a) It is connected with *purification*. It is the fire which purifies the base metal; the alloy is separated and the metal left pure. Fire then will mean everything which purifies life, the discipline by which sin is conquered, the experiences of life which purify and strengthen the sinews of the soul. In that case this will mean: 'The life which is acceptable to God is the life which has been cleansed and purified by the discipline of Christian obedience and Christian acceptance of the guiding hand of God.'

(b) Fire is connected with *destruction*. In that case this saying will have to do with *persecution*. It will mean that the life which has undergone the trials and hardships and perils of persecution is the life which is acceptable to God. Anyone who has voluntarily faced the danger of the destruction of possessions and even the destruction of life itself because of loyalty to Jesus Christ is dear to God.

We may take this first saying of Jesus to mean that the life which is purified by discipline and has faced the danger of persecution because of its loyalty is the sacrifice which is precious to God.

(2) Salt is good, but if the salt has become saltless, with what will you season it? This is an even harder saying to interpret. We would not say that there are no other possible

interpretations, but we would suggest that it may be understood on the following lines. Salt has two characteristic virtues. First, it lends *flavour* to things. An egg without salt is an insipid thing. Anyone knows how unpleasant many dishes are when the salt which should have been included is accidentally omitted in the preparation. Second, salt was the earliest of all *preservatives*. To keep a thing from going rotten, salt was used. The Greeks used to say that salt acted like a soul in a dead body. Dead meat left to itself went bad, but, pickled in salt, it retained its freshness. The salt seemed to put a kind of life into it. Salt defended against corruption.

Now the Christian was sent into a pagan society to do something for it. That society had two characteristics. First, it was bored and world-weary. The very luxuries and excesses of that ancient world were a proof that in its bored weariness it was looking for some thrill in a life from which all thrill had gone. As Matthew Arnold wrote in 'Obermann Once More':

> On that hard pagan world, disgust
> And secret loathing fell;
> Deep weariness and sated lust
> Made human life a hell.
> In his cool hall, with haggard eyes,
> The Roman noble lay;
> He drove abroad in furious guise
> Along the Appian Way;
> He made a feast, drank fierce and fast,
> And crowned his hair with flowers –
> No easier nor no quicker passed
> The impracticable hours.

Into that bored and weary world Christianity came, and it was the task of the Christian to impart to society a new flavour and a new thrill as salt does to the dish with which it is used.

Second, that ancient world was corrupt. No one knew that better than the ancients themselves. Juvenal likened Rome to a filthy sewer. Purity was gone and chastity was unknown. Into that corrupt world Christianity came, and it was the task of the Christian to bring an antiseptic to the poison of life, to bring a cleansing influence into that corruption. Just as salt defeated the corruption which inevitably attacked dead meat, so Christianity was to attack the corruption of the world.

So, in this saying, Jesus was challenging the Christian. 'The world', he said, 'needs the flavour and the purity that only the Christian can bring. And if Christians themselves have lost the thrill and the purity of the Christian life, where will the world ever get these things?' Unless Christians, in the power of Christ, defeat world-weariness and world corruption, these things must flourish unchecked.

(3) Have salt in yourselves and live at peace with each other. Here we must take salt in the sense of *purity*. The ancients declared that there was nothing in the world purer than salt because it came from the two purest things, the sun and the sea. The very glistening whiteness of salt was a picture of purity. So this will mean, 'Have within yourselves the purifying influence of the Spirit of Christ. Be purified from selfishness and self-seeking, from bitterness and anger and grudge-bearing. Be cleansed from irritation and moodiness and self-centredness, and then, and then only, you will be able to live in peace with your neighbours.' In other words, Jesus is saying that it is only the life that is cleansed of self and filled with Christ which can live in real fellowship with others.

FOR BETTER OR FOR WORSE

Mark 10:1–12

> Leaving there, Jesus came into the hill country of Judaea
> and to the district across the Jordan, and once again
> crowds came together to him. As his custom was, he
> again continued to teach them. Some Pharisees came to
> him and asked him if it was lawful for a man to put
> away his wife. They asked this question to test him. He
> asked them, 'What commandment did Moses lay down
> for you?' They answered, 'Moses allowed a man to
> write a bill of divorcement and then to put her away.'
> Jesus said to them, 'It was to meet the hardness of your
> heart that he wrote this commandment for you. From
> the beginning of creation male and female he created
> them. For this cause a man will leave his father and his
> mother and will cleave to his wife. And the two will
> become one flesh, so that they are no longer two but
> one flesh. So then what God has joined together let not
> man separate.' In the house his disciples again asked
> him about this. He said to them, 'Whoever puts away
> his wife and marries another woman commits adultery
> against her. And if a woman divorces her husband and
> marries another man, she commits adultery.'

JESUS was pursuing his way south. He had left Galilee and
had come into Judaea. He had not yet entered Jerusalem, but
step by step and stage by stage he was approaching the final
scene.

Certain Pharisees came with a question about divorce, by
which they hoped to test him. There may have been more
than one motive behind their question. Divorce was a burning
question, a crux of Rabbinic discussion, and it may well be
that they honestly wished for Jesus' opinion on it. They may

have wished to test his orthodoxy. It may well be that Jesus
had already had something to say on this matter. Matthew
5:31–2 shows us Jesus speaking about marriage and remarriage, and it may be that these Pharisees had the hope
that he might contradict himself and entangle himself in his
own words. It may be that they knew what he would answer
and wished to involve him in enmity with Herod, who had in
fact divorced his wife and married another. It may well be
that they wished to hear Jesus contradict the law of Moses,
as indeed he did, and thereby to formulate a charge of heresy
against him. One thing is certain – the question they asked
Jesus was no academic one of interest only to the Rabbinic
schools. It was a question which dealt with one of the most
acute issues of the time.

In theory nothing could be higher than the Jewish ideal of
marriage. Chastity was held to be the greatest of all the virtues.
'We find that God is long-suffering to every sin except the
sin of unchastity.' 'Unchastity causes the glory of God to
depart.' 'Every Jew must surrender his life rather than commit
idolatry, murder or adultery.' 'The very altar sheds tears when
a man divorces the wife of his youth.' The ideal was there
but practice fell very far short.

The basic fact that impaired the whole situation was that
in Jewish law a woman was regarded as a thing. She had no
legal rights whatever but was at the complete disposal of the
male head of the family. The result was that a man could
divorce his wife on almost any grounds, while there were
very few on which a woman could seek divorce. At best she
could only ask her husband to divorce her. 'A woman may be
divorced with or without her will, but a man only with his
will.' The only grounds on which a woman could claim a
divorce were if her husband became a leper, if he engaged in
a disgusting trade such as that of a tanner, if he sexually

assaulted a virgin, or if he falsely accused her of pre-nuptial sin.

The law of Jewish divorce goes back to Deuteronomy 24:1. That passage was the foundation of the whole matter. It runs thus: 'Suppose a man enters into marriage with a woman, but she does not please him because he finds something objectionable in her, and so he writes her a certificate of divorce, puts it in her hand, and sends her out of his house.'

At first the bill of divorcement was very simple. It read like this: 'Let this be from me thy writ of divorce and letter of dismissal and deed of liberation, that thou mayest marry whatsoever man thou wilt.' In later days the bill became more elaborate: 'On the . . . day, of the . . . week, of the . . . month, year . . . of the world, according to the calculation in use in the town of . . ., situated by the river . . ., I, A.B., son of C.D., and by whatsoever name I am called here, present this day . . ., native of the town of . . ., acting of my free will, and without any coercion, do repudiate, send back, and put away thee E.F., daughter of G.H., and by whatsoever name thou art called, and until this present time my wife. I send thee away now E.F., daughter of G.H., so that thou art free and thou canst at thy pleasure marry whom thou wilt and no one will hinder thee. This is thy letter of divorce, act of repudiation, certificate of separation, according to the law of Moses and of Israel.' In New Testament times it took a skilled Rabbi to draw up this document. It was afterwards proved by a court of three Rabbis, and then lodged with the Sanhedrin. But the process of divorce remained on the whole exceedingly easy, and at the entire discretion of the man.

But the real crux of the problem was the interpretation of the law as it is in Deuteronomy 24:1. There it is laid down that a man can divorce his wife if he finds *something objectionable* in her. How was that phrase to be interpreted? There were in this matter two schools of thought.

There was the school of Shammai. They interpreted the matter with utter strictness. Something objectionable was adultery and adultery alone. Let a woman be as bad as Jezebel, unless she was guilty of adultery there could be no divorce.

The other school was the school of Hillel. They interpreted that crucial phrase as widely as possible. They said that it could mean if the wife spoiled a dish of food, if she spun in the streets, if she talked to a strange man, if she spoke disrespectfully of her husband's relatives in his hearing, if she was an argumentative woman (who was defined as a woman whose voice could be heard in the next house). Rabbi Akiba even went so far as to say that it meant if a man found a woman who was fairer in his eyes than his wife was.

Human nature being as it is, it was the laxer view which prevailed. The result was that divorce for the most trivial reasons, or for no reason at all, was tragically common. Things had come to such a pass that, in the time of Jesus, women hesitated to marry at all because marriage was so insecure. When Jesus spoke as he did, he was speaking on a subject which was a burning issue, and he was striking a blow for women by seeking to restore marriage to the position it ought to have.

Certain things are to be noted. Jesus quoted the Mosaic regulation, and then he said that Moses laid that down only 'to meet the hardness of your hearts'. That may mean one of two things. It may mean that Moses laid it down because it was the best that could be expected from people such as those for whom he was legislating. Or, it may mean that Moses laid it down in order to try to control a situation which even then was degenerating, that in fact it was not so much a permission to divorce as it was in the beginning an attempt to control divorce, to reduce it to some kind of law, and to make it more difficult.

In any event Jesus made it quite clear that he regarded Deuteronomy 24:1 as being laid down for a definite situation and being in no sense permanently binding. The authorities which he quoted went much further back. For his authorities he went right back to the Creation story and quoted Genesis 1:27 and 2:24. It was his view that in the very nature of things marriage was a permanency which indissolubly united two people in such a way that the bond could never be broken by any human laws and regulations. It was his belief that in the very constitution of the universe marriage is meant to be an absolute permanency and unity, and no Mosaic regulation dealing with a temporary situation could alter that.

The difficulty is that in the parallel account in Matthew there is a difference. In Mark, Jesus' prohibition of divorce and remarriage is absolute. In Matthew 19:3–9, he is shown as absolutely forbidding remarriage, but as permitting divorce on one ground – adultery. Almost certainly the Matthew version is correct, and it is indeed implied in Mark. It was Jewish law that adultery did in fact compulsorily dissolve any marriage. And the truth is that infidelity does in fact dissolve the bond of marriage. Once adultery has been committed the unity is in any case destroyed and divorce merely attests the fact.

The real essence of the passage is that Jesus insisted that the loose sexual morality of his day must be mended. Those who sought marriage only for pleasure must be reminded that marriage is also for responsibility. Those who regarded marriage simply as a means of gratifying their physical passions must be reminded that it was also a spiritual unity. Jesus was building a defence around the home.

OF SUCH IS THE KINGDOM OF HEAVEN

Mark 10:13–16

> They brought little children to Jesus that he might touch
> them. But the disciples rebuked them. When Jesus saw
> what they were doing he was vexed and said to them,
> 'Let the little children come to me, and don't try to stop
> them for of such is the kingdom of God. This is the
> truth I tell you, whoever does not receive the kingdom
> of God as a little child will not enter into it.' And he
> took them up in the crook of his arm and blessed them
> and laid his hands upon them.

IT was natural that Jewish mothers should wish their children
to be blessed by a great and distinguished Rabbi. Especially
they brought their children to such a person on their first
birthday. It was in this way that they brought the children to
Jesus on this day.

We will fully understand the almost poignant beauty of
this passage only if we remember when it happened. Jesus
was on the way to the cross – and he knew it. Its cruel shadow
can never have been far from his mind. It was at such a time
that he had time for the children. Even with such a tension in
his mind as that, he had time to take them in his arms and he
had the heart to smile into their faces and maybe to play with
them for a while.

The disciples were not boorish and ungracious men. They
simply wanted to protect Jesus. They did not quite know what
was going on, but they knew quite clearly that tragedy lay
ahead and they could see the tension under which Jesus
laboured. They did not want him to be bothered. They could
not conceive that he could want the children about him at such
a time as that. But Jesus said, 'Let the children come to me.'

Incidentally, this tells us a great deal about Jesus. It tells us that he was the kind of person who cared for children and for whom children cared. He could not have been a stern and gloomy and joyless person. There must have been a kindly sunshine on him. He must have smiled easily and laughed joyously. Somewhere the writer George Macdonald says that he does not believe in people's Christianity if the children are never to be found playing around their doors. This little, precious incident throws a flood of light on the human kind of person Jesus was.

'Of such', said Jesus 'is the kingdom of God.' What is it about children that Jesus liked and valued so much?

(1) There is the child's *humility*. There is the child who is an exhibitionist, but such a child is rare and almost always the product of misguided adult treatment. Ordinarily children are embarrassed by prominence and publicity. They have not yet learned to think in terms of place and pride and prestige. They have not yet learned to discover the importance of themselves.

(2) There is the child's *obedience*. True, children are often disobedient, but, paradox though it may seem, their natural instinct is to obey. They have not yet learned the pride and the false independence which separate us from one another and from God.

(3) There is the child's *trust*. That is seen in two things.

(a) It is seen in the child's acceptance of authority. There is a time when children believe that their father and mother know everything and that they are always right. To our shame, they soon grow out of that. But instinctively children realize their own ignorance and their own helplessness and trust the ones who, as they think, know.

(b) It is seen in the child's confidence in other people. Children do not expect people to be bad. They will make friends with a perfect stranger. A great man once said that the greatest compliment ever paid him was when a little boy came up to him, a complete stranger, and asked him to tie his shoelace. Children have not yet learned to suspect the world. They still believe the best about others. Sometimes that very trust leads them into danger, for there are those who are totally unworthy of it and who abuse it, but that trust is a lovely thing.

(4) The child has *a short memory*. Children have not yet learned to bear grudges and nourish bitterness. Even when they are unjustly treated – and who among us is not sometimes unjust to their children? – they forget, and forget so completely that they do not even need to forgive.

Indeed, of such is the kingdom of God.

HOW MUCH DO YOU WANT GOODNESS?

Mark 10:17–22

As Jesus was going along the road, a man came running to him and threw himself at his feet and asked him, 'Good teacher, what am I to do to inherit eternal life?' Jesus said to him, 'Why do you call me good? There is no one who is good, except one – God. You know the commandments. You must not kill, you must not commit adultery, you must not steal, you must not bear false witness, you must not defraud anyone, you must honour your father and mother.' He said to him, 'Teacher, I have kept all these from my youth.' When Jesus looked at him he loved him, and he said to him, 'You still lack one thing. Go, sell all that you have, and give it to the poor and you will have treasure in heaven. And come! Follow me!' But he was grieved at this saying, and he went away in sadness, for he had many possessions.

HERE is one of the most vivid stories in the gospels.

(1) We must note how the man came and how Jesus met him. He came running. He flung himself at Jesus' feet. There is something amazing in the sight of this rich, young aristocrat falling at the feet of the penniless prophet from Nazareth, who was on the way to being an outlaw. 'Good teacher!' he began. And straightaway Jesus answered back, 'No flattery! Don't call me good! Keep that word for God!' It looks almost as if Jesus was trying to pour cold water on that young enthusiasm.

There is a lesson here. It is clear that this man came to Jesus in a moment of overflowing emotion. It is also clear that Jesus exercised a personal fascination over him. Jesus did two things that every evangelist and every preacher and every teacher ought to remember and to copy.

First, he said in effect, 'Stop and think! Don't get carried away by your excitement. I don't want you swept to me by a moment of emotion. Think calmly what you are doing.' Jesus was not cold-shouldering the man. He was telling him even at the very outset to count the cost.

Second, he said in effect, 'You cannot become a Christian by devotion to me. *You must look at God.*' Preaching and teaching always mean the conveying of truth through personality, and thereby lies the greatest danger of the greatest teachers. The danger is that the pupil, the scholar, the young person may form a personal attachment to the teacher or the preacher and think that it is an attachment to God. Teachers and preachers must never point to themselves. They must always point to God. There is in all true teaching a certain self-obliteration. True, we cannot keep personality and warm personal loyalty out of it altogether, and we would not if we could. But the matter must not stop there. Teachers and preachers are in the last analysis only pointers to God.

(2) Never did any story so lay down the essential Christian truth that *respectability is not enough*. Jesus quoted the commandments which were the basis of the decent life. Without hesitation the man said he had kept them all. Note one thing – with one exception they were all negative commandments, and that one exception operated only in the family circle. In effect the man was saying. 'I never in my life did anyone any harm.' That was perfectly true. But the real question is, 'What good have you done?' And the question to this man was even more pointed, 'With all your possessions, with your wealth, with all that you could give away, what positive good have you done to others? How much have you gone out of your way to help and comfort and strengthen others as you might have done?' Respectability, on the whole, consists in *not doing things*; Christianity consists in *doing things*. That was precisely where this man – like so many of us – fell down.

(3) So Jesus confronted him with a challenge. In effect he said, 'Get out of this moral respectability. Stop looking at goodness as consisting in not doing things. Take yourself and all that you have, and spend everything on others. Then you will find true happiness in time and in eternity.' The man could not do it. He had great possessions, which it had never entered his head to give away; and when it was suggested to him, he could not. True, he had never stolen, and he had never defrauded anyone – but neither had he ever been, nor could he compel himself to be, positively and sacrificially generous.

It may be respectable never to take away from anyone. It is Christian to give to someone. In reality, Jesus was confronting this man with a basic and essential question – 'How much do you want real Christianity? Do you want it enough to give your possessions away?' And the man had to answer in effect, 'I want it – but I don't want it as much as all that.'

Robert Louis Stevenson in *The Master of Ballantrae* draws a picture of the master leaving the ancestral home of Durrisdeer for the last time. Even he is sad. He is talking to the faithful family steward. 'Ah! M'Kellar,' he said, 'Do you think I have never a regret?' 'I do not think,' said M'Kellar, 'that you could be so bad a man unless you had all the machinery for being a good one.' 'Not all,' said the master, 'not all. It is there you are in error. *The malady of not wanting.*'

It was the failing of not wanting enough which meant tragedy for the man who came running to Jesus. It is the failing from which most of us suffer. We all want goodness, but so few of us want it enough to pay the price.

Jesus, looking at him, loved him. There were many things in that look of Jesus.

(a) There was the appeal of love. Jesus was not angry with him. He loved him too much for that. It was not the look of anger but the appeal of love.

(b) There was the challenge to moral courage. It was a look which sought to pull the man out of his comfortable, respectable, settled life into the adventure of being a real Christian.

(c) It was the look of grief. And that grief was the sorest grief of all – the grief of seeing a man deliberately choose not to be what he might have been and had it in him to be.

Jesus looks at us with the appeal of love and with the challenge to have the courage of our convictions and boldly take up the Christian way. God grant that he may never have to look at us with sorrow for a loved one who refuses to be all that he or she might have been and could have been.

THE PERIL OF RICHES

Mark 10:23-7

> Jesus looked round and said to his disciples, 'With what
> difficulty will those who have money enter into the
> kingdom of God!' His disciples were amazed at his
> words. Jesus repeated, 'Children, how difficult it is for
> those who trust in money to enter into the kingdom of
> God! It is easier for a camel to go through the eye of
> a needle than for a rich man to enter the kingdom of
> God.' They were exceedingly astonished. 'Who then',
> they said to him, 'can be saved?' Jesus looked at them
> and said, 'With man it is impossible, but not with God.
> All things are possible with God.'

THE ruler who had refused the challenge of Jesus had walked
sorrowfully away, and, no doubt, the eyes of Jesus and the
company of the apostles followed him until his figure receded
into the distance. Then Jesus turned and looked round his
own disciples. 'How very difficult it is', he said, 'for someone
who has money to enter into the kingdom of God.' The
word used for money is *chremata*, which is defined by
Aristotle as, 'All those things of which the value is measured
by coinage.'

We may perhaps wonder why this saying so astonished
the disciples. Twice their amazement is stressed. The reason
for their amazement was that Jesus was turning accepted
Jewish standards completely upside down. Popular Jewish
morality was simple. It believed that prosperity was the
sign of a good man. If a man was rich, God must have
honoured and blessed him. Wealth was proof of excellence
of character and of favour with God. The psalmist sums it
up, 'I have been young, and now am old, yet I have not seen

the righteous forsaken or their children begging bread' (Psalm 37:25).

No wonder the disciples were surprised! They would have argued that the more prosperous people were, the more certain they were of entry into the kingdom. So Jesus repeated his saying in a slightly different way to make clearer what he meant. 'How difficult it is', he said, 'for those who have put their trust in riches to enter the kingdom.'

No one ever saw the dangers of prosperity and of material things more clearly than Jesus did. What are these dangers?

(1) Material possessions tend to fix our hearts to this world. We have so large a stake in it, we have so great an interest in it, that it is difficult for us to think beyond it, and it is specially difficult for us to contemplate leaving it. Dr Johnson was once shown round a famous castle and its lovely grounds. After he had seen it all, he turned to his friends and said, 'These are the things that make it difficult to die.' The danger of possessions is that they fix our thoughts and interests to this world.

(2) If our main interest is in material possessions, it tends to make us think of everything in terms of price. A hill shepherd's wife wrote a most interesting letter to a newspaper. Her children had been brought up in the loneliness of the hills. They were simple and unsophisticated. Then her husband got a position in a town, and the children were introduced to the town. They changed very considerably – and they changed for the worse. The last paragraph of her letter read – 'Which is preferable for a child's upbringing – a lack of worldliness, but with better manners and sincere and simple thoughts, or worldliness and its present-day habit of knowing the price of everything and the true value of nothing?'

If our main interest is in material things, we will think in terms of price and not in terms of value. We will think in terms of what money can get. And we may well forget that there are values in this world far beyond money, that there are things which have no price, and that there are precious things that money cannot buy. It is fatal to begin to think that everything worth having has a monetary value.

(3) Jesus would have said that the possession of material goods is two things.

(a) It is an acid test of character. For every 100 who can stand adversity only one can stand prosperity. Prosperity can so very easily make people arrogant, proud, self-satisfied, worldly. It takes a really big and good person to bear it worthily.

(b) It is a responsibility. We will always be judged by two standards – how we got our possessions and how we use them. The more we have, the greater the responsibility that rests upon us. Will we use what we have selfishly or generously? Will we use it as if we had undisputed possession of it, or remembering that we hold it in stewardship from God?

The reaction of the disciples was that if what Jesus was saying was true, to be saved at all was well-nigh impossible. Then Jesus stated the whole doctrine of salvation in a nutshell. 'If', he said, 'salvation depended on a person's own efforts it would be impossible for anyone. But salvation is the gift of God and all things are possible to him.' Those who trust in themselves and in their possessions can never be saved. Those who trust in the saving power and the redeeming love of God can enter freely into salvation. This is the thought that Jesus stated. This is the thought that Paul wrote in letter after letter. And this is the thought which is still for us the very foundation of the Christian faith.

CHRIST IS NO ONE'S DEBTOR

Mark 10:28–31

> Peter began to say to him, 'Look now! We have left
> everything and have become your followers.' Jesus said,
> 'This is the truth I tell you – there is no one who has left
> house or brothers or sisters or mother or father or
> children or lands for my sake and for the sake of the
> good news who will not get it back 100 times over in
> this present time – homes and brothers and sisters and
> mothers and children and lands – with persecutions, and
> in the world to come eternal life. But many who are
> first will be last, and the last first.'

PETER's mind had been working, and, characteristically, his
tongue could not stay still. He had just seen a man deliberately
refuse Jesus' 'Follow me!' He had just heard Jesus say in
effect that that man by his action had shut himself out from
the kingdom of God. Peter could not help drawing the contrast
between that man and himself and his friends. Just as the
man had refused Jesus' 'Follow me!' he and his friends had
accepted it, and Peter with that almost crude honesty of his
wanted to know what he and his friends were to get out of it.
Jesus' answer falls into three sections.

(1) He said that no one ever gave up anything for the sake
of himself and of his good news without getting it back a
hundredfold. It so happened that in the early Church that was
literally true. A person's Christianity might involve the loss
of home and friends and loved ones, but entry into the
Christian Church brought with it a family far greater and
wider than the one left behind – a new spiritual family.

We see this actually happening in the life of Paul. No
doubt, when Paul became a Christian the door of his home

slammed in his face and his family disowned him. But equally without doubt there was city upon city, town upon town, village upon village in Europe and in Asia Minor where he could find a home waiting for him and a family in Christ to welcome him. It is strange how he often speaks in terms of family. In Romans 16:13, he tells how the mother of Rufus was as good as a mother to him. In Philemon 10, he speaks of Onesimus as the son whose father he had become during his imprisonment.

It would be so of all Christians in the early days. When their own families rejected them, they entered into the wider family of Christ.

When Egerton Young first preached the gospel to the native Americans in Saskatchewan, the idea of the fatherhood of God fascinated people who had hitherto seen God only in the thunder and the lightning and the storm blast. An old chief said to Egerton Young, 'Did I hear you say to God "Our Father"?' 'I did,' said Egerton Young. 'God is your Father?' asked the chief. 'Yes,' said Egerton Young. 'And', continued the chief, 'he is also my Father?' 'He certainly is,' said Egerton Young. Suddenly the chief's face lit up with a new radiance. His hand went out. 'Then', he said with the tone of someone making a dazzling discovery, 'you and I are brothers.'

Becoming a Christian may mean sacrificing ties that are very dear, but anyone who does so becomes a member of a family as wide as earth and heaven.

(2) Jesus added two things. First, he added the simple words *and persecutions*. Straightaway these words remove the whole matter from the world of *quid pro quo*. They take away the idea of a material reward for a material sacrifice. They tell us of two things. They speak of the utter honesty of Jesus. He never offered an easy way. He made it clear that to

be a Christian is a costly thing. Second, they tell us that Jesus never used a *bribe* to make people follow him. He used a *challenge*. It is as if he said, 'Certainly you will get your reward, but you will have to show yourself big enough and brave enough to get it.' The second thing that Jesus added was the idea of the world to come. He never promised that within this world of space and time there would be a kind of squaring up of the balance sheet and settlement of accounts. He did not call men and women to win the rewards of time. He called them to earn the blessings of eternity. God has not only this world in which to repay.

(3) Then Jesus added one warning epigram – 'Many who are first shall be last, and the last first.' This was in reality a warning to Peter. It may well be that by this time Peter was estimating his own worth and his own reward and assessing them high. What Jesus was saying was, 'The final standard of judgment is with God. Many may stand well in the judgment of the world, but the judgment of God may upset the world's judgment. Still more – many may stand well in their own judgment, and find that God's evaluation of them is very different.' It is a warning against all pride. It is a warning that the ultimate judgments belong to God who alone knows the motives of human hearts. It is a warning that the judgments of heaven may well upset the reputations of earth.

THE APPROACHING END

Mark 10:32–4

> They were on the road, on their way up to Jerusalem, and Jesus was walking ahead of them. They were in a state of astonished bewilderment, and, as they followed him, they were afraid. Once again he took the Twelve

to him, and began to tell them what was going to happen
to him. 'Look you!' he said. 'We are going up to
Jerusalem, and the Son of Man will be handed over to
the chief priests and experts in the law, and they will
condemn him to death, and they will hand him over to
the Gentiles, and they will make a jest of him, and they
will spit on him, and they will scourge him and they
will kill him. And after three days he will rise again.'

HERE is a vivid picture, all the more vivid because of the
stark economy of words with which it is painted. Jesus and
his disciples were entering upon the last scene. Jesus had set
his course definitely and irrevocably to Jerusalem and the
cross. Mark marks the stages very definitely. There had been
the withdrawal to the north, to the territory round Caesarea
Philippi. There had been the journey south, and the brief halt
in Galilee. There had been the way to Judaea and the time in
the hill country and beyond Jordan. And now there is the
final stage, the road to Jerusalem.

This picture tells us something about Jesus.

(1) It tells us of the loneliness of Jesus. They were going
along the road and he was out ahead of them – alone. And
they were so amazed and bewildered, so conscious of the
sense of impending tragedy, that they were afraid to go up to
him. There are certain decisions which can only be taken
alone. Had Jesus tried to share this decision with the Twelve
their only contribution would have been to try to stop him.
There are certain things which must be faced alone. Matthew
Arnold, in his poem 'Isolation', speaks of

> This truth – to prove and make thine own:
> 'Thou hast been, shalt be, art alone'.

There are certain decisions which must be taken and certain
roads that must be walked in the awful loneliness of our own

souls. And yet, in the deepest sense of all, even in these times
we are not alone, for never is God nearer to us. The American
poet John Greenleaf Whittier writes of such a time:

> Nothing before, nothing behind.
>   The steps of faith
> Fall on the seeming void, and find
>   The rock beneath.

Here we see the essential loneliness of Jesus, a loneliness
that was comforted by God.

(2) It tells us of the courage of Jesus. Three times Jesus
foretold the things that were to happen to him in Jerusalem,
and as Mark tells of these warnings, each time they grow
grimmer and some further detail of horror is included. At
first (Mark 8:31) it is the bare announcement. At the second
time the hint of betrayal is there (Mark 9:31). And now at the
third time the jesting, the mocking and the scourging appear.
It would seem as if the picture became ever clearer in the
mind of Jesus as he became more and more aware of the cost
of redemption.

There are two kinds of courage. There is the courage which
is a kind of instinctive reaction, almost a reflex action, the
courage of those who are confronted out of the blue with a
crisis to which they instinctively react, scarcely having time
to think. Many have performed acts of great bravery in the
heat of the moment. There is also the courage of those who
see the grim thing approaching far ahead, who have plenty of
time to turn back, who could, if they chose, evade the issue,
and who yet go on. There is no doubt which is the higher
courage – this known deliberate facing of the future. That is
the courage Jesus showed. If no higher verdict was possible,
it would still be true to say of Jesus that he ranks with the
heroes of the world.

(3) It tells us of the personal magnetism of Jesus. It is quite clear that by this time the disciples did not know what was going on. They were sure that Jesus was the Messiah. They were equally sure that he was going to die. To them these two facts did not make sense when put together. They were completely bewildered, *and yet they followed*. To them everything was dark except one thing – they loved Jesus, and, however much they wished to, they could not leave him. They had learned something which is of the very essence of life and faith – they loved so much that they were compelled to accept what they could not understand.

THE REQUEST MADE OUT OF AMBITION

Mark 10:35–40

> James and John, the sons of Zebedee, came to Jesus. 'Teacher,' they said, 'we want you to do for us whatever we ask you.' 'What do you want me to do for you?' he said to them. They said to him, 'Grant to us that, in your glory, we may sit one on your right hand and one on your left.' 'You do not know what you ask,' Jesus said to them. 'Can you drink the cup which I am drinking? Or, can you go through the experience through which I am going?' 'We can,' they said to him. Jesus said to them, 'You will drink the cup which I am drinking. You will go through the experience through which I am going. But to sit on my right hand and on my left is not mine to give you. That place belongs to those for whom it has been prepared.'

THIS is a very revealing story.

(1) It tells us something about Mark. Matthew tells this story (Matthew 20:20–3), but in his version the request for the first places is made not by James and John, but by their mother Salome. Matthew must have felt that such a request was unworthy of an apostle, and, to save the reputation of James and John, he attributed it to the natural ambition of their mother. This story shows us the honesty of Mark. It is told that a court painter painted the portrait of Oliver Cromwell. Cromwell was afflicted with warts on the face. Thinking to please him, the painter omitted the warts in the painting. When Cromwell saw it, he said, 'Take it away! and paint me warts and all!' It is Mark's aim to show us the disciples, warts and all. And Mark was right, because the Twelve were not a company of saints. They were ordinary men. It was with people like ourselves that Jesus set out to change the world – and did it.

(2) It tells us something about James and John.

(a) It tells us that they were ambitious. When the victory was won and the triumph was complete, they aimed at being Jesus' chief ministers of state. Maybe their ambition was kindled because more than once Jesus had made them part of his inner circle, the chosen three. Maybe they were a little better off than the others. Their father was well enough off to employ hired servants (Mark 1:20), and it may be that they rather snobbishly thought that their social superiority entitled them to the first place. In any event they show themselves as men in whose hearts there was ambition for the first place in an earthly kingdom.

(b) It tells us that they had completely failed to understand Jesus. The amazing thing is not the fact that this incident happened, but *the time* at which it happened. It is the juxtaposition of Jesus' most definite and detailed forecast of his death and this request that is staggering. It shows, as nothing else could, how little they understood what Jesus was saying to them. Words were powerless to rid them of the idea of a Messiah of earthly power and glory. Only the cross could do that.

(c) But when we have said all that is to be said against James and John, this story tells us one shining thing about them – bewildered as they might be, *they still believed in Jesus*. It is amazing that they could still connect glory with a Galilaean carpenter who had incurred the enmity and the bitter opposition of the orthodox religious leaders and who was apparently heading for a cross. There is amazing confidence and amazing loyalty there. Misguided James and John might be, but their hearts were in the right place. They never doubted Jesus' ultimate triumph.

(3) It tells us something of Jesus' standard of greatness. The Revised Standard Version gives a literally accurate reading of what Jesus said – 'Are you able to drink the cup that I drink, or to be baptized with the baptism with which I am baptized?' Jesus uses two Jewish metaphors here.

It was the custom at a royal banquet for the king to hand the cup to his guests. *The cup* therefore became a metaphor for the life and experience that God handed out to men and women. 'My cup overflows,' said the psalmist (Psalm 23:5), when he spoke of a life and experience of happiness given to him by God. 'In the hand of the Lord there is a cup,' said the psalmist (Psalm 75:8), when he was thinking of the fate in store for the wicked and the disobedient. Isaiah, thinking of the disasters which had come upon the people of Israel, describes them as having drunk 'at the hand of the Lord the cup of his wrath' (Isaiah 51:17). *The cup* speaks of the experience allotted to men and women by God.

The other phrase which Jesus uses is actually misleading in the literal English version. He speaks of the baptism with which he was baptized. The Greek verb *baptizein* means *to dip*. Its past participle (*bebaptismenos*) means *submerged*, and it is regularly used of being *submerged in any experience*. For instance, a spendthrift is said to be *submerged* in debt. A drunk person is said to be *submerged* in drink. A grief-stricken person is said to be *submerged* in sorrow. A pupil before a cross-examining teacher is said to be *submerged* in questions. The word is regularly used for a ship that has been wrecked and *submerged* beneath the waves. The metaphor is very closely related to a metaphor which the psalmist often uses. In Psalm 42:7 we read, 'All your waves and your billows have gone over me.' In Psalm 124:4 we read, 'Then the flood would have swept us away, the torrent would have gone over us.' The expression, as Jesus used it here, had nothing to do with technical baptism. What he is saying is, 'Can you bear to go through the terrible experience which I have to go through? Can you face being submerged in hatred and pain and death, as I have to be?' He was telling these two disciples that without a cross there can never be a crown. The standard of greatness in the kingdom is the standard of the cross. It was true that in the days to come they did go through the experience of their Master, for James was beheaded by Herod Agrippa (Acts 12:2), and, though John was probably not martyred, he suffered much for Christ. They accepted the challenge of their Master – even if they did so blindly.

(4) Jesus told them that the ultimate issue of things belonged to God. The final assignment of destiny was his prerogative. Jesus never usurped the place of God. His whole life was one long act of submission to God's will, and he knew that in the end that will was supreme.

THE PRICE OF SALVATION

Mark 10:41–5

> When the ten heard about this, they began to be vexed
> about the action of James and John. Jesus called them
> to him. 'You are well aware', he said, 'that those who
> are esteemed good enough to rule over the Gentiles lord
> it over them, and their great ones exercise authority over
> them. It is not so among you, but, among you, whoever
> wishes to be great will be your servant, and among you,
> whoever wishes to be first will be the slave of all. For
> the Son of Man did not come to be served but to serve,
> and to give his life a ransom for many.'

INEVITABLY the action of James and John aroused deep
resentment among the other ten. It seemed to them that they
had tried to steal a march and to take an unfair advantage.
Immediately the old controversy about who was to be greatest
began to rage again.

This was a serious situation. The fellowship of the apostolic
band might well have been wrecked, had Jesus not taken
immediate action. He called them to him, and made quite
clear the different standards of greatness in his kingdom and
in the kingdoms of the world. In the kingdoms of the world
the standard of greatness was power. The test was: how many
people does a man control? How great an army of servants
has he at his beck and call? On how many people can he
impose his will? Not very much later than this, Galba was to
sum up the pagan idea of kingship and greatness when he
said that now he was emperor he could do what he liked and
do it to anyone. In the kingdom of Jesus the standard was
that of service. Greatness consisted not in reducing others to
one's service, but in reducing oneself to their service. The

test was not what service can I extract?, but, what service can I give?

We tend to think of this as an ideal state of affairs, but, in point of fact, it is the soundest common sense. It is in fact the first principle of ordinary everyday business life. It has been pointed out that the basis on which some motor companies will claim the patronage of prospective customers is that they will crawl under your car oftener and get themselves dirtier than any of their competitors. They are in other words prepared to give more service. It is also pointed out that although the ordinary office worker may go home at 5.30 pm, the light will be seen burning in the office of the chief executive long into the night. It is that willingness to give the extra service that marks out the head of the company.

The basic trouble is that it is human nature to want to do as little as possible and to get as much as possible. It is only when we are filled with the desire to put into life more than we take out that life for ourselves and for others will be happy and prosperous. Rudyard Kipling has a poem called 'Mary's Son' which is advice on the spirit in which work must be done:

> If you stop to find out what your wages will be
>   And how they will clothe and feed you,
> Willie, my son, don't you go to the Sea,
>   For the Sea will never need you.
>
> If you ask for the reason of every command,
>   And argue with people about you,
> Willie, my son, don't you go on the Land,
>   For the Land will do better without you.
>
> If you stop to consider the work that you've done
>   And to boast what your labour is worth, dear,
> Angels may come for you, Willie, my son.
>   But you'll never be wanted on earth dear!

The world needs people whose ideal is service – that is to say it needs people who have realized what sound sense Jesus spoke.

To clinch his words Jesus pointed to his own example. With such powers as he had, he could have arranged life entirely to suit himself, but he had spent himself and all his powers in the service of others. He had come, he said, *to give his life a ransom for many*. This is one of the great phrases of the gospel, and yet it has been sadly mishandled and maltreated. People have tried to erect a theory of the atonement on what is a saying of love.

It was not long before people were asking to whom this ransom of the life of Christ had been paid. Origen asked the question, 'To whom did he give his life a ransom for many? It was not to God. Was it not then to the evil one? For the devil was holding us fast until the ransom should be given to him, even the life of Jesus, for he was deceived with the idea that he could have dominion over it and did not see that he could not bear the torture involved in retaining it.' It is an odd conception that the life of Jesus was paid as a ransom to the devil so that he should release human beings from the bondage in which he held them, but that the devil found that in demanding and accepting that ransom, he had, so to speak, bitten off more than he could chew.

In the fourth century, Gregory of Nyssa saw the flaw in that theory, namely that it really puts the devil on an equality with God. It allows him to make a bargain with God on equal terms. So Gregory conceived of the extraordinary idea of *a trick* played by God. The devil was tricked by the seeming weakness of the incarnation. He mistook Jesus for a mere man. He tried to exert his authority over him and, by trying to do so, lost it. Again it is an odd idea – that God should conquer the devil by a trick.

Another 200 years passed and Gregory the Great took up the idea. He used a fantastic metaphor. The incarnation was a divine stratagem to catch the great leviathan. The deity of Christ was the hook, his flesh was the bait. When the bait was dangled before Leviathan, the devil, he swallowed it, and tried to swallow the hook, too, and so was overcome forever.

Finally, in the twelfth century, Peter the Lombard brings this idea to its most grotesque and repulsive. 'The cross', he said, 'was a mousetrap to catch the devil, baited with the blood of Christ.' All this simply shows what happens when a lovely and precious picture is taken and attempts are made to make a cold theology out of it.

Suppose we say, 'Sorrow is the *price* of love,' we mean that love cannot exist without the possibility of sorrow, but we never even think of trying to explain to whom that *price* is paid. Suppose we say that freedom can be obtained only at the *price* of blood, toil, tears and sweat, we never think of investigating to whom that *price* is paid. This saying of Jesus is a simple and pictorial way of saying that it cost the life of Jesus to bring men and women back from their sin into the love of God. It means that the cost of our salvation was the cross of Christ. Beyond that we cannot go, and beyond that we do not need to go. We know only that something happened on the cross which opened for us the way to God.

A MIRACLE BY THE WAYSIDE

Mark 10:46–52

> They went to Jericho. As Jesus was passing through
> Jericho, on his way out of the city – his disciples and a
> great crowd were with him – Bartimaeus, the son of

Timaeus, a blind beggar, was sitting by the roadside.
When he heard that Jesus of Nazareth was there he
began to shout. 'Son of David!' he cried, 'Jesus! Have
pity on me!' Many rebuked him and told him to be quiet.
But he shouted all the more, 'Son of David! Have pity
on me!' Jesus came to a stop. 'Call him here!' he said.
They called the blind man. 'Courage!' they said to him.
'Get up! He is calling you!' He threw off his cloak and
leapt up and came to Jesus. Jesus said to him, 'What do
you want me to do for you?' The blind man said to him,
'Master teacher! My prayer is that I might see again.'
Jesus said to him, 'Go! Your faith has cured you.'
Immediately he saw again, and he followed him upon
the road.

FOR Jesus the end of the road was not far away. Jericho was
only about fifteen miles from Jerusalem. We must try to
visualize the scene. The main road ran right through Jericho.
Jesus was on his way to the Passover. When a distinguished
Rabbi or teacher was on such a journey it was the custom
that he was surrounded by a crowd of people, disciples and
learners, who listened to him as he discoursed while he
walked. That was one of the commonest ways of teaching.

It was the law that every male Jew over twelve years of
age who lived within fifteen miles of Jerusalem must attend
the Passover. It was clearly impossible that such a law should
be fulfilled and that everyone should go. Those who were
unable to go were in the habit of lining the streets of towns
and villages through which groups of Passover pilgrims must
pass to bid them godspeed on their way. So then the streets of
Jericho would be lined with people, and there would be even
more than usual, for there would be many eager and curious
to catch a glimpse of this audacious young Galilaean who
had pitted himself against the assembled might of orthodoxy.

Jericho had one special characteristic. There were attached
to the Temple over 20,000 priests and as many Levites.
Obviously they could not all serve at the one time. They were
therefore divided into twenty-six courses which served in
rotation. Very many of these priests and Levites resided in
Jericho when they were not on actual temple duty. There must
have been many of them in the crowd that day. At the Passover
all were on duty for all were needed. It was one of the rare
occasions when all did serve. But many would not have
started yet. They would be doubly eager to see this rebel who
was about to invade Jerusalem. There would be many cold
and bleak and hostile eyes in the crowd that day, because it
was clear that if Jesus was right, the whole Temple worship
was one vast irrelevance.

At the northern gate sat a beggar, Bartimaeus by name. He
heard the tramp of feet. He asked what was happening and
who was passing. He was told that it was Jesus. There and
then he set up an uproar to attract Jesus' attention to him. To
those listening to Jesus' teaching as he walked, the uproar
was an offence. They tried to silence Bartimaeus, but no one
was going to take from him his chance to escape from his
world of darkness, and he cried with such violence and
persistence that the procession stopped, and he was brought
to Jesus.

This is a most illuminating story. In it we can see many of
the things which we might call the conditions of miracle.

(I) There is the sheer persistence of Bartimaeus. Nothing
would stop his clamour to come face to face with Jesus. He
was utterly determined to meet the one person whom he
longed to confront with his trouble. In the mind of Bartimaeus
there was not just a vague, wistful, sentimental wish to see
Jesus. It was a desperate desire, and it is that desperate desire
that gets things done.

(2) His response to the call of Jesus was immediate and
eager, so eager that he cast off his hindering cloak to run to
Jesus the more quickly. Many people hear the call of Jesus,
but say in effect, 'Wait until I have done this,' or 'Wait until I
have finished that.' Bartimaeus came like a shot when Jesus
called. Certain chances happen only once. Bartimaeus instinctively knew that. Sometimes we have a wave of longing
to abandon some habit, to purify life of some wrong thing, to
give ourselves more completely to Jesus. So very often we
do not seize the moment to act on it – and the chance is gone,
perhaps never to come back.

(3) He knew precisely what he wanted – his sight. Too
often our admiration for Jesus is a vague attraction. When we
go to the doctor it is to have something specific dealt with.
When we go to the dentist we do not ask to have *any* tooth
extracted, but the one that is diseased. It should be so with us
and Jesus. And that involves the one thing that so few people
wish to face – *self-examination*. When we go to Jesus, if we
are as desperately definite as Bartimaeus, things will happen.

(4) Bartimaeus had a quite inadequate conception of Jesus.
Son of David, he insisted on calling him. Now that was a
messianic title, but it has in it all the thought of a conquering
Messiah, a king of David's line who would lead Israel to
national greatness. That was a very inadequate idea of Jesus.
But, in spite of that, Bartimaeus had *faith*, and faith made
up a hundredfold for the inadequacy of his theology. The
demand is not that we should fully understand Jesus. That, in
any event, we can never do. The demand is for *faith*. A wise
writer has said, 'We must ask people to think, but we should
not expect them to become theologians before they are
Christians.' Christianity begins with a personal reaction to
Jesus, a reaction of love, feeling that here is the one person
who can meet our need. Even if we are never able to think

things out theologically, that response of the human heart is enough.

(5) In the end there is a precious touch. Bartimaeus may have been a beggar by the wayside but he was a man of gratitude. Having received his sight, he followed Jesus. He did not selfishly go on his way when his need was met. He began with need, went on to gratitude, and finished with loyalty – and that is a perfect summary of the stages of discipleship.

THE COMING OF THE KING

Mark 11:1-6

> When they were coming near to Jerusalem, to Bethphage and to Bethany, Jesus despatched two of his disciples, and said to them, 'Go into the village opposite you, and as soon as you come into it, you will find tethered there a colt, on which no man has ever yet sat. Loose it and bring it to me. And if anyone says to you, "Why are you doing this?" say, "The Lord needs it," and immediately he will send it.' And they went away and they found the colt tethered, outside a door, on the open street, and they loosed it. And some of those who were standing by said to them, 'What are you doing loosing this colt?' They said to them what Jesus had told them to say, and they let them go.

WE have come to the last stage of the journey. There had been the time of withdrawal around Caesarea Philippi in the far north. There had been the time in Galilee. There had been the stay in the hill country of Judaea and in the regions beyond Jordan. There had been the road through Jericho. Now comes Jerusalem.

We have to note something without which the story is almost unintelligible. When we read the first three gospels we get the idea that this was actually Jesus' first visit to Jerusalem. They are concerned to tell the story of Jesus' work in Galilee. We must remember that the gospels are very short. Into their short compass is crammed the work of three years, and the writers were bound to select the things in which they were interested and of which they had special knowledge. And when we read the Fourth Gospel we find Jesus frequently in Jerusalem (John 2:13, 5:1, 7:10). We find in fact that he regularly went up to Jerusalem for the great feasts.

There is no real contradiction here. The first three gospels are specially interested in the Galilaean ministry, and the fourth in the Judaean. In fact, moreover, even the first three have indications that Jesus was not infrequently in Jerusalem. There is his close friendship with Martha and Mary and Lazarus at Bethany, a friendship which speaks of many visits. There is the fact that Joseph of Arimathaea was his secret friend. And above all there is Jesus' saying in Matthew 23:37 that often he would have gathered together the people of Jerusalem as a hen gathers her chickens under her wings but they were unwilling. Jesus could not have said that unless there had previously been more than one appeal which had met with a cold response.

This explains the incident of the colt. Jesus did not leave things until the last moment. He knew what he was going to do and long ago he had made arrangements with a friend. When he sent forward his disciples, he sent them with a password that had been pre-arranged – 'The Lord needs it now.' This was not a sudden, reckless decision of Jesus. It was something to which all his life had been building up.

Bethphage and Bethany were villages near Jerusalem. Very probably *Bethphage* means *house of figs* and *Bethany* means *house of dates.* They must have been very close because we know from the Jewish law that Bethphage was one of the circle of villages which marked the limit of a Sabbath day's journey, that is, less than a mile, while Bethany was one of the recognized lodging places for pilgrims to the Passover when Jerusalem was full.

The prophets of Israel had always had a very distinctive method of getting their message across. When words failed to move people they did something dramatic, as if to say, 'If you will not hear, you must be compelled to see' (cf. specially I Kings 11:30-2). These dramatic actions were what we might call acted warnings or dramatic sermons. That method was what Jesus was employing here. His action was a deliberate dramatic claim to be the Messiah.

But we must be careful to note just what he was doing. There was a saying of the prophet Zechariah (Zechariah 9:9), 'Rejoice greatly, O daughter Zion! Shout aloud, O daughter Jerusalem! Lo, your king comes to you; triumphant and victorious is he, humble and riding on a donkey, on a colt, the foal of a donkey.' The whole impact is that *the King was coming in peace.* In Palestine the donkey was not a despised animal, but a noble one. When a king went to war he rode on a horse, when he came in peace he rode on a donkey.

G. K. Chesterton has a poem in which he makes the modern donkey speak:

> When fishes flew and forests walk'd
>   And figs grew upon thorn,
> Some moment when the moon was blood
>   Then surely I was born.
>
> With monstrous head and sickening cry
>   And ears like errant wings,
> The devil's walking parody
>   Of all four-footed things.

> The tatter'd outlaw of the earth
>> Of ancient crooked will;
> Starve, scourge, deride me, I am dumb,
>> I keep my secret still.

> Fools! For I also had my hour,
>> One far fierce hour and sweet;
> There was a shout about my ears,
>> And palms before my feet.

It is a wonderful poem. Nowadays the donkey is an animal of amused contempt, but in the time of Jesus it was the animal used to bear kings. But we must note *what kind of a king Jesus was claiming to be*. He came meek and lowly. He came in peace and for peace. They greeted him as the Son of David, but they did not understand.

It was just at this time that the Hebrew poems, The Psalms of Solomon, were written. They represent the kind of Son of David whom people expected. Here is their description of him:

> Behold, O Lord, and raise up unto them their king, the
>> son of David,
>>> At the time, in which thou seest, O God, that he
>>>> may reign over Israel, thy servant.
> And gird him with strength that he may shatter
>> unrighteous rulers,
>>> And that he may purge Jerusalem from nations
>>>> that trample her down to destruction.
> Wisely, righteously he shall thrust out sinners from
>> the inheritance,
>>> He shall destroy the pride of sinners as a
>>>> potter's vessel.
> With a rod of iron he shall break in pieces all their
>> substance.

He shall destroy the godless nations with the
    word of his mouth.
At his rebuke nations shall flee before him,
    And he shall reprove sinners for the thoughts of
        their hearts.

                    . . .

All nations shall be in fear before him,
For he will smite the earth with the word of his mouth
    forever.

                    (Psalms of Solomon 17:21-5, 39)

That was the kind of poem on which the people nourished
their hearts. They were looking for a king who would shatter
and smash and break. Jesus knew it – and he came meek and
lowly, riding upon a donkey.

When Jesus rode into Jerusalem that day, he claimed to be
king, but he claimed to be King of peace. His action was a
contradiction of everything that was hoped for and expected.

THE ONE WHO IS COMING

Mark 11:7-10

They brought the colt to Jesus, and they put their
garments on it, and mounted him on it. Many of them
spread their garments on the road. Others cut branches
from the fields and spread them on the road. And those
who were going before and those who were following
kept shouting, 'Save now! Blessed is the coming
kingdom of our father David! Send thy salvation from
the heights of heaven!'

THE colt they brought had never been ridden upon. That was
fitting, for an animal to be used for a sacred purpose must
never have been used for any other purpose. It was so with

the red heifer whose ashes cleansed from pollution (Numbers 19:2f.; Deuteronomy 21:3f.).

The whole picture is of a people who misunderstood. It shows us a crowd of people thinking of kingship in the terms of conquest in which they had thought of it for so long. It is oddly reminiscent of how Simon Maccabaeus entered Jerusalem 150 years before, after he had blasted Israel's enemies in battle. 'On the twenty-third day of the second month, in the one hundred and seventy-first year, the Jews entered it with praise and palm branches, and with harps, and cymbals, and stringed instruments, and with hymns and songs, because a great enemy had been crushed and removed from Israel' (1 Maccabees 13:51). It was a conqueror's welcome they sought to give to Jesus, but they never dreamed of the kind of conqueror he wished to be.

The very shouts which the crowd raised to Jesus showed how their thoughts were running. When they spread their garments on the ground before him, they did exactly what the crowd did when that man of blood Jehu was anointed king (2 Kings 9:13). They shouted, 'Blessed is the one who comes in the name of the Lord!' That is a quotation from Psalm 118:26, and should really read a little differently, 'Blessed in the name of the Lord is the one who is coming!'

There are three things to note about that shout.

(1) It was the regular greeting with which pilgrims were addressed when they reached the Temple on the occasion of the great feasts.

(2) 'The one who comes' was another name for the Messiah. When the Jews spoke about the Messiah, they talked of him as *the One who is Coming*.

(3) But it is the whole origin of the Psalm from which the words come that makes them supremely suggestive. In 167 BC there had arisen an extraordinary king in Syria called

Antiochus. He had conceived it his duty to be a missionary of Hellenism and to introduce Greek ways of life, Greek thought and Greek religion wherever he could, even, if necessary, by force. He tried to do so in Palestine.

For a time he conquered Palestine. To possess a copy of the law or to circumcise a child were crimes punishable by death. He desecrated the Temple courts. He actually instituted the worship of Zeus where Yahweh had been worshipped. With deliberate insult he offered pig's flesh on the great altar of the burnt offering. He made the chambers round the Temple courts into brothels. He did everything he could to wipe out the Jewish faith.

It was then that Judas Maccabaeus arose; and, after an amazing career of conquest, in 163 BC he drove Antiochus out and repurified and reconsecrated the Temple, an event which the Feast of the Dedication, or the Feast of Hanukkah, still commemorates. And in all probability Psalm 118 was written to commemorate that great day of purification and the battle which Judas Maccabaeus won. *It is a conqueror's psalm.*

Again and again we see the same thing happening in this incident. Jesus had claimed to be the Messiah, but in such a way as to try to show that the popular ideas of the Messiah were misguided. But the people did not see it. Their welcome was one which befitted not the King of love but the conqueror who would shatter the enemies of Israel.

In verses 9 and 10 there is the word *Hosanna*. The word is consistently misunderstood. It is quoted and used as if it meant *Praise*; but it is a simple transliteration of the Hebrew for *Save now!* It occurs in exactly the same form in 2 Samuel 14:4 and 2 Kings 6:26, where it is used by people seeking for help and protection at the hands of the king. When the people shouted *Hosanna* it was not a cry of praise to Jesus, which it often sounds like when we quote it. It was a cry to God to break in and save his people now that the Messiah had come.

No incident so shows the sheer courage of Jesus as this does. In the circumstances one might have expected him to enter Jerusalem secretly and to keep hidden from the authorities who were out to destroy him. Instead he entered in such a way that the attention of every eye was focused upon him. One of the most dangerous things that anyone can do is to go to people and tell them that all their accepted ideas are wrong. Anyone who tries to tear up by the roots a people's nationalistic dreams is in for trouble. But that is what Jesus was deliberately doing. Here we see Jesus making the last appeal of love and making it with a courage that is heroic.

THE QUIET BEFORE THE STORM

Mark 11:11

> And he came into Jerusalem into the Temple. After he
> had looked round everything, when it was now late, he
> went out to Bethany with the Twelve.

THIS simple verse shows us two things about Jesus which were typical of him.

(1) It shows us Jesus deliberately summing up his task. The whole atmosphere of the last days was one of deliberation. Jesus was not recklessly plunging into unknown dangers. He was doing everything with his eyes wide open. When he looked round everything, he was like a commander summing up the strength of the opposition and his own resources preparatory to the decisive battle.

(2) It shows us where Jesus got his strength. He went back to the peace of Bethany. Before he joined battle with the

world, he sought the presence of God. It was only because each day he faced God that he could face the world's challenge with such courage.

This brief passage also shows us something about the Twelve. They were still with him. By this time it must have been quite plain to them that Jesus was committing suicide, as it seemed to them. Sometimes we criticize them for their lack of loyalty in the last days, but it says something for them, that, little as they understood what was happening, they still stood by him.

THE FRUITLESS FIG TREE

Mark 11:12–14, 20–1

> When, on the next day, they were coming out from Bethany, Jesus was hungry. From a distance he saw a fig tree in leaf, and he went to it to see if he would find anything on it. When he came to it he found nothing except leaves, for it was not yet the season of figs. He said to it, 'Let no one eat fruit from you forever.' And the disciples heard him say it ... When they were going along the road early in the morning, they saw the fig tree withered from the roots. Peter remembered what Jesus had said the day before and said, 'Teacher! Look! The fig tree which you cursed has withered away!'

ALTHOUGH in Mark's gospel the story of the fig tree is divided into two, we take it as one. The first part of the story happened on the morning of one day, and the second part on the morning of the next day, and, chronologically, the cleansing of the Temple came in between. But, when we are trying to see the meaning of the story, we are better to take it as one.

There can be no doubt that this, without exception, is the most difficult story in the gospel narrative. To take it as literal history presents difficulties which are well-nigh insuperable.

(1) The story does not ring true. To be frank, the whole incident does not seem worthy of Jesus. There seems a certain peevishness in it. It is just the kind of story that is told of other wonder-workers but never of Jesus. Further, we have this basic difficulty. Jesus had always refused to use his miraculous powers for his own sake. He would not turn the stones into bread to satisfy his own hunger. He would not use his miraculous powers to escape from his enemies. He *never* used his power for his own sake. And yet here he uses his power to blast a tree which had disappointed him when he was hungry.

(2) Worse, the whole action was unreasonable. This was the Passover Season, that is, the middle of April. The fig tree in a sheltered spot may bear leaves as early as March, but never did a fig tree bear figs until late May or June. Mark says that it was not the season for figs. Why blast the tree for failing to do what it was not possible for it to do? It was both unreasonable and unjust. Some commentators, to save the situation, say that what Jesus was looking for was green figs, half-ripe figs in their early stages, but such unripe fruit was unpleasant and was never eaten.

The whole story does not seem to fit Jesus at all. What are we to say about it?

If we are to take this as the story of something which actually happened, we must take it as *an enacted parable*. We must in fact take it as one of those prophetic, symbolic, dramatic actions. If we take it that way, it may be interpreted as the condemnation of two things.

(1) It is the condemnation of *promise without fulfilment*. The leaves on the tree might be taken as the promise of fruit,

but there was no fruit there. It is the condemnation especially of the people of Israel. All their history was a preparation for the coming of God's chosen one. The whole promise of their national record was that when the chosen one came they would be eager to receive him. But when he did come, that promise was tragically unfulfilled.

The nineteenth-century English essayist Charles Lamb tells of a certain man called Samuel le Grice. In his life there were three stages. When he was young, people said of him, 'He will do something.' As he grew older and did nothing, they said of him, 'He could do something if he tried.' Towards the end they said of him, 'He might have done something if he had tried.' His life was the tale of a promise that was never fulfilled. If this incident is an enacted parable it is the condemnation of unfulfilled promise.

(2) It is the condemnation of *profession without practice*. It might be taken that the tree with its leaves professed to offer something and did not. The whole cry of the New Testament is that we can be known only by the fruits of our lives. 'You will know them by their fruits' (Matthew 7:16). 'Bear fruits worthy of repentance' (Luke 3:8). It is not the person who piously says, 'Lord, Lord,' who will enter into the kingdom but the one who does God's will (Matthew 7:21). Unless our religion makes us better and more useful people, makes our homes happier, makes life better and easier for those with whom we are brought into contact, it is not religion at all. We cannot claim to be followers of Jesus Christ and remain entirely unlike the Master whom we profess to love.

If this incident is to be taken literally and is an enacted parable, that must be the meaning. But, relevant as these lessons may be, it seems difficult to extract them from the incident, because it was quite unreasonable to expect the fig tree to bear figs when the time for figs was still six weeks away.

What then are we to say? Luke does not relate this incident at all, but he has the parable of the fruitless fig tree (Luke 13:6–9). Now that parable ends indecisively. The master of the vineyard wished to root up the tree. The gardener pleaded for another chance. The last chance was given; and it was agreed that if the tree bore fruit it should be spared, and if not it should be destroyed. May it not be that this incident is a kind of continuation of that parable? The people of Israel had had their chance. They had failed to bear fruit. And now was the time for their destruction. It has been suggested – and it is quite possible – that on the road from Bethany to Jerusalem there was a lonely blasted fig tree. It may well be that Jesus said to his disciples, 'You remember the parable I told you about the fruitless fig tree? Israel is still fruitless and will be blasted as that tree.' It may well be that that lonely tree became associated in people's minds with a saying of Jesus about the fate of fruitlessness, and so the story arose.

Let readers take it as they will. To us there seem insuperable difficulties in taking it literally. It seems to us to be in some way connected with the parable of the fruitless tree. But in any event the whole lesson of the incident is that uselessness invites disaster.

THE WRATH OF JESUS

Mark 11:15–19

> They came into Jerusalem, and when Jesus had come into the sacred precincts, he began to cast out those who sold and bought in the sacred place, and he overturned

the tables of the money-changers and the seats of those who sold doves, and he would not allow that anyone should carry their gear through the sacred precincts. The burden of his teaching and speaking was, 'Is it not written, my house shall be called a house of prayer for all nations, but you have made it a brigands' cave?' The chief priests and the experts in the law heard him, and they sought a way to destroy him, for they were afraid of him, for the whole crowd was astonished at his teaching.

And when evening came he went out of the city.

WE will visualize this far better if we have in our mind's eye a picture of the layout of the Temple precincts. There are two closely connected words used in the New Testament. The first is *hieron*, which means *the sacred place*. This included the whole Temple area. The Temple area covered the top of Mount Zion and was about thirty acres in extent. It was surrounded by great walls which varied on each side, 1,300 to 1,000 feet in length. There was a wide outer space called the *Court of the Gentiles*. Into it anyone, Jew or Gentile, might come. At the inner edge of the Court of the Gentiles was a low wall with tablets set into it which said that if a Gentile passed that point the penalty was death. The next court was called the *Court of the Women*. It was so called because unless women had come actually to offer sacrifice they might not proceed further. Next was the *Court of the Israelites*. In it the congregation gathered on great occasions, and from it the offerings were handed by the worshippers to the priests. The inmost court was the *Court of the Priests*.

The other important word is *naos*, which means *the Temple proper*, and it was in the Court of the Priests that the Temple stood. The whole area, including all the different Courts, was the sacred precincts (*hieron*). The special building within the Court of the Priests was the Temple (*naos*).

This incident took place in the Court of the Gentiles. Bit by bit the Court of the Gentiles had become almost entirely secularized. It had been meant to be a place of prayer and preparation, but there was in the time of Jesus a commercialized atmosphere of buying and selling which made prayer and meditation impossible. What made it worse was that the business which went on there was sheer exploitation of the pilgrims.

Every Jew had to pay a temple tax of one half-shekel a year. That was equivalent to nearly two days' wages for a working man. That tax had to be paid in one particular kind of coinage. For ordinary purposes Greek, Roman, Syrian, Egyptian, Phoenician and Tyrian coinages were all equally valid. But this tax had to be paid in shekels of the sanctuary. It was paid at the Passover time. Jews came from all over the world to the Passover and with all kinds of currencies. When they went to have their money changed they had to pay a fee, and should their coin exceed the tax, they had to pay another fee before they got their change. Most pilgrims had to pay this extra commission before they could pay their tax, and the commission amounted to half a day's wage, which for most people was a great deal of money.

As for the sellers of doves – doves entered largely into the sacrificial system (Leviticus 12:8, 14:22, 15:14). A sacrificial victim had to be without blemish. Doves could be bought cheaply enough outside, but the Temple inspectors would be sure to find something wrong with them, and worshippers were advised to buy them at the Temple stalls. The price of a pair of doves inside could be as much as fifteen times the price that might be paid outside. Again it was sheer imposition, and what made matters worse was that this business of

buying and selling belonged to the family of Annas who had
been high priest.

The Jews themselves were well aware of this abuse. The
Talmud tells us that Rabbi Simon ben Gamaliel, on hearing
that a pair of doves inside the Temple cost a gold piece,
insisted that the price be reduced to a silver piece. It was
the fact that poor, humble pilgrims were being swindled
which moved Jesus to wrath. M. J. Lagrange, the great biblical
scholar, who knew the middle east so well, tells us that
precisely the same situation still obtains in Mecca. Pilgrims,
seeking the divine presence, find themselves in the middle of
a noisy uproar, where the one aim of the sellers is to exact as
high a price as possible and where the pilgrims argue and
defend themselves with equal fierceness.

Jesus used a vivid metaphor to describe the Temple court.
The road from Jerusalem to Jericho was notorious for its
robbers. It was a narrow winding road, passing between rocky
gorges. Among the rocks were caves where the brigands lay
in wait, and Jesus said, 'There are worse brigands in the Temple
courts than ever there are in the caves of the Jericho road.'

Verse 16 has the odd statement that Jesus would not allow
anyone to carry his gear through the Temple court. In point
of fact the Temple court provided a short cut from the eastern
part of the city to the Mount of Olives. The Mishnah itself
lays down, 'A man may not enter into the Temple mount
with his staff or his sandal or his wallet, or with the dust
upon his feet, *nor may he make of it a short by-path.*' Jesus
was reminding the Jews of their own laws. In his time, Jews
thought so little of the sanctity of the outer court of the Temple
that they used it as a thoroughfare on their business errands.
It was to their own laws that Jesus directed their attention,
and it was their own prophets that he quoted to them (Isaiah
56:7; Jeremiah 7:11).

What moved Jesus to such wrath?

(1) He was angry at the exploitation of the pilgrims. The Temple authorities were treating them not as worshippers, not even as human beings, but as things to be exploited for their own ends. The exploitation of one human being by another always provokes the wrath of God, and doubly so when it is made under the cloak of religion.

(2) He was angry at the desecration of God's holy place. The sense of the presence of God in the house of God had been lost. Commercialization of the sacred was violating it.

(3) Is it possible that Jesus had an even deeper anger? He quoted Isaiah 56:7, 'My house shall be called a house of prayer *for all peoples.*' Yet in that very same house there was a wall beyond which to pass was, for the Gentile, death. It may well be that Jesus was moved to anger by the exclusiveness of Jewish worship and that he wished to remind them that God loved not the Jews but *the world*.

THE LAWS OF PRAYER

Mark I I:22–6

> Jesus answered, 'Have faith in God. This is the truth I tell you – whoever will say to this mountain, "Be lifted up and be cast into the sea," and who in his heart does not doubt, but believes that what he says is happening, it will be done for him. So then I tell you, believe that you have received everything for which you pray and ask, and it will be done for you. And whenever you stand praying, if you have anything against anyone, forgive it, so that your Father who is in heaven may forgive you your trespasses.'

WE return now to sayings which Mark attaches to the story of the blasting of the fig tree. We have noticed more than once how certain sayings of Jesus stuck in people's minds although the occasion on which he said them had been forgotten. It is so here. The saying about the faith which can remove mountains also occurs in Matthew 17:20 and in Luke 17:6, and in each of the gospels it occurs in a quite different context. The reason is that Jesus said it more than once and its real context had often been forgotten. The saying about the necessity of forgiving one another occurs in Matthew 6:12 and 14 again in a quite different context. We must approach these sayings as not so much having to do with particular incidents, but as general rules which Jesus repeatedly laid down.

This passage gives us three rules for prayer.

(1) It must be the prayer of faith. The phrase about removing mountains was a quite common Jewish phrase. It was a regular, vivid phrase for *removing difficulties*. It was specially used of wise teachers. A good teacher who could remove the difficulties which the minds of his scholars encountered was called *a mountain-remover.* One who heard a famous Rabbi teach said that 'he saw Resh Lachish as if he were *plucking up mountains*'. So the phrase means that if we have real faith, prayer is a power which can solve any problem and make us able to deal with any difficulty. That sounds very simple, but it involves two things.

First, it involves that we should be willing to take our problems and our difficulties to God. That in itself is a very real test. Sometimes our problems are that we wish to obtain something we should not desire at all, that we wish to find a way to do something we should not even think of doing, that we wish to justify ourselves for doing something to which we should never lay our hands or apply our minds. One of the greatest tests of any problem is simply to say, 'Can I take it to God and can I ask his help?' Second, it involves that we should be ready to accept God's guidance when he gives it. It is the commonest thing in the world for people to ask for advice when all they really want is approval for some action that they are already determined to take. It is useless to go to God and to ask for his guidance unless we are willing to be obedient enough to accept it. But if we do take our problems to God and are humble enough and brave enough to accept his guidance, there does come the power which can conquer the difficulties of thought and of action.

(2) It must be the prayer of expectation. It is the universal fact that anything tried in the spirit of confident expectation has a more than double chance of success. The patient who goes to a doctor and has no confidence in the prescribed remedies has far less chance of recovery than the patient who is confident that the doctor can provide a cure. When we pray, it must never be a mere formality. It must never be a ritual without hope.

A scene from Leonard Merrick's book, *Conrad in Quest of His Youth*, provides a good illustration: '"Do you think prayers are ever answered?" inquired Conrad. "In my life I have sent up many prayers, and always with the attempt to persuade myself that some former prayer had been fulfilled. But I knew. I knew in my heart none ever had been. Things that I wanted have come to me, but – I say it with all reverence – too late . . ." Mr Irquetson's fine hand wandered across his brow. "Once," he began conversationally, "I was passing with a friend through Grosvenor Street. It was when in the spring the tenant's fancy lightly turns to coats of paint, and we came to a ladder leaning against a house that was being redecorated. In stepping to the outer side of it my friend lifted his hat to it. You may know the superstition. He was a university man, a man of considerable attainments. I said, 'Is it possible you believe in that nonsense?' He said, 'N-no, I don't exactly

believe in it, but I never throw away a chance'." Suddenly
the vicar's inflexion changed, his utterance was solemn,
stirring, devout, "I think, sir, that most people pray on my
friend's principle – they don't believe in it, but they never
throw away a chance." '

There is much truth in that. For many people prayer is
either a pious ritual or a forlorn hope. It should be a thing of
burning expectation. Maybe our trouble is that what we want
from God is *our* answer, and we do not recognize *his* answer
when it comes.

(3) It must be the prayer of charity. The prayers of bitter
people cannot penetrate the wall of their own bitterness. Why?
If we are to speak with God there must be some bond between
us and God. There can never be any intimacy between two
people who have nothing in common. The principle of God
is love, for he *is* love. If the ruling principle of our hearts is
bitterness, we have erected a barrier between ourselves and
God. In such circumstances, if our prayers are to be answered
we must first ask God to cleanse our hearts from the bitter
spirit and put into them the spirit of love. Then we can speak
to God and God can speak to us.

A CUNNING QUESTION AND
A PIERCING ANSWER

Mark 11:27–33

> Once again they came to Jerusalem, and, when Jesus
> was walking in the Temple, the chief priests and the
> experts in the law and the elders came to him, and said
> to him, 'By what kind of authority do you do these
> things? Or, who gave you authority to do these things?'
> Jesus said, 'I will put one point to you, and, if you

answer me, I will tell you by what kind of authority I
do these things. Was the baptism of John from heaven?
Or was it from men? Answer me!' They discussed the
matter among themselves. 'If', they said, 'we say,
"From heaven," he will say, "Why did you not believe
in it?" But, are we to say, "From men"?' – for they
were afraid of the people, for all truly held that John
was a prophet. So they answered Jesus, 'We do not
know.' So Jesus said to them, 'Neither do I tell you by
what kind of authority I do these things.'

IN the sacred precincts there were two famous cloisters, one
on the east and one on the south side of the Court of the
Gentiles. The one on the east was called Solomon's Porch. It
was a magnificent arcade made by Corinthian columns
thirty-five feet high. The one on the south was even more
splendid. It was called the Royal Cloister. It was formed by
four rows of white marble columns, each six feet in diameter
and thirty feet high. There were 162 of them. It was common
for Rabbis and teachers to stroll in these columns and to teach
as they walked. Most of the great cities of ancient times had
these cloisters. They gave shelter from the sun and the wind
and the rain, and, in point of fact, it was in these places that
most of the religious and philosophic teaching was done. One
of the most famous schools of ancient thought was that of the
Stoics. They received their name from the fact that Zeno,
their founder, taught as he walked in the *Stoa Poikilē*, the
Painted Porch, in Athens. The word *stoa* means *porch* or
arcade and the Stoics were the school of the porch. It was in
these cloisters in the Temple that Jesus was walking and
teaching.

   To him there came a deputation of the chief priests and the
experts in the law, that is the scribes, Rabbis and elders. This
was in reality a deputation from the Sanhedrin, of which these

three groups formed the component parts. They asked a most natural question. For a private individual, all on his own, to clear the Court of the Gentiles of its accustomed and official traders was a staggering thing. So they asked Jesus, 'By what kind of authority do you act like that?'

They hoped to put Jesus into a dilemma. If he said he was acting under his own authority they might well arrest him as a megalomaniac before he did any further damage. If he said that he was acting on the authority of God they might well arrest him on an obvious charge of blasphemy, on the grounds that God would never give anyone authority to create a disturbance in the courts of his own house. Jesus saw quite clearly the dilemma in which they sought to involve him, and his reply put them into a dilemma which was still worse. He said that he would answer on condition that they would answer one question for him, 'Was John the Baptist's work, in your opinion, human or divine?'

This impaled them on the horns of a dilemma. If they said it was divine, they knew that Jesus would ask why they had stood out against it. Worse than that – if they said it was divine, Jesus could reply that John had in fact pointed every- one to him, and that therefore he was divinely attested and needed no further authority. If these members of the Sanhedrin agreed that John's work was divine, they would be compelled to accept Jesus as the Messiah. On the other hand, if they said that John's work was merely human, now that John had the added distinction of being a martyr, they knew quite well that the listening people would cause a riot. So they were compelled to say weakly that they did not know, and thereby Jesus escaped the need to give them any answer to their question.

The whole story is a vivid example of what happens to those who will not face the truth. They have to twist and wriggle and in the end get themselves into a position in which they are so helplessly involved that they have nothing to say. Those who face the truth may have the humiliation of saying that they were wrong, or the peril of standing by it, but at least the future for them is strong and bright. Those who will not face the truth have nothing but the prospect of deeper and deeper involvement in a situation which renders them helpless and ineffective.

REJECTION AND RETRIBUTION

Mark 12:1-12

> Jesus began to speak to them in parables. A man planted a vineyard. He put a hedge round about it, and dug a wine vat, and built a tower. He let it out to cultivators and went abroad. At the right time he sent a servant to the cultivators that he might receive from the cultivators his share of the fruits of the vineyard. They took him and beat him and sent him away empty-handed. Again he sent another servant to them. They wounded him in the head, and treated him shamefully. He sent yet another. They killed him. So they treated many others, beating some and killing others. He had still one person left to send, his beloved son. Last of all he sent him to them. 'They will respect my son,' he said. But these cultivators said to each other, 'This is the heir. Come, let us kill him, and the inheritance will be ours.' So they took him and killed him and threw him out of the vineyard. What, then will the owner of the vineyard do? He will come and he will destroy the cultivators and he will give the vineyard to others. Have you not read this passage of Scripture, 'The stone which the builders rejected, this has become the headstone of the

corner. This came from God, and it is in our eyes an amazing thing'? They tried to find a way to get hold of Jesus, for they feared the crowd, for they were well aware that he spoke this parable against them. So they let him alone and went away.

WE said that a parable must never be treated as an allegory, and that a meaning must not be sought for every detail. Originally, Jesus' parables were not meant to be read but to be spoken, and their meaning was that which flashed out when first they were heard. But to some extent this parable is an exception. It is a kind of hybrid, a cross between an allegory and a parable. Not all the details have an inner meaning, but more than usual have. And this is because Jesus was talking in pictures which were part and parcel of Jewish thought and imagery.

The owner of the vineyard is *God*; the *vineyard* itself is *the people of Israel*. This was a picture with which the Jews were perfectly familiar. In the Old Testament it is vividly used in Isaiah 5:1–7, a passage from which some of the details and the language of this passage are taken. This vineyard was given every equipment. There was a wall to mark out its boundaries, to keep out robbers and to defend it from the assaults of the wild boars. There was a wine vat. In a vineyard there was a wine press in which the grapes were trodden down with the feet. Beneath the wine press was a wine vat into which the pressed-out juice flowed. There was a tower. In this the wine was stored, the cultivators had their lodging, and, from this, watch was kept for robbers at harvest time. *The cultivators* stand for *the rulers of Israel* throughout the history of the nation. The *servants* whom the owner sent stand for the *prophets*. *Servant* or *slave* of God is a regular title. So Moses was called (Joshua 14:7). So David was called (2 Samuel 3:18). And the title occurs regularly in the books of the prophets (Amos 3:7; Jeremiah 7:25; Zechariah 1:6). *The son* is *Jesus himself*. Even on the spur of the moment the hearers could have made these identifications because the thoughts and the pictures were all so familiar to them.

The story itself is of what might well happen in Palestine in the time of Jesus. The country had much labour unrest and many absentee landlords. The owner of such a vineyard might be a Jew who had sought a more comfortable land than Palestine, or he might be a Roman who regarded the vineyard as an investment for his money. If the owner followed the law, the first time for collecting the rental would be five years after the planting of the vineyard (Leviticus 19:23–5). In such a case the rental was paid in kind. It might be a fixed and agreed percentage of the crop, or it might be a stated amount, irrespective of what the crop came to. The story is by no means improbable and tells of the kind of thing which did actually happen.

The parable is so full of truths that we can note them only in the briefest way.

It tells us certain things about God.

(1) It tells us of *the generosity* of God. The vineyard was equipped with everything that was necessary to make the work of the cultivators easy and profitable. God is generous in the life and in the world that he gives to men and women.

(2) It tells us of *the trust* of God. The owner went away and left the cultivators to run the vineyard themselves. God trusts us enough to give us freedom to run life as we choose. As someone has said, 'The lovely thing about God is that he allows us to do so much for ourselves.'

(3) It tells us of *the patience* of God. Not once or twice but many times the master gave the cultivators the chance to pay the debt they owed. He treated them with a patience they little deserved.

(4) It tells us of the ultimate triumph of *the justice* of God. We might take advantage of the patience of God, but in the end come judgment and justice. God may bear disobedience and rebellion for a long time, but in the end he acts.

This parable tells us something about Jesus.

(1) It tells us that Jesus regarded himself *not as a servant but as a son*. He deliberately removes himself from the succession of the prophets. They were servants. He was son. In him God's last and final word was being spoken. This parable was a deliberate challenge to the Jewish authorities because it contains the unmistakable claim of Jesus to be the Messiah.

(2) It tells us that *Jesus knew that he was to die*. The cross did not come to him as a surprise. He knew that the way he had chosen could have no other ending. It is the greatness of his courage that he knew that and still went on.

(3) It tells us that *Jesus was sure of his ultimate triumph*. He also knew that he would be maltreated and killed, but he also knew that would not be the end, that after the rejection would come the glory.

This parable tells us something about human nature.

(1) There could be only one reason why the cultivators thought they could kill the son and then enter into possession of the vineyard. They must have thought that the owner was too far away to act, or that he was dead and out of the reckoning. Some people still think they can act against God and get away with it. But God is very much alive. Human beings seek to trade on their own freedom and his patience, but the day of reckoning comes.

(2) If people refuse their privileges and their responsibilities, they pass on to someone else. The parable has in it the whole germ of what was to come – the rejection of the Jews and the passing of their privileges and responsibilities to the Gentiles.

The parable closes with an Old Testament quotation which became very dear to the Church. The quotation about the stone that was rejected is from Psalm 118:22–3. The rejected stone had become the stone that bound the corners of the building together, the keystone of the arch, the most important stone of all. This passage fascinated the early Christian writers. It is quoted or referred to in Acts 4:11; 1 Peter 2:4, 7; Romans 9:32–3; Ephesians 2:20. Originally, in the Psalm, the reference was to the people of Israel. The great nations which had thought of themselves as architects of the structure of the world had regarded the people of Israel as unimportant and unhonoured. But, as the psalmist saw it, the nation which had been regarded as of no importance would, some day, in God's economy, become the greatest nation in the world. The Christian writers saw in the psalmist's dream something which was perfectly fulfilled in the death and resurrection of Jesus.

CAESAR AND GOD

Mark 12:13–17

> They sent to Jesus some of the Pharisees and Herodians to try to trap him in his speech. They came to him and said, 'Teacher, we know that you are genuine, and that you do not allow yourself to be influenced by anyone, for you are no respecter of persons, and you teach the way of God in truth. Is it right to pay tax to Caesar? Or not? Are we to pay? Or, are we not to pay?' Jesus knew well that they were acting a part. 'Why are you trying to test me?' he said. 'Bring me a denarius and let me see it.' So they brought him one. He said to them, 'Whose portrait is this, and whose inscription is on it?' 'Caesar's,' they said to him. Jesus said to them, 'Render

to Caesar the things which belong to Caesar, and to
God the things that belong to God.' And they were
completely astonished at him.

THERE is history behind this shrewd question, and bitter
history too. Herod the Great had ruled all Palestine as a
Roman tributary king. He had been loyal to the Romans, and
they had respected him and given him a great deal of freedom.
When he died in 4 BC, he divided his kingdom into three. To
Herod Antipas he gave Galilee and Peraea. To Herod Philip
he gave the wild district up in the north-east round Trachonitis
and Ituraea and Abilene. To Archelaus he gave the south
country including Judaea and Samaria.

Antipas and Philip soon settled in and on the whole ruled
wisely and well. But Archelaus was a complete failure. The
result was that in AD 6 the Romans had to step in and introduce
direct rule. Things were so unsatisfactory that southern
Palestine could no longer be left as a semi-independent
tributary kingdom. It had to become a province governed by
a procurator.

Roman provinces fell into two classes. Those which were
peaceful and required no troops were governed by the senate
and ruled by proconsuls. Those which were trouble centres
and required troops were the direct sphere of the emperor
and were governed by procurators. Southern Palestine fell
naturally into the second category, and tribute was in fact
paid directly to the emperor.

The first act of the governor, Cyrenius, was to take a census
of the country, in order that he might make proper provision
for fair taxation and general administration. The calmer
section of the people accepted this as an inevitable necessity.
But one Judas the Gaulonite raised violent opposition. He
thundered that 'taxation was no better than an introduction to

slavery'. He called on the people to rise, and said that God would favour them only if they resorted to all the violence they could muster. He took the high ground that for the Jews God was the only ruler. The Romans dealt with Judas with their customary efficiency, but his battle cry never died out. 'No tribute to the Romans' became a rallying cry of the more fanatical Jewish patriots.

The actual taxes imposed were three.

(1) A ground tax, which consisted of one-tenth of all the grain and one-fifth of the wine and fruit produced. This was paid partly in kind and partly in money.

(2) An income tax which amounted to one per cent of a man's income.

(3) A poll tax, which was levied on all men between the ages of fourteen and sixty-five, and on all women from twelve to sixty-five. This poll tax was one *denarius*, the daily wage of a working man. It was the tax which everyone had to pay simply for the privilege of existing.

The approach of the Pharisees and Herodians was very subtle. They began with flattery. That flattery was designed to do two things. It was designed to disarm the suspicions that Jesus might have had, and to make it impossible for him to avoid giving an answer without losing his reputation completely.

In view of all the circumstances the question which the Pharisees and Herodians put to Jesus was a masterpiece of cunning. They must have thought that they had him impaled on the horns of a completely inescapable dilemma. If he said that it was lawful to pay tribute, his influence with the people would be gone forever, and he would be regarded as a traitor and a coward. If he said that it was not lawful to pay tribute, they could report him to the Romans and have him arrested as a revolutionary. They must have been sure that they had Jesus in a trap from which there was no escape.

Jesus said, 'Show me a *denarius*.' We may note in the passing that he himself did not possess even one coin of his own. He asked whose image was on it. The image would be that of Tiberius, the reigning emperor. All the emperors were called Caesar. Round the coin there would be the title which declared that this was the coin 'of Tiberius Caesar, the divine Augustus, son of Augustus', and on the reverse would be the title 'pontifex maximus', 'the high priest of the Roman nation'.

We must understand the ancient view of coinage if this incident is to be intelligible. In regard to coinage the ancient peoples held three consistent principles.

(1) Coinage is the sign of power. When anyone conquered a nation or was a successful rebel, the first thing he did was to issue his own coinage. That and that alone was the final guarantee of kingship and power.

(2) Where the coin was valid the king's power held good. A king's sway was measurable by the area in which his coins were valid currency.

(3) Because a coin had the king's head and inscription on it, it was held, at least in some sense, to be his personal property. Jesus' answer therefore was, 'By using the coinage of Tiberius you in any event recognize his political power in Palestine. Apart altogether from that, the coinage is his own because it has his name on it. By giving it to him you give him what is in any event his own. Give it to him but remember that there is a sphere in life which belongs to God and not to Caesar.'

Never did anyone lay down a more influential principle. It conserved at one and the same time the civil and the religious power. A. J. Rawlinson, the 1920s Bishop of Derby, reminds us that Lord Acton, the great historian, said of this, 'Those words ... gave to the civil power, under the protection of conscience, a sacredness it had never enjoyed and bounds it had never acknowledged, and they were the repudiation of absolutism and the inauguration of freedom.' At one and the same time these words asserted the rights of the state and the liberty of conscience.

On the whole the New Testament lays down three great principles with regard to the individual Christian and the state.

(1) The state is ordained by God. Without the laws of the state life would be chaos. Human beings cannot live together unless they agree to obey the laws of living together. Without the state there are valuable services that no one could enjoy. Individuals could not have their own water supply, their own sewage system, their own transport system, their own social security organization. The state is the origin of many of the things which make life livable.

(2) No one can accept all the benefits which the state gives and then opt out of all the responsibilities. It is beyond question that the Roman government brought to the ancient world a sense of security it never had before. For the most part, except in certain notorious areas, the seas were cleared of pirates and the roads of brigands, civil wars were changed for peace and capricious tyranny for Roman impartial justice. As E. J. Goodspeed wrote, 'It was the glory of the Roman Empire that it brought peace to a troubled world. Under its sway the regions of Asia Minor and the East enjoyed tranquillity and security to an extent and for a length of time unknown before and probably since. This was the *pax Romana*. The provincial, under Roman sway, found himself in a position to conduct his business, provide for his family, send his letters, and make his journeys in security, thanks to the strong hand of Rome.' It is still true that people cannot

honourably receive all the benefits which living in a state confers upon them and then opt out of all the responsibilities of citizenship.

(3) But there is a limit. E. A. Abbott, the New Testament scholar, has a suggestive thought. The coin had Caesar's *image* upon it, and therefore belonged to Caesar. Human beings have God's *image* upon them – God created them in his own image (Genesis 1:26–7) – and therefore belong to God. The inevitable conclusion is that if the state remains within its proper boundaries and makes its proper demands, individuals must give it their loyalty and their service; but in the last analysis both state and human beings belong to God, and, therefore, should their claims conflict, loyalty to God comes first. But it remains true that, in all ordinary circumstances, our Christianity should make us better citizens.

THE WRONG IDEA OF THE LIFE TO COME

Mark 12:18–27

> There came to Jesus Sadducees, who are a party who say that the resurrection of the dead does not exist. They put the following problem to him. 'Teacher,' they said, 'Moses wrote the law for us, that, if a man's brother dies and leaves behind him a wife, and does not leave a family, the law is that the brother should take his wife, and should raise up a family to his brother. There were seven brothers. The first took a wife, and died, and left no family. The second took her, and he died, and left behind no family. The third did the same. The seven left no family. Last of all, the woman died. At the resurrection whose wife will she be? For the seven had her as wife.' Jesus said to them, 'Are you not in error and for this reason – because you do not know the

Scriptures, nor do you know the power of God? When people rise from the dead, they neither marry, nor are they given in marriage, but they are like the angels in heaven. With regard to the dead, and the fact that they do rise, have you not read in the Book of Moses, in the passage about the bush, how God said to him, "I am the God of Abraham, and the God of Isaac, and the God of Jacob." God is not the God of the dead, but the God of the living. You are far wrong.'

THIS is the only time in Mark's gospel that the Sadducees appear, and their appearance is entirely characteristic of them. The Sadducees were not a large Jewish party. They were aristocratic and wealthy. They included most of the priests; the office of high priest was regularly held by a Sadducee. Being the wealthy and aristocratic party, they were not unnaturally collaborationist, for they wished to retain their comforts and their privileges. It was from them that there came those who were prepared to collaborate with the Romans in the government of the country.

They differed very widely from the Pharisees in certain matters. First, they accepted only the written Scriptures and attached more importance to the Pentateuch, the first five books of the Old Testament, than to all the rest. They did not accept the mass of oral law and tradition, the rules and regulations which were so dear to the Pharisees. It was on the written Mosaic law that they took their stand. Second, they did not believe in immortality, nor in spirits and angels. They said that in the early books of the Bible there was no evidence for immortality, and they did not accept it.

So the Sadducees came to Jesus with a test question designed to make the belief in individual resurrection look ridiculous. The Jewish law had an institution called levirate marriage. Its regulations are laid down in Deuteronomy

25:5–10. If a group of brothers lived together – that is a point that is omitted in the Sadducees' quotation of the law – and if one of them died and left no issue, it was the duty of the next to take his brother's widow as wife and to raise up issue to his brother. Theoretically this would go on as long as there were brothers left and as long as no child was born. When a child was born, the child was held to be the offspring of the *original* husband.

It is clear that the whole point of this law was to ensure two things – first, that the family name continued, and second, that the property remained within the family. As a matter of fact, strange as the matter seems to us, there were certain not dissimilar regulations in Greek law. If a Greek father had a considerable estate and had only a daughter, she, being a woman, could not inherit directly. Either her husband or her son would be the direct heir. But if the daughter was un-married, the father could leave his property *and his daughter* to anyone he chose. Such a person, in order to inherit the property, had to marry the heiress, even if he had to divorce an already existing wife to do so. And, if in such circum-stances, a father died without making a will, the nearest relation could claim the heiress daughter as his wife. It is the same principle again. The whole thing is designed to maintain the family and to retain the property within the family.

The question that the Sadducees asked, therefore, may have presented an exaggerated case, with the story of the *seven* brothers, but it was a question founded on a well-known Jewish law.

The question of the Sadducees was simply this – if, in accordance with the regulations governing levirate marriage, one woman has been married in turn to seven brothers, if there is a resurrection of the dead, whose wife is she when that resurrection comes? They thought that by asking that question they rendered the idea of resurrection completely ridiculous.

Jesus' answer really falls into two parts.

First, he deals with what we might call *the manner* of the resurrection. He lays it down that when a person rises again, the old laws of physical life no longer obtain. The risen are like the angels, and physical things like marrying and being married no longer enter into the case. Jesus was saying nothing new. In 1 Enoch the promise is, 'You shall have great joy as the angels of heaven.' In the Apocalypse of Baruch it is said that the righteous shall be made 'like unto the angels'. And the Rabbinic writings themselves said that in the life to come 'there is no eating and drinking, no begetting of children, no bargaining, jealousy, hatred and strife, but that the righteous sit with crowns on their heads, and are satisfied with the glory of God'. It is Jesus' point that the life to come cannot be thought of in terms of this life at all.

Second, he deals with *the fact* of the resurrection. Here he meets the Sadducees on their own ground. They insisted that in the Pentateuch, by which they set so much store, there was no evidence for immortality. From the Pentateuch Jesus draws his proof. In Exodus 3:6, God calls himself the God of Abraham, the God of Isaac and the God of Jacob. If God is the God of these patriarchs even now, it means that they must still be alive, for the living God must be the God of living people, and not of those who are dead. And if the patriarchs are alive then the resurrection is proved. On their own grounds, and with an argument to which they could find no answer, Jesus defeated the Sadducees.

This passage may seem to deal with a matter which is recondite and remote. It is an argument on terms which are out of the orbit of our experience. In spite of that, two eternally valid truths emerge.

(1) The Sadducees made the mistake of creating heaven in the image of earth. That has always been a human failing. The native Americans, who were by nature hunters, conceived of a heaven which was a happy hunting-ground. The Vikings, who were by nature warriors, thought of a Valhalla where they would fight all day, where at night the dead would be raised and the wounded made whole again, and they would spend the evening in banquets, drinking wine from cups made from the skulls of their conquered foes. The Muslims were desert people living in circumstances where luxury was unknown. They conceived of heaven as a place where life would be replete with every sensual and bodily pleasure. The Jews hated the sea and thought of heaven as a place where there would be no more sea. Everyone shrank from sorrow and from pain, and heaven would be a place where the tears were wiped from every eye and there would be no more pain.

There has always been a tendency to create in thought a heaven to suit human desires. Sometimes that idea can be poignantly beautiful. During the First World War, *The Westminster Gazette* printed a lovely little poem about those who had died for their country:

> They left the fury of the fight,
>> And they were tired.
> The gates of heaven were open quite,
>> Unguarded and unwired.
> There was no sound of any gun,
>> The land was still and green,
> Wide hills lay silent in the sun,
>> Blue valleys slept between.
> They saw far off a little wood
>> Stand up against the sky.
> Knee deep in grass a great tree stood,
>> Some lazy cows went by.

> There were some rooks sailed overhead,
>   And once a church bell pealed.
> 'God, but it's England!' someone said,
>   'And there's a cricket field'.

There is wistful beauty there and real truth. But we do well to remember that Paul was right (1 Corinthians 2:9) when he took the words of the prophet (Isaiah 64:4) and made them his own, 'What no eye has seen, nor ear heard, nor the human heart conceived, what God has prepared for those who love him.' The life of the heavenly places will be greater than any conception this life can supply.

(2) In the end, Jesus based his conviction of the resurrection on the fact that the relationship between God and a good man or a good woman is one that nothing can break. God was the friend of Abraham, Isaac and Jacob when they lived. That friendship could not cease with death. 'God', as the French theologian Alfred Loisy said, 'cannot cease to be the God of those who served him and loved him.' As the psalmist said, 'I am continually with you; You hold my right hand. You guide me with your counsel, and afterwards you will receive me [to glory]' (Psalm 73:23–4). It is inconceivable that that relationship with God can ever be broken.

In a word, there is only one immortal thing – and that is love.

LOVE FOR GOD AND LOVE FOR NEIGHBOUR

Mark 12:28–34

> One of the experts in the law, who had listened to the discussion, and who realized that Jesus had answered them well, approached him and asked him, 'What is the

> first commandment of all?' Jesus answered, ' "The Lord
> thy God is one Lord, and you must love the Lord your
> God with your whole heart, and your whole soul, and
> your whole mind, and your whole strength." This is the
> second, "You must love your neighbour as yourself."
> There is no other commandment which is greater than
> these.' The expert in the law said to him, 'Teacher, you
> have in truth spoken well, because God is one, and there
> is no other except him, and to love him with your whole
> heart, and your whole understanding, and your whole
> strength, and to love your neighbour as yourself is
> better than all burnt offerings of whole victims and
> sacrifices.' When Jesus saw that he had answered
> wisely, he said to him, 'You are not far from the
> kingdom of God.' And no one any longer dared to ask
> him any questions.

No love was lost between the expert in the law and the
Sadducees. The profession of the scribes was to interpret the
law in all its many rules and regulations. Their trade was to
know and to apply the oral law, while, as we have seen, the
Sadducees did not accept the oral law at all. The expert in the
law would no doubt be well satisfied with the discomfiture of
the Sadducees.

This scribe came to Jesus with a question which was often
a matter of debate in the Rabbinic schools. In Judaism there
was a kind of double tendency. There was the tendency to
expand the law limitlessly into hundreds and thousands of
rules and regulations. But there was also the tendency to try
to gather up the law into one sentence, one general statement
which would be a compendium of its whole message. Rabbi
Hillel was once asked by a proselyte, a convert to Judaism,
to instruct him in the whole law while he stood on one leg.
Hillel's answer was, 'What thou hatest for thyself, do not to
thy neighbour. This is the whole law, the rest is commentary.

Go and learn.' Rabbi Akiba had already said, '"Thou shalt
love thy neighbour as thyself" – this is the greatest general
principle in the law.' Simon the Righteous had said, 'On three
things stands the world – on the law, on the worship, and on
works of love.'

Sammlai had taught that Moses received 613 precepts on
Mount Sinai, 365 according to the days of the sun year, and
248 according to the generations. David reduced the 613 to
11 in Psalm 15.

> O Lord, who may abide in your tent? Who may dwell
> on your holy hill?
> 1. Those who walk blamelessly.
> 2. And do what is right.
> 3. And speak truth from their hearts.
> 4. Who do not slander with their tongues.
> 5. And do no evil to their friends.
> 6. Nor take up a reproach against their neighbours.
> 7. In whose eyes the wicked are despised.
> 8. But who honour those who fear the Lord.
> 9. Who stand by their oath even to their hurt.
> 10. Who do not lend money at interest.
> 11. And do not take a bribe against the innocent.

Isaiah reduced them to six (Isaiah 33:15).

> 1. Those who walk righteously.
> 2. And speak uprightly.
> 3. Who despise the gain of oppressions.
> 4. Who wave away a bribe instead of accepting it.
> 5. Who stop their ears from hearing of bloodshed.
> 6. And shut their eyes from looking on evil.
> They will live on the heights.

Micah reduced the six to three (Micah 6:8).

> He has told you, O mortal, what is good; and what does
> the Lord require of you?

1. To do justice.
2. To love kindness.
3. To walk humbly with your God.

Once again Isaiah brought the three down to two (Isaiah 56:1).

1. Maintain justice.
2. Do what is right.

Finally Habakkuk reduced them all to one (Habakkuk 2:4).

The righteous live by their faith.

It can be seen that Rabbinic ingenuity did try to contract as well as to expand the law. There were really two schools of thought. There were those who believed that there were lighter and weightier matters of the law, that there were great principles which were all important to grasp. As Augustine later said, 'Love God – and do what you like.' But there were others who were much against this, who held that every smallest principle was equally binding and that to try to distinguish between their relative importance was highly dangerous. The expert who asked Jesus this question was asking about something which was a living issue in Jewish thought and discussion.

For answer Jesus took two great commandments and put them together.

(1) 'Hear, O Israel: The Lord is our God, the Lord alone.' That single sentence is the real creed of Judaism (Deuteronomy 6:4). It had three uses. It is called *the Shema*. *Shema* is the imperative of the Hebrew verb *to hear*, and it is so called from the first word in the sentence.

(*a*) It was the sentence with which the service of the synagogue always began and still begins. The full Shema is Deuteronomy 6:4–9, 11:13–21; Numbers 15:37–41. It is the declaration that God is the only God, the foundation of Jewish monotheism.

(b) The three passages of the Shema were contained in the *phylacteries* (Matthew 23:5), little leather boxes which devout Jews wore on their foreheads and on their wrists when they were at prayer. As they prayed they reminded themselves of their creed. The warrant for wearing *phylacteries* is found in Deuteronomy 6:8.

(c) The Shema was contained in a little cylindrical box called the *Mezuzah*, which was and still is affixed to the door of every Jewish house and the door of every room within it, to remind Jewish families of God as they went out and as they came in.

When Jesus quoted this sentence as the first commandment, every devout Jew would agree with him.

(2) 'You shall love your neighbour as yourself.' That is a quotation from Leviticus 19:18. Jesus did one thing with it. In its original context it has to do only with *fellow Jews*. It would not have included the Gentiles, whom it was quite permissible to hate. But Jesus quoted it without qualification and without limiting boundaries. He took an old law and filled it with a new meaning.

The new thing that Jesus did was to put these two commandments together. No Rabbi had ever done that before. There is only one suggestion of connection previously. Round about 100 BC there was composed a series of tractates called The Testaments of the Twelve Patriarchs, in which an unknown writer put into the mouths of the patriarchs some very fine teaching. In the Testament of Issachar (5:2), we read:

> Love the Lord and love your neighbour,
> Have compassion on the poor and weak.

In the same testament (7:6), we read:

> I loved the Lord,
> Likewise also every man with my whole heart.

In the Testament of Dan (5:3), we read:

> Love the Lord through all your life,
> And one another with a true heart.

But no one until Jesus put the two commandments together and made them one. Religion to him was loving God and loving one another. He would have said that the only way to prove love for God is by showing love for others.

The scribe willingly accepted this, and went on to say that such a love was better than all sacrifices. In that, he was in line with the highest thought of his people. Long, long ago Samuel had said, 'Has the Lord as great delight in burnt offerings and sacrifices, as in obedience to the voice of the Lord? Surely, to obey is better than sacrifice, and to heed than the fat of rams' (1 Samuel 15:22). Hosea had heard God say, 'I desire steadfast love and not sacrifice' (Hosea 6:6).

But it is always easy to let ritual take the place of love. It is always easy to let worship become a matter of the church building instead of a matter of the whole life. The priest and the Levite could pass by the wounded traveller because they were eager to get on with the ritual of the Temple. This scribe had risen beyond his contemporaries, and that is why he found himself in sympathy with Jesus.

There must have been a look of love in Jesus' eyes, and a look of appeal as he said to him, 'You have gone so far. Will you not come further and accept my way of things? Then you will be a true citizen of the kingdom.'

THE SON OF DAVID

Mark 12:35–37a

> While Jesus was teaching in the sacred precincts, he
> said, 'How can the experts in the law say that God's
> Anointed One is the Son of David? David himself,
> moved by the Holy Spirit, said, "The Lord said to my
> Lord, Sit at my right hand until I make your enemies a
> footstool for your feet." David himself calls him Lord.
> And how then can he be his son?'

FOR us this is a difficult passage to understand, because it uses
thoughts and methods of argument which are strange to us.
But it would not be at all difficult for the crowd who heard it
in the Temple precincts in Jerusalem, for they were well accustomed to just such ways of arguing and of using Scripture.

We may begin by noting one thing which helps to make
the passage clearer. The Revised Standard Version translates
verse 35, 'How can the scribes say that the Christ is the son
of David?' In the early parts of the New Testament Christ is
never a proper name, as it has since come to be. It has in fact
in this passage the definite article before it and so is translated
as *the Christ*. *Christos* and *Messiah* are the Greek and the
Hebrew for the same word, and both mean *the Anointed
One*. The reason for the use of the title is that in ancient
times a man was made king by being anointed with oil – a
practice that still continues in modern coronation ceremonies.
Christos and *Messiah* then both mean *God's anointed king*,
the great one who is to come from God to save his people. So
when Jesus asks, 'How can the scribes say that the Christ is
the son of David?' he is not directly referring to himself. He
is really saying, 'How can the scribes say that God's anointed
king who is to come is the Son of David?'

The argument which Jesus puts forward in support is this. He quotes Psalm 110:1 – 'The Lord says to my lord, "Sit at my right hand."' The Jews at this time assumed that all the Psalms came from the hand of David. They also held that this Psalm referred to the coming Messiah. In this verse, David refers to this coming one as *his lord*. How, asks Jesus, if he is his son can David address him by the title of Lord?

What is Jesus seeking to teach here? Of all titles for the Messiah, the commonest was Son of David. At all times, the Jews looked forward to a God-sent deliverer who would be of David's line (Isaiah 9:2–7, 11:1–9; Jeremiah 23:5ff., 33:14–18; Ezekiel 34:23ff., 37:24; Psalm 89:20ff.). It was by that title that Jesus himself was often addressed, especially by the crowds (Mark 10:47ff.; Matthew 9:27, 12:23, 15:22, 21:9, 15). All through the New Testament, the conviction that Jesus was in fact the Son of David in his physical descent occurs (Romans 1:3; 2 Timothy 2:8; Matthew 1:1–17; Luke 3:23–38). The genealogies of Jesus given in the passages from Matthew and Luke which we have cited are to show that Jesus was in fact of the lineage of David. What Jesus is doing is this – he is not denying that the Messiah is the Son of David, nor is he saying that he himself is not the Son of David. What he is saying is that he is the Son of David – *and far more*, not only David's son but *David's Lord*.

The trouble was that the title Son of David had got itself inextricably entangled with the idea of a conquering Messiah. It had got involved in political and nationalistic hopes and dreams, aims and ambitions. Jesus was saying that the title *Son of David*, as it was popularly used, is a quite inadequate description of himself. He was *Lord*. This word *Lord* (the Greek *kurios*) is the regular translation of Yahweh (Jehovah) in the Greek version of the Hebrew Scriptures. Always its use would turn people's thoughts to God. What Jesus was saying was that he came not to found any earthly kingdom but *to bring men and women to God.*

Jesus is doing here what he so constantly tried to do. He is trying to take from people's minds their idea of a conquering warrior Messiah who would found an earthly empire, and seeking to put into them the idea of a Messiah who would be the servant of God and bring to them the love of God.

THE WRONG KIND OF RELIGION

Mark 12:37b–40

> The mass of the people listened to him with pleasure. And in his teaching he said, 'Beware of the experts in the law, who like to walk about in flowing robes, and who like greetings in the market places, and the front seats in the synagogue, and the places of highest honour at meals, men who devour widows' houses, and who, in pretence, pray at great length. These will receive a more abundant condemnation.'

THE first sentence of this passage most probably goes with this section and not, as in the Revised Standard Version, with the passage which goes before. The verse divisions of the New Testament were first inserted by Stephanus in the sixteenth century. It was said that he put them in while riding from his house to his printing factory. They are by no means always the most suitable divisions, and this seems to be one requiring change. It is far more likely that the mass of the people listened with pleasure to a denunciation of the scribes than they did to a· theological argument. There are certain minds to which invective is always attractive.

In this passage Jesus makes a series of charges against the scribes. They liked to walk about in flowing robes. A long robe which swept the ground was the sign of a notable person. It was the kind of robe in which no one could either hurry or work, and was the sign of the leisured man of honour. It may be that the phrase has another meaning. In obedience to Numbers 15:38, Jews wore tassels at the edge of their outer robe. These tassels were to remind them that they were the people of God. Quite possibly these legal experts wore outsize tassels for special prominence (cf. Matthew 23:5). At all events they liked to dress in such a way that it drew attention to themselves and to the honour they enjoyed.

They liked greetings in the market place. The scribes loved to be greeted with honour and with respect. The very title *Rabbi* means 'My great one'. To be so addressed was agreeable to their vanity.

They liked the front seats in the synagogue. In the synagogue, in front of the ark where the sacred volumes were kept and facing the congregation, there was a bench where the specially distinguished sat. It had the advantage that no one who sat there could possibly be missed, being in full view of the admiring congregation.

They liked the highest places at feasts. At feasts precedence was strictly fixed. The first place was that on the right of the host, the second that on the left of the host, and so on, alternating right and left, round the table. It was easy to tell the honour in which people were held by the places at which they sat.

They devoured widows' houses. This is a savage charge. Josephus, who was himself a Pharisee, says of certain times of intrigue in Jewish history, that 'the Pharisees valued themselves highly upon their exact skill in the law of their fathers, and made men believe that they [the Pharisees] were highly favoured by God', and that 'they inveigled' certain women into their schemes and plottings. The idea behind this seems to be this. An expert in the law could take no pay for his teaching. He was supposed to have a trade by which he earned his daily bread. But these legal experts had managed to convey to people that there was no higher duty and privilege than to support a Rabbi in comfort; that, in fact, such support would undoubtedly entitle him or her who gave it to a high place in the heavenly academy. It is a sad fact that religious charlatans have always preyed upon vulnerable people, and it would seem that these scribes and Pharisees imposed on people who could ill afford to support them.

The long prayers of the scribes and Pharisees were notorious. It has been said that the prayers were not so much offered to God as offered to other people. They were offered in such a place and in such a way that no one could fail to see how pious they were who offered them.

This passage, as stern as Jesus ever spoke, warns against three things.

(1) It warns against the desire for prominence. It is still true that many accept office in the Church because they think they have earned it, rather than through any desire to render selfless service to the house and the people of God. Office in the Church may still be regarded by some as a privilege rather than a responsibility.

(2) It warns against the desire for deference. Almost everyone likes to be treated with respect. And yet a basic fact of Christianity is that it ought to produce the desire to obliterate self rather than to exalt it. There is a story of a monk in the old days, a very holy man, who was sent to take up office as abbot in a monastery. He looked so humble a person that, when he arrived, he was sent to work in the kitchen washing the dishes, because no one recognized him. Without a word of protest and with no attempt to take his position, he went and washed the dishes and did the most

menial tasks. It was only when the bishop arrived a considerable time later that the mistake was discovered and the humble monk took up his true position. Those who enter upon office for the respect which will be given to them have begun in the wrong way, and cannot, unless they change, ever be in any sense *the servants* of Christ and of their neighbours.

(3) It warns against the attempt to make a traffic of religion. It is still possible to use religious connections for self-gain and self-advancement. But this is a warning to all who are in the Church for what they can get out of it and not for what they can put into it.

THE GREATEST GIFT

Mark 12:41-4

When Jesus had sat down opposite the treasury, he was watching how the crowd threw their money into the treasury, and many rich people threw in large sums. A poor widow came and threw in two mites which make up half a penny. He called his disciples and said to them, 'This is the truth I tell you – this poor widow has thrown in more than all the people who threw money into the treasury, for all of them threw their contributions in out of their abundance, but she out of her lack has thrown in everything that she had, all she had to live on.'

BETWEEN the Court of the Gentiles and the Court of the Women there was the Gate Beautiful. It may well be that Jesus had gone to sit quietly there after the argument and the tension of the Court of the Gentiles and the discussions in the cloisters. In the Court of the Women there were thirteen collecting boxes called 'The Trumpets', because they were so shaped. Each of them was for a special purpose, for instance to buy corn or wine or oil for the sacrifices. They were for contributions for the daily sacrifices and expenses of the Temple. Many people threw in quite considerable contributions. Then came a widow. She flung in two mites. The coin so called was a *lepton*, which literally means *a thin one*. It was the smallest of all coins. And yet Jesus said that her tiny contribution was greater than all the others, for the others had thrown in what they could spare easily enough and still have plenty left, while the widow had flung in everything she had.

Here is a lesson in giving:

(1) Real giving must be sacrificial. The amount of the gift never matters so much as its cost to the giver; not the size of the gift, but the sacrifice. Real generosity gives until it hurts. For many of us it is a real question if ever our giving to God's work is any sacrifice at all. Few people will do without their pleasures to give a little more to the work of God. It may well be a sign of the decadence of the Church and the failure of our Christianity that gifts have to be coaxed out of church people, and that often they will not give at all unless they get something back in the way of entertainment or of goods. There can be few of us who read this story without shame.

(2) Real giving has a certain recklessness in it. The woman might have kept one coin. It would not have been much but it would have been something, yet she gave everything she had. There is a great symbolic truth here. It is our tragedy that there is so often some part of our lives, some part of our activities, some part of ourselves which we do not give to Christ. Somehow there is nearly always something we hold back. We rarely make the final sacrifice and the final surrender.

(3) It is a strange and lovely thing that the person whom the New Testament and Jesus hand down to history as a pattern of generosity was a person who gave a gift of so little value in monetary terms. We may feel that we have not much in the way of material gifts or personal gifts to give to Christ, but if we put all that we have and are at his disposal, he can do things with it and with us that are beyond our imaginings.

THE THINGS TO COME

MARK 13 is one of the most difficult chapters in the New Testament for a modern reader to understand. That is because it is one of the most Jewish chapters in the Bible. From beginning to end it is thinking in terms of Jewish history and Jewish ideas. All through it Jesus is using categories and pictures which were very familiar to the Jews of his day, but which are very strange, and, indeed, unknown, to many modern readers. Even so, it is not possible to disregard this chapter because it is the source of many ideas about the second coming of Jesus. The difficulty about the doctrine of the second coming is that nowadays people are apt either completely to disregard it or to be so completely unbalanced about it that it becomes for them practically the only doctrine of the Christian faith. It may be that if we study this chapter with some care we shall come to a sane and correct view about this doctrine.

We will first of all glance at the Jewish background against which this chapter must be read. We will then try to make an analysis of the various elements which go to make it up. We will then study it section by section in the usual way. Finally, we will try to extract from it the great truths which are permanently valid.

The Day of the Lord

This whole chapter must be read with one thing in mind. Again and again we have to return to this matter because there is so much of the New Testament which is not intelligible without it. The Jews never doubted that they were the chosen people, and they never doubted that one day they would occupy the place in the world which the chosen people, as they saw it, deserved and were bound to have in the end. They had long since abandoned the idea that they could ever win that place by human means, and they were confident that in the end God would directly intervene in history and win it for them. The day of God's intervention was *the day of the Lord*. Before that day of the Lord, there would be a time of terror and trouble when the world would be shaken to its foundations and judgment would come. But it would be followed by the new world and the new age and the new glory.

In one sense, this idea is the product of unconquerable optimism. The Jews were quite certain that God would break in. In another sense, it was the product of bleak *pessimism*, because it was based on the idea that this world was so utterly bad that only its complete destruction and the emergence of a new world would suffice. They did not look for reformation. They looked for a re-creating of the entire scheme of things.

Let us look at some of the Old Testament passages about the day of the Lord. Amos writes (5:16–18, 20):

> In all the squares there shall be wailing; and in all the
> streets they shall say, 'Alas! alas!' They shall call the
> farmers to mourning, and those skilled in lamentations
> to wailing, in all the vineyards there shall be wailing,
> for I will pass through the midst of you, says the Lord.
> Alas for you who desire the day of the Lord! Why do

you want the day of the Lord? Is not the day of the Lord darkness, not light, and gloom with no brightness in it?

Isaiah (13:6, 9–10, 13) has a terrible passage about the day of the Lord:

> Wail, for the day of the Lord is near; it will come like destruction from the Almighty! . . . See, the day of the Lord comes, cruel, with wrath and fierce anger, to make the earth a desolation, and to destroy its sinners from it. For the stars of the heavens and their constellations will not give their light; the sun will be dark at its rising, and the moon will not shed its light . . . Therefore I will make the heavens tremble, and the earth will be shaken out of its place, at the wrath of the Lord of hosts on the day of his fierce anger.

The second and third chapters of Joel (2:1–2, 30–1) are full of terrible descriptions of the day of the Lord:

> The day of the Lord is coming . . . a day of darkness and gloom, a day of clouds and thick darkness . . . I will show portents in the heavens and on the earth, blood and fire and columns of smoke. The sun shall be turned to darkness, and the moon to blood, before the great and terrible day of the Lord comes.

Again and again such passages of terror meet us in the Old Testament. The day of the Lord will be sudden, shattering, terrifying. The world will reel with destruction. The very course of nature will be uprooted, and God, the judge, will come.

Between the Old and the New Testaments there was a time when the Jews knew no freedom. It was therefore only natural that their hopes and dreams of the day of the Lord would become even more vivid. In that time a kind of popular religious literature grew up. Jesus would know it. All the Jews would be familiar with its picture. The writings of which this literature consisted were called *Apocalypses*. *Apokalupsis* means *an unveiling*. These books were dreams and visions of what would happen when the day of the Lord came and in the terrible time immediately before it. They continued to use the Old Testament imagery, and to supplement it with new details. But, it must be noted, all these books were dreams and visions. They were attempts to paint the unpaintable and to speak the unspeakable. They were poetry, not prose. They were visions, not science. They were dreams, not history. They were never meant to be taken prosaically as maps of the future and timetables of events to come.

We will see that every single detail in this chapter can be paralleled in the visions of the Old Testament and of the literature between the Testaments. Jesus was taking the language, the imagery, the apparatus of apocalyptic literature, and using it to try to make people understand. He was working with the only ideas that people knew. But he knew, as they knew, that these things were only pictures, for no one could really tell what would happen when God broke in.

The Different Strands

Further, in this chapter there are various strands of thought. The gospel writers had a way of collecting Jesus' sayings on any subject. It was a wise way to write and excellent for teaching purposes. Here Mark, as it were, collects *Jesus' sayings about the future*. Now even a cursory reading, with no special knowledge, shows that though all these sayings were about the future, they were not all about the same things. There are in fact in this chapter *five* different strands.

(1) *There are prophecies of the destruction of Jerusalem.* We get them in verses 1–2 and 14–20. Jesus foresaw the end

of the holy city. As we shall see, Jesus was right. Jerusalem fell in AD 70. The Temple was destroyed and the most terrible things happened.

(2) *There is warning of persecution to come.* We get that in verses 9–13. Jesus foresaw that his followers would have to go through the most heartbreaking and soul-searing experiences, and he warned them in advance.

(3) *There are warnings of the dangers of the last days.* We get them in verses 3–6 and 21–2. Jesus saw quite clearly that men would come who would twist and adulterate the Christian faith. It was bound to be so, for people are always inclined to listen to their own proud minds rather than to the voice of God. He wished to defend his people in advance from the heresies and lies which would invade the Church.

(4) *There are warnings of the second coming.* Now, these warnings of the second coming are dressed in the language which has to do with the day of the Lord. We get them in verses 7–8 and 24–7. The imagery of the day of the Lord and of the second coming are inextricably mixed up. It had to be so, because no one could possibly know what would happen in either case. It is with visions and dreams that we have to deal. The only pictures Jesus could use about his second coming were those which prophets and apocalyptists had already used about the day of the Lord. They are not meant to be taken literally. They are meant as impressionistic pictures, as seer's visions, designed to impress upon people the greatness of that event when it should come.

(5) *There are warnings of the necessity to be on the watch.* We get them in verses 28–37. If men and women live in the shadow of eternity, if they live with the constant possibility of the intervention of God, if they live with the prospect of the consummation of the coming of Christ always before

them, if the times and the seasons are known only to God, there is the necessity always to be ready.

This chapter will make far more sense if we remember these various strands in it and remember that every strand is unfolded in language and imagery which go back to the Old Testament and apocalyptic pictures of the day of the Lord.

Because that is so, we will study the chapter not in consecutive verses, but in the various passages of which the various strands consist.

A CITY'S DOOM

Mark 13:1-2

> As they were going out of the sacred precincts, one of his disciples said to Jesus, 'Teacher, see! What stones and what buildings!' Jesus said to him, 'You see this great building? Not one stone will be left on another which will not be thrown down!'

WE begin with the prophecies of Jesus which foretold the doom of Jerusalem. The Temple which Herod built was one of the wonders of the world. It was begun in 20-19 BC and in the time of Jesus was not yet completely finished. It was built on the top of Mount Moriah. Instead of levelling off the summit of the mountain, a kind of vast platform was formed by raising up walls of massive masonry and enclosing the whole area. On these walls a platform was laid, strengthened by piers which distributed the weight of the superstructure. Josephus tells us that some of these stones were 40 feet long by 12 feet high by 18 feet wide. It would be some of these vast stones that moved the Galilaean disciples to such wondering amazement.

The most magnificent entrance to the Temple was at the south-west angle. Here between the city and the Temple hill there stretched the Tyropoeon Valley. A marvellous bridge spanned the valley. Each arch was 41½ feet and there were stones used in the building of it which measured 24 feet long. The Tyropoeon valley was no less than 225 feet below. The breadth of the cleft that the bridge spanned was 354 feet, and the bridge itself was 50 feet in breadth. The bridge led straight into the Royal Porch. The porch consisted of a double row of Corinthian pillars all 37½ feet high and each one cut out of one solid block of marble.

Of the actual Temple building itself, the holy place, Josephus writes, 'Now the outward face of the Temple in its front wanted nothing that was likely to surprise men's minds or their eyes, for it was covered all over with plates of gold of great weight, and, at the first rising of the sun, reflected back a very fiery splendour, and made those who forced themselves to look upon it to turn their eyes away, just as they would have done at the sun's own rays. But this Temple appeared to strangers, when they were at a distance, like a mountain covered with snow, for, as to those parts of it which were not gilt, they were exceeding white . . . Of its stones, some of them were forty-five cubits in length, five in height and six in breadth.' (A cubit was eighteen inches.)

It was all this splendour that so impressed the disciples. The Temple seemed the summit of human art and achievement, and seemed so vast and solid that it would stand forever. But Jesus made the astonishing statement that the day was coming when not one of these stones would stand upon another. In less than fifty years his prophecy came tragically true. As Robert Bridges wrote so eloquently in that great hymn, 'All my hope on God is founded':

Pride of man and earthly glory,
   Sword and crown betray his trust;
What with care and toil he buildeth,
   Tower and temple, fall to dust.
     But God's power,
     Hour by hour,
Is my temple and my tower.

A CITY'S AGONY

Mark 13:14–20

'When you see the abomination of desolation standing where he ought not (let him who reads understand), then let those who are in Judaea flee to the mountains. Let him who is on the housetop not come down, nor let him go in to take anything out of his house. And let him who is working in the field not turn back to pick up his cloak. Woe to women who are with child and to those whose babes are at their breasts in these days! Pray that it may not happen in the stormy weather. These days will be a tribulation such as has never happened from the beginning of the creation which God has created until now, and such as will never happen again. Unless the Lord had shortened the days no living creature could have survived. But, for the sake of the chosen ones whom he chose, he shortened the days.'

JESUS forecasts some of the awful terror of the siege and the final fall of Jerusalem. It is his warning that when the first signs of it came people ought to flee, not even waiting to pick up their clothes or to try to save their goods. In fact the people did precisely the opposite. They crowded into Jerusalem, and death came in ways that are almost too terrible to think about.

The phrase *the abomination of desolation* has its origin in
the book of Daniel (9:27, 11:31, 12:11). The Hebrew expression literally means *the profanation that appals*. The origin
of the phrase was in connection with Antiochus. We have
already seen that he tried to stamp out the Jewish religion
and introduce Greek thought and Greek ways. He desecrated
the Temple by offering pig's flesh on the great altar and by
setting up public brothels in the sacred courts. Before the
very Holy Place itself, he set up a great statue of Olympian
Zeus and ordered the Jews to worship it. In connection with
that, the writer of 1 Maccabees says (1:54, Revised Standard
Version), 'Now the fifteenth day of the month Casleu, in the
hundred and forty-fifth year, they set up the abomination of
desolation upon the altar and builded idol altars throughout
the cities of Juda on every side.' The phrase *the abomination
of desolation*, *the profanation that appals*, originally described the pagan image and all that accompanied it with
which Antiochus desecrated the Temple. Jesus prophesies
that the same kind of thing is going to happen again. It very
nearly happened in the year AD 40. Caligula was then Roman
emperor. He was an epileptic and mad. But he insisted that
he was a god. He heard of the imageless worship of the
Temple of Jerusalem and planned to set up his own statue in
the Holy Place. His advisers begged him not to do so, for
they knew that if he did, a bloody civil war would result. He
was obstinate, but fortunately he died in AD 41 before he could
carry out his plan of desecration.

What does Jesus mean when he speaks about *the abomination of desolation*? People expected not only a Messiah,
but also the emergence of a power who would be the very
incarnation of evil and who would gather up into himself
everything that was against God. Paul called that power *the
Man of Lawlessness* (2 Thessalonians 2:3). John of the

Revelation identified that power with Rome (Revelation 17). Jesus is saying, 'Some day, quite soon, you will see the very incarnate power of evil rise up in a deliberate attempt to destroy the people and the Holy Place of God.' He takes the old phrase and uses it to describe the terrible things that are about to happen.

It was in AD 70 that Jerusalem finally fell to the besieging army of Titus, who was to be emperor of Rome. The horrors of that siege form one of the grimmest pages in history. The people crowded into Jerusalem from the countryside. Titus had no alternative but to starve the city into subjection. The matter was complicated by the fact that even at that terrible time there were sects and factions inside the city itself. Jerusalem was torn without and within.

Josephus tells the story of that terrible siege in the fifth book of *The Jewish Wars*. He tells us that 97,000 were taken captive and 1,100,000 perished by slow starvation and the sword. He tells us, 'Then did the famine widen its progress and devoured the people by whole houses and families. The upper rooms were full of women and children dying of starvation. The lanes of the city were full of the dead bodies of the aged. The children and the young men wandered about the market places like shadows, all swelled with famine, and fell down dead wheresoever their misery seized them. As for burying them, those that were sick themselves were not able to do it. And those that were hearty and well were deterred by the great multitude of the dead, and the uncertainty when they would die themselves, for many died as they were burying others, and many went to their own coffins before the fatal hour. There was no lamentation made under these calamities . . . the famine confounded all natural passions . . . A deep silence and a kind of deadly night had seized upon the city.'

To make it still grimmer, there were the inevitable ghouls who plundered the dead bodies. Josephus tells grimly how when not even any herbs were available 'some persons were driven to such terrible distress as to search the common sewers and old dunghills of cattle, and to eat the dung which they got there, and what they could not endure so much as to see, they now used for food'. He paints a grim picture of men gnawing the leather of straps and shoes, and tells a terrible story of a woman who killed and roasted her child, and offered a share of that terrible meal to those who came seeking food.

The prophecy that Jesus made of terrible days ahead for Jerusalem came most abundantly true. Those who crowded into the city for safety died by the 100,000, and only those who took his advice and fled to the hills were saved.

THE HARD WAY

Mark 13:9–13

'Take heed to yourselves, for they will hand you over to councils, and they will scourge you in synagogues, and you will stand before governors and kings for my sake, and it will be your opportunity to bear your witness to them. The gospel must first be preached to all nations. And when they hand you over and bring you before authorities, do not worry beforehand about what you will say, but speak whatever is given you in that hour, for it is not you who speak but the Holy Spirit. Brother shall hand over brother to death, and father child. All children will rise up against parents, and will kill them. And you will be hated of all for the sake of my name. But the man who has endured to the end, he will be saved.'

Now we come to the warnings of persecution to come. Jesus never left his followers in any doubt that they had chosen a hard way. No one could claim that the conditions of Christ's service had not been explained.

The handing over to councils and the scourging in synagogues refer to Jewish persecution. In Jerusalem there was the great Sanhedrin, the supreme court of the Jews, but every town and village had its local Sanhedrin. Before such local Sanhedrins the self-confessed heretics would be tried, and in the synagogues they would be publicly scourged. The governors and kings refer to trials before the Roman courts, such as Paul faced before Felix and Festus and Agrippa.

It was a fact that the Christians were wonderfully strengthened in their trials. When we read of the trials of the martyrs, even though they were often uneducated men and women, the impression often is that it was the judges and not the Christians who were on trial. Their Christian faith enabled them to fear God so much that they were never afraid to stand up to anyone.

It was true that people were even sometimes betrayed by members of their own family. In the early Roman Empire one of the curses was the informer (*delator*). There were those who, in their attempts to curry favour with the authorities, would not hesitate to betray their own family and friends. That must have been the sorest blow of all.

In Hitler's Germany a man was arrested because he stood for freedom. He endured imprisonment and torture with stoic and uncomplaining fortitude. Finally, with spirit still unbroken, he was released. Some short time afterwards he committed suicide. Many wondered why. Those who knew him well knew the reason – he had discovered that his own son was the person who had informed against him. The treachery of his own flesh and blood broke him in a way that the cruelty of his enemies was unable to achieve.

This family and domestic hostility was one of the regular items in the catalogue of terror of the last and terrible days, 'Friends shall conquer one another' (4 Ezra [2 Esdras] 5:9). 'And they shall hate one another and provoke one another to fight' (2 Baruch 70:3). 'And they shall strive with one another, the young with the old, and the old with the young, the poor with the rich, the lowly with the great, the beggar with the prince' (Jubilees 23:19). 'Children shall shame the elders, and the elders shall rise up before the children' (the Mishnah, Sotah 9:15). 'For the son treats the father with contempt, the daughter rises up against her mother, the daughter-in-law against her mother-in-law; your enemies are members of your own household' (Micah 7:6).

Life becomes a hell upon earth when personal loyalties are destroyed and when love is a source of suspicion rather than trust.

It was true that the Christians were hated. One Roman historian, Tacitus, talked of Christianity as an accursed superstition; another, Suetonius, called it a new and evil superstition. The main reason for the hatred was the way in which Christianity cut across family ties. The fact was that love for Christ had to come before love for father or mother, or son or daughter. And the matter was complicated by the way that the Christians were much slandered. It is beyond doubt that the Jews encouraged these slanders. The most serious was the charge that the Christians were cannibals, a charge supported by the words of the sacrament which speak of eating Christ's body and drinking his blood.

In this, as in all other things, it is the one who endures to the end who is saved. Life is not a short, sharp sprint; it is a marathon race. Life is not a single battle; it is a long campaign.

The Glasgow minister, Dr G. J. Jeffrey, tells of a famous man who refused to have his biography written when he was still alive. 'I have seen too many men fall out on the last lap of the race,' he said. Life is never safe until it reaches journey's end. It was John Bunyan who, in his dream, saw that from the very gates of heaven there was a way to hell. It is the one who endures *to the end* who will be saved.

THE DANGERS OF THE LAST DAYS

Mark 13:3–6, 21–3

> As he was sitting on the Mount of Olives, opposite the sacred precincts of the Temple, Peter and James and John and Andrew privately asked Jesus, 'Tell us, when shall these things be? And what sign will there be when these things are going to be completed?' Jesus began to say to them, 'See that no one misleads you. Many will come in my name, and say, "I am he," and they will lead many astray.'
>
> 'And if someone then says to you, "See! Here is the Messiah!" or, "See! There he is!" do not believe them. For false Messiahs and false prophets will arise, and they will produce signs and wonders to lead the elect astray, if it is possible. But do you look to yourselves! See! I have told you beforehand all that will happen.'

JESUS was well aware that, before the end, heretics would arise; and, indeed it was not long before the Church had its heretics. Heresy arises from five main causes.

(1) It arises from constructing doctrine to suit oneself. The human mind has an infinite capacity for wishful thinking. In a famous sentence, the psalmist said, 'Fools say in their

hearts, "There is no God"' (Psalm 14:1). The fools about whom the psalmist was speaking were not fools in the sense that they had no intelligence. They were *moral* fools. The statement that there was no God was made because they did not wish God to be. If God existed, so much the worse for them; therefore they eliminated him from their doctrine and from their universe.

One particular heresy has always been with us, and that is *antinomianism*. Antinomians begin with the principle that law has been abolished – and in a sense they are right. They go on to say that there is nothing but *grace* – and again in a sense they are right. They then go on to argue – as Paul shows us in Romans 6 – on lines like these. 'You say that God's grace is wide enough to cover every sin?' 'Yes.' 'You say that God's grace can forgive any sin?' 'Yes.' 'You say that God's grace is the greatest and the most wonderful thing in the universe?' 'Yes.' 'Then', they conclude, 'let us go on sinning to our hearts' content, for the more we sin, the more chances we give to God's amazing grace to operate. Sin is a good thing, for sin gives grace a chance to work. Therefore, let us do whatever we like.' The grace of God has been twisted to suit those who want to sin.

The same kind of argument is used by those who declare that the only important thing in life is the soul and that the body does not matter. If that is so, the argument runs, then we can do what we like with our bodies. If we are so inclined, we can sate our physical desires.

One of the commonest ways to arrive in heresy is to mould Christian truth to suit ourselves. Can it be that the doctrine of hell and the doctrine of the second coming have dropped out of much religious thought because they are both uncomfortable doctrines? No one would wish to bring either back in its crude form, but can it be that they have dropped *too far* out of Christian thought because it does not suit us to believe in them?

(2) Heresy arises from overstressing one part of the truth. It is, for instance, always wrong to overstress one attribute of God. If we think only of God's *holiness*, we can never attain to any intimacy with him, but rather tend to a deism in which he is entirely remote from the world. If we think only of God's *justice*, we can never be free of the fear of God. We become haunted and not helped by our religion. If we think only of God's *love*, religion can become a very easy-going sentimental thing. There is more in the New Testament than Luke 15.

Always there is paradox in Christianity. God is love, yet God is justice. We are free, yet God is in control. We are creatures of time, yet also creatures of eternity. G. K. Chesterton said that orthodoxy was like walking along a knife-edge ridge with a yawning chasm on either side. One step too much to right or left and disaster follows. We must, as the Greeks insisted, see life steady and see it *whole*.

(3) Heresy arises from trying to produce a religion which will suit people, one which will be popular and attractive. To do that it has to be watered down. The sting, the condemnation, the humiliation, the moral demand have to be taken out of it. It is not our job to alter Christianity to suit people, but to alter people to suit Christianity.

(4) Heresy arises from divorcing oneself from the Christian fellowship. Anyone who thinks alone runs a grave danger of thinking astray. There is such a thing as the tradition of the Church. There is such a conception as the Church being the guardian of truth. If people find that their thinking separates them from the fellowship of others, the chances are that there is something wrong with their thinking. It is the Roman Catholic principle that we cannot have God for our

Father unless we have the Church for our mother – and there is truth there.

(5) Heresy arises from the attempt to be completely intelligible. Here is one of the great paradoxes. We are duty-bound to try to understand our faith. But because we are finite and God is infinite we can never fully understand. For that very reason a faith that can be neatly stated in a series of propositions and neatly proved in a series of logical steps like a geometrical theorem is a contradiction in terms. As G. K. Chesterton said, 'It is only the fool who tries to get the heavens inside his head, and not unnaturally his head bursts. The wise man is content to get his head inside the heavens.' Even at our most intellectual we must remember that there is a place for the ultimate mystery before which we can only worship, wonder and adore.

> How could I praise,
> If such as I could understand?

'I believe', as Tertullian said, 'because it is impossible.'

HIS COMING AGAIN

Mark 13:7–8, 24–7

> Jesus said, 'When you hear of wars and reports of wars, do not be disturbed. These things must happen. But the end is not yet. Nation shall rise against nation, and kingdom against kingdom. In certain places there will be earthquakes. There will be famines. These things are the beginning of the birth-pangs of the new age.'

> 'And in those days, after that tribulation, the sun will be darkened, and the moon will not give its light, and the stars will be falling from heaven, and the powers in

the heavens will be shaken. And then they will see the
Son of Man coming in the clouds with much power and
glory. And then he will send his angels and they will
gather the chosen ones from the four winds, from the
edge of the earth to the edge of the heaven.'

HERE Jesus unmistakably speaks of his coming again. But –
and this is important – he clothes the idea in three pictures
which are part and parcel of the apparatus connected with the
day of the Lord.

(1) The day of the Lord was to be preceded by a time of
wars. Fourth Ezra [2 Esdras] declares that before the day of
the Lord there will be

> Earthquakes
> Tumult of peoples,
> Intrigues of nations,
> Wavering of leaders,
> Confusion of princes. (9:3)

The same book says,

> And bewilderment of mind shall come over those who
> inhabit the earth. They shall plan to make war against
> one another, city against city, place against place,
> people against people, and kingdom against kingdom.
> (13:30–1)

The Sibylline Oracles foresee that

> King captures king and takes his land, and nations
> ravage nations and potentates people, and rulers all flee
> to another land, and the land is changed in men and a
> barbarian empire ravages Hellas and drains the rich land
> of its wealth, and men come face to face in strife.
> (3:635–41)

Second Baruch has the same ideas. In 27:2–13, this book
singles out twelve things which will precede the new age.

In the first part there will be the beginning of commotions. In the second part there shall be the slayings of great ones. In the third part the fall of many by death. In the fourth part the sending of the sword. In the fifth part famine and withholding of rain. In the sixth part earthquakes and terrors . . . [there is a blank in the manuscript here] . . . In the eighth part a multitude of spectres and attacks of the evil spirits. In the ninth part the fall of fire. In the tenth part rapine and much oppression. In the eleventh part wickedness and unchastity. In the twelfth part confusion from the mingling together of all those things aforesaid.

All the inhabitants of the earth shall be moved against one another. (48:32)

And they shall hate one another,
And provoke one another to fight.

. . .

And it shall come to pass that whosoever comes safe
    out of the war shall die in the earthquake,
And whosoever gets safe out of the earthquake shall be
    burned by the fire,
And whosoever gets safe out of the fire shall be
    destroyed by famine. (70:9-10)

It is abundantly clear that when Jesus spoke of wars and rumours of wars he was using pictures which were part and parcel of Jewish dreams of the future.

(2) The day of the Lord was to be preceded by the darkening of sun and moon. The Old Testament itself is full of that (Amos 8:9; Joel 2:10, 3:15; Ezekiel 32:7-8; Isaiah 13:10, 34:4); again the popular literature of Jesus' day is full of it, too.

371

> And the sun shall suddenly begin to shine at night,
> > And the moon during the day,
> > > . . .
> and the stars shall fall. (4 Ezra [2 Esdras] 5:4–5)

Second Baruch 32:1 speaks of 'the time in which the mighty one is to shake the whole creation'. The Sibylline Oracles (3:796–806) talk of a time when 'swords in the star-lit heaven appear by night towards dusk and towards dawn . . . and all the brightness of the sun fails at midday from the heaven, and the moon's rays shine forth and come back to earth, and a sign comes from the rocks with dripping streams of blood'. The Assumption of Moses foresees a time when:

> The horns of the sun shall be broken and he shall be
> > turned into darkness,
> And the moon shall not give her light, and be turned
> > wholly into blood,
> And the circle of the stars shall be disturbed. (10:5)

Once again it is clear that Jesus is using the popular language which everyone knew.

(3) It was a regular part of the imagery that the Jews were to be gathered back to Palestine from the four corners of the earth. The Old Testament itself is full of that idea (Isaiah 27:13, 35:8–10; Micah 7:12; Zechariah 10:6–11); once more the popular literature loves the idea:

> Blow ye in Zion on the trumpet to summon the saints,
> > Cause ye to be heard in Jerusalem the voice of him
> > > that bringeth good tidings,
> > For God hath had pity on Israel in visiting them.
> Stand on the height, O Jerusalem, and behold thy
> > children,
> > From the East and the West gathered together by
> > > the Lord.
> > > > (Psalms of Solomon 11:1–3)

The Lord will gather you together in faith through His tender mercy, and for the sake of Abraham and Isaac and Jacob.

(The Testament of Asher 7:7)

When we read the pictorial words of Jesus about the second coming, we must remember that he is giving us neither a map of eternity nor a timetable to the future, but that he is simply using the language and the pictures that many Jews knew and used for centuries before him.

But it is extremely interesting to note that the things Jesus prophesied were in fact happening. He prophesied wars, and the dreaded Parthians were in fact pressing in on the Roman frontiers. He prophesied earthquakes, and within forty years the Roman world was aghast at the earthquake which devastated Laodicaea and at the eruption of Vesuvius, which buried Pompeii in lava. He prophesied famines, and there was famine in Rome in the days of Claudius. It was in fact such a time of terror in the near future that when Tacitus began his histories he said that everything happening seemed to prove that the gods were seeking not salvation but vengeance on the Roman Empire.

In this passage, the one thing that we must retain is the fact that Jesus did foretell that he would come again. The imagery we can disregard.

BE ON THE WATCH

Mark 13:28–37

Jesus said, 'Learn the lesson the fig tree offers you. As soon as its branches become tender, and it puts forth its leaves, you know that summer is near. So must you too

know, when you see these things happening, that the
end is near at the doors. This is the truth I tell you – this
generation will not pass away until these things happen.
Heaven and earth will pass away but my words will
never pass away. But no man knows about that day and
that hour, not even the angels in heaven, not even the
Son, no one except the Father. Be watchful, be wakeful,
be praying, for you do not know when the time is. It is
like when a man goes abroad, and leaves his home, and
puts his servants in charge, and orders the doorkeeper
to be on the watch. So then be watchful! For you do not
know when the master of the house comes, late in the
evening, at midnight, at cock-crow, or in the early day.
Watch! in case he comes suddenly and finds you
sleeping. What I say to you, I say to all – be on the
watch!'

THERE are three special things to note in this passage.

(1) It is sometimes held that when Jesus said that these
things were to happen within this generation he was in
error. But Jesus was right, for this sentence does not refer
to the second coming. It could not when the next sentence
says he does not know when that day will be. It refers to
Jesus' prophecies about the fall of Jerusalem and the
destruction of the Temple, and they were abundantly fulfilled.

(2) Jesus says that he does not know the day or the hour
when he will come again. There were things which even he
left without questioning in the hand of God. There can be no
greater warning and rebuke to those who work out dates and
timetables as to when he will come again. Surely it is nothing
less than blasphemy for us to inquire into that of which our
Lord consented to be ignorant.

(3) Jesus draws a practical conclusion. We are like those
who know that their master will come, but who do not know

when. We live in the shadow of eternity. That is no reason for fearful and hysterical expectation. But it means that day by day our work must be completed. It means that we must so live that it does not matter when he comes. It gives us the great task of making every day fit for him to see and being at any moment ready to meet him face to face. All life becomes a preparation to meet the King.

We began by saying that this was a very difficult chapter, but that in the end it had permanent truth to tell us.

(1) It tells us that only God's people can see into the secrets of history. Jesus saw the fate of Jerusalem although others were blind to it. Leaders of real stature must be men and women of God. To guide any country its leaders must be themselves God-guided. Only those who know God can enter into something of the plan of God.

(2) It tells us two things about the doctrine of the second coming.

(a) It tells us that it contains a fact we forget or disregard at our peril.

(b) It tells us that the imagery in which it is clothed is the imagery of Jesus' own time, and that to speculate on it is useless, when Jesus himself was content not to know. The one thing of which we can be sure is that history is going somewhere; there is a consummation to come.

(3) It tells us that of all things to forget God and to become immersed in material concerns is most foolish. The truly wise never forget that they must be ready when the summons comes. For those who live in that memory, the end will not be terror, but eternal joy.

THE LAST ACT BEGINS

Mark 14:1-2

> The Feast of the Passover and of Unleavened Bread
> was due in two days' time. And the chief priests and
> experts in the law were trying to find some way to seize
> Jesus by some stratagem and to kill him, for they said,
> 'This must not be done at the Feast itself in case there
> should be a disturbance of the people.'

THE last crowded act of Jesus' life was now about to open.
The Feast of the Passover and the Feast of Unleavened Bread
were really two different things. The Feast of the Passover
fell on 14th Nisan, that is, about 14th April. The Feast of
Unleavened Bread consisted of the seven days following the
Passover. The Passover itself was a major feast and was kept
like a Sabbath. The Feast of Unleavened Bread was called a
minor festival, and, although no new work could be begun
during it, such work as was 'necessary for public interest or
to provide against private loss' was allowable. The really great
day was Passover Day.

The Passover was one of the three compulsory feasts. The
others were the Feast of Pentecost and the Feast of
Tabernacles. To these feasts every male adult Jew who lived
within fifteen miles of Jerusalem was bound to come.

The Passover had a double significance.

(a) It had a *historical significance* (Exodus 12). It commemorated the deliverance of the children of Israel from their
bondage in Egypt. God had sent plague after plague on Egypt,
and as each plague came, Pharaoh promised to let the people
go. But when each plague abated, he hardened his heart and
went back on his word. Finally there came a terrible night
when the angel of death was to walk through the land of

Egypt and slay every first-born son in every home. The Israelites were to slay a lamb. Using a bunch of hyssop they were to smear the lintel of the doorpost with the blood of the lamb, and when the angel of death saw the doorpost so marked, he would *pass over* that house and its occupants would be safe. Before they went upon their way the Israelites were to eat a meal of a roasted lamb and unleavened bread. It was that 'passover', that deliverance and that meal that the Feast of the Passover commemorated.

(b) It had an *agricultural significance*. It marked the gathering in of the barley harvest. On that day a sheaf of barley had to be waved before the Lord (Leviticus 23:10–11). Not till after that had been done could the barley of the new crop be sold in the shops or bread made with the new flour be eaten.

Every possible preparation was made for the Passover. For a month beforehand its meaning was expounded in the synagogue, and its lesson was taught daily in the schools. The aim was that no one should come ignorant and unprepared to the feast. The roads were all put in order; the bridges repaired. One special thing was done. It was very common to bury people beside the road. Now if any pilgrims had touched one of these wayside tombs they would technically have been in contact with a dead body and so rendered unclean and unable to take part in the feast. So, before the Passover, all the wayside tombs were whitewashed so that they would stand out and the pilgrims could avoid them. Psalms 120–34 are entitled *Psalms of Degree*, and it may well be that these were the psalms which the pilgrims sang on their way to the feast, as they sought to lighten the road with their music. It is said that Psalm 122 was the one which they actually sang as they climbed the hill to the Temple on the last lap of their journey.

As we have already seen, it was compulsory for every adult male Jew who lived within fifteen miles of Jerusalem to come to the Passover, but far more than these came. It was the one ambition of all Jews to eat at least one Passover in Jerusalem before they died. Therefore from every country in the world pilgrims came flocking to the Passover Feast. During the Passover all lodging was free. Jerusalem could not hold the crowds, and Bethany and Bethphage were two of the outlying villages where pilgrims lodged.

A passage in Josephus gives us an idea of how many pilgrims actually came. He tells that Cestius, governor of Palestine round about AD 65, had some difficulty in persuading Nero of the great importance of the Jewish religion. To impress him, he asked the then high priest to take a census of the lambs slain at the Passover in one year. The number, according to Josephus, was 256,500. The law was that there must be a minimum party of ten people to one lamb, so that there must have been close on 3,000,000 pilgrims in Jerusalem.

It was just there that the problem of the Jewish authorities lay. During the Passover, feelings ran very high. The remembrance of the old deliverance from Egypt made the people long for a new deliverance from Rome. At no time was nationalist feeling so intense. Jerusalem was not the Roman headquarters in Judaea. The governor had his residence and the soldiers were stationed in Caesarea. During the Passover time special detachments of troops were drafted into Jerusalem and quartered in the Tower of Antonia, which overlooked the Temple. The Romans knew that at Passover anything might happen and they were taking no chances. The Jewish authorities knew that in an inflammable atmosphere like that, the arrest of Jesus might well provoke a riot. That is why they sought some secret stratagem to arrest him and have him in their power before the people knew anything about it.

The last act of Jesus' life was to be played out in a city crammed with Jews who had come from the ends of the earth. They had come to commemorate the event whereby their nation was delivered from slavery in Egypt long ago. It was at that very time that God's deliverer of all humanity was crucified upon his cross.

LOVE'S EXTRAVAGANCE

Mark 14:3-9

> While Jesus was in Bethany, while he was reclining at a table in the house of Simon the leper, there came a woman who had a phial of ointment of pure nard. She broke the phial and poured it over his head. Some of them said indignantly to each other, 'To what purpose is the waste of this ointment? This ointment could have been sold for more than 300 denarii, and the money could have been given to the poor.' And they were angry at her. Jesus said, 'Let her be! Why do you trouble her? It is a lovely thing that she has done to me. You have always got the poor with you, and you can do something for them any time you like, but you have not got me always. She has done what she could. She has taken my body and anointed it beforehand against my burial. This is the truth I tell you – wherever the good news shall be proclaimed throughout the whole world, the story of what she has done will be told, so that she will always be remembered.'

THE poignancy of this story lies in the fact that it tells us of almost the last kindness that Jesus had done to him.

He was in the house of a man called Simon the leper, in the village of Bethany. People did not sit to eat; they reclined on low couches. They lay on the couch resting on the left elbow and using the right hand to take their food. Anyone coming up to those who were lying like this would stand well above them. To Jesus there came a woman with an alabaster phial of ointment. It was the custom to pour a few drops of perfume on a guest when he arrived at a house or when he sat down to a meal. This phial held nard which was a very precious ointment made from a rare plant that came from far-off India. But it was not a few drops that this woman poured on the head of Jesus. She broke the flask and anointed him with the whole contents.

There may be more than one reason why she broke the flask. Maybe she broke it as a sign that all was to be used. There was a custom in the middle east that if a glass was used by a distinguished guest, it was broken so that it would never again be touched by the hand of any lesser person. Maybe there was something of that in the woman's mind. But there was one thing not in her mind which Jesus saw. It was also the custom in this part of the world, first to bathe, then to anoint the bodies of the dead. After the body had been anointed, the flask in which the perfume had been contained was broken and the fragments were laid with the dead body in the tomb. Although she did not mean it so, that was the very thing this woman was doing.

Her action provoked the grudging criticism of some of the bystanders. The flask was worth more than 300 *denarii*. A *denarius* was a Roman coin which was a working man's daily wage. It would have cost an ordinary man almost a year's pay to buy the flask of ointment. To some it seemed a shameful waste; the money might have been given to the poor. But Jesus understood. He quoted their own Scriptures to them. As the Revised Standard Version has it, 'The poor will never cease out of the land' (Deuteronomy 15:11). 'You can help the poor any time,' Jesus said, 'but you have not long to do anything for me now.' 'This', he said, 'is like anointing my body beforehand for its burial.'

This story shows the action of love.

(1) Jesus said that it was a *lovely* thing the woman had done. In Greek there are two words for *good*. There is *agathos*, which describes a thing which is morally good; and there is *kalos*, which describes a thing which is not only good but *lovely*. A thing might be *agathos*, and yet be hard, stern, austere, unattractive. But a thing which is *kalos* is captivating and lovely, with a certain bloom of charm upon it. The nineteenth-century church historian Gavin Struthers used to say that it would do the Church more good than anything else if Christians would sometimes 'do a bonnie thing'. That is exactly what *kalos* means, something that is fine and attractive; and that is exactly what this woman did. Love does not do only good things. Love does lovely things.

(2) If love is true, there must always be a certain extravagance in it. It does not nicely calculate the less or more. It is not concerned to see how little it can decently give. If it gave all it had, the gift would still be too little. There is a recklessness in love which refuses to count the cost.

(3) Love can see that there are things, the chance to do which comes only once. It is one of the tragedies of life that often we are moved to do something fine and do not do it. It may be that we are too shy and feel awkward about it. It may be that second thoughts suggest a more prudent course. It occurs in the simplest things – the impulse to send a letter of thanks, the impulse to tell someone of our love or gratitude,

the impulse to give some special gift or speak some special word. The tragedy is that the impulse is so often strangled at birth. This world would be so much lovelier if there were more people like this woman, who acted on her impulse of love because she knew in her heart of hearts that if she did not do it then she would never do it at all. How that last extravagant, impulsive kindness must have uplifted Jesus' heart.

(4) Once again we see the invincible confidence of Jesus. The cross loomed close ahead now but he never believed that it would be the end. He believed that the good news would go all round the world. And with the good news would go the story of this lovely thing, done with reckless extravagance, done on the impulse of the moment, done out of a heart of love.

THE TRAITOR

Mark 14:10-11

> Judas Iscariot, the man who was one of the Twelve,
> went away to the chief priests to betray Jesus to them.
> When they had listened to his offer, they were delighted,
> and they promised to give him money. So he began to
> search for a convenient method of betraying him.

It is with consummate artistry that Mark sets side by side the anointing at Bethany and the betrayal by Judas – the act of generous love and the act of terrible treachery.

There is always a shudder of the heart as we think of Judas. Dante sets him in the lowest of all hells, a hell of cold and ice, a hell designed for those who were not hot sinners swept away by angry passions, but cold, calculating, deliberate offenders against the love of God.

Mark tells the story with such economy of words that he leaves us no material for speculation. But at the back of Judas' action we can distinguish certain things.

(1) There was *covetousness*. Matthew 26:15 actually tells us that Judas went to the authorities and asked what price they were prepared to pay and drove a bargain with them for thirty pieces of silver. John 11:57 drops a hint. That verse tells us that the authorities had asked for information as to where Jesus could be found so as to arrest him. It may well be that by this time Jesus was to all intents and purposes an outlaw with a price upon his head, and that Judas knew it and wished to acquire the offered reward. John is quite definite. He tells us that Judas was the treasurer of the apostolic band and used his position to pilfer from the common purse (John 12:6).

It may be so. The desire for money can be a terrible thing. It can make people blind to decency and honesty and honour. It can make them have no care how they get so long as they get. Judas discovered too late that some things cost too much.

(2) There was *jealousy*. Friedrich Klopstock, the German poet, thought that Judas, when he joined the Twelve, had every gift and every virtue which might have made him great, but that bit by bit he became consumed with jealousy of John, the beloved disciple, and that this jealousy drove him to his terrible act. It is easy to see that there were tensions in the Twelve. The rest were able to overcome them, but it may well be that Judas had an unconquerable and uncontrollable demon of jealousy within his heart. Few things can wreck life for ourselves and for others as jealousy can.

(3) There was *ambition*. Again and again we see how the Twelve thought of the kingdom in earthly terms and dreamed of high position in it. Judas must have been like that. It may well be that, while the others still clung to them, he came to

see how far wrong these dreams were and how little chance they ever had of any earthly fulfilment. And it may well be that in his disillusionment the love he once bore to Jesus turned to hate. In *Henry VIII* Shakespeare makes Wolsey say to Thomas Cromwell:

> Cromwell, I charge thee, fling away ambition;
> By that sin fell the angels; how can man then,
> The image of his Maker, hope to win by it?
> Love thyself last.

There is an ambition which will trample on love and honour and all lovely things to gain the end it has set its heart upon.

(4) Minds have been fascinated by the idea that it may be that Judas did not want Jesus to die at all. It is almost certain that Judas was a fanatical nationalist and that he had seen in Jesus the one person who could make his dreams of national power and glory come true. But now he saw Jesus drifting to death on a cross. So it may be that in one last attempt to make his dream come true, he betrayed Jesus *in order to force his hand*. He delivered him to the authorities with the idea that now Jesus would be compelled to act in order to save himself, and that action would be the beginning of the victorious campaign he dreamed of. It may be that this theory is supported by the fact that when Judas saw what he had done he flung the accursed money at the feet of the Jewish authorities and went out and hanged himself (Matthew 27:3–5). If that is so, the tragedy of Judas is the greatest in history.

(5) Both Luke and John say quite simply that the devil entered into Judas (Luke 22:3; John 13:27). In the last analysis that is what happened. Judas wanted Jesus to be what he wanted him to be and not what Jesus wanted to be. In reality Judas attached himself to Jesus, not so much to become a follower as to use Jesus to work out the plans and desires of

his own ambitious heart. So far from surrendering to Jesus, he wanted Jesus to surrender to him; and when Jesus took his own way, the way of the cross, Judas was so incensed that he betrayed him. The essence of sin is pride; the core of sin is independence; the heart of sin is the desire to do what we like and not what God likes. That is what the devil, Satan, the evil one stands for. He stands for everything which is against God and will not bow to him. That is the spirit which was incarnate in Judas.

We shudder at Judas. But let us think again – covetousness, jealousy, ambition, the dominant desire to have our own way of things. Are we so very different? These are the things which made Judas betray Jesus, and these are the things which still make people betray him.

PREPARING FOR THE FEAST

Mark 14:12–16

> On the first day of the Feast of Unleavened Bread, when they were sacrificing the Passover Lamb, Jesus' disciples said to him, 'Where do you wish us to go and make the necessary preparations for you to eat the Passover?' He despatched two of his disciples, and said to them, 'Go into the city, and there will meet you a man carrying an earthen pitcher of water. Follow him, and wherever he enters in, say to the householder, "The teacher says, 'Where is my room, where I may eat the Passover with my disciples?'" He will show you a large upper room, furnished and prepared. There get things ready for us.' So the disciples went away, and they came into the city, and found everything just as he had told them. And they got everything ready for the Passover Feast.

IT may seem an unusual word to use in connection with Jesus, but, as we read the narrative of the last week of his life, we cannot help being struck with his efficiency of arrangement. Again and again we see that he did not leave things until the last moment. Long before, he had arranged that the colt should be ready for his ride into Jerusalem; and here again we see that all his arrangements had been made long beforehand.

His disciples wished to know where they would eat the Passover. Jesus sent them into Jerusalem with instructions to look for a man carrying an earthen pitcher of water. That was a pre-arranged signal. To carry a water pot was a woman's duty. It was a thing that no man ever did. A man with a water pot on his shoulder would be very easy to pick out in any crowd. Jesus did not leave things until the last minute. Long ago he had arranged a last meeting place for himself and for his disciples, and had arranged just how it was to be found.

The larger Jewish houses had upper rooms. Such houses looked exactly like a smaller box placed on top of a bigger box. The smaller box was the upper room, and it was approached by an outside stair, making it unnecessary to go through the main room. The upper room had many uses. It was a storeroom, it was a place for quiet and meditation, it was a guest room for visitors. But in particular it was the place where a Rabbi taught his chosen band of intimate disciples. Jesus was following the custom that any Jewish Rabbi might follow.

We must remember the Jewish way of reckoning days. The new day began at 6 pm. Up until 6 pm it was 13th Nisan, the day of the preparation for the Passover. But 14th Nisan, the Passover day itself, began at 6 pm. In other words, *Friday* the 14th began at 6 pm on *Thursday* the 13th.

What were the preparations that a Jew made for the Passover?

First was *the ceremonial search for leaven*. Before the Passover, every particle of leaven must be banished from the house. That was because the first Passover in Egypt (Exodus 12) had been eaten with unleavened bread. (Unleavened bread is not like bread at all. It is like a water biscuit.) It had been used in Egypt because it can be baked much more quickly than a loaf baked with leaven, and the first Passover, the Passover of escape from Egypt, had been eaten in haste, with everyone ready for the road. In addition, leaven was the symbol of corruption. Leaven is fermented dough, and Jews identified fermentation with putrefaction, and so leaven stood for rottenness. The day before the Passover, the master of the house took a lighted candle and ceremonially searched the house for leaven. Before the search he prayed,

> Blessed art thou, Yahweh, our God, King of the Universe, who hast sanctified us by thy commandments, and commanded us to remove the leaven.

At the end of the search the householder said,

> All the leaven that is in my possession, that which I have seen and that which I have not seen, be it null, be it accounted as the dust of the earth.

Next, on the afternoon before the Passover evening, came *the sacrifice of the Passover Lamb*. All the people came to the Temple. The worshipper must slay his own lamb, thereby, as it were, making his own sacrifice. But in Jewish eyes all blood was sacred to God, because Jews equated the blood and the life. It was quite natural to do so because, if a person or an animal is wounded, as the blood flows away, so does life. So in the Temple the worshipper slew his own lamb. Between the worshippers and the altar were two long lines of priests, each with a gold or silver bowl. As the lamb's throat was slit the blood was caught in one of these bowls, and passed up the line, until the priest at the end of the line dashed it upon the altar. The carcass was then flayed, the entrails and the fat extracted, because they were part of the necessary sacrifice, and the carcass handed back to the worshipper. If the figures of Josephus are anywhere nearly correct, and there were more than 250,000 lambs slain, the scene in the Temple courts and the blood-stained condition of the altar can hardly be imagined. The lamb was carried home to be roasted. It must not be boiled. Nothing must touch it, not even the sides of a pot. It had to be roasted over an open fire on a spit made of pomegranate wood. The spit went right through the lamb from mouth to vent, and the lamb had to be roasted entire with head and legs and tail still attached to the body.

The table itself was shaped like a square with one side open. It was low and the guests reclined on couches, resting on their left arms with their right arms free for eating.

Certain things were necessary and these were the things the disciples would have to get ready.

(1) There was the *lamb*, to remind them of how their houses had been protected by the badge of blood when the angel of death passed through Egypt.

(2) There was the *unleavened bread* to remind them of the bread they had eaten in haste when they escaped from slavery.

(3) There was a *bowl of salt water*, to remind them of the tears they had shed in Egypt and of the waters of the Red Sea through which they had miraculously passed to safety.

(4) There was a collection of *bitter herbs* – horseradish, chicory, endive, lettuce, horehound – to remind them of the bitterness of slavery in Egypt.

(5) There was a paste called *charosheth*, a mixture of apples, dates, pomegranates and nuts, to remind them of the

clay of which they had made bricks in Egypt. Through it there were sticks of cinnamon to remind them of the straw with which the bricks had been made.

(6) There were *four cups of wine*. The cups contained a little more than half a pint of wine, but three parts of wine were mixed with two of water. The four cups, which were drunk at different stages of the meal, were to remind them of the four promises in Exodus 6:6–7:

> I will free you from the burdens of the Egyptians
>   and deliver you from slavery to them.
> I will redeem you with an outstretched arm
>   and with mighty acts of judgment.
> I will take you as my people,
>   and I will be your God.

Such were the preparations which had to be made for the Passover. Every detail spoke of that great day of deliverance when God liberated his people from their bondage in Egypt. It was at that feast that he who liberated the world from sin was to sit at his last meal with his disciples.

LOVE'S LAST APPEAL

Mark 14:17–21

> When it was evening, Jesus came with the Twelve. As they were reclining at table and eating, Jesus said, 'This is the truth I tell you – one of you will betray me, one who is eating with me.' They began to be grieved, and to say to him, one by one, 'Surely it cannot be I?' He said to them, 'One of the Twelve, one who dips his hand with me into the dish. The Son of Man goes as it stands written about him, but woe to that man through whom the Son of Man is betrayed. It had been good for him, if that man had not been born.'

THE new day began at 6 pm, and when the Passover evening had come, Jesus sat down with the Twelve. There was only one change in the old ritual which had been observed so many centuries ago in Egypt. At the first Passover Feast in Egypt, the meal had been eaten standing (Exodus 12:11). But that had been a sign of haste, a sign that they were slaves escaping from slavery. In the time of Jesus, the regulation was that the meal should be eaten reclining, for that was the sign of free people, with a home and a country of their own.

This is a poignant passage. All the time, there was a text running in Jesus' head. 'Even my bosom friend in whom I trusted, who ate of my bread, has lifted the heel against me' (Psalm 41:9). These words were in his mind all the time. We can see certain great things here.

(1) Jesus knew what was going to happen. That is his supreme courage, especially in the last days. It would have been easy for him to escape, and yet undeterred he went on. Homer relates how the great warrior Achilles was told that if he went out to his last battle he would surely be killed. His answer was, 'Nevertheless I am for going on.' With a full knowledge of what lay ahead, Jesus was for going on.

(2) Jesus could see into the heart of Judas. The curious thing is that the other disciples seem to have had no suspicions. If they had known what Judas was engaged on, it is certain that they would have stopped him even by violence. Here is something to remember. There may be things we succeed in hiding from other people, but we cannot hide them from Jesus Christ. He is the searcher of human hearts. He knows what is in each one of us. In J. G. Whittier's words:

> Our thoughts lie open to thy sight;
>   And naked to thy glance.
> Our secret sins are in the light
>   Of thy pure countenance.

Blessed indeed are the pure in heart.

(3) In this passage, we see Jesus offering two things to Judas.

(a) He is making love's last appeal. It is as if he is saying to Judas, 'I know what you are going to do. Will you not stop even now?'

(b) He is offering Judas a last warning. He is telling him in advance of the consequences of the thing that it is in his heart to do. But we must note this, for it is of the essence of the way in which God deals with us – *there is no compulsion*. Without a doubt, Jesus could have stopped Judas. All he had to do was tell the other eleven what Judas was planning, and Judas would never have left that room alive.

Here is the whole human situation. God has given us wills that are free. His love appeals to us. His truth warns us. But there is no compulsion. We hold the awful responsibility that we can spurn the appeal of God's love and disregard the warning of his voice. In the end, there is no one but ourselves responsible for our sins.

In Greek legend, two famous travellers passed the rocks where the Sirens sang. The Sirens sat on these rocks and sang with such sweetness that they lured mariners irresistibly to their doom. Ulysses sailed past these rocks. His method was to stop the sailors' ears so that they could not hear and order them to bind himself to the mast with ropes so that, however much he struggled, he would not be able to answer to that seductive sweetness. He resisted by compulsion. The other traveller was Orpheus, the sweetest musician of all. His method was to play and sing with such surpassing sweetness as his ship passed the rocks where the Sirens were, that the attraction of the song of the Sirens was never even felt because of the attraction of the song he sang. His method was to answer the appeal of seduction with a still greater appeal.

God's is the second way. He does not stop us, whether we like it or not, from sin. He seeks to make us love him so much that his voice is more sweetly insistent to us than all the voices which call us away from him.

THE SYMBOL OF SALVATION

Mark 14:22–6

> As they were eating, Jesus took a loaf and gave thanks for it, and broke it and gave it to them and said, 'Take this. This is my body.' And, after he had given thanks, he took a cup and gave it to them, and they all drank from it. And he said to them, 'This is the blood of the new covenant which is being shed for many. Truly I tell you, I will no longer drink of the fruit of the vine, until that day when I drink it new in the kingdom of God.' And, after they had sung the Psalm, they went out to the Mount of Olives.

WE must first set out the various steps of the Passover Feast, so that in our mind's eye we can follow what Jesus and his disciples were doing. The steps came in this order.

(1) *The cup of the Kiddush. Kiddush* means sanctification or *separation*. This was the act which, as it were, separated this meal from all other common meals. The head of the family took the cup and prayed over it, and then all drank of it.

(2) *The first handwashing*. This was carried out only by the person who was to celebrate the feast. Three times he had to wash his hands in the prescribed way which we have already described when studying chapter 7.

(3) A piece of parsley or lettuce was then taken and dipped in the bowl of salt water and eaten. This was an appetizer to the meal, but the parsley stood for the hyssop with which the

lintel had been smeared with blood, and the salt stood for the tears of Egypt and for the waters of the Red Sea through which Israel had been brought in safety.

(4) *The breaking of bread.* Two blessings were used at the breaking of bread. 'Blessed be thou, O Lord, our God, King of the Universe, who bringest forth from the earth.' Or, 'Blessed art thou, our Father in heaven, who givest us today the bread necessary for us.' On the table lay three circles of unleavened bread. The middle one was taken and broken. At this point only a little was eaten. It was to remind the Jews of the bread of affliction that they ate in Egypt and it was broken to remind them that slaves had never a whole loaf, but only broken crusts to eat. As it was broken, the head of the family said, 'This is the bread of affliction which our forefathers ate in the land of Egypt. Whosoever is hungry let him come and eat. Whosoever is in need let him come and keep the Passover with us.' (In the modern celebration in strange lands, here is added the famous prayer, 'This year we keep it here, next year in the land of Israel. This year as slaves, next year as free.')

(5) Next came the *relating* of the story of deliverance. The youngest person present had to ask what made this day different from all other days and why all this was being done. And the head of the house had thereupon to tell the whole story of the history of Israel down to the great deliverance which the Passover commemorated. The Passover could never become a ritual. It was always a commemoration of the power and the mercy of God.

(6) Psalms 113 and 114 were sung. Psalms 113–18 are known as *the Hallel*, which means the praise of God. All these psalms are praising psalms. They were part of the very earliest material which a Jewish boy had to commit to memory.

(7) The second cup was drunk. It was called *the cup of Haggadah*, which means the cup of explaining or proclaiming.

(8) All those present now washed their hands in preparation for the meal.

(9) A grace was said. 'Blessed art thou, O Lord, our God, who bringest forth fruit from the earth. Blessed art thou, O God, who has sanctified us with thy commandment and enjoined us to eat unleavened cakes.' Thereafter small pieces of the unleavened bread were distributed.

(10) Some of the *bitter herbs* were placed between two pieces of unleavened bread, dipped in the *charosheth* and eaten. This was called *the sop*. It was the reminder of slavery and of the bricks that once they had been compelled to make.

(11) Then followed the meal proper. The whole lamb must be eaten. Anything left over must be destroyed and not used for any common meal.

(12) The hands were cleansed again.

(13) The remainder of the unleavened bread was eaten.

(14) There was a prayer of thanksgiving, containing a petition for the coming of Elijah to herald the Messiah. Then the third cup was drunk, called *the cup of thanksgiving*. The blessing over the cup was, 'Blessed art thou, O Lord, our God, King of the Universe, who hast created the fruit of the vine.'

(15) The second part of *the Hallel* – Psalms 115–18 – was sung.

(16) The fourth cup was drunk, and Psalm 136, known as *the great Hallel*, was sung.

(17) Two short prayers were said:

> All thy works shall praise thee, O Lord, our God. And
> thy saints, the righteous, who do thy good pleasure, and
> all thy people, the house of Israel, with joyous song, let

them praise and bless and magnify and glorify and exalt
and reverence and sanctify and scribe the Kingdom to
thy name, O God, our King. For it is good to praise
thee, and pleasure to sing praises to thy name, for from
everlasting unto everlasting thou art God.

The breath of all that lives shall praise thy name, O
Lord, our God. And the spirit of all flesh shall con-
tinually glorify and exalt thy memorial, O God, our
King. For from everlasting unto everlasting thou art
God, and beside thee we have no king, redeemer or
saviour.

Thus ended the Passover Feast. If the feast that Jesus and
his disciples sat at was the Passover it must have been items
(13) and (14) that Jesus made his own, and (16) must have
been the hymn they sang before they went out to the Mount
of Olives.

Now let us see what Jesus was doing, and what he was
seeking to impress upon his disciples. More than once we
have seen that the prophets of Israel resorted to symbolic,
dramatic actions when they felt that words were not enough.
That is what Ahijah did when he rent the robe into twelve
pieces and gave ten to Jeroboam in token that ten of the tribes
would make him king (1 Kings 11:29-32). That is what
Jeremiah did when he made bonds and yokes and wore them
in token of the coming servitude (Jeremiah 27). That is what
the prophet Hananiah did when he broke the yokes that
Jeremiah wore (Jeremiah 28:10-11). That is the kind of thing
that Ezekiel was continually doing (Ezekiel 4:1-8, 5:1-4). It
was as if words were easily forgotten, but a dramatic action
would print itself on the memory.

That is what Jesus did, and he allied this dramatic action
with the ancient feast of his people so that it would be the
more imprinted on the minds of the Twelve. He said, 'Look!

Just as this bread is broken, my body is broken for you! Just as this cup of red wine is poured out, my blood is shed for you.'

What did he mean when he said that the cup stood for a new covenant? The word *covenant* is a common word in the Jewish religion. The basis of that religion was that God had entered into a *covenant* with Israel. The word means something like an arrangement, a bargain, a relationship. The acceptance of *the old covenant* is set out in Exodus 24:3–8; and from that passage we see that the covenant was entirely dependent on Israel keeping the law. If the law was broken, the covenant was broken and the relationship between God and the nation shattered. *It was a relationship entirely dependent on law and on obedience to law.* God was judge. And since no one can keep the law the people were always in default. But Jesus says, 'I am introducing and ratifying *a new covenant*, a new kind of relationship between God and human beings. And it is not dependent on *law*, it is dependent on *the blood that I will shed.*' That is to say, it is dependent solely on *love.* The new covenant was a relationship between human beings and God, dependent not on law but on love. In other words Jesus says, 'I am doing what I am doing to show you how much God loves you.' Men and women are no longer simply *under the law of God.* Because of what Jesus did, they are forever *within the love of God.* That is the essence of what the sacrament says to us.

We note one thing more. In the last sentence we see again the two things we have so often seen. Jesus was sure of two things. He knew he was to die, and he knew his kingdom would come. He was certain of the cross, but just as certain of the glory. And the reason was that he was just as certain of God's love as he was of human sin; and he knew that in the end that love would conquer that sin.

THE FAILURE OF FRIENDS

Mark 14:27–31

> Jesus said to them, 'You will all fall away from me, for
> it stands written, "I will smite the shepherd and the sheep
> will be scattered." But after I have been raised to life
> again, I will go before you into Galilee.' Peter said to
> him, 'All the others may fall away from you, but I will
> not.' Jesus said to him, 'This is the truth I tell you –
> today, this night, before the cock crows twice you will
> deny me three times.' Peter began to insist vehemently,
> 'If I must die with you I will not deny you.' So, too,
> they all said.

IT is a tremendous thing about Jesus that there was nothing
for which he was not prepared. The opposition, the mis-
understanding, the enmity of the orthodox religious people,
the betrayal by one of his own inner circle, the pain and the
agony of the cross – he was prepared for them all. But perhaps
what hurt him most was the failure of his friends. It is when
we are up against it that we need our friends most, and that
was exactly when Jesus' friends left him all alone and let him
down. There was nothing in the whole gamut of physical
pain and mental torture that Jesus did not pass through.

Sir Hugh Walpole wrote a great novel called *Fortitude*. It
is the story of one called Peter, whose creed was, 'It isn't life
that matters, but the courage you bring to it.' Life did
everything that it possibly could to him. At the end, on his
own mountain top, he heard a voice, 'Blessed be pain and
torment and every torture of the body. Blessed be all loss and
the failure of friends and the sacrifice of love. Blessed be all
failure and the ruin of every earthly hope. Blessed be all
sorrow and torment, hardships, and endurances that demand
courage. Blessed be these things – for of these things cometh

the making of a man.' Peter fell to praying, 'Make of me a man . . . to be afraid of nothing, to be ready for everything. Love, friendship, success . . . to take it if it comes, to care nothing if these things are not for me. Make me brave. Make me brave.'

Jesus had supremely, more than anyone who ever lived, this quality of fortitude, this ability to remain erect no matter with what blows life assaulted him, this serenity when there was nothing but heartbreak behind and torture in front. Inevitably every now and then we find ourselves catching our breath at his sheer heroism.

When Jesus foretold this tragic failure of loyalty, Peter could not believe that it would happen. In the eighteenth century during the Stewart troubles the Cock of the North, the Marquis of Huntly, was captured. His captors pointed at the block and the axe and told him that unless he abandoned his loyalty he would be executed then and there. His answer was, 'You can take my head from my shoulders but you will never take my heart from my king.' That is what Peter said that night.

There is a lesson in the word that Jesus used for 'fall away'. The Greek verb is *skandalizein*, from *skandalon* or *skandalēthron* which meant the bait in a trap, the stick on to which the animal was lured and which snapped the trap when the animal stepped on it. So the word *skandalizein* came to mean to entrap, or to trip up by some trick or guile. Peter was too sure. He had forgotten the traps that life can lay for even the best among us. He had forgotten how easy it is to step on a slippery place and fall. He had forgotten his own human weakness and the strength of the devil's temptations. But there is one thing to be remembered about Peter – *his heart was in the right place*. Better a Peter with a flaming heart of love, even if that love did for a moment fail most shamefully, than a Judas with a cold heart of hate. Let those people condemn Peter who never broke a promise, who were never disloyal in thought or action to a pledge. Peter loved Jesus, and even if his love failed, it rose again.

YOUR WILL BE DONE

Mark 14:32-42

> They came to a place the name of which is Gethsemane. Jesus said to his disciples, 'Sit here while I pray.' He took Peter and James and John with him, and began to be in great distress and trouble of mind. He said to them, 'My soul is sore grieved even to death. Stay here and watch.' He went on a little farther and fell on the ground and prayed that, if it was possible, this hour might pass from him. He said, 'Abba, Father, everything is possible to you. Take this cup from me – but not what I wish, but what you wish.' He came and found them sleeping and he said to Peter, 'Simon, are you sleeping? Could you not stay awake for one hour? Watch and pray lest you enter into some testing time. The spirit is willing but the flesh is weak.' And again he went away and prayed in the same words. And again he came and found them sleeping, for their eyes were weighed down with sleep. And they did not know how to answer him. And he came the third time and said to them, 'Sleep on now. Take your rest. It is enough. The hour has come. See! The Son of Man is betrayed into the hands of sinners. Rise! Let us be going! He who betrays me has come!'

THIS is a passage we almost fear to read, for it seems to intrude into the private agony of Jesus.

To have stayed in the upper room would have been danger-ous. With the authorities on the watch for him, and with Judas bent on treachery, the upper room might have been raided at any time. But Jesus had another place to which to go. The fact that Judas knew to look for him in Gethsemane shows that Jesus was in the habit of going there. In Jerusalem itself there were no gardens. The city was too crowded, and there was a strange law that the city's sacred soil might not be polluted with manure for the gardens. But some of the rich people possessed private gardens out on the Mount of Olives, where they took their rest. Jesus must have had some wealthy friend who gave him the privilege of using his garden at night.

When Jesus went to Gethsemane there were two things he sorely desired. He wanted *human fellowship* and he wanted *God's fellowship*. 'It is not good that the man should be alone,' God said in the beginning (Genesis 2:18). In time of trouble we want friends with us. We do not necessarily want them to do anything. We do not necessarily even want to talk to them or have them talk to us. We only want them there. Jesus was like that. It was strange that men who so short a time before had been protesting that they would die for him could not stay awake for him one single hour. But none can blame them, for the excitement and the tension had drained their strength and their resistance.

Certain things are clear about Jesus in this passage.

(1) He did not want to die. He was thirty-three and no one wants to die with life just opening on to the best of the years. He had done so little and there was a world waiting to be saved. He knew what crucifixion was like and he shuddered at the thought of it. He had to compel himself to go on – just as we have so often to do.

(2) He did not fully understand why this had to be. He only knew beyond a doubt that this was the will of God and that he must go on. Jesus, too, had to make the great venture

of faith, he had to accept – as we so often have to do – what he could not understand.

(3) He submitted to the will of God. *Abba* is the Aramaic for *my father*. It is that one word which made all the difference. Jesus was not submitting to a God who made a cynical sport of men and women. Thomas Hardy finishes his novel *Tess of the D'Urbervilles*, after telling of her tragic life, with the terrible sentence, 'The President of the Immortals had finished his sport with Tess.' But Jesus was not submitting to a God who was an iron fate such as Edward Fitzgerald portrays in *The Rubaiyat of Omar Khayyam*:

> But helpless pieces of the game he plays,
> Upon this chequer board of nights and days,
> Hither and thither moves and checks and slays –
> And one by one back in the closet lays.

God was not like that. Even in this terrible hour, when he was making this terrible demand, God was *father*. When Richard Cameron, the covenanter, was killed, his head and hands were cut off by one Murray and taken to Edinburgh. 'His father being in prison for the same cause, the enemy carried them to him, to add grief unto his former sorrow, and inquired if he knew them. Taking his son's head and hands, which were very fair (being a man of a fair complexion like himself) he kissed them and said, "I know them – I know them. They are my son's – my own dear son's. It is the Lord. Good is the will of the Lord, who cannot wrong me nor mine, but hath made goodness and mercy to follow us all our days."' If we can call God *father* everything becomes bearable. Time and again we will not understand, but always we will be certain that 'The Father's hand will never cause his child a needless tear.' That is what Jesus knew. That is why he could go on – and it can be so with us.

We must note how the passage ends. The traitor and his gang had arrived. What was Jesus' reaction? Not to run away, although even then, in the night, it would have been easy to escape. His reaction was *to face them*. To the end, he would neither turn aside nor turn back.

THE ARREST

Mark 14:43–50

> And immediately, while he was still speaking, Judas, one of the Twelve arrived, and with him a crowd with swords and cudgels from the chief priests, and the experts in the law, and the elders. The betrayer had given them this sign. 'Whom I shall kiss,' he said, 'that is he. Seize him and take him away securely.' So when he had come, immediately he stepped forward. 'Rabbi!' he said – and kissed him as a lover would. They laid hands on him and seized him. One of those standing by drew his sword and struck the high priest's servant and cut off his ear. Jesus said to them, 'Have you come out with swords and cudgels to arrest me as you would come against a brigand? Daily I was with you teaching in the Temple precincts, and you did not seize me – but, let it be, that the Scriptures may be fulfilled.' And they all left him and fled.

HERE is sheer drama – and, even in Mark's economy of words, the characters stand out before us.

(1) There is Judas, the traitor. He was aware that the people knew Jesus well enough by sight. But he felt that in the dim light of the garden, with the darkness of the trees lit in pools of light by the flare of the torches, they needed a definite indication of who they were to arrest. And so he chose that most terrible of signs – a kiss. It was customary to greet a

Rabbi with a kiss. It was a sign of respect and affection for a well-loved teacher. But there is a dreadful thing here. When Judas says, 'Whom I shall kiss, that is he,' he uses the word *philein* which is the ordinary word. But when it is said that he came forward and kissed Jesus, the word is *kataphilein*. The *kata-* is intensive and suggests that the kiss was prolonged in order to give a clear signal. But more than that, it was not a mere formal greeting. It was the greeting of a friend. That is the grimmest and most awful thing in all the gospel story.

(2) There is the arresting mob. They came from the chief priests, the scribes and the elders. These were the three sections of the Sanhedrin, and Mark means that they came from the Sanhedrin. Even under Roman jurisdiction, the Sanhedrin had certain police rights and duties in Jerusalem and had its own police force. No doubt an assorted rabble had attached itself to them on the way. Somehow Mark manages to convey the pent-up excitement of those who came to make the arrest. Maybe they had come prepared for bloodshed with nerves taut and tense. It is they who emanate terror – not Jesus.

(3) There is the man of the forlorn hope who drew his sword and struck one blow. John (18:10) tells us that it was Peter. It sounds like Peter, and Mark very likely omitted the name because it was not yet safe to write it down. In the scuffle no one saw who struck the blow; it was better that no one should know. But when John wrote forty years later it was then quite safe to write it down. It may be wrong to draw a sword and hack at a man, but somehow we are glad that there was one man there who, at least on the impulse of the moment, was prepared to strike a blow for Jesus.

(4) There are the disciples. Their nerve cracked. They could not face it. They were afraid that they too would share the fate of Jesus, and so they fled.

(5) There is Jesus himself. The strange thing is that in all this disordered scene Jesus was the one oasis of serenity. As we read the story it reads as if he, not the Sanhedrin police, was directing affairs. For him the struggle in the garden was over, and now there was the peace of the man who knows that he is following the will of God.

A CERTAIN YOUNG MAN

Mark 14:51–2

> And a certain young man was following him, clothed
> in a linen sheet over his naked body. And they tried to
> seize him, but he left the linen sheet and escaped naked.

THESE are two strange and fascinating verses. At first sight they seem completely irrelevant. They seem to add nothing to the narrative and yet there must be some reason for them being there.

We saw in the Introduction that Matthew and Luke used Mark as the basis of their work and that they include in their gospels practically everything that is in Mark. But they do not include these two verses. That would seem to show that this incident was interesting to Mark and not really interesting to anyone else. Why then was this incident so interesting to Mark that he felt he must include it? The most probable answer is that the young man was Mark himself, and that this is his way of saying, 'I was there', without mentioning his own name at all.

When we read Acts we find that the meeting place and headquarters of the Jerusalem church was apparently in the house of Mary, the mother of John Mark (Acts 12:12). If that is so, it is at least probable that the upper room in which the Last Supper was eaten was in that same house.

There could be no more natural place than that to be the centre of the Church. If we can assume that, there are two possibilities.

(1) It may be that Mark was actually present at the Last Supper. He was young, just a boy, and maybe no one really noticed him. But he was fascinated with Jesus, and when the company went out into the dark, he slipped out after them when he ought to have been in bed, with only the linen sheet over his naked body. It may be that all the time Mark was there in the shadows listening and watching. That would explain where the Gethsemane narrative came from. If the disciples were all asleep, how did anyone know about the struggle of soul that Jesus had there? It may be that the one witness was Mark as he stood silent in the shadows, watching with a boy's reverence the greatest hero he had ever known.

(2) From John's narrative, we know that Judas left the company before the meal was fully ended (John 13:30). It may be that it was to the upper room that Judas meant to lead the Temple police so that they might secretly arrest Jesus. But when Judas came back with the police, Jesus and his disciples were gone. Naturally there was recrimination and argument. The uproar wakened Mark. He heard Judas propose that they should try the garden of Gethsemane. Quickly Mark wrapped his bedsheet about him and sped through the night to the garden to warn Jesus. But he arrived too late, and in the scuffle that followed was very nearly arrested himself.

Whatever may be true, we may take it as fairly certain that Mark put in these two verses because they were about himself. He could never forget that night. He was too humble to put his own name in, but in this way he wrote his signature and said, to anyone who could read between the lines, 'I, too, when I was a boy, was there.'

THE TRIAL

Mark 14:53, 55–65

> They took Jesus away to the high priest, and all the
> chief priests and experts in the law and elders assembled
> with him . . . The chief priests and the whole Sanhedrin
> were trying to find some evidence against Jesus, in order
> to put him to death, and they could not find any, for
> there were many who bore false witness against him,
> but their evidence did not agree. Some stood up and
> bore false witness against him. 'We heard him saying,'
> they said, '"I will destroy this Temple made with hands
> and in three days' time I will build another not made
> with hands".' But not even so did their evidence agree.
> So the high priest stood up in the midst and questioned
> Jesus. 'Do you give no answer?' he said. 'What is the
> evidence that these men are alleging against you?' Jesus
> remained silent and gave no answer. Again the high
> priest questioned him, and said to him, 'Are you God's
> Anointed One, the Son of the Blessed One?' Jesus said,
> 'I am, and you will see the Son of Man seated on the
> right hand of power, and coming with the clouds of
> heaven.' The high priest rent his garments. 'What need',
> he said, 'have we of witnesses? You have listened to
> blasphemy. How does it seem to you?' And they all
> adjudged him to be liable to death. And some began to
> spit upon him, and to cover his face, and to buffet him,
> and to say to him, 'Prophesy!' And the servants received
> him with blows.

THINGS were moving quickly to their inevitable end.

At this time the powers of the Sanhedrin were limited
because the Romans were the rulers of the country. The
Sanhedrin had full power over religious matters. It seems
also to have had a certain amount of police-court power. But

it had no power to inflict the death penalty. If what Mark describes was a meeting of the Sanhedrin, it must be compared to a grand jury. Its function was not to condemn, but to prepare a charge on which the criminal could be tried before the Roman governor.

There is no doubt that in the trial of Jesus the Sanhedrin broke all its own laws. The regulations for the procedure of the Sanhedrin are in one of the tractates of the Mishnah. Naturally enough, some of these regulations are ideals than rather actual practices; but, even allowing for that, the whole procedure of this night was a series of flagrant injustices.

The Sanhedrin was the supreme court of the Jews and was composed of seventy-one members. Within its membership there were Sadducees – the priestly classes were all Sadducees – Pharisees and scribes, who were experts in the law, and respected men who were elders. It appears that any vacancies in the court were filled by co-option. The high priest presided over the court. The court sat in a semi-circle in such a way that any member could see any other member. Facing it sat the students of the Rabbis. They were allowed to speak on behalf of the person on trial but not against him. The official meeting place of the Sanhedrin was the Hall of Hewn Stone which was within the Temple precincts, and the decisions of the Sanhedrin were not valid unless reached at a meeting held in that place. The court could not meet at night, nor could it meet at any of the great feasts. When evidence was taken, witnesses were examined separately and their evidence, to be valid, must agree in every detail. Each individual member of the Sanhedrin must give his verdict separately, beginning from the youngest and going on to the eldest. If the verdict was a verdict of death, a night must elapse before it was carried out, so that the court might have a chance to change its mind and its decision towards mercy.

It can be seen that on point after point the Sanhedrin broke its own rules. It was not meeting in its own building. It was meeting at night. There is no word of individually given verdicts. A night was not allowed to elapse before the penalty of death was inflicted. In their eagerness to eliminate Jesus, the Jewish authorities did not hesitate to break their own laws.

At first the court could not get even false witnesses to agree. The false witnesses accused Jesus of having said that he would destroy the Temple. It may well be that someone had overheard him speaking as he did in Mark 13:2, and had maliciously twisted the saying into a threat to destroy the Temple. There is an old legend which tells how the Sanhedrin could get plenty of the kind of evidence they did not want, for man after man came forward saying, 'I was a leper and he cleansed me. I was blind and he made me able to see. I was deaf and he made me able to hear. I was lame and he made me able to walk. I was paralysed and he gave me back my strength.'

At last the high priest took the matter into his own hands. When he did, he asked the very kind of question that the law completely forbade. He asked a leading question. It was forbidden to ask questions by answering which the person on trial might incriminate himself. No man could be asked to condemn himself, but that was the very question the high priest asked. Bluntly he asked Jesus if he was the Messiah. Clearly Jesus felt that it was time that the whole wretched business was ended. Without hesitation he answered that he was. Here was a charge of blasphemy, insult against God. The Sanhedrin had what it wanted, a charge which merited the death penalty, and they were savagely content.

Once again we see the two great characteristics of Jesus emerge.

(1) We see his *courage*. He knew that to make that answer was to die, and yet unhesitatingly he made it. Had he

denied the charges they would have been powerless to touch him.

(2) We see his *confidence*. Even with the cross now a certainty, he still continued to speak with complete confidence of his ultimate triumph.

Surely it is the most terrible of tragedies to see him who came to offer love to all people denied even bare justice, and humiliated by the crude and cruel horseplay of the Sanhedrin servants and guards.

COURAGE AND COWARDICE

Mark 14:54, 66–72

> And Peter followed him at a distance, right into the courtyard of the high priest's house, and he was sitting there with the servants, warming himself at the fire . . . When Peter was below in the courtyard, one of the maid servants of the high priest came up, and when she saw Peter warming himself, she looked closely at him. 'You, too,' she said, 'were with the Nazarene, with Jesus.' He denied it. 'I do not know,' he said, 'or understand what you are saying.' He went out into the porch, and the cock crew. The maid servant saw him and again began to say to the bystanders, 'This man was one of them.' But he again denied it. Soon afterwards the bystanders said to Peter, 'In truth you are one of them, for you are a Galilaean.' He began to curse and to swear, 'I do not know the man you are talking about.' And immediately cock-crow sounded. And Peter remembered the word, how Jesus had said to him, 'Before the cock crow twice you will deny me three times.' And he flung his cloak about his head and wept.

SOMETIMES we tell this story in such a way as to do Peter far less than justice. The thing we so often fail to recognize is that up to the very last, Peter's career this night had been one of fantastically reckless courage. He had begun by drawing his sword in the garden with the reckless courage of a man prepared to take on a whole mob by himself. In that scuffle he had wounded the servant of the high priest. Common prudence would have urged that Peter should lie very low. The last place anyone would have dreamed that he would go to would be the courtyard of the high priest's house – yet that is precisely where he did go. That in itself was sheer audacity. It may be that the others had fled, but Peter was keeping his word. Even if the others had gone he would stick to Jesus.

Then the peculiar mixture of human nature emerged. He was sitting by the fire, for the night was cold. No doubt he was huddled in his cloak. Maybe someone poked the fire or flung a fresh log upon it, and it flared up with a fitful flame and Peter was recognized. Straightaway he denied all con- nection with Jesus. *But* – and here is the forgotten point – any prudent man would then have left that courtyard as fast as his legs could carry him – but not Peter. The same thing happened again. Again Peter denied Jesus and again he would not go. It happened once more. Again Peter denied Jesus; Peter did not curse Jesus' name. What he did was to swear he did not know Jesus and to call down curses on himself if he was not telling the truth. Still it seems he did not mean to move. But something else happened.

Very probably it was this. The Roman night was divided into four watches from 6 pm to 6 am. At the end of the third watch, at 3 am, the guard was changed. When the guard was changed there was a bugle call which was called the *gallicinium*, which is the Latin for the *cock-crow*. Most likely what happened was that as Peter spoke his third denial, the clear note of the bugle call rang out over the silent city, and Peter heard it. He remembered and his heart broke.

Make no mistake – Peter fell to a temptation which would have come only to a man of fantastic courage. It ill becomes the more prudent and safety-seeking among us to criticize Peter for falling to a temptation which would never, in the same circumstances, have come to them at all. Everyone has a breaking point. Peter reached his here, but 999 men out of every 1,000 would have reached theirs long before. We would do well to be amazed at Peter's courage rather than to be shocked at his fall.

But there is another thing. There is only one source from which this story could have come – and that is Peter himself. We saw in the introduction that Mark's gospel is the preaching material of Peter. That is to say, over and over again Peter must have told the story of his own denial. 'That is what I did,' he must have said, 'and this amazing Jesus never stopped loving me.'

There was an evangelist called Brownlow North. He was a man of God, but in his youth he had lived a wild life. One Sunday he was to preach in Aberdeen. Before he entered the pulpit, a letter was handed to him. The writer recounted a shameful incident in Brownlow North's life before he became a Christian and stated that if he dared to preach he would rise in the church and publicly proclaim what once he had done. Brownlow North took the letter into the pulpit with him. He read it to the congregation. He told them that it was perfectly true. Then he told them how through Christ he had been forgiven, how he had been enabled to overcome himself and put the past behind him, how through Christ he was a new creature. He used his own shame as a magnet to draw others to Christ. That is what Peter did. He told people, 'I hurt him and I let him down like that, and still he loved and forgave me – and he can do the same for you.'

When we read this passage with understanding, the story of Peter's cowardice becomes an epic of courage and the story of his shame becomes a tale of glory.

THE SILENCE OF JESUS

Mark 15:1-5

> Immediately, early in the morning, the chief priests, together with the elders and the experts in the law – that is to say, the whole Sanhedrin – held a consultation. They bound Jesus and took him away and handed him over to Pilate. Pilate asked him, 'Are you the King of the Jews?' Jesus answered, 'It is you who say so.' The chief priests made many accusations against him. Pilate again questioned him. 'Have you no answer to make?' he said. 'See how many accusations they have made against you.' Jesus answered nothing further, and Pilate was amazed.

As soon as it was light, the Sanhedrin met to confirm the conclusions they had arrived at during their meeting in the night. They themselves had no power to carry out the death penalty. That had to be imposed by the Roman governor and carried out by the Roman authorities.

It is from Luke that we learn how deep and determined the bitter malice of the Jews was. As we have seen, the charge at which they had arrived was one of blasphemy, of insulting God. But that was not the charge on which they brought Jesus before Pilate. They knew well that Pilate would have had nothing to do with what he would have considered a Jewish religious argument. When they brought Jesus to him they charged him with perverting the people, forbidding them to give tribute to Caesar and calling himself a king (Luke 23:1-2). They had to evolve a political charge or Pilate would not have listened. They knew the charge was a lie – and so did Pilate.

Pilate asked Jesus, 'Are you the King of the Jews?' Jesus gave him a strange answer. He said, 'It is you who say so.' Jesus did not say yes or no. What he did say was, 'I may have claimed to be the King of the Jews, but you know very well that the interpretation that my accusers are putting on that claim is not my interpretation. I am no political revolutionary. My kingdom is a kingdom of love.' Pilate knew that perfectly well. Pilate went on to question Jesus more, and the Jewish authorities went on to multiply their charges – and Jesus remained completely silent.

There is a time when silence is more eloquent than words, for silence can say things that words can never say.

(1) There is the silence of *wondering admiration*. It is a compliment for any performance or oration to be greeted with thunderous applause, but it is a still greater compliment for it to be greeted with a hushed silence which knows that applause would be out of place. It is a compliment to be praised or thanked in words, but it is a still greater compliment to receive a look of the eyes which plainly says there are no words to be found.

(2) There is the silence of *contempt*. It is possible to greet someone's statements or arguments or excuses with a silence which shows they are not worth answering. Instead of answering someone's protestations the listener may turn on his heel and contemptuously leave them be.

(3) There is the silence of *fear*. People may remain silent for no other reason than that they are afraid to speak. The cowardice of their souls may stop them saying the things

they know they ought to say. Fear may gag them into a shameful silence.

(4) There is the silence of *the heart that is hurt*. When people have been really wounded they do not break into protests and recriminations and angry words. The deepest sorrow is a dumb sorrow, which is past anger and past rebuke and past anything that speech can say, and which can only silently look its grief.

(5) There is the silence of *tragedy*, and that is silent because there is nothing to be said. That was why Jesus was silent. He knew there could be no bridge between himself and the Jewish leaders. He knew that there was nothing in Pilate to which he could ultimately appeal. He knew that the lines of communication were broken. The hatred of the Jews was an iron curtain which no words could penetrate. The cowardice of Pilate in face of the mob was a barrier no words could pierce. It is a terrible thing when a person's heart is such that even Jesus knows it is hopeless to speak. God save us from that!

THE CHOICE OF THE MOB

Mark 15:6–15

> At the time of the Feast, it was the custom for the governor to release to the people a prisoner, whom they were accustomed to choose. There was a man called Barabbas, confined with the revolutionaries, who had committed murder during the insurrection. The crowd approached Pilate's judgment seat and began to request that he should carry out the customary procedure for them. Pilate answered, 'Do you wish me to release to you the King of the Jews?' For he knew that the chief

priests had handed him over to him through sheer
malice. The chief priests stirred up the mob to demand
the release of Barabbas all the more. Pilate again asked
them, 'What shall I do to the man you call the King of
the Jews?' Again they shrieked, 'Crucify him!' Pilate
said to them, 'What harm has he done?' They shrieked
the more vehemently, 'Crucify him!' Pilate wished to
please the mob, and he released Barabbas for them, and,
when he had scourged Jesus, he handed him over to
them to be crucified.

OF Barabbas we know nothing other than what we read in
the gospel story. He was not a thief, he was a brigand. He
was no petty pilferer but a bandit, and there must have been a
rough audacity about him that appealed to the crowd. Perhaps
we may guess what he was. Palestine was filled with insur-
rections. It was an inflammable land. In particular there was
one group of Jews called the *Sicarii*, which means the
dagger-bearers, who were violent, fanatical nationalists. They
were pledged to murder and assassination. They carried their
daggers beneath their cloaks and used them as they could. It
is very likely that Barabbas was a man like that, and, thug
though he was, he was a brave man, a patriot, and it is
understandable that he was popular with the mob.

People have always felt it a mystery that less than a week
after the crowd was shouting a welcome when Jesus rode
into Jerusalem, they were now shrieking for his crucifixion.
There is no real mystery. The reason is quite simply that this
was a different crowd. Think of the arrest. It was deliberately
secret. True, the disciples fled and must have spread the news,
but they could not have known that the Sanhedrin was going
to violate its own laws and carry out a travesty of a trial by
night. There can have been very few of Jesus' supporters in
that crowd.

Who then were there? Think again. The crowd knew that there was this custom whereby a prisoner was released at the Passover time. It may well be that this was a crowd which had assembled with the deliberate intention of demanding the release of Barabbas. They were in fact a *mob of Barabbas' supporters*. When they saw the possibility that Jesus might be released and not Barabbas they went mad. To the chief priests this was a heaven-sent opportunity. Circumstances had played into their hands. They fanned the popular clamour for Barabbas and found it easy, for it was the release of Barabbas that that crowd had come to claim. It was not that the crowd was fickle. It was that it was a different crowd.

Nonetheless, they had a choice to make. Confronted with Jesus and Barabbas, they chose Barabbas.

(1) They chose *lawlessness instead of law*. They chose the law-breaker instead of Jesus. One of the New Testament words for sin is *anomia*, which means lawlessness. In the human heart there is a streak which resents law, which desires to do as it likes, which wants to smash the confining barriers and kick over the traces and refuse all discipline. There is something of that in each of us. Rudyard Kipling makes the old soldier say in 'Mandalay':

> Ship me somewheres east of Suez, where the best is
> 　like the worst,
> Where there aren't no Ten Commandments an' a man
> 　can raise a thirst.

There are times when most of us wish there were no Ten Commandments. The mob was the representative of human frailty when it chose lawlessness instead of law.

(2) They chose *war instead of peace*. They chose the man of blood instead of the Prince of Peace. In almost 3,000 years of history there have been less than 130 years where there

has not been a war raging somewhere. Human beings, in their incredible folly, have persisted in trying to settle things by war which settles nothing. The mob was doing what has been done so often when they chose the warrior and rejected the man of peace.

(3) They chose *hatred and violence instead of love*. Barabbas and Jesus stood for two different ways. Barabbas stood for the heart of hate, the stab of the dagger, the violence of bitterness. Jesus stood for the way of love. As so often has happened, hate reigned supreme in human hearts, and love was rejected. The people insisted on taking their own way to conquest, and refused to see that the only true conquest was the conquest of love.

There can be hidden tragedy in a word. 'When he had scourged him' is one word in the Greek. The Roman scourge was a terrible thing. The criminal was bent and bound in such a way that his back was exposed. The scourge was a long leather thong, studded here and there with sharpened pieces of lead and bits of bone. It literally tore a man's back to ribbons. Sometimes it tore a man's eye out. Some men died under it. Some men emerged from the ordeal raving mad. Few retained consciousness through it. That is what they inflicted on Jesus.

THE SOLDIERS' MOCKERY

Mark 15:16–20

> The soldiers led Jesus away into the hall, which is the Praetorium, and they called together the whole company. They clad him in a purple robe, and they plaited a crown of thorns and put it on him, and they began to salute him, 'Hail! King of the Jews!' And they struck

his head with a reed, and they spat on him, and they
knelt down before him and worshipped him. And after
they had made sport of him, they took off the purple
robe, and clad him in his own clothes. And they led
him away to crucify him.

THE Roman ritual of condemnation was fixed. The judge said
Illum duci ad crucem placet, 'The sentence is that this man
should be taken to a cross.' Then he turned to the guard and
said, *I, miles, expedi crucem*, 'Go, soldier, and prepare the
cross.' It was when the cross was being prepared that Jesus
was in the hands of the soldiers. The Praetorium was the
residence of the governor, his headquarters, and the soldiers
involved would be the headquarters' cohort of the guard. We
would do well to remember that Jesus had already undergone
the agony of scourging before this horseplay of the soldiers
began.

It may well be that of all that happened to him this hurt
Jesus least. The actions of the Jews had been venomous with
hatred. The consent of Pilate had been a cowardly evasion of
responsibility. There was cruelty in the action of the soldiers
but no malice. To them Jesus was only another man for a
cross, and they carried out their barrack-room pantomime of
royalty and worship, not with any malice, but as a coarse
jest.

It was the beginning of much mockery to come. Always
the Christian was liable to be regarded as a jest. Scribbled
on the walls of Pompeii, whose walls are still chalked
with coarse jests today, there is a picture of a Christian
kneeling before a donkey and below it scrawled the words,
'Anaximenes worships his God.' If people ever make a jest
of our Christianity, it will help to remember that they did it
to Jesus in a way that is worse than anything likely to happen
to us.

THE CROSS

Mark 15:21–8

> And they impressed into service a man called Simon of
> Cyrene, who was passing by, on his way in from the
> country, the father of Alexander and Rufus, and they
> made him carry his cross. So they brought him to the
> place Golgotha, which means the place of a skull. They
> offered him wine mingled with myrrh, but he would
> not take it. They crucified him. And they divided out
> his garments, throwing dice for them to decide who
> should take what. It was 9 am when they crucified him.
> And the inscription of the charge against him was
> written on the cross – 'The King of the Jews'. With him
> they crucified two brigands, one on his right hand and
> one on his left.

THE routine of crucifixion did not alter. When the cross was
prepared the criminal had himself to carry it to the place of
execution. He was placed in the middle of a hollow square of
four soldiers. In front marched a soldier carrying a board
stating the crime of which the prisoner was guilty. The board
was afterwards affixed to the cross. They took not the shortest
but the longest way to the place of execution. They followed
every possible street and lane so that as many as possible
should see and take warning. When they reached the place of
crucifixion, the cross was laid flat on the ground. The prisoner
was stretched upon it and nailed to it. The nails were usually
driven through the wrists. The feet were not nailed but only
loosely bound. Between the prisoner's legs projected a ledge
of wood called the saddle, to take his weight when the cross
was raised upright – otherwise the nails would have torn
through the wrists. The cross was then lifted upright and set
in its socket – and the criminal was left to die. The cross was

not tall. It was shaped like the letter T, and had no top piece at all. Sometimes prisoners hung for as long as a week, slowly dying of hunger and of thirst, suffering sometimes to the point of actual madness.

This must have been a grim day for Simon of Cyrene. Palestine was an occupied country and any man might be pressed into the Roman service for any task. The sign of this was a tap on the shoulder with the flat of a Roman spear. Simon was from Cyrene in Africa. No doubt he had come from that far-off land for the Passover. No doubt he had scraped and saved for many years in order to come. No doubt he was gratifying the ambition of a lifetime to eat one Passover in Jerusalem. Then this happened to him.

At the moment Simon must have bitterly resented it. He must have hated the Romans, and hated this criminal whose cross he was being forced to carry. But we may legitimately speculate what happened to Simon. It may be that it was his intention when he got to Golgotha to fling the cross down on the ground and hasten as quickly as he could from the scene. But perhaps it did not turn out that way. Perhaps he lingered on because something about Jesus fascinated him.

He is described as *the father of Alexander and Rufus*. The people for whom the gospel was written must have been meant to recognize him by this description. It is most likely that Mark's gospel was first written for the church at Rome. Now let us turn to Paul's letter to Rome and read Romans 16:13. 'Greet Rufus, chosen in the Lord; and greet his mother – a mother to me also.' Rufus was so eminent a Christian that he was *chosen in the Lord*. The mother of Rufus was so dear to Paul that he could call her his own mother. Things must have happened to Simon on Golgotha.

Now turn to Acts 13:1. There is a list of the men of Antioch who sent Paul and Barnabas out on that epoch-making first mission to the Gentiles. The name of one is *Simeon who was called Niger. Simeon* is another form of *Simon. Niger* was the regular name for a man of dark skin who came from Africa, and Cyrene is in Africa. Here it may well be that we are meeting Simon again. Maybe Simon's experience on the way to Golgotha bound his heart forever to Jesus. Maybe it made him a Christian. Maybe in the after days he was a leader in Antioch and instrumental in the first mission to the Gentiles. Maybe it was because Simon was compelled to carry the cross of Jesus that the first mission to the Gentiles took place. That would mean that *we* are Christians because one day a Passover pilgrim from Cyrene, to his bitter resentment at the time, was pressed by a nameless Roman officer to carry his cross for Jesus.

They offered Jesus drugged wine and he would not drink it. A company of pious and merciful women in Jerusalem came to every crucifixion and gave the criminals a drink of drugged wine to ease the terrible pain. They offered this to Jesus – and he refused it. When Dr Johnson was ill with his last illness, he asked his doctor to tell him honestly if he could recover. The doctor said he could not without a miracle. 'Then', said Johnson, 'I will take no more physic, not even opiates, for I have prayed that I may render up my soul to God unclouded.' Jesus was resolved to taste death at its bitterest and to go to God with open eyes.

The soldiers threw dice for his clothes. We have seen how the prisoner was marched to the place of crucifixion amid the four soldiers. These soldiers had as their 'perk' the clothes of the criminal. Now a Jew wore *five* articles of clothing – the inner robe, the outer robe, the sandals, the girdle and the turban. When the four lesser things had been assigned, that left the great outer robe. It would have been useless to cut it up, so the soldiers gambled for it in the shadow of the cross.

Jesus was crucified between two thieves. It was a symbol of his whole life that even at the end he kept company with sinners.

THE LIMITLESS LOVE

Mark 15:29–32

> Those who were passing by hurled their insults at him, wagging their heads at him. 'Aha!' they said, 'you who are going to pull down the Temple and build it in three days, come down from the cross and save yourself!' Even so the chief priests jested with each other, with the experts in the law. 'He saved others,' they said. 'He cannot save himself. Let this Anointed One of God, this King of Israel, come down from the cross, so that we may see it and believe.' And those who were crucified with him flung their taunts at him.

THE Jewish leaders flung one last challenge at Jesus. 'Come down from the cross,' they said, 'and we will believe in you.' It was precisely the wrong challenge. As General William Booth of the Salvation Army said long ago, 'It is because Jesus did *not* come down from the cross that we believe in him.' The death of Jesus was absolutely necessary and the reason was this. Jesus came to tell people of the love of God; more, he was himself the incarnate love of God. If he had refused the cross or if in the end he had come down from the cross, it would have meant that there was a limit to God's love, that there was something which that love was not prepared to suffer for men and women, that there was a line beyond which it would not go. But Jesus went the whole way and died on the cross, and this means that there is literally no limit to God's love, that there is nothing in all the universe which that love is not prepared to suffer for us, that there is nothing, not even death on a cross, which it will refuse to bear for us.

When we look at the cross, Jesus is saying to us, 'God loves you like that, with a love that is limitless, a love that will bear every suffering earth has to offer.'

TRAGEDY AND TRIUMPH

Mark 15:33-41

> When it was 12 noon, there came a darkness over the whole earth, and it lasted until 3 pm. And at 3 pm Jesus cried with a great voice, 'Eloi, Eloi, lama sabachthani?' which means, 'My God! My God! Why have you abandoned me?' When certain of the bystanders heard it, they said, 'See! He is calling for Elijah!' Someone ran and soaked a sponge in vinegar and gave him a drink. 'Let be!' he said, 'till we see if Elijah is going to come and take him down.' Jesus uttered a great shout – and died. And the veil of the Temple was rent in two from top to bottom. When the centurion who was standing opposite him saw that he died like this, he said, 'Truly this man was the Son of God.' There were some women watching from a distance, among whom were Mary of Magdala, and Mary the mother of James the little and of Joses, and Salome. They had accompanied him in Galilee and had attended to his needs. And there were many others who had come up with him to Jerusalem.

HERE comes the last scene of all, a scene so terrible that the sky was unnaturally darkened and it seemed that even nature could not bear to look upon what was happening. Let us look at the various people in this scene.

(1) There was Jesus. Jesus said two things.

(a) He uttered the terrible cry, 'My God! My God! Why have you abandoned me?' There is a mystery behind that cry which we cannot penetrate. Maybe it was like this. Jesus had taken this life of ours upon him. He had done our work and faced our temptations and borne our trials. He had suffered all that life could bring. He had known the failure of friends, the hatred of foes, the malice of enemies. He had known the most searing pain that life could offer. Up to this moment, Jesus had gone through every experience of life *except one – he had never known the consequence of sin*. Now if there is one thing sin does, it separates us from God. It puts between us and God a barrier like an unscalable wall. That was the one human experience through which Jesus had never passed, because he was without sin.

It may be that at this moment that experience came upon him – not because he had sinned, but because in order to be identified completely with our humanity he had to go through it. In this terrible, grim, bleak moment, Jesus really and truly identified himself with human sin. Here we have the divine paradox – Jesus knew what it was to be a sinner. And this experience must have been doubly agonizing for Jesus, because he had never known what it was to be separated from God by this barrier.

That is why he can understand our situation so well. That is why we need never fear to go to him when sin cuts us off from God. Because he has gone through it, he can help others who are going through it. There is no depth of human experience which Christ has not plumbed.

(b) There was the great shout. Both Matthew (27:50) and Luke (23:46) tell of it. John does not mention the shout but he tells us that Jesus died having said, 'It is finished' (John 19:30). In the original that would be one word; and *that one word was the great shout.* 'Finished!' Jesus died with the cry of triumph on his lips, his task accomplished, his work completed, his victory won. After the terrible dark there came the light again, and he went home to God a victor triumphant.

(2) There was the bystander who wished to see if Elijah would come. He had a kind of morbid curiosity in the face of the cross. The whole terrible scene did not move him to awe or reverence or even pity. He wanted to experiment while Jesus died.

(3) There was the centurion. A hard-bitten Roman soldier, he was the equivalent of a regimental sergeant-major. He had fought in many a campaign and he had seen many men die. But he had never seen men die like this and he was sure that Jesus was the Son of God. If Jesus had lived on and taught and healed he might have attracted many, but it is the cross which speaks straight to the hearts of men and women.

(4) There were the women in the distance. They were bewildered, heartbroken, drenched in sorrow – *but they were there.* They loved so much that they could not leave him. Love clings to Christ even when the intellect cannot understand. It is only love which can give us a hold on Christ that even the most bewildering experiences cannot break.

There is one other thing to note. 'The curtain of the Temple was torn in two, from top to bottom.' This was the curtain which shut off the Holy of Holies, into which no one might go. Symbolically that tells us two things.

(a) The way to God was now wide open. Into the Holy of Holies only the high priest could go, and he only once a year on the Day of Atonement. But now, the curtain was torn and the way to God was wide open to everyone.

(b) Within the Holy of Holies dwelt the very essence of God. Now with the death of Jesus the curtain which hid God was torn and he could be seen face to face. No longer was

God hidden. There was no longer any need to guess and grope. Anyone who looked at Jesus could say, 'That is what God is like. God loves me like that.'

THE MAN WHO GAVE JESUS A TOMB

Mark 15:42–7

> When it was now evening, since it was the day of Preparation, that is, the day before the Sabbath, Joseph of Arimathaea, a respected member of the council, and a man who was himself waiting for the kingdom of God, ventured to go to Pilate and asked for the body of Jesus. Pilate was amazed that he was already dead. He summoned the centurion, and asked if he had been long dead. And when he had learned the facts from the centurion, he granted the body to Joseph. And Joseph bought fine linen, and he took him down from the cross and wrapped him in the linen, and put him in a tomb which had been hewn out of rock, and he rolled a stone against the door of the tomb. And Mary of Magdala and Mary the mother of Joses saw where he had been laid.

JESUS died at 3 pm on the Friday and the next day was the Sabbath. We have already seen that the new day started at 6 pm. Therefore when Jesus died, it was already the time of preparation for the Sabbath, and there was very little time to waste, for after 6 pm the Sabbath law would operate and no work could be done.

Joseph of Arimathaea acted quickly. It frequently happened that the bodies of criminals were never buried at all, but were simply taken down and left for the vultures and the scavenging wild dogs to deal with. In fact it has been suggested that

Golgotha may have been called the place of a skull because it was littered with skulls from previous crucifixions. Joseph went to Pilate. It often happened that criminals hung for days on their crosses before they died, and Pilate was amazed that Jesus was dead only six hours after he had been crucified. But when he had checked the facts with the centurion, he gave the body to Joseph.

Joseph is a curious case.

(1) It may well be that it is from Joseph that all the information came about the trial before the Sanhedrin. Certainly none of the disciples was there. The information must have come from some member of the Sanhedrin, and it is probable that Joseph was the one. If that is so, he had a very real share in the writing of the gospel story.

(2) There is a certain tragedy about Joseph. He was a member of the Sanhedrin and yet we have no hint that he spoke one word in Jesus' favour or intervened in any way on his behalf. Joseph is the man who gave Jesus a tomb when he was dead but was silent when he was alive. It is one of the commonest tragedies of life that we keep our wreaths for people's graves and our praises until they are dead. It would be infinitely better to give them some of these flowers and some of these words of gratitude when they are still alive.

(3) But we cannot blame Joseph too much, for he was another of those people for whom the cross did what not even the life of Jesus could do. When he had seen Jesus alive, he had felt his attraction but had gone no further. But when he saw Jesus die – and he must have been present at the crucifixion – his heart was broken in love. First the centurion, then Joseph – it is an amazing thing how soon Jesus' words came true that when he was lifted up from the earth he would draw all people to himself (John 12:32).

TELL PETER

Mark 16:1-8

> When the Sabbath had passed, Mary of Magdala and
> Mary the mother of James and Salome bought spices to
> go and anoint his body. Very early in the morning on
> the first day of the week, when the sun was rising, they
> went to the tomb. They kept saying to each other, 'Who
> will roll away the stone from the door of the tomb for
> us?' They looked up and they saw that the stone had
> been rolled away, for it was very large. And they
> went into the tomb, and they saw a young man sitting
> on the right side, clothed in a long, white robe. They
> were utterly amazed. He said to them, 'Do not be
> amazed. You are looking for Jesus of Nazareth, who
> was crucified. He is risen. He is not here. See! There is
> the place where they laid him. But go! Tell his disciples
> and Peter, "He goes before you into Galilee. There you
> will see him as he told you."' And they went out and
> fled from the tomb, for fear and astonishment gripped
> them. And they told no one anything for they were
> afraid.

THERE had not been time to render the last services to the
body of Jesus. The Sabbath had intervened and the women
who wished to anoint the body had not been able to do so. As
early as possible after the Sabbath had passed, they set out to
perform this sad task.

They were worried about one thing. Tombs had no doors.
When the word door is mentioned it really means *opening*.
In front of the opening was a groove, and in the groove ran a
circular stone as big as a cartwheel; and the women knew
that it was quite beyond their strength to move a stone like
that. But when they reached the tomb, the stone was rolled

away, and inside was a messenger who gave them the un-
believable news that Jesus had risen from the dead.

One thing is certain – if Jesus had not risen from the dead,
we would never have heard of him. The attitude of the women
was that they had come to pay the last tribute to a dead body.
The attitude of the disciples was that everything had finished
in tragedy. By far the best proof of the resurrection is the
existence of the Christian Church. Nothing else could have
changed sad and despairing men and women into people
radiant with joy and aflame with courage. The resurrection is
the central fact of the whole Christian faith. Because we
believe in the resurrection certain things follow.

(1) Jesus is not a figure in a book but a living presence. It
is not enough to study the story of Jesus like the life of any
other great historical figure. We may begin that way but we
must end by meeting him.

(2) Jesus is not a memory but a presence. The dearest
memory fades. The Greeks had a word to describe time meaning *time which wipes all things out*. Long since, time would
have wiped out the memory of Jesus unless he had been a
living presence forever with us. As J. G. Whittier's hymn
'Immortal Love' has it:

> And warm, sweet, tender, even yet
>   A present help is he;
> And faith has still its Olivet,
>   And love its Galilee.

Jesus is not someone to discuss so much as someone to meet.

(3) The Christian life is not a matter of *knowing about*
Jesus, but of *knowing* Jesus. There is all the difference in the
world between *knowing about* a person and *knowing* a person.
Most people *know about* the Queen or the President of the
United States but not so many *know* them. The greatest

scholar in the world who knows everything about Jesus is less than the humblest Christian who knows him.

(4) There is an endless quality about the Christian faith. It should never stand still. Because our Lord is a living Lord there are new wonders and new truths waiting to be discovered all the time.

But the most precious thing in this passage is in two words which are in no other gospel. 'Go,' said the messenger. 'Tell his disciples *and Peter.*' How that message must have cheered Peter's heart when he received it! He must have been tortured with the memory of his disloyalty, and suddenly there came a special message for him. It was characteristic of Jesus that he thought not of the wrong Peter had done him but of the remorse he was undergoing. Jesus was far more eager to comfort the penitent sinner than to punish the sin. Someone has said, 'The most precious thing about Jesus is the way in which he trusts us on the field of our defeat.'

THE COMMISSION OF THE CHURCH

Mark 16:9–20

> When he had risen early on the first day of the week, he appeared first to Mary of Magdala, out of whom he had cast seven devils. She went and told the news to those who had been with him, who were mourning and weeping. When they heard that he was alive and had been seen by her, they did not believe.
>
> After that he appeared in another form to two of them as they walked, as they were on their way to the country. And they went away and told the news to the rest, but they did not believe it.
>
> Later he appeared to the eleven as they were sitting at meat and rebuked them for their disbelief and the

obtuseness of their minds, because they had not believed
those who saw him after he had risen. He said to them,
'Go into the whole world and preach the goodness. He
who believes and is baptized will be saved. He who
does not believe will be condemned. These signs will
accompany those who believe. By my name they will
cast out devils. They will speak with new tongues. They
will lift serpents, and even if they drink any deadly thing
it will not hurt them. They will place their hands on the
infirm and they will be well.'
So the Lord Jesus, after he had spoken to them, was
taken up into heaven, and sat down at the right hand of
God.
They went out and preached everywhere, while the
Lord worked with them, and confirmed their message
by the signs that accompanied it.

As we saw in the Introduction, Mark's gospel really stops at
verse 8. We have only to read this passage to see how different
it is from the rest of the gospel, and it appears in none of the
great manuscripts of the gospel. It is a later summary which
replaces the ending which either Mark did not live to write or
which at some time went astray.

Its great interest is the picture of the duty of the Church
that it gives to us. Whoever wrote this concluding section
obviously believed that the Church had certain tasks
committed to it by Jesus.

(1) The Church has a preaching task. It is the duty of the
Church, and that means that it is the duty of every Christian,
to tell the story of the good news of Jesus to those who have
never heard it. The Christian duty is to be the herald of Jesus.

(2) The Church has a healing task. Here is a fact we have
seen again and again. Christianity is concerned with bodies
as well as minds. Jesus wished to bring health to the body
and health to the soul.

(3) The Church has a source of power. We need not take everything literally. We need not think that the Christian is literally to have the power to lift venomous snakes and drink poisonous liquids and come to no harm. But at the back of this picturesque language is the conviction that the Christian is filled with a power to cope with life that others do not possess.

(4) The Church is never left alone to do its work. Always Christ works with it and in it and through it. The Lord of the Church is still in the Church and is still the Lord of power.

And so the gospel finishes with the message that the Christian life is lived in the presence and the power of him who was crucified and rose again.